THE PRIVATE DIPLOMACY OF SHIBUSAWA EIICHI

FIGURE 1   Shibusawa Eiichi (1840–1931), at seventy.
Photo: Shibusawa Memorial Museum.

The Private Diplomacy of
Shibusawa Eiichi

VISIONARY ENTREPRENEUR AND
TRANSNATIONALIST OF MODERN JAPAN

ᔆ

by

Shibusawa Masahide

Translated by the Center for Intercultural Communication

RENAISSANCE BOOKS

The Private Diplomacy of Shibusawa Eiichi
Visionary Entrepreneur and Transnationalist of Modern Japan

Original Japanese edition first published 1970 by the Yomiuri Shimbun 太平洋に
かける橋―渋沢栄一の生涯―』

First English edition published 2018 by
RENAISSANCE BOOKS
P O Box 219
Folkestone
Kent CT20 2WP

Renaissance Books is an imprint of Global Books Ltd

ISBN 978-1-898823-81-0 Hardback
      978-1-898823-82-7 e-Book

British Library Cataloguing in Publication Data
A catalogue record for this book is available
from the British Library

Set in Garamond 11 on 12.5 pt by Dataworks
Printed and bound by CPI Group (UK) Ltd, Croydon CR0 4YY

For Chako
for her everlasting support

Originally published as *Taiheiyō ni kakeru hashi: Shibusawa Eiichi no shōgai* (Building Bridges over the Pacific). Tokyo: Yomiuri Shinbunsha, 1970. Translation by Lynne E. Riggs, Takechi Manabu, and Julie Kuma; further editing and adaptation by Lynne E. Riggs and Brian Bridges with the advice and supervision of the author. The Shibusawa Eiichi Memorial Foundation provided research support and other assistance.

Editorial Notes: Japanese, Chinese and Korean names are written in customary order, surname first. Chinese names are romanized by the Pinyin system. Place names, especially in China and Korea, are generally spelled according to current official usage but some familiar places as well as historical personalities are given spellings current at the time of the events. The book draws extensively on the archives of the Shibusawa Eiichi Memorial Foundation, the catalogue to which can be accessed online. For details about the collection, see pp. 374–75.

CONTENTS

ജ

List of Figures		*ix*
Foreword by Akira Iriye		*xiii*
Preface		*xv*
Chapter 1	Awakening to a Wider World	1
Chapter 2	Launching Private-Sector Diplomacy	31
Chapter 3	World Tour Before the Storm	63
Chapter 4	Flattery without Scruple	101
Chapter 5	Promoting Goodwill in the United States	127
Chapter 6	The Roots of the Anti-Japanese Movement	152
Chapter 7	Cultivating the Friendship of Giants	185
Chapter 8	The Japanese-American Relations Committee	232
Chapter 9	The Washington Naval Conference	276
Chapter 10	The Sunset of Private-Sector Diplomacy	313
Chapter 11	Rainbows over the Ocean	349
References		*383*
Index		*397*

LIST OF FIGURES

ﾐﾝ

Frontispiece

1. Shibusawa Eiichi (1840–1931), at seventy.   ii

Preface

2. The *Shibusawa Eiichi denki shiryō* (Shibusawa Eiichi
   Biographical Materials).   xix

Chapter 1

3. Gyokusenji temple, Shimoda, where Townsend Harris
   lived 1856–1857.   6
4. Townsend Harris (1804–1878), first American consul
   general in Japan.   7
5. Shibusawa Eiichi in samurai garb (in France, 1867).   11
6. Fukuchi Gen'ichirō (1841–1906; penname Ōchi),
   Eiichi's close friend, journalist and author.   13

Chapter 2

7. Ōkuma Shigenobu (1838–1922; left) as minister of
   finance with Itō Hirobumi (1841–1909; right), home affairs
   minister, around 1878.   34
8. Ulysses S. Grant (1822–1885), eighteenth president
   of the United States.   37
9. Sketch of Grant's audience with Emperor Meiji, 1879.   47
10. The Shintomi theater in Kyōbashi where Grant and
    his party were entertained.   50
11. Eiichi's first wife, Chiyo (1841–1882), probably as she
    looked when Grant visited.   53

12. The Shibusawa Asukayama residence (1879–1945), which served as an important stage for Eiichi's personal international exchange endeavors for over 50 years. Photo: Shibusawa Memorial Museum   54

13. Hashimoto Chikanobu, *Entertaining Grant at Ueno Park,* 1879.   43

Chapter 3

14. Shibusawa Eiichi during his 1902 tour in the United States and Europe; at the Waltham Watch Company, Massachusetts.   65
15. Eiichi's second wife, Kaneko (1852–1934).   66
16. Inoue Kaoru (1836–1915), member of the Meiji oligarchy.   69

Chapter 4

17. Kodama Gentarō (1852–1906), Imperial Army General.   102
18. Ōkubo Toshimichi (1830–1878), leader of the Meiji government.   103
19. William Howard Taft (1857–1930), U.S. Secretary of War; later 27th president.   111

Chapter 5

20. Komura Jutarō (1855–1911), statesman and diplomat.   128
21. Map of the itinerary of the 1909 business delegation to the United States.   140
22. The honorary commissioners after visiting the Edison Electric Company in Chicago, Illinois.   141
23. Itō Hirobumi, who was first governor-general of Korea under Japanese colonial rule.   148

Chapter 6

24. Ushijima Kinji (George Shima; 1864–1926), first president of the Japanese Association of America.   167
25. Woodrow Wilson (1856–1924) became president of the United States in 1913.   178

Chapter 7

26. Sun Yat-sen (1866–1925), founder of the Nationalist
    Party of China.   186
27. A September 18, 1924 letter from Sun yat-sen to Eiichi. 193
28. Tokugawa Yoshinobu (1837–1913), last of the
    Tokugawa shoguns.   194
29. Yuan Shikai (1859–1916), leader of China when
    Eiichi visited in 1914.   200
30. Katō Takaaki (1860–1926), foreign minister in 1914
    at the outbreak of World War I.   206
31. Yuaikai president Suzuki Bunji.   210
32. Frank A. Vanderlip (1864–1928), American banker
    and journalist.   221

Chapter 8

33. Ōkura Kihachirō (1837–1926), founder of
    the Ōkura *zaibatsu*.   233
34. Sasaki Yūnosuke (1854–1943), second president of the
    Dai-ichi Bank.   234
35. Robert Lansing (1864–1928), U.S. Secretary of State.   240
36. Terauchi Masatake (1852–1919), prime minister.   244
37. Wallace M. Alexander (1869–1939), chairman of the
    American-Japanese Relations Committee of San Francisco. 255
38. Fujiyama Raita (1863–1938), president of the Tokyo
    Chamber of Commerce.   259
39. Hara Takashi (1856–1921), prime minister from 1918
    to 1921.   261
40. Sakatani Yoshirō (1863–1941), Eiichi's son-in-law.   269

Chapter 9

41. Katō Tomosaburō (1861–1923), navy minister and chief
    commissioner plenipotentiary of the Japanese delegation
    to the Washington Naval Conference.   288
42. Shidehara Kijūrō (1872–1951), Japan's ambassador to the
    United States and member of the Japanese delegation
    to the Washington Naval Conference.   289

43. Zumoto Motosada (1863–1943), journalist and
    member of the Diet.   290
44. Watch received from John Wanamaker.   301

Chapter 10

45. Nitobe Inazō (1862–1933), agricultural economist,
    educator, diplomat, and Christian.   341
46. Dan Takuma (1858–1932), M.I.T.-educated
    businessman who was director of the Mitsui zaibatsu.   342

Chapter 11

47. Ceremony unveiling the stone monument dedicated to
    Townsend Harris at Gyokusenji temple, Shimoda,
    site of the first U.S. consulate.   354
48. Chiang Kai-shek (1887–1975), Chinese statesman
    who visited Japan in 1927.   358
49. Chiang Kai-shek and Shibusawa Keizō (1956).   362
50. Thomas Edison letter to Eiichi (1928).   364
51. Eiichi (center) addresses guests at a celebration of
    his 88th birthday (1928).   365

FOREWORD

by

Akira Iriye

ဢ

THE FOLLOWING PAGES offer an account of the life of Shibusawa Eiichi, who may be considered the first "internationalist" in modern Japan, written by his great grandson Masahide and published in 1970 under the title, *Taiheiyō ni kakeru hashi* (Building Bridges over the Pacific").

Japan had a tortuous relationship with internationalism between 1840, when Shibusawa was born, and 1931, the year the nation invaded Manchuria and when he passed away. The author shows that the key to understanding Shibusawa's thoughts against the background of this history lies in the concept of "people's diplomacy," namely an approach to international relations through non-governmental connections. Such connections entail more transnational than international relations. In that sense, Shibusawa was more a transnationalist than an internationalist thinker.

Internationalism presupposes the prior existence of sovereign states cooperating to establish a peaceful order. The best examples are the League of Nations and the United Nations. Transnationalism, in contrast, goes beyond the framework of sovereign nations and promotes connections among individuals and non-governmental organizations. It was what in the 1990s came to be known as "globalism" in the sense that transnationalism aims at building bridges across the globe apart from independent nation-states. In that sense Shibusawa was a pioneering globalist.

It was only in the 1990s that expressions like globalism and globalization came to be widely used. This was more than sixty years after Shibusawa Eiichi's death, which suggests how pioneering his thoughts were.

We should also note the key importance of the 1970s, when the book was first published. Whereas earlier the nation had provided the key identity to individuals throughout most of the world, after around 1970 non-national identities such as gender, ethnicity, age, and religion came to be considered equally important determinants. People became connected across national boundaries on the basis of these and other identities. A worldwide conference of women, for instance, would be convened, and individuals in their eighties and nineties would develop a sense of common affinity regardless of their nationalities. It is, therefore, quite fitting that this book, which documents Shibusawa's transnationalism, should have first been published in 1970.

PREFACE

෨

THIS BOOK IS an exploration of Shibusawa Eiichi's (1840–1931) private-sector diplomacy, activities in a field then far ahead of his time that dominated the last thirty years of his life. I became interested in this particular part of my great-grandfather's life back in 1970 because I wanted to understand the ideas, convictions, and way of life that lay behind the efforts that consumed him even in advanced age. Even now, forty years later, I think, Eiichi's concerns and activities are sure to shed light on the precarious position of Japan in the world in the first thirty years of the twentieth century and on what we could learn from that time in guiding our path one century later. We are now living in an era when world politics is not just about state-to-state relations, but in which an increasingly wide range of actors – corporations, non-governmental organizations, and individuals included – can and do play an active role in how different peoples and countries engage with each other. As such, Eiichi's pioneering activities are both relevant and instructive for all of us.

Many have written about the extraordinary revolution known as the Meiji Restoration and the dramatic process through which Japan's society and economy were transformed and modernized. Of the numerous able and talented leaders who contributed to the transformation, Shibusawa Eiichi is remarkable in terms of the broad scope of his activities, the diversity of his ideas, and the scale of his achievements. For example, he established the First National Bank, overcoming all sorts of difficulties to create East Asia's first Western-style financial institution. Laboring in a context still deeply influenced by the feudal institutions through which the country had been governed for centuries, he negotiated and energized the building of a modern economy based on democratic principles, involving himself in the founding and management of several hundred enterprises and establishing various industrial associations. He made core contributions to the modern infrastructure of the country, and many of his activities were well ahead of his time.

These achievements were to win Eiichi such epithets as Japan's "founder of modern capitalism" and "grand old man" of the financial world, but his concerns did not stop with business and finance. His endeavors in the cultural realm were of surprising breadth and diversity as well. He remained involved long-term in the management of nonprofit, public-benefit enterprises such as the Tokyo Yōikuin orphanage, of which he was chairman, and in education, where he helped administer and develop educational institutions including what are today Hitotsubashi University and Japan Women's University. Another personal commitment was to Tokugawa Yoshinobu (1837–1913), whom Eiichi served as a retainer in the final days of the Tokugawa shogunate and respected as his mentor to the end of his life. Yoshinobu became the fifteenth and last of the Tokugawa shoguns, whose 264-year rule was overthrown by supporters of the restoration of sovereignty to the emperors, under the reigning Emperor Meiji. The forces of history may have led to the end of the Tokugawa government, but Yoshinobu had merely been the last person to hold the title of shogun, and Eiichi remained devoted to restoring the honor of his former lord through the several-decades-long project of completing Yoshinobu's biography.[1]

Against the diverse backdrop of these activities of his early and middle career, as Eiichi entered the latter years of his life, he felt a keen sense of crisis regarding Japan's relationship with the United States and China. For several decades after the Meiji Restoration – or Meiji Revolution, some call it – of 1868, Japan had busied itself domestically with the drive to modernize, but its foreign affairs had taken a sharp aggressive turn when it waged war against China in 1894–1895 and then against Russia in 1904–1905. After 1910 when Japan annexed Korea and began to overtly intervene in the internal affairs of Manchu-

---

[1]   Published in 1918 in 8 volumes as *Tokugawa Yoshinobu kō den* (Biography of Duke Tokugawa Yoshinobu).

ria and China, the advanced nations of the West suddenly began to notice that this small nation in the Far East was mustering strength with inordinate speed. The United States as a nation had been quite pro-Japan since it had forced open the country's doors in 1854, and the American government maintained a friendly stance toward Japan, but among the populace of the United States there was a swelling of anti-Japanese sentiment.

Shibusawa Eiichi had been intimately involved in the growth of Japan's modern economy from his youth, and he knew well that, while it had grown tremendously in size, the country was still essentially quite weak. He knew that the slightest error in judgment could lead to its demise. Japan was in no position to pick fights with mammoth neighbors like China and the United States.

Inherently conscientious and endowed with an awareness of the importance of strategy rare among people in the private sector, Eiichi tackled these problems with all his resources. Not only did he cultivate exchange and dialogue with people outside Japan as an individual, he also held discussions in the Japanese organizations with which he was closely associated (such as the Tokyo Chamber of Commerce and the Tokyo Bankers Association), taking every opportunity to involve them in support of his causes. Through these activities, he was able to raise the awareness of top-level members of the business world and deepen their understanding of "Japan in the world." These efforts also dovetailed with the goal to which he devoted his whole life, which was the education and cultivation of the caliber of people running the Japanese business world.

By involving other industrial leaders in his private diplomatic endeavors, meanwhile, Eiichi was able to exercise influence backed by the common intentions and will of the business world that made his endeavors inherently different from the efforts of other individuals of a more "grass roots" nature.

The people whom Eiichi influenced, engaged, and mobilized are colorful and diverse, populating the absorbing drama of the three decades of this part of his life. They include heroic figures like Yuan Shikai (1859–1916), Sun Yat-sen (1866–1925), and

Chiang Kai-shek (1887–1975), men who built the groundwork of the history of modern China. There were also four successive U.S. presidents – Theodore Roosevelt, William Howard Taft, Woodrow Wilson, and Warren G. Harding. Many of the brilliant business magnates who exercised control over the American economy and were active in that extraordinary period of growth appear in the story, as do idiosyncratic individuals like American Federation of Labor leader Samuel Gompers (1850–1924) and inventor Thomas Edison (1847–1931).

On the other hand, the Japanese names that crop up in Eiichi's story include founders of the modern Meiji state like Itō Hirobumi (1841–1909) and Ōkuma Shigenobu (1838–1922), outstanding diplomats like Komura Jutarō, Shidehara Kijūrō, and Yoshida Shigeru, and alongside the many leaders of the business world who were his steady comrades, there appear figures like Suzuki Bunji, trailblazer of Japan's labor movement. It was diverse people like these who set in motion the vast drama of the history of Asia and the Pacific in the latter years of Eiichi's life.

Ultimately, it was a drama to be followed by tragedy. Already by the early 1910s (the end of the Meiji era), an insidious black cloud hung over Japan-U.S. relations, and exactly as Eiichi had worried, the cloud was steadily extending its shadow. No matter what people like him might try to do, the powerful current of destiny could not be changed. With 1931, the year Eiichi died, as the turning point, Japan plunged rapidly into a reckless war.

The opportunity to unravel the threads of the multifarious activities Eiichi engaged in during his final thirty years and write a book about them came to me in the spring of 1970, when I received a request from the Yoshida International Education Foundation and the Yomiuri Shimbunsha newspaper company to write about Eiichi's efforts at private-sector diplomacy. The request came just as I was about to set off on a month-long trip to the United States, so I gathered together various materials while I was there, and after returning to Japan began reading whatever I could find on the subject in the 68-volume Shibusawa Eiichi Biographical Materials and a mountain of other works. As I did so, I began to see a clearer figure of Eiichi emerge: a spirited

FIGURE 2
The *Shibusawa Eiichi
denki shiryō* (Shibusawa
Eiichi Biographical
Materials), 68 volumes,
published 1955 to 1971.
Photo: Shibusawa
Memorial Museum.

and committed fighter for his causes of conscience began to take
clear shape against the backdrop of history in the late nineteenth
and early twentieth centuries (Japan's Meiji, Taishō and early-
Shōwa eras).

As a man born in 1840, who grew to manhood nourished by
the culture of a feudal system of domains controlled by the shogunate headquartered in Edo, Eiichi was a product of the *"Analects* and abacus"-oriented education of his time quite different
from today. He was well versed in the Confucian classics and traditional East Asian thought, and believed in them. Eiichi often
cited the passage in the *Analects* (2.10) that states: "Observe what
a man does. Mark his motives. See whether he enjoys what he
is doing. How can a man conceal his character?" When Eiichi
needed to observe others and evaluate their actions, he is said to
have taken Confucius as his guide.

By observing what it was that Eiichi was striving for through
his thirty years of efforts at private-sector diplomacy, I believe

we will have a somewhat better understanding of the foundation and expanse of his life. Although many of his efforts may
have been destined to end in failure, it seems to me that his
failures were, in a sense, the failures of Japan. Eiichi's limits were,
in other words, the limits of Japan and showed where Meiji-era
modernization succeeded and failed. Nonetheless, his activities
devoted to promoting better relations within the Pacific triangle
of Japan, China and the United States have inspired me to think
deeply about – and hopefully in some small way to contribute
to – Japan's contemporary interactions with its neighbors. My
own sense of curiosity about the past and the linkages between
the past and present – and, indeed, the future – have encouraged
me to offer this interpretation of Eiichi's life as a contribution
to the ongoing and important debates about Japan's role in the
world today.

I wish to acknowledge the contributions of several individuals.
Jun'etsu Komatsu first suggested publishing an English language
version of the book, and his enthusiasm and hard work on mul-
tiple fronts were critical to the success of the project. I am deeply
indebted to Lynne E. Riggs for her sensitive and skillful editing of the translation. The translation greatly benefited from
the comments and suggestions of five readers of the draft: Brian
Bridges, Gil Latz, Jorge Leon, James Runsdorf, John Sagers,
and David Welch. Professor Iriye Akira has added perspective
to the book with his thoughtful Foreword. Brian Bridges and
James Runsdorf contributed immensely to the final proofreading
and polishing of the book. Inoue Jun, Kato Ruri, and the other
members of the Shibusawa Foundation staff provided indispensable research and background support.

Shibusawa Masahide
April 2018

CHAPTER 1

AWAKENING TO A WIDER WORLD

છ

SHIBUSAWA EIICHI WAS thirteen when Commodore Matthew Calbraith Perry led his fleet of steam-powered warships into the port at Uraga in 1853. The reaction within Japan to the aggressive approaches of unknown "invaders" was violent and convulsive. Just as we would react if aliens from outer space were to land a powerful spaceship on earth, people had no idea what these visitors were thinking. The strangers seemed to be saying they were there on a mission of friendship and amity, but that was hardly to be taken at face value. Japan knew well what was happening not far away in China. Only recently, their giant neighbor had been cleverly conned and humiliated by the British in the Opium Wars, and forced into handing over various territories and concessions. The United States was unlikely to be different; there was no knowing what the Americans were scheming. Anti-foreign sentiment seethed all over the country.

Like Japan itself, Eiichi was just beginning to be aware of the wider world. He had begun to help with his father's indigo business from boyhood, and in 1858 at the age of 18 he had married a cousin, Odaka Chiyo. Their daughter Utako was born in 1863. And that was the very year, when he was 23, that he was swept up in the reaction against the foreign incursions.

The zeal to protect the country against the outside world was widespread in Japan, and was felt even in the Musashino countryside north of Edo, the capital of Japan. Eiichi, together with a group of other young hot-blooded rural men of high aspirations (*shishi*) centered in his hometown of Chiaraijima in what is now Saitama prefecture, formulated a plot to attack and burn the foreign settlement in Yokohama. In the autumn of that year he and his co-conspirators collected weapons, clothing, and equipment and stored them discreetly, waiting for the right time to carry out the mission. From their base in northern Saitama, where the cold, dry winds sweep across the plains from the heights of Mt. Akagi, their plan was this: one night in early winter a group of about 60 comrades would take up arms and march on and seize the local castle at Takasaki. They would then travel swiftly southward down the Kamakura highway to attack the foreign settlement in Yokohama. If the plot had been carried out, Eiichi and other leaders would have been quickly killed, for however loyalty to country might be approved, violence against the people who had been permitted to reside in the settlement would not be condoned. Fortunately, however, a cousin, who had been in Kyoto and had observed the situation closer to the center of events, returned just before they set out and argued with Eiichi and his cohorts that their plan was rash and should be aborted. He faced stiff resistance from Eiichi and his friends, who had worked up quite a bit of momentum for their plan, but in the end his fierce opposition convinced them, and Eiichi called off their rebellion.

Knowing full well that if the plot he had instigated were to become known, not only he but his whole family would be in danger, Eiichi had previously determined to leave his home, going so far as to ask his father to disown him in order to place distance between himself and his family, and he decided to depart immediately for Kyoto, leaving his young wife and infant daughter behind. It is said that Chiyo, instructed by her brother and close friend of Eiichi Odaka Atsutada, accepted Eiichi's aspirations for change in the country and faithfully prepared for his departure, sending him off with brave words, while having no idea whether he would ever return.[2]

In Kyoto, Eiichi took up the life of a young and independent knight of the new cause and was seen with various activists of the time including prominent figures like Saigō Takamori

---

[2]   For more details about Chiyo and her role in Eiichi's life, see *Three Women of the Shibusawa Family*, by Shibusawa Masahide.

(1828–1877), for a while eking out the existence of a "masterless" samurai. It then transpired that Eiichi was offered a position serving the household of Hitotsubashi Yoshinobu (who was a member of a collateral branch of the Tokugawa family and thus in line to succeed as shogun), and in 1864, Eiichi entered the service of the Hitotsubashi family as a financial officer.

Those were the days when the European powers were converging on Japan with obviously imperialistic intent and ambitions. The British, at the urging of their envoy Harry Smith Parkes, supported the position of the Satsuma and Chōshū domains who were pushing for the restoration of imperial rule and the ending of the shogunate, while France's consul Léon Roches served Emperor Napoleon III's aspirations by making overtures to the Tokugawa shogunate, offering weapons and munitions and providing military instructors. The ulterior motive of both countries, foreseeing internal ruptures and political collapse within Japan, was to encourage the trend and take advantage of the ensuing chaos to carve out territory and obtain various concessions in Japan.

Although not cognizant of the details of the wheeling and dealing of modern diplomacy, Hitotsubashi Yoshinobu was among those on the shogunate side who earliest detected the essentially imperialistic designs of the foreign powers. Among opponents of the shogunate who supported the restoration of imperial rule, leading figures including Saigō Takamori, Iwakura Tomomi, and Katsura Kogorō had begun to realize what the Europeans were up to as well. The fact that the situation in Japan changed very rapidly, with the turmoil at the end of the shogunate resolved almost immediately and with a new government launched without delay, can be considered evidence of the recognition by such people of the danger from outside the country. The solidarity they forged in the face of that danger ended up transcending internal divisions and rivalries.

AMERICA AS FRIEND

The United States at that early stage seemed to be driven by different motives than those of the other foreign powers in Asia and behaved somewhat differently from the European states. Officials in the shogunate, which was directly involved in negotiating a treaty with the representatives of the United States, were the first to notice the difference – which began as something like a rumor and then became well-established knowledge – and what had prompted that awareness were the actions of first American consul-general in Japan, Townsend Harris (1804–1878). They were impressed by his handling of the first diplomatic crisis between the two countries, the so-called Heusken affair of 1861.

Townsend Harris

Harris was a solitary and sober-minded person who had been assigned to the mission without any previous diplomatic experience. He was charged with concluding American treaties with a government that had long shut out direct contact with most countries of the Western world. Residing in Japan for six long years, he represented the values of the West and the Anglo-Saxon principles of action. Distrust and suspicion of foreigners was deeply ingrained among Japanese, and his task was essentially to convince them that Westerners were human beings just like themselves. Harris was disinclined to compromise; he was very grave and rather lacking in personal charm, but these qualities, while angering and perplexing his hosts on a number of occasions, turned out to win Japanese hearts much more than even he expected, and in the end, he succeeded in gaining their lasting respect.

When in 1854 Commodore Perry sailed into the Japanese port of Uraga a second time, the shogunate signed the Treaty of Kanagawa, agreeing that the United States would establish a consulate 18 months later at Shimoda. Townsend Harris had been working in trade among ports in India, the Malay peninsula, the Philippines, and China, and when he heard of these plans, he apparently became convinced that the opening of Japan was tied up with his own destiny. He immediately began to lobby to be appointed the first American consul there.

Harris had reached the age of 49, and until then, while cultivated and well educated, had been living a life of inertia, drifting about Asia for several years. We do not know whether there was something special about Japan that he might have been attracted by, but in any case, he immediately returned to the United States, wrote a letter directly to President Franklin Pierce asking to be named consul to Japan, and met with Senator William H. Seward (later Secretary of State) and Commodore Perry to persuade them to support his application.

Harris's efforts were successful, and on August 21, 1856, he landed at Shimoda and took up residence in the priest's quarters of an old temple named Gyokusenji, accompanied by his secretary and interpreter the Dutch-American Henry Heusken. (Dutch, rather than English, was at this point in Japan's history the key language of international communication with Japanese.) Troubled by mosquitoes, "*enormous* in size," he spent his first fitful night in Japan. On August 25, the *San Jacinto*, the ship that had brought them, fired a 13-gun salute in honor of the establishment of the first U.S. consulate in Japan and sailed away.[3] That was the beginning of Harris's long and isolated sojourn serving as consul in Japan. Other than Heusken, he met no other Americans and received no letters from home for 18 months. The Japanese he associated with during that time were mostly low-ranking members of the bureaucracy of the Tokugawa government. These samurai saw Harris through the heavy veil of bias inculcated in them over three centuries while the country was cut off from the outside world, observing this troublesome intruder and doing their best to make what must have seemed like a creature from outer space fit into their own fixed order of authority.

If the samurai of 1854 were to appear before us today, it is quite likely that even Japanese would find them extremely difficult to deal with. They were men shaped by a society that had developed over several hundred years isolated from the rest of the world perhaps more than any other place on earth. Everything about the values and authority that governed their thinking and behavior was forged within extremely rigid structures of power

---

[3] *Complete Journal of Townsend Harris*, p. 207.

FIGURE 3   Gyokusenji temple, Shimoda, where Townsend Harris lived 1856–1857.
Photo: Courtesy of Gyokusenji Temple, Shizuoka prefecture.

so overblown and elaborate that they were practically incomprehensible to those outside their hierarchy.

It must have been very difficult to carry on any sort of candid dialogue on the level of one human being and another with people of that sort. It took Harris nearly two years to obtain approval of his request to go to Edo, have an audience with the shogun, and negotiate a treaty for trade and commerce. Anything new and unknown was alarming and fearsome, and the samurai of the feudalistic regime's cumbersome bureaucracy did their best to keep such things at arm's length. No one had ever heard of a lowly foreigner attempting to meet the august shogun, and so they sought to put off answering his demand, apparently imagining that if they ignored him long enough he would abandon the enterprise. They came up with every possible excuse, sometimes quoting the most transparent lies, in hopes of convincing him to give up.

In the face of their bluffing Harris always responded only by trying to be honest with them, but he refused to bargain. When it was obvious the samurai were lying, he made no attempt to soften his language, but called them out in so many words. Regarding his own demands, he insisted on them with inexhaustible resolve and patience and was determined that no matter how long it

FIGURE 4
Townsend Harris (1804–1878),
first American consul general in
Japan. Painting in the collection
of Gyokusenji temple. Photo:
Courtesy of Gyokusenji
Temple, Shizuoka prefecture.

might take and no matter how complicated the protocol might be, he would not retreat.

A great many months passed, but gradually the Japanese around Harris began to understand his attitude and develop a sense of trust and respect for his character. It was the first time in three centuries that the spark of understanding and kindred human feeling was lit between Japanese and Westerners.

The representatives of Britain, France, and other European countries were all very smart bargainers, but they were all servants of a higher master and were concerned entirely with trying to make their boss in the home country happy. Doing so was both a form of self-defense and the path to success and higher status, so if necessary for their purposes they would without hesitation deceive others into believing white to be black. The samurai working for the shogunate, who were in the same position as they, were well attuned to that sort of thing; they were quick to sniff the signs of knavery. Townsend Harris, by contrast, put priority on being a person over being a diplomat. He was stubborn, uncompromising, and rather prickly, but the things he said, which expressed what he really thought, were forthright and made sense.

The Treaty of Amity and Commerce between the United States and Japan was signed in July 1858, before any of the other Western countries, against the backdrop of the trust that high officials of the shogunate had begun to place in Harris. Of course, the signing of what came to be known as the "Harris Treaty" set off a political explosion that ultimately led to the downfall of the Tokugawa government. Nevertheless, the role that Harris played in concluding the treaty, the particular posture he took toward his Japanese hosts, and his distinctive personality would have a major influence on Japanese-American relations for a long time thereafter. The great test of Harris's character came when Henry Heusken, his indispensable interpreter and staunch companion over four years of many hardships, was killed.

Heusken was returning on horseback from the Shiba Akabane-bashi area to the consulate at Zenpukuji in the Azabu area on a cold wintry night in January 1861 when he was set upon and mortally wounded by a group of anti-foreign *ronin* led by Kiyo-kawa Hachirō. The government samurai who were supposed to be guarding Heusken fled the scene, and the attackers did their deed and left the scene without being apprehended. Heusken was Dutch and had only recently become an American citizen. The treaty may have been signed, but anti-foreign sentiment was rife in the country around this time.[4]

The incident immediately stirred up an international frenzy. The foreign diplomats stationed in Edo at the time were all infuriated and pounced upon the shogunate for its impotence and irresponsibility in allowing such a murder to take place. They began to argue that the foreign consulates should all move to Yokohama and take measures to defend themselves by bringing troops ashore from their warships. The British consul-general

---

[4]   For a detailed account of this incident, see Hesselink, "The Assassination of Henry Heusken," pp. 331–51.

Rutherford Alcock was especially adamant on the matter and the French and Dutch officials agreed with him.

In those days, the European powers were quick to exploit such incidents as the pretext upon which they would take up arms, obtain extraterritorial privileges over port and harbor areas, then demand further concessions through treaties, and ultimately assume complete control of a country. It had become the established imperialist pattern. The matter of the safety of the lives of the diplomats in Japan aside, the murder of Heusken handed to them a useful card for negotiating treaties with Japan advantageous to their interests, and they all began jockeying to put pressure on the shogunate.

But Townsend Harris, who was Heusken's immediate superior and leader of the victim consulate, was opposed to the moves advocated by the other powers. He argued that the Japanese government was suffering great difficulties at the time, and that it was not the time to use the incident as the pretext for impossible demands. The shogunate had made it clear over and over how dangerous it was to go out at night, and since Heusken had not followed its orders, it was his own fault that he had been attacked. Citing the recent incident in Naples when the French ambassador had been killed in a riot and the culprit had not been apprehended, Harris noted that one did not hear of France making such moves as to close its embassy or bring in its own troops to protect it. So, Harris declared, he could not agree to the idea of using the incident as a pretext for bringing in foreign troops, creating a predicament for the government. He said he would stay where he was in Edo and he hoped that the representatives of the other countries would follow his example.

When it turned out that Harris, head of the longest-standing consulate in Japan and the one most directly affected by the murder, did not agree with their position, the British and French representatives were indignant and withdrew to Yokohama anyway. Ultimately chided by their home governments for bungling the situation, they were later forced to move back to Edo.[5]

---

[5] See Statler, *Shimoda Story*, pp. 566–70.

Harris's unwillingness to condemn the Japanese government, which had already been in a weak and difficult position, but to recognize that the blame lay on Heusken's side as well made a strong impression on Japanese. The American consul's decision to remain in Edo despite the personal danger he must have felt, moreover, displayed a courage and integrity that resonated with the spirit of bushido that guided the values of the samurai. His response – suggesting that there were people of the West who might even share their values – was something fresh and new to those in the shogunal government and elsewhere who learned of it.

Harris remained in Japan after the treaty's signing, but his six years of solitary struggle had worn him down. With the unfamiliar food and environment, he was often ill. In 1861, it turned out that a Republican president – Abraham Lincoln – had assumed office in the United States, and turning aside the shogunate's repeated requests that he stay on, he submitted his resignation. When he left Japan, the shogun presented him with a fine samurai sword in recognition of his distinguished service. It is said that Harris later gave that sword to Civil War hero Ulysses S. Grant. Harris went back to live in his native New York and passed away there largely unknown in 1878.

Eiichi Sees the World

In February 1867 (the first month of Keiō 3), Eiichi was aboard the French steamer *Alphée* headed for France. He had been chosen to join the entourage of Shogun Tokugawa Yoshinobu's younger brother Akitake, who had been assigned to attend the international exposition organized by Napoleon III in Paris as Japan's representative and then go on to study in France. Talking with his companions during the voyage, Eiichi had continued to spout off his anti-foreign views, lumping together all foreigners, Americans included, as untrustworthy. When one of the other samurai on board argued that "the Americans are different" and explained the events involving Townsend Harris and Henry Heusken's murder, Eiichi expe-

Figure 5
Shibusawa Eiichi in samurai
garb (in France, 1867). Photo:
Shibusawa Memorial Museum.

rienced a tremendous shock, and recorded that he was overcome with embarrassment. Apparently, his view of the United States made an about-face from that time. Yoshinobu's selection of Eiichi reflected both his trust in the young man and his confidence that the opportunity would contribute to Eiichi's future. Indeed, it was that experience that launched Eiichi on his career in business and industry. From that time on, Eiichi kept in mind what Harris had experienced and achieved in launching Japan-U.S. relations.

In 1867, while Eiichi was in Europe, the Tokugawa regime came to an end, and the new Meiji government took power under the restored sovereign power of the emperor. Eiichi returned in November 1868, and the following year he was invited to serve in the new government's finance ministry where he was involved in drawing up the blueprints for fiscal and financial institutions for the new government and putting them into practice.

In 1871, the so-called Iwakura Mission was sent on an 18-month-long tour of the United States and Europe to survey and study Western institutions and systems. Japan had undergone a revolution and established a new government, but it had little experience with modern administration and its officials were groping in the dark as far as what the institutions of their modern state should be like. It was time to send a large mission to learn more about conditions in the advanced countries of the West, and based on their example, work to bring their own government up to the standard of the rest of the "civilized world." In addition to Iwakura Tomomi, leader of the mission, Kido Takayoshi, Ōkubo Toshimichi, Itō Hirobumi, and other central figures of the new government, members of each of the ministries were included in the 48-member mission.

From the finance ministry, Eiichi's colleague Fukuchi Gen'ichirō (1841–1906) was to join the mission in order to study fiscal and financial systems. Formerly a direct vassal of the Tokugawa family, he was a particularly close friend of Eiichi's, and when he departed, he placed his family in Eiichi's charge, repeatedly begging him to watch over them in his absence.

Fukuchi kept in touch with Eiichi throughout the journey, and the letters he wrote to Eiichi painted a vivid picture of what he saw abroad and the goings-on within the mission.[6] Fukuchi was an expert writer – indeed, he later left the ministry and founded the *Tokyo Nichinichi shinbun* newspaper – and he wrote a great deal during his sojourn with the mission. What interested Eiichi in particular was the startling difference in the attitudes toward Japan between the United States and Britain. The United States was freewheeling and spontaneous and unbelievably kind toward the mission.

---

6   A total of 19 letters to Eiichi from Fukuchi during the Iwakura Mission's journey are preserved, and his gossip about the personalities and dynamics within the group makes quite interesting reading. For example, he describes the mission leader Iwakura as "very meticulous and always nagging," deplores bad terms between deputy ambassadors Kido Takayoshi and Ōkubo Toshimichi, and praises Itō Hirobumi for his growth as a person after he joined the mission.

FIGURE 6
Fukuchi Gen'ichirō (1841–
1906; penname Ōchi), Eiichi's
close friend, journalist and
author. Photo: National Diet
Library, Japan.

Japan was essentially a backward country at that time with little
that could be called "technology" in the modern sense. One of
Fukuchi's assignments in the United States was to have currency
and bond certificates printed and sent to Japan. The U.S. Mint
was quick to agree to the task. It even put several specialists
in charge, who undertook everything from the design work to
selection of paper, printing, and shipping to Japan, assuming
responsibility just as if they were doing all this for their own
country. The result of their work was excellent, and Fukuchi
wrote that their quality was even better than the currency circulating in the United States, so his accomplishment of this task
did much to heighten his reputation.

When the mission crossed over to Britain, however, the government there was noticeably cold and unhelpful. No matter
what the members tried to study or learn about, people refused
to tell them anything, treating the Japanese with disdain, as if

they did not have the right to ask questions. The contrast with the United States, where people had responded as if they were directly involved with Japan's modernization, was striking.

The British being so parsimonious about information, the Japanese ended up relying mainly on the United States for their models and sources of information for modernization, and that led to an overwhelming portion of the foreign advisors hired by the Meiji government being invited from the United States. During the period when the Iwakura Mission was in the United States, Fukuchi had decided on several people who would be hired to serve as specialists on taxation and customs-related matters. It was also around that time that then president Ulysses S. Grant sent his current secretary of agriculture, Horace Capron, to serve as a top advisor for the Hokkaido development project. At Capron's recommendation, Japan later hired William S. Clark, president of the Massachusetts Agricultural College in Amherst, Massachusetts, to establish the Sapporo Agricultural College. Clark's achievements during his short stay of eight months, including founding the college and instituting the education that produced such outstanding figures as Uchimura Kanzō and Nitobe Inazō, are well known.

From the time of the Perry Expedition onward, the United States seemed to have looked upon Japan with a special sentiment stemming from its role in prying open the doors of the long-secluded country and ushering it into the modern world. Among the countries of Asia, most of which the European powers had violently invaded and freely plundered, Japan alone remained virgin territory. At this stage, the United States developed a sort of chivalrous spirit, considering it a mission entrusted to it by history to help Japan and pass on to it the bounty of civilization and enlightenment.

At the time of the Iwakura Mission, the United States had not exacted any imperialist demands for territory or concessions from any other countries. Having expanded all across the western part of the continent and even to as-yet-undeveloped Alaska, the United States was momentarily satiated as far as territory was concerned. Still, it was by no means indifferent to the interests in

Asia from which other powers were profiting handsomely. Like a child who isn't included in the mischief of a gang of troublemakers and lets off steam by calling them names, the United States criticized the colonialism of Britain and France and made a display of its own behavior as "different" from the others – attempting to be the virtuous one in the region.

In 1862, four Englishmen had been killed by Satsuma domain samurai at a place called Namamugi in the suburbs of Yokohama. In typical fashion, the British, French and other foreign consuls all clamored for an attack on the shogunate and the Satsuma domain, but Harris's successor, Robert Hewson Pruyn, took the side of the Japanese, saying that the Englishmen had been crossing on horseback through the procession of Shimazu Hisamitsu, father of the current lord of Satsuma, which was a clear violation of Japanese customs and if they suffered the consequences that could not be helped.

The following year, 1863, Chōshū forces bombarded the warships of four countries, England, France, Holland and the United States, and Japan was forced to pay reparations amounting to 3 million dollars. Later, however, a movement arose in the United States to return its share of the reparations, and in 1883 a resolution was passed in both Houses of Congress and the U.S. did return some 780,000 dollars to the Japanese government. Japan was deeply grateful for this extraordinary step, and used the money for the building of a dyke at Yokohama.

At the time, U.S. policy in the Far East emphasized commerce over politics, and was focused on obtaining opportunities for future trade before the European powers had completely spoiled the East Asian market. The three main elements of the policy were: (1) equal commercial opportunity for Americans; (2) no territorial concessions for the United States; (3) a strong Eastern Asia to resist a designing Europe.[7] These policies agreed with the national interests of Japan at that time, resulting in a brief interlude that may be called the "U.S.-Japan honeymoon."

---

[7]   See Griswold, *The Far Eastern Policy of the United States*, see p. 8.

AMERICA AS FOE

As the nineteenth century drew to an end, however, American national power had grown considerably and its aggressive, imperialistic ambitions were more manifest, markedly shifting the course of its policy in the Far East. Its most concrete and indeed shocking move was the takeover of the Philippines.

In 1898, no sooner had war broken out in the Caribbean between the United States and Spain over Cuba and Puerto Rico when the U.S. Far Eastern Fleet under the command of Admiral George Dewey entered Manila Bay. Within a day it had "liberated" the Philippines from Spanish control. At first there was celebration, as the native people thought the Americans had given them independence, but hope soon changed to despair as it became clear the Americans were bent on making the Philippines their own territory. Emilio Aguinaldo, who had been the leader of the war for independence under Spanish rule, created a line of Filipino resistance, and a long-running guerrilla war began against the U.S. forces.

The United States sought to suppress the guerillas by sheer firepower and force their way into assuming control of the Philippines, and the author of this policy was then undersecretary of the navy Theodore Roosevelt. It was also promoted by Senator Henry Cabot Lodge and other influential "hawks" in Congress.

Opposition to the American annexation of the Philippines was quite strong in the United States. Arguing that maintaining colonies went against their country's founding spirit, leading businessmen such as Andrew Carnegie, labor leaders like Samuel Gompers, writer Mark Twain, and many other prominent people were against the move. Citing evidence of the U.S. forces' cruel suppression of the resistance put up by the native peoples, they fiercely attacked the government.

The guerrilla war that unfolded was as intense and violent as that in Vietnam was to be several decades later. The United States sent nearly 100,000 regular troops to the Philippines and used gruesome tactics such as those remembered in the My Lai massacre during the Vietnam War, but on a countrywide scale. The total death toll covering both sides is said to have been between 200,000 and 250,000.

There was lively debate over the issue both inside and outside the Congress and views were divided just about half and half. Ultimately U.S. President William McKinley's hand was forced by the hawks and he decided on annexation, and with that decision, the United States became a bona fide member of the imperialist camp in the Pacific as of December 1898.

One factor that caused McKinley to commit himself to making the Philippines a U.S. possession was that Germany had been extending its ambitions into East Asia, and if the United States were to withdraw, there were signs that the Germans would quickly take over the archipelago. Fearing that scenario, Britain was tacitly encouraging the United States to go ahead with its ambitions. But in the backdrop of that step, too, was the general acceptance of expansionism then gradually spreading among Americans.

One of the most influential advocates of imperialism at that critical juncture was naval strategist, historian, and admiral Alfred Thayer Mahan. In order to protect itself from the invasion by Asian forces that many people believed was only a matter of time in coming, Mahan argued that the United States needed to establish bases at Hawai'i and other locations in the Pacific to serve as outposts of American culture. In 1890, Mahan published *The Influence of Sea Power on History, 1660–1783*, in which he railed against the pacifism that then prevailed, declaring that Americans could not afford to shut themselves up and indulge in their own safety and prosperity.

Mahan pointed to the way Britain had built itself into the world's greatest empire out of its brave mastery of the "seven seas." History showed that a country that did not develop its sea power never was able to expand its national strength. Passivity, he declared, inevitably led to the demise of a state. A mercantile state could only prosper from trade if it had a fleet of merchant ships and in order to protect such merchant ships, a country had to have military strength. It had to have a large navy, and in order to keep such ships fueled and supplied it had to be assured of access to ports at strategic points around the globe, and so on.

Mahan's books soon became best sellers, and the English editions were followed by French, German, and Russian editions. They were even translated into Japanese and strategists pored over them in Europe and Japan. The German Kaiser is said to have set to rebuilding the German navy in earnest after reading Mahan's writings, and in Japan as well, Fleet Admiral Tōgō Heihachirō, not to mention the chiefs of staff of the navy, assiduously studied Mahan's ideas.

Mahan had in fact visited Japan in his youth. The story takes us back in history again, to the time of the battle of Toba-Fushimi that took place in the first month of Meiji 1 (January 1868) in Kyoto. During the shogunate's last-ditch effort to launch an attack on Kyoto and remove the forces of the Satsuma and Chōshū domains that were attempting to lead the formation of a new government under the emperor, Shogun Tokugawa (the former Hitotsubashi) Yoshinobu, who was in the Osaka castle, suddenly lost his will to fight. Abandoning the shogunal forces and the battlefield, he planned to return to Edo and turn his allegiance to the court, ending the war. Under cover of night, Yoshinobu left the castle with other leaders of the fight who happened to be there, including the lord of the Aizu domain Matsudaira Katamori, the lord of the Kuwana domain Matsudaira Sadaaki, and senior councillors Itakura Katsushige and Sakai Utanokami. They planned to take a boat from Tenma in order to board the *Kaiyō*, a shogunal ship that was supposed to be moored off Tenpōzan.

In the dark of night, however, the fugitives could not locate the *Kaiyō*. They did find the American ship *Iroquois*, however, and decided to request refuge there for the night. The crew of the *Iroquois* was startled by this sudden visitation of illustrious guests, but did their best to be hospitable. It was the young Alfred Mahan, a senior officer on the *Iroquois*, who entertained the refugee shogun and his companions. In his recollections he describes the scene – one of the most dramatic moments in the history of Japan – with a rather detached pity: "the poor fellows presented a moving picture of human misery, and certainly were under a heavy accumulation of misfortunes: a lost battle, and probably a lost cause; flying for life, and now on an element totally new; surrounded by those who could not speak their language."[8]

Mahan remained in Japan for a half year after that, stationed off the coast. A man of intense curiosity, he made many excursions to land and observed much going on in a Japan then in the throes of an unprecedented convulsion of change. On one occasion, he writes: "I was tempted by curiosity, once while on the station, to attend the execution of some ordinary criminals; and I can testify to the deftness and instantaneousness with which one head fell, in the flash of a sword or the twinkling of an eye. I did not care to view the fates of the three others condemned, but it was clear that no judicial death could be more speedy and merciful."[9]

After returning to the United States, Mahan became instructor at the U.S. Naval Academy and later president of the Naval War College.

From around the time of the end of the first Sino-Japanese War (1894–1895), fear of emerging power in East Asia gave rise to the term "the yellow peril," which is believed to have been first used by Kaiser Wilhelm of Germany. Mahan did not mention the "yellow peril" per se, but his writings present a forceful argument regarding the relationship between the East and the West. In an essay published in *Harper's Magazine* in 1897 entitled "A Twentieth-Century Outlook," he foresaw that jealousy in the East of the wealth and power of the West would certainly boil over in the twentieth century. If it became clear that such wealth and power could only be taken by force, then they would bring force to obtain it. Before that happened, he argued, the West had to be prepared to turn back the attack. Mahan could see clearly the threat that would be posed by Asia once the hundreds of millions of people in the Asian region awoke to the reality of the world.

---

[8]   Mahan, *From Sail to Steam*, p. 243.
[9]   Mahan, *From Sail to Steam*, p. 249.

Mahan warned that, "The great task now before the world of civilized Christianity, its great mission, which it must fulfil or perish, is to receive into its own bosom and raise to its own ideals those ancient and different civilizations by which it is surrounded and outnumbered – the civilizations at the head of which stand China, India, and Japan."[10] And yet Mahan did not hold out much hope for the conversion of East Asia to Christianity. He felt that it would be difficult to get the region to accept both Western spiritual values and technology. He argued that in order to protect Christian civilization, the West must duly be prepared to defend itself for at least one or two generations.

AMERICAN HUBRIS UNLEASHED

The annexation of the Philippines turned out, however, to be a much greater burden on the United States, both materially and in terms of conscience, than had been expected.

The guerilla war continued even after the negotiations for the transfer of the territory from Spain to the United States had been concluded and American forces found they could not quell the rebellion. Suppression of the guerillas as well as protection of the new territories required sending a massive military force across the Pacific where it remained stationed for a long time.

Experience with the American forces in the Philippines turned out to be the training ground of a number of men who later became top leaders in the U.S. military. World War I hero John J. Pershing, along with George Marshall, Douglas MacArthur, Dwight D. Eisenhower, and Chester Nimitz were among the famous generals and admirals who served in the Philippines.

As long as there was a guerilla war to contend with, the United States could not hope to use the islands as a base to fend off outside threats to its sphere of influence, so negotiations with countries likely to have territorial ambitions toward the Philippines took on great importance. For the time being, the prime concern was Japan, so the United States had to do its utmost, whether it might involve threats or conciliation, to forestall

---

[10] *Harpers New Monthly Magazine* 95 (September 1897), p. 527.

any ideas that Japanese might have of invading the Philippines. The "honeymoon" between the two countries ended as the two became first partners in imperialism and later competitors destined for confrontation.

Young as the new government still was under the Meiji Emperor at the turn of the century, Japan had gained quite a bit of knowledge and experience regarding imperialism. Indeed, Japan's diplomacy was sternly forged according to the principle of survival of the fittest. At first its fervent wish was only to defend itself from the predations of the big powers, but it was not long before its national policy became focused on joining the European powers in the dividing up of rights and interests on the continent. The most dangerous threat to Japan was from Russia. Russia's strong interests in Manchuria and Korea meant it was just a matter of time until serious conflict arose between the two countries.

Britain, the veteran among imperialists, was steadily and systematically making its moves to expand its interests in the Middle East, India, Singapore, Hong Kong, Shanghai and along the delta reaches of the Yangtze river. No other country was as calculating and shrewd, but on the other hand, if one made a large enough compromise, Britain was sure to sufficiently reward it.

When the United States first joined in the competition for interests in Asia, Japan did not attempt to deny or oppose its actions. It remained the weakest of the imperialist powers, and intervention from the United States, with which Japan at that time had good relations, seemed actually welcome as a kind of brake vis-à-vis the more callous actions of the European powers. But Japanese observers, Eiichi included, were aware of the tremendous power of the United States and concerned about its tendency for startling moves, as evidenced by the invasion of the Philippines.

While the United States had gained the Philippines, it still had no foothold in China. Following the scramble for concessions in China by European powers that ensued after the end of the Sino-Japanese War, there was little left in the way of resources that America could avail itself of. That was when the United States came up with its policy of "the open door and territorial integrity [of China]." This was exactly the "startling" sort of thing that Eiichi had expected, and it became the cause of much consternation, not only for Japan but the other imperial powers. In 1899, American Secretary of State John Hay dispatched to his European counterparts what was called the "Open Door Notes," in which he called on those countries to agree to keep China open to trade with all countries on an equal basis and protect the territorial integrity of China – a rare showing of moral rectitude in those days of plunder and exploitation.

The Open Door Notes were about as effective as a traffic safety slogan: while there was no overt opposition, they were not expected, from the outset, to really change anything. It was typical of the United States that it seemed convinced that such an appeal meant anything at all in the world of international diplomatic bargaining. The situation in China was exceedingly complex, and the stratagems of the big powers were not limited to clearly defined matters such as division of territory and discriminatory tariff rates. Their intrigues involved all sorts of things, like obtaining rights to build railway lines and rights to open and operate mines as well as the transfer of some police rights and rights to station troops in order to maintain and protect such facilities. They were far from being simple enough to be dealt with by slogans like "the open door" and "territorial integrity." The big powers knew that very well, and therefore were at a loss as to what the United States was up to; for some time, they watched and waited to see what the others would do, and then indicated their willingness to agree if the other countries did so.

To their surprise, the United States took the conditional responses of the other countries at face value and assumed that the other countries had agreed with the moral principles it advocated. It concluded that China's independence would be established and peace defended in East Asia. The Americans thought they had won a shining victory for U.S. diplomacy.

The "open door" policy may have been the "right" and just policy, but for the still-young United States, it was just an idea it espoused. From the beginning, the Americans had no intention of assuming any economic or military responsibility. Ultimately, they could do little to rein in the self-interested actions of the other powers. Nevertheless, having set forth its declaration of the "open door," the United States acquired a rather self-righteous confidence that it was involved on the continent not for the purpose of fulfilling territorial ambitions but as a moral force devoted to defending China's independence.

This American hubris governed U.S. Far Eastern diplomacy for a long time thereafter, and by the time World War I ended it had escalated to the stage at which Americans had come to believe that thwarting Japanese imperialist designs and defending the independence of China was the responsibility of the American people.

FACE TO FACE WITH RACIAL DISCRIMINATION

With the turn into the twentieth century, the honeymoon between Japan and the United States ended and Japanese were keenly aware that relations had entered a new phase. As long as Japan was small and weak, the United States went out of its way to stand by it and stand up for it, but once that country grew up to be stronger and more mature, all at once it became a rival and competitor. The same pattern, indeed, has been repeated several times after that. We saw that same trend when we look at the Japan-U.S. negotiations over the issues of textile exports in the late 1960s and early 1970s and capital liberalization in the late 1980s and early 1990s.

At the beginning of the twentieth century, another very serious issue was unfolding: the exclusion of Japanese immigrants from the United States. Even though that problem was to be an extremely difficult thorn in relations between Japan and the United States for more than 30 years from then on, Japanese of that time were not sufficiently aware of its significance.

Before Japanese became the targets of immigration exclusion, Chinese had been excluded, so it was only to be expected that the same thing would happen to Japanese. At the time, however, Japanese were of the impression that Chinese were being excluded because of the low cultural standard of living of the Chinese in the United States, most of whom were laborers, and they rather simplistically and arrogantly thought that they themselves were more sophisticated and well educated, so they raised not a finger in protest when Chinese were excluded from the United States. By the time they realized the naïveté of their assumptions, it was too late to do anything about the situation, and Japanese were like ants that have fallen into the antlion's pit; no matter how they might scramble they would end up becoming ever-more deeply mired in the pit.

Other than the Native Americans whose ancestors had spread over the continent before the coming of the Europeans, the United States is a nation of immigrants – people who flooded to the continent under the banner of freedom and equality in search of happiness and prosperity. Since its founding, the United States developed as a multiethnic nation like no other: Massive numbers of black Africans were herded out of the depths of Africa and into slave ships that brought them to work on plantations in the South. Mexicans, Chinese, and Japanese later arrived in large numbers as contract workers and in other ways.

From Asia, the earliest migrant laborers were Chinese. In the mid-nineteenth century when the Gold Rush began, there was a severe shortage of labor. Filling that need, Chinese laborers, farmers, and retail merchants first came in 1848, and they played an important role in the opening up of the new territories. Within only five years, by 1853, there were 25,000 Chinese living in California.

Development continued after that, and when construction began on the Central Pacific Railroad, demand for labor increased steadily again. The Seward-Burlingame Treaty of 1868[11] was signed allowing Chinese free immigration and travel in the United States. The number of migrant Chinese swelled and in the 1880s the number of Chinese immigrants had surpassed 130,000.

---

[11] Signed by Secretary of State William Seward and Anson Burlingame acting on behalf of China (who had formerly been in the employ of the State Department but resigned and was hired by the Chinese government to represent it in dealings with the Western powers).

As long as labor was in short supply, the Chinese were welcomed, but as the Gold Rush slacked off and the railroad building was more or less complete, the labor market in the West was suddenly in surplus, and unemployed white laborers had to compete with Chinese coolies and contract workers. Once the land was more or less opened up, moreover, and people had begun to settle down, the mainstream society of whites was disturbed to find farms, shops, and restaurants run by Chinese appearing everywhere in their communities.

While the United States was already a multiethnic society, in fact the prevailing sense since the country was founded was that it was "a white man's country." People of Anglo-Saxon stock from England did indeed occupy the highest status in terms of wealth and power, as well as in population numbers, and joining them as "white people" were those of German, French, and Scandinavian stock. Among Europeans, however, migrants from Italy, Poland, Greece, and other countries were considered second-class minority groups.

People of non-white ethnic groups were not treated as full citizens under the law or in American society. Even after the emancipation of the slaves following the Civil War, a rigid framework of racial discrimination strictly limited the rights and freedoms of blacks. People from East Asia, too, were considered inferior to whites and were seen as people who ought to serve the interests of the white majority society. Given such realities, when it became clear that Chinese workers might be taking away the jobs of white workers, there was much outcry and a sense of the threat posed to the safety and authority of white society.

In 1858, the California State Legislature passed a law barring Chinese from entering the state. The exclusion law was eventually struck down by the state supreme court, which argued that immigration measures fell within the scope of national trade and commerce (matters that were under the jurisdiction of the federal government), and stated that it would be unconstitutional for state law to attempt to control such matters. The decision reflected awareness of the fact that the Seward-Burlingame treaty was still in effect.

Illegal as the exclusion they insisted on might be, Californians were furious at the court's decision and there were demonstrations against Chinese immigration and incidents of violence. A group of white workers in San Francisco went on a rampage in Chinatown, shouting "Chinese go home," and looting, setting fire to buildings, and beating up people in their path. The violence spread to Seattle, Tacoma, and east to Wyoming, and many innocent Chinese saw their shops burned and their property stolen. There were lynchings as well.[12]

In 1869, journalist and writer Ambrose Bierce, who was known for his satires, published an article describing the way whites were behaving in those days:

> On last Sunday afternoon a Chinaman passing guilelessly along Dupont Street was assailed with a tempest of bricks and stones from the steps of the First Congregational Church. At the completion of this devotional exercise the Sunday scholars retired within the hallowed portals of the sanctuary, to hear about Christ Jesus and him crucified. (*San Francisco News Letter*, August 7, 1869)[13]

Bierce's writings bitterly attacked the discriminatory treatment of Chinese in the Western states and the hypocrisy of the white majority.

Racial discrimination was inseparable from the issue of maintaining the purity of blood lines, and whites feared above all the interbreeding of their daughters with blacks. The same was true regarding Chinese. Liaisons between white women and Chinese men were sensationalized in the newspapers of the day and made into all-absorbing scandals. It was a time when readers were willing to believe claims that Chinese men possessed a curious power to ensnare white women.

Bierce's writings lampooned the supposedly fine city gentlemen who passed around such rumors while they themselves

---

[12] For an overview of the anti-Chinese movement in the United States, see "The Chinese Exclusion Act of 1882 and Racial Discrimination in the United States," by Aris Teon, dated 10 February 2017, in *The Greater China Journal*, online at https://china-journal.org/2017/02.

[13] https://thegrandarchive.wordpress.com/the-town-crier-26/

could be seen at night, their overcoat collars turned up and hat brims pulled down, visiting gaily dressed Chinese prostitutes in the backstreets of Chinatown. Famous for his *Tom Sawyer* and *Huckleberry Finn*, Mark Twain too, showed his indignation at the hypocrisy and deceit of his fellow Americans. In *Roughing It*, he writes:

> He is a great convenience to everybody – even to the worst class of white men, for he [the Chinaman] bears the most of their sins, suffering fines for their petty thefts, imprisonment for their robberies, and death for their murders. Any white man can swear a Chinaman's life away in the courts, but no Chinaman can testify against a white man. Ours is the "land of the free" – nobody denies that – nobody challenges it. [Maybe it is because we won't let other people testify.] As I write, news comes that in broad daylight in San Francisco, some boys have stoned an inoffensive Chinaman to death, and that although a large crowd witnessed the shameful deed, no one interfered.[14]

Their efforts to shut out Chinese thwarted by the federal government and its treaty with China, the California State Legislature launched a powerful movement to push through its demands by lobbying in the Congress. The state's population increased and as its status in the union rose, the influence of its exclusionist movement grew stronger, and by the time of the 1876 presidential election, the candidates for both the Republican and Democratic parties could not but pledge themselves in support of Chinese immigration exclusion. In 1882 the Chinese Exclusion Act was passed in Congress and though President Chester A. Arthur made an effort to veto it as a diplomatic gesture, the only change made was to reduce the term of validity to 10 from 20 years before it went into effect on May 6.

The stance on immigration taken in the United States at that time denied and contradicted the essential nature of democracy and the values Americans supposedly stood for. The Christian teachings of love and compassion they followed in their daily lives and the

---

[14] Twain, *Roughing It.*

freedom, equality, and respect for rights upon which they had built their nation applied to everything that pertained to the interests of the white-centered society, but if those interests were threatened, such teachings and ideals were as if non-existent, and people showed only their zeal to protect their vested interests. Moreover, in order to whitewash the injustices they were perpetrating, they found excuses to go even further in attacking their targets.

The charge that Chinese were incapable of assimilating into American society was the most convenient fuel for their arguments. They claimed that Chinese did not have the capacity or the will to ever assimilate into the white man's American society and join in the nation building of America. Conveniently forgetting that it was their own discriminatory behavior that encouraged the immigrants to stay in their ghettoes, they declared that Chinese clustered together in their own communities and made no attempt to blend in with the wider society. There would be no benefit, it was argued, to the United States to allow such people to live among them. Cruel treatment of such people, the logic went, was justified as "self-defense."

The highhanded tactic of forcing on others ideas arbitrarily deemed to be right and using that sense of right as if it legitimized armed attack could be seen in every conflict between the West and non-West. It was behind the behavior of the British in China at the time of the Opium Wars, and may indeed be seen as a proclivity inherent in the nature of Western Christian civilization itself. It is a characteristic observed over and over until this very day that undermines the credibility of Christianity itself.

The government of China frequently protested the unilateral actions of the United States regarding the immigration exclusion laws, but to no avail. The Chinese empire at that time was weak and, kept busy dealing with the predations of the European powers on its own soil, it could not negotiate effectively regarding its migrants on the opposite side of the Pacific. The United States took advantage of the situation, ignoring Chinese protests and forcing its ideas on Beijing, regardless of anything China might have had to say.

In 1887 the Chinese government protested to the American ambassador residing in Beijing at the time that Chinese in the United States were being mistreated. In 1888 the U.S. government, however, far from addressing the protest, retaliated by pressing China to sign a treaty prohibiting all Chinese immigration to the United States. Then, even as China had reluctantly signed the treaty, the Senate demanded that a clause be added to the treaty that would deny Chinese migrants who had gone back to visit China the right of reentry to the United States.

Unwilling to accept such an unreasonable addition to the treaty, China refused to ratify it. In response, the Congress notified China of its decision to make the treaty effective regardless of whether it was ratified or not, and the president and the Supreme Court went along with the decision. The State Department, responsible for foreign affairs, was thus forced to submit to political pressure and had to act as if it did not know what was going on. In response to China's protests, it replied mechanically with pat phrases to the effect that the protests would be "seriously considered."

Eiichi was himself to come face to face with racial discrimination in 1902, when he visited the United States, but it would not be until years later that the reality of what he had seen would sink in. During his visit to San Francisco, he saw a sign at the Golden Gate Bridge beach park saying, "No Japanese allowed." Quick to be aroused by anything that might smack of discrimination, he demanded, "What is the meaning of this?" His guide, then Japanese consul in San Francisco Ueno Suesaburō, grimaced and explained "Oh, there were some young Japanese-American boys who apparently swam underwater and touched the legs of some of the white women, creating a scandal that led to this rule. It's been quite a headache for me."[15]

Was the rule necessary because of such a minor prank? Eiichi had a strong sense that there was much more to the matter than that. Unfair and discriminatory treatment was very difficult for

---

[15] *Ryūmon zasshi* vol. 310 (March 1914), p. 21; "Nichibei kokkō to yo no kankei" (My Involvement in Japan–U.S. Relations (Seien Sensei), *Shibusawa denki shiryō*, vol. 25, pp. 477–78.

Japanese to bear, then as now. Worried as he was about what might happen from then on, he commiserated with Ueno on the difficulty of his job and encouraged him to do his best. He made no more fuss over the matter at the time, but the memory of that sign was hard to get out of his mind, and when a few years later the movement to exclude Japanese immigrants reared its head, Eiichi knew his concern had been on the mark.

Alfred Mahan died in 1914 at the age of 74, but just before he died, he had written that America's youth was over. The light-hearted, happy-go-lucky days of a new nation were gone, never to return. From now on, he declared, it would inevitably face in full measure the sufferings and misery of a mature country.

Mahan's prophecy proved true not only in the case of the United States but also of Japan and of relations between the two countries. Until then Japan had been like a young man, serious of purpose and intent on the future, making its way forward with grit and determination. It eventually found itself in the complex adult world as a country with power and ambition. With the opening of the twentieth century, misunderstanding, mistrust, and hatred infused relations between the two countries, leading to complex and dangerous developments.

CHAPTER 2

LAUNCHING PRIVATE-SECTOR DIPLOMACY

හ

IN THE SUMMER of 1879, former U.S. president Ulysses S. Grant visited Japan on his way back to the United States from a pleasure trip to Europe and other parts of Asia. Grant was a world celebrity. He had received many honors for having led the Union armies to victory in the American Civil War over the forces of the Confederate war hero Robert E. Lee. After the war ended, he had served as president for two terms from 1869 to 1877. He was the most illustrious guest, in both status and fame, that Japan had received since it opened itself to the world only two decades earlier.

This was a time when a trip around the world took half a year, traveling by ship. It was completely unprecedented for a former president of a big country like the United States to pay a visit to a small country like Japan in the remote Far East. The news that Grant planned to visit Japan ignited much excitement, with both the government and private individuals planning various gala welcomes for him half a year in advance.

Japan's own civil war, known as the Bōshin War, in which forces of the former Tokugawa shogunate were defeated by the troops of the new regime, had ended only eleven years earlier, and the country had just begun its first efforts to modernize under the leadership of the twenty-seven-year-old Emperor Meiji. The government was led by Grand Minister of State Sanjō Sanetomi (1837–1891) and Minister of the Right Iwakura Tomomi (1825–1883), and under the guidance of *sangi* councilors, including Ōkubo Toshimichi, Yamagata Aritomo, and Itō Hirobumi, the country was pouring strenuous effort into nation-building. Only two years previously, the Satsuma Rebellion had posed a major threat to the established order, so the new country was hardly on a steady footing.

The Western powers remained skeptical in their views of the country's progress toward modernization, rejecting Japan's most-fervent efforts to renegotiate the unequal treaties signed in the final years of the Tokugawa shogunate. Their skepticism was understandable, as little more than a decade had passed since the country was governed in completely feudal fashion by a ruling class of two-sword-carrying samurai, not a few of whom had sworn to cut down any foreigner they might come upon.

Today, the developed countries tend to be quite considerate of the rights of the developing countries in Asia, Africa, and elsewhere; far from imposing unequal treaties on such countries, they find it virtually their duty to extend them military protection and economic assistance. But in the nineteenth century, the attitude of the Western powers toward the less-developed countries was unsentimental and harsh. It was a time when Westerners simply assumed that only they were civilized; other peoples were dismissed as not quite part of the human race. In the face of such attitudes, Japanese gritted their teeth, determined to show that they could modernize their country on their own and resist the pressures placed upon them from the West. The visit of a famous person such as Ulysses S. Grant offered an unbelievably good opportunity to show off what Japan really had to offer. Everyone was determined to take advantage of the chance to display their success at modernizing their country under the banner of "civilization and enlightenment" (*bunmei kaika*) and make a good impression on the popular former president.

And Japanese were – and are – a people who love entertaining guests. It is a trait that might come naturally to inhabitants of a remote archipelago well off the beaten track of mainstream civilization and seldom visited by people of world importance.

With a long tradition of welcoming guests, Japanese would do whatever they could to entertain this important American visitor, no matter what the sacrifices might be. Grant's visit provided the first grand-scale chance since the regime change of 1868 for putting that tradition into action.

One challenge Japan faced in 1879 was the custom that had been observed in Western countries when state guests were entertained and welcome extended, not only by royalty or by leaders of the government, but by the citizens of the land. Such welcomes by the citizenry were considered a feature of a truly democratic state, so if Japan wished to impress Grant with its modernity, it would have to produce some sort of citizen-led welcome. Without it, Grant might conclude that while the ruler might have changed from the Tokugawa shoguns to the imperial house, the political system was as much a dictatorship as it had been before. Somehow, the welcome program needed a dimension sponsored by the private sector.

It would be a difficult feat, given that up until only ten or so years earlier the country had been firmly in the grip of the feudalistic *bakuhan* system with a rigid social system separating the ruling aristocratic and samurai class, the farmer landowning and tenant agrarian class, and the urban artisan and merchant class. There were essentially no private organizations that represented "the will of the people." Minister of Finance Ōkuma Shigenobu must have realized this lack when he was negotiating with British envoy Sir Harry Parkes on tariffs several years earlier. The export and import taxes at the time had been forced on Japan by the Western powers in the waning years of the Tokugawa shogunate, and without any previous experience regarding tariffs, Japan found itself in very disadvantageous positions. Changing these arrangements, too, was part of the process of obtaining revisions of the treaties that had been signed. To counter Parkes's unilateral and unfair assertion of Britain's terms, Ōkuma did his best to bluff, declaring that what he was saying was not just his own opinion. "Public opinion in Japan wouldn't accept such terms." To this Parkes, who was by then quite familiar with Japan, is said to have expressed doubt that "public opinion" even existed in

FIGURE 7
Ōkuma Shigenobu (1838–1922;
left) as minister of finance with
Itō Hirobumi (1841–1909;
right), home affairs minister,
around 1878. Photo: Courtesy of
Hirobumi Ito Museum, Hikari,
Yamaguchi prefecture.

Japan, disdaining Ōkuma's claims as the notion of mere tradesmen serving the government.[16]

Around 1878, the year before Grant was to visit, Ōkuma must have realized that something had to be done to rally "public opinion." He consulted with Minister of Home Affairs Itō Hirobumi and they decided to call in Shibusawa Eiichi, who had been an official in the Ministry of Finance until a few years earlier and had left the government to work in the private sector. They held a meeting with him at which they asked him to create

---

[16] *Ryūmon zasshi* 509 (February 1931), pp. 28–34. See also, William Miles Fletcher, *The Japanese Business Community and National Trade Policy, 1920–1942*, p. 10: "When [Japanese] diplomats told the British ambassador, Harry Parkes, that public opinion would not tolerate the treaties, Parkes had replied pointedly that no organized commercial groups existed in Japan to voice public opinion on economic matters! Hence arose the sudden fascination with chambers of commerce."

an organization that would represent the views of the merchants – the modern business world.[17]

As it happened, Eiichi had had his eye on the Yokohama Foreign Chamber of Commerce that had earlier been established by the foreign residents of the open treaty port of Yokohama to handle the various problems they shared in dealing with trade issues or matters of daily life. He had become convinced that Japan needed an organization of that kind as well. With Ōkuma's request as added incentive, in March 1878 he founded the Tokyo Chamber of Commercial Law (Tōkyō Shōhō Kaigisho; later renamed the Tōkyō Shōgyō Kaigisho or Tokyo Chamber of Commerce). He himself became its president and brought in associates Fukuchi Gen'ichirō and Masuda Takashi (1848–1938) to serve as vice presidents.[18]

Then, in rather last-minute fashion, with members chosen from the Tokyo Prefectural Assembly and the Tokyo Chamber of Commercial Law, a Tokyo Welcome Committee was formed to play the role of planning and carrying out a citizens' welcome for Grant. This was the launching of private-sector diplomacy in Japan. The members of the committee, in addition to the above three, were Ōkura Kihachirō (1837–1928; later, founder of the Ōkura *zaibatsu* financial combine), Yasuda Zenjirō (1838–1921; founder of the Yasuda *zaibatsu*), Minomura Risuke (1843–1901; son-in-law of Rizaemon, founder of the Mitsui *zaibatsu*), Yonekura Ippei (1831–1904; leader of the Tokyo Rice Exchange), Asabuki Eiji (1849–1918; a leading figure of Mitsui Group), and Narushima Ryūhoku (1837–1884; president of the popular rights-oriented newspaper *Chōya shinbun*).

---

[17] *Shibusawa denki shiryō*, vol. 25, pp. 523–27.

[18] The three of them had formerly worked in the Ministry of Finance and left the government in 1873. Eiichi had been absorbed with managing the just-founded Dai-ichi Bank and the Ōji Paper Company and Fukuchi was a pioneer in the field of journalism, managing the *Tōkyō Nichinichi shinbun* while serving as a member of the Tokyo Prefectural Assembly (no election law yet existed in Japan at the time, so all the members were appointed by the government). Masuda was the founder of the Senshū-Gaisha that was the predecessor of the Mitsui Bussan trading company. Ibid.

THE HONORED VISITORS ARRIVE

At 10:40 a.m. on the 3rd of July, 1879, Grant and his wife Julia, and their son Colonel Frederick Grant arrived at Yokohama on the naval ship *USS Richmond*. It was a clear early summer day. Cannons boomed in salute and a display of 170 fireworks lit up the sky. All the leading members of the government were on the quay to meet them – Minister of Foreign Affairs Mori Arinori, Minister of the Right Iwakura Tomomi, and councilors Itō Hirobumi, Saigō Tsugumichi, and Inoue Kaoru – and they all soon headed for Tokyo on a special train.

In Tokyo, people were waiting with bated breath for the arrival of the honored guests, having done everything possible in preparation. From Shimbashi Station to the Enryōkan (later Shiba Detached Palace) where the Grants would be lodged, the soldiers of the first regiment of the Tokyo Garrison lined the street. The houses and shops along the way were decked out gaily with Japanese and American flags. Here and there were large welcome arches covered with green leaves, one of them featuring the initials "USG" formed with hydrangea blossoms.

When the special train arrived at Shimbashi Station at 2:00 p.m., music swelled from the band assembled on the immaculately prepared platform. With Tokyo Prefectural Governor Kusumoto Masataka in the lead, Eiichi and the other members of the city hospitality committee members advanced to greet the party. When the Grants alighted from the train, Eiichi read out the official welcome as their representative.

In 1867, Eiichi had visited England accompanying 13-year-old Tokugawa Akitake, who served as envoy to Europe on behalf of his brother and last shogun Tokugawa Keiki (Yoshinobu). When their ship had arrived at Dover, a representative of the citizens had come out to welcome Akitake and made a welcome speech. Following the model of that occasion as Eiichi recalled it, the speech praised Grant's exploits in battle and his high moral example, expressed appreciation for the friendly stance he had shown toward the Japanese people during his administration as president, and wrapped up with eloquent phrases honoring him and welcoming him to Tokyo.

FIGURE 8
Ulysses S. Grant
(1822–1885), eigh-
teenth president of the
United States. Photo:
National Diet Library,
Japan.

Grant's journey around the world, even allowing for the
relatively undeveloped state of means of transport at the
time, was an extremely long one. He took about two years,
traveling through Europe and Northern Africa, touring
countries in the Middle and Near East, and continuing to
India, China, and Japan before returning home. Also part of
Grant's party was a *New York Herald Tribune* journalist named
John Russell Young.

Grant was known throughout his life as a man of few words,
and even during his presidencies, it had been difficult to determine what he thought in interviews and on other occasions.
The *Herald Tribune* was famous for its scoop of a few years
earlier when its reporter Henry Morton Stanley traveled into
the African jungles and "found" David Livingstone, the famed
missionary and explorer who had "vanished" there. Now the
paper reasoned that in the course of the former president's

long trip, he would express his thoughts on this and that and perhaps even give the paper a scoop of some sort, so it had sent Young along. Young fulfilled his mission, not only by writing several hundred dispatches for the *Herald*, but by also publishing the two-volume, 1,200-page *Around the World with General Grant* (1879).

Born in the state of Ohio in 1822, Grant graduated from the U.S. military academy at West Point in 1843, but it took him 10 years to be promoted to captain. He then left the army and became a farmer for a time, but the Civil War began and his fortunes changed completely, placing him right at the center of historic events.

The U.S. Army leaders found Grant a puzzling figure as a leader of troops. He was short in stature, by no means a formidable presence among others. In ordinary times, he was often oblivious to the most ordinary things, exhibiting a slightly distracted air that made him seem even a bit dull. When presented with a challenging or difficult situation, however, he grasped the crux of the problem with unexpected perceptivity and good judgment, and invariably emerged victorious.

Grant is remembered for his role in the Civil War battles in Kentucky, Tennessee, and Jackson, Mississippi, and for his great victory at Chattanooga, after which he was made lieutenant general. He remained at the center of the war until 1865 brought him to Virginia and the final encounter with the Confederate general Robert E. Lee, whose forces he defeated, securing the Union victory signed at Appomattox in April that year. In addition to his vigorous fighting spirit and decisiveness as well as fearlessness in battle, Grant was also known for his warm-heartedness, as demonstrated by the story of the way he respected Robert E. Lee, even to the point of fighting with the government when it threatened to put Lee on trial for treason.

Grant did not cut a particularly illustrious figure as president of the United States. U.S. presidents, chosen as they are by a citizenry likely to be critical at every turn, tend to be flamboyant figures of one sort or other. Some, such as George Washington and Abraham Lincoln, were later idolized, and others included shrewd politicians such as Theodore Roosevelt or brilliant leaders such as Woodrow Wilson and John Kennedy. Grant was one of several presidents who had formerly distinguished themselves as military leaders, but compared to most others, his record as a diplomat was initially rather unimpressive.

Preoccupied by domestic issues, Grant had not been much involved or interested in world affairs as president, but that changed immediately after he set off on his trip abroad. What he saw of the world in the Middle East, India, China, and elsewhere deeply affected him. His traveling companion Young records him as saying,

> . . . since I left India I have seen things that made my blood boil, in the way the European powers attempt to degrade the Asiatic nations. I would not believe such a policy possible. It seems to have no other aim than the extinction of the independence of the Asiatic nations.[19]

In Northeast Asia at the time, only China and Japan had somehow managed to maintain some degree of independence, but all the other countries had succumbed to the rule of one or other of the European powers. Swelled with the arrogance of power built on science, technology, and modern industry, Western states grasped control, established colonial administrations, and plundered the resources of countries all over Asia and Africa, entirely for the profit of their home countries. The ethical and moral traditions of Christianity and Western culture not only did nothing to restrain such arrogance and avarice, they were actively mobilized to justify the actions of the colonial powers.

Billions of people around the world, simply because they were not "Western" and were not followers of Christianity, were stamped with the label of "inferior races" and their rights and traditions trampled on. Moreover, the politics and economy of the world were managed in such a way as to make such treatment seem as if it were perfectly natural. Probably in no other era before or since have human civiliza-

---

[19] From Young, *Around the World with General Grant*, p. 543.

tions been betrayed on such a vast scale. For the small island country of Japan striving to defend its autonomy at the far eastern edge of the colonialized world and amid the overt scheming governed by colonial values, nation building was no easy task.

Ulysses S. Grant may not have been brilliant, but he retained a healthy spirit of honesty and sincerity that allowed him to perceive the difficult situation Japan faced. He both sympathized and believed that the West could not keep up such evil ways for long and would eventually suffer the repercussions of their transgressions. The account of his impressions of Japan continues:

> Japan is rapidly reaching a condition of independence and if it had now to be done over such treaties as exist could not be forced upon her . . . I can readily conceive that there are many foreigners, particularly those interested in trade, who do not look beyond the present and who would like to have the present condition remain, only grasping more from the East, . . . I have so much sympathy for the good of their children if not for them, that I hope the two countries will not disappoint them.[20]

A century later, the posterity of the white colonialists was indeed facing the consequences of the transgressions of the past. The war in Vietnam was part of those consequences; the civil wars in Africa and the wars in the Middle East are also their extension. Amid the current of fundamental changes taking place in the world order, the cost the West is faced with paying grows only larger and the suffering and injustice it exacts in the process are far more intense than ever expected.

Grant, being a man of the kind of convictions and sensibilities expressed in the passage above, was a person who would quite naturally receive an enthusiastic welcome in Japan. Japanese had an intuitive capacity to see beyond surface impressions and detect the true nature of visitors from overseas. And if their own feelings matched well with a visitor, they would open up completely in welcome.

---

[20] See Baxter, "Informal Diplomacy in Meiji Japan," p. 223.

THE WELCOME PARTY AND BALL

> You are cordially invited to attend a ball to be held in honor of U.S. President Grant on the 8th of this month [July], at the Imperial College of Engineering in Toranomon. Please present yourself at the venue at 9:00 p.m.
>
> > Respectfully yours,
> > Shibusawa Eiichi
> > Fukuchi Gen'ichirō
> > On behalf of the Tokyo Welcome Committee
>
> Dress should be Western evening attire or *haori* and *hakama* Japanese attire. Please inform us whether you will attend or not as soon as possible by writing to Tokyo Welcome Committee at the Tokyo Chamber of Commercial Law, 10-chōme Kobikichō.

This is a translation of what was probably the first invitation to such a grand ball to welcome a foreign guest hosted by citizens of Tokyo in the history of Japan. The venue, the Imperial College of Engineering (Kōbu Daigakkō; predecessor of the Faculty of Engineering of the University of Tokyo) in Toranomon in central Tokyo, was then the largest Western-style building in the city.

The Tokyo Welcome Committee planners of citizen's hospitality for Grant were ambitious. Their program started off with a grand ball at the Imperial College building. They chartered the Shintomi kabuki playhouse in Kyōbashi on July 16th to host an evening at the theater for the Grants, and then on August 25th, the country's very first lantern parade (*chōchin gyōretsu*) featured in an elaborate welcome pageant, a colorful and impressive program to which even the emperor was invited as a guest of the citizens of Tokyo.[21]

The budget drawn up for these events was the then huge sum of 30,000 yen in the currency of the time (something like 74 million yen today) and all of it was covered by donations.

Eiichi took a leading role in the fund-raising. One anecdote passed down is that at a gathering of businessmen at which

---

[21] As reported by Hoshino Takeo in *Tengyō minpō*, June 15, 1930; see *Shibusawa denki shiryō*, vol. 25, p. 537.

Eiichi was present, the conversation shifted to the expenses for the Grant welcome program. It happened that Iwasaki Yatarō, the head of the fabulously wealthy Mitsubishi enterprise, was absent, but Eiichi went up to his younger brother Yanosuke, who was in attendance, and challenged him, saying: "I'm planning to donate 5,000 yen. You folks made a lot of money from the Seinan War [Satsuma Rebellion of 1877], so why don't you get your brother to give us 10,000 yen for the fund?"

When Yanosuke appeared hesitant, Eiichi pressed him, "Don't tell me you can't afford it; just say 'yes'!"

His pride perhaps hurt, Yanosuke declared, "Who's saying we can't afford it!" and the two of them, still young at the time, practically came to fisticuffs before someone stepped in to calm their tempers. Yanosuke promised – whatever his brother decided to do – to put up 3,000 yen. The veracity of such a story is doubtful, but it nevertheless gives us a sense of the atmosphere among the businessmen excited by the preparations to welcome General Grant.[22]

In fact, their enthusiasm was such that too much money was collected and a most unusual advertisement was placed in the daily newspaper *Tōkyō Nichinichi shinbun* on July 7:

In preparation for the visit of former U.S. president Grant to Tokyo, in addition to the lavish hospitality to be provided by the Grand Council of State [central government], we decided – for the sake of friendly interchange with other countries – that we, the people of Tokyo prefecture, ought not to simply stand by idly, so, inadequate as we might be, assumed the office of members of a [private] welcome committee. We decided to issue a call throughout the prefecture for public contributions to cover the expenses of our program, but before that a number of those supporting this plan made generous contributions. When we calculated the amount of money needed against the amount that had already been collected, we found that we would have no concern about shortage of funds. So, thanks to the large amount that was unexpectedly and expeditiously collected, we found that we did not need to trouble the good people of Tokyo for further contributions. We hereby undertake to entertain Japan's illustrious visitor on behalf of the people of Tokyo.

---

[22] Ihara, *Meiji engekishi*, pp. 243–45.

We therefore inform you about that with a report on the above developments. With sincere wishes for the public happiness.

Tokyo Welcome Committee, July 1879

The invitation to the grand ball at the Imperial College of Engineering included urging the guests – especially those who were members of the welcome committee – to have their wives and daughters attend as well. This traditionally unheard-of idea caused a sensation in the businessmen's households, where women had almost never attended public occasions with their husbands. Eiichi's daughter Utako, who was 17 at the time (she later married Hozumi Nobushige, recipient of the country's first doctorate of law), appeared in public for the first time at this ball. One can only imagine her amazement at the immensity of the grand auditorium with its lofty ceiling and stout pillars along both sides, all gaily decorated for the occasion. For the diminutive Utako seeing an example of Western architecture for the first time, it must have been quite overwhelming.[23]

The raised podium at the head of the hall was decorated for the seating of the guests of honor. On one side were the seats for other important guests. The more than 1,500 guests who assembled that evening included ambassadors from various countries, imperial family members, and the government people who were invited by Tokyo citizens as well as ministers of state, *sangi* councilors, high-ranking members of the bureaucracy, elite members of the army and navy, journalists, respected religious leaders, doctors and many more.

Despite the special invitation, the number of women who attended the ball was small. Grand Minister of State Sanjō Sanetomi's wife arrived in full formal Japanese-style attire (*keiko uchikake*), an unusual sight that Utako recalled left her staring with fascination.

---

[23] For Hozumi Utako's recollections of the Grant visit, see *Ryūmon zasshi* 509 (February 1931), pp. 35–39. *Shibusawa denki shiryō*, vol. 25, pp. 492–93. See also Hozumi, *Hozumi utako nikki*.

At the time, it was only the wives of diplomats or others with some special connection to other countries who might appear outside the home at such social events, and even then, only rarely. The women of ordinary households had only limited occasions for dressing formally, such as at the weddings of family members or relatives or when participating in the Buddhist memorial ceremonies held for deceased family members; they almost never attended other large banquets.

The hosts of the party had quite explicitly instructed that, since it was a ball, the women's dress should be lavish and colorful, but their efforts were mostly in vain. At the time, if one wanted to purchase new and colorful fabrics, unlike in our current era of mass consumption, even the most venerable and well-stocked kimono shops like the Echigoya (later Mitsukoshi Department Store) or Daimaru did not have large stocks, and there was not enough time. Eiichi's wife Chiyo was forced to make do with a formal silk-gauze overkimono with family crests that she had, and for the young Utako a new *kokumochi*-type kimono (black fabric with family crest dyed in white circles) was made by Echigoya with a pattern around the hem.

The wives of the welcome committee members might have been expected to play active roles at the ball as hostesses alongside their husbands, but this was very much the first time for this sort of thing, and they had no idea how to comport themselves. Although they might want to rely on their husbands, the men had all gone ahead to the venue, leaving them behind. Not wanting the awkwardness of straggling in one at a time, a number of them decided to gather at a tea room near the Imperial College and set out from there together.

Hozumi Utako's memories of that evening contributed to the *Ryūmon zasshi* in February 1931,[24] tell that "Fifteen or sixteen gathered, including the wives of Masuda Takashi and Ōkura Kihachirō and the daughter of Yonekura Ippei, but Mrs. Fukuchi did not appear that day. They were like completely raw recruits going off to a battle they knew nothing about."

---

[24] Quoted passages translated from *Ryūmon zasshi* 509 (February 1931), pp. 36–38.

Eiichi led the welcome committee group ushering General Grant to the venue. Fukuchi accompanied Mrs. Grant. Utako had expected that Westerners were all so tall as to look down on her short-statured father, but to her surprise, he did not look out of place beside the relatively short general. In the lines of his neck and shoulders, too, General Grant even seemed to resemble Eiichi, making her feel an affinity with him right away.

> The general was very reserved and placid in demeanor, registering so little emotion as to even seem somewhat unfriendly. I was struck that he seemed less typical of an American gentleman and more like a *taijin* (man of great character) of the East . . . I am sure that I shook hands with Mrs. Grant as well, but I cannot clearly remember. Mrs. Grant, too, seemed a very modest and graceful lady.

When the program of formal addresses of welcome and responses from the Grants was over, a meal was served in a separate room.

> The refreshments served at the party were very diverse and had clearly been prepared with extra special care. There were cold meats, aspic, salads, and such, and everything was completely new to me, but I found I liked everything very much. Surely there are not many who are accustomed to occasions like this. That's probably why the food was brought out to us arranged on individual plates. At the end came a mound of something yellow in color. We wondered what it could be. If it were butter, there was far too much to eat. As we gazed at it, without picking up our spoons, the yellow mass began to melt. All we could think was that it was a very strange food.

A few weeks later, she would learn that it was ice cream.

> After that there were toasts and the like, and then the ball began. Many American and European residents [in Japan] came out to dance and there were three or four numbers of square dance and round dance music. The only Japanese woman in Western dress dancing among them was public works minister Inoue Kaoru's daughter. Minister Inoue was a staunch supporter of Western-style education for women, and we heard that he had sent his daughter to live in the household of a foreign gentleman to learn these things. We other women lined up along the wall, gazing with startled looks at the scene, thinking to our-

selves of the wide world about which we knew nothing. In a daze, all I could think was the tremendous effort it would take for a Japanese woman to make even one step into such a world.

It was four years later that the famous Rokumeikan was built for entertainment of foreign guests. The so-called "Rokumeikan age" is sometimes taken as a synonym for frivolity, but that was not necessarily the case. Inoue Kaoru's words that "We must change our country and people so that our country is the same as the European countries and our people are the same as European peoples," were not intended to make a superficial imitation of the West but were an expression of the strong awareness and conviction that modernization meant Westernization. Without Westernizing itself, Japan would not be accorded respect in an intensely survival-of-the-fittest world; people felt this sense of crisis in the early years of Meiji – they knew the country's independence was at stake.

While this was a position taken in the face of the arrogance of the Western powers, the fact that Japanese of the time instinctively grasped the reality of the world in that way and made Westernization the focus of their civic efforts is noteworthy. Would Westernization really be good for the country? Would it bring the people genuine happiness? General Grant may have had misgivings on that score, but he accepted the all-out welcome he received with gratitude and sincerity and sought to do whatever he could for Japan.

OCCASION FOR ENTERTAINMENT AND EXCHANGE OF VIEWS

Emperor Meiji appears to have felt an affinity with the elder statesman visiting from afar. Not only did he provide one of the imperial detached palaces, the Enryōkan, for the Grants' lodgings, but went to visit Grant there for extended conversations.

Grand Minister of State Sanjō Sanetomi, other ministers and councilors, and high-ranking government officials took time out of their duties to show Grant the sights of Nikkō, and while entertaining him at various venues, lent quite a receptive ear to whatever advice he had. One of the topics that came up in

FIGURE 9   Sketch of Grant in audience with Emperor Meiji, 1879, in *Personal Memoirs of U.S.Grant*, New York, C. L. Webster & Co., 1885–86.

their discussions was the dispute between Japan and Qing China over ownership of the Ryukyu islands that stretched south of the main Japanese islands, including modern-day Okinawa. Before coming to Japan, Grant had met with the Regent Prince Gong (1833–1898) and then Chinese prime minister Li Hongzhang (1823–1901) in China and had been asked by them to intercede on their behalf with Japan on the issue.[25]

Grant reminded the Chinese repeatedly that he was no longer in office and had no qualifications for acting as mediator in political negotiations. The U.S. Embassy in Tokyo, too, went so far as to issue a statement saying that Grant's trip was a private affair and that his remarks did not represent the position or intentions of the United States government. Grant was surprised to find, however, that the leaders both in Beijing and Tokyo made little effort to understand that distinction.

To political leaders of the time in East Asia, it did not make sense that someone who had once been the leader of a country could revert to being no more than an ordinary private citizen after leaving office. The story goes that when Fukuzawa Yukichi

---

[25] See Baxter, "Informal Diplomacy," pp. 218, 222.

crossed the Pacific to the United States on the *Kanrin-maru* in 1860 and learned that ordinary American citizens did not even know anything about the descendants of first president George Washington, he found it difficult to believe. He equated it with what he knew of Japan. It would have been unthinkable for ordinary Japanese not to know anything about the descendants of Tokugawa Ieyasu, who was founder of the Tokugawa shogunate (they continued to rule Japan until 1867).

So, while repeatedly reminding his hosts that he was simply expressing his views as an individual, Grant firmly emphasized that it would not be to the advantage of either state to confront each other on the Ryukyu issue. Any clash between the two countries for whatever reason would only hand the European powers the opportunity they were waiting for to intervene in their affairs. Arguing that there were more risks than advantages to be had from territorial disputes, he urged them to promote an Asian version of the Monroe doctrine, as follows:

> American statesmen have long since perceived the danger of European interference in the political affairs of North and South America. So guard against this danger. And as a measure of self-protection it has become the settled policy of the United States that no European power shall be permitted to enlarge its domination or extend its influence by any interference in American affairs. It is likewise the policy of America in the Orient, I may say it is the law of our empire in the Pacific, that the integrity and independence of China and Japan should be preserved and maintained.[26]

Explaining in detail the sequence of events by which Britain made incursions into the independence of Egypt by allowing it to run up enormous debts, Grant advised Japan above all to be careful not to be tempted into raising foreign loans in European countries, thus playing into the hands of imperialists.

The British minister plenipotentiary at the time, Sir Harry Parkes observed indignantly that "General Grant is here and is turning the Japanese heads."[27] His complaint was apparently that Grant's

---

[26] Treat, *Japan and the United States,* quoting Grant, p. 108.
[27] Treat, *Japan and the United States,* p. 109.

encouragement of the Japanese spirit of independence would have gone against the purposes of Britain's colonialist policies.

Negotiations on the Ryukyu issue were subsequently continued along the lines that Grant proposed, but due to several circumstances, the problem could not be solved amicably. Grant's assertion at the time that harmony between China and Japan was the indispensable condition for peace and independence in Asia is of great interest. After Grant, U.S. policy in Asia shifted markedly toward policies intended to check Japan, threaten and challenge it in the name of defending China's independence. Those policies laid the foundations for the outbreak of the Pacific War. Then, after the war was over, when the United States found that China was not going in a direction America favored, it reversed itself and switched to a strategy of using Japan as a lever and "outpost" against the threat of China.

In any case, the notion of furthering Japan-China amity ceased to be part of America's Asia policy in the late nineteenth-early twentieth century decades. If greater teamwork had been realized between China and Japan, the efforts of the Western powers including the United States to intervene in Asian interests and their chances of snatching exorbitant profits for themselves would have been quickly preempted.

Things would not have stopped there. If a truly friendly relationship had been forged between Japan and China, the balance of power between East and West and between the white man and people of color would have been decisively different. I cannot help thinking that the leaders of the American government in the post-Grant era and American public as well instinctively realized that possibility and made deliberate decisions that would prevent such an eventuality.

THE EVENING AT THE THEATER

On July 16, there was a grand performance at the Shintomi theater. It featured the three greatest actors of the Meiji world of kabuki – Ichikawa Danjūrō IX (1838–1903), Onoe Kikugorō V (1844–1903), and Ichikawa Sadanji I (1842–1904) along with all the

FIGURE 10   The Shintomi theater in Kyōbashi where Grant and his party were entertained. Photo: Shibusawa Memorial Museum.

other leading performers of their generation: Nakamura Sōjūrō (1835–1889), Iwai Hanshirō VIII (1829–1882), and Ichimura Kakitsu IX (1847–1893).

Great care had gone into the preparation of the theater. The pillars and wainscotting were wrapped with the red-and-white striped silk cloth used for very special occasions. Front-row seats before the stage were prepared for the Grant party, members of the imperial family, and state ministers and councilors attending. The lower galleries on the east and west sides and the boxes in the rear (*taka-doma*) were prepared with seating for people related to the government and the boxes in the vicinity of the stage (*doma*) for the Tokyo citizens who had contributed funds for the Grant welcome events. In consideration of the needs of foreign guests, special toilets were installed in one location on both east and west sides and carbolic acid was applied over and over in the ordinary toilets in an effort to control unpleasant smells.

Quite a few members of the imperial family were in attendance and the princesses appeared in splendid traditional court garb, with their long hair arranged over their shoulders and their brocade *keiko* robes over their kimono filling the theater with glitter and color. Probably this was the first and last time this kind of splendid attire would be seen in a Tokyo theater. The box where the Grants sat was popularly known as the "Grant Box" for a long time after that memorable event.

The program featured "Go-sannen Ōshū gunki" (Martial Tale of the Later Three Years' War in Ōshū) based on an original story written by Fukuchi Gen'ichirō and adapted by Kawatake Mokuami for the kabuki theater. The plot depicts Minamoto no Yoshiie's arduous early-eleventh-century campaign to overpower the fractious brothers Kiyohara no Takehira and Yasuhira in the tough Ōshū northeastern frontier, with Ichikawa Danjūrō in the leading role. With the Minamoto role intended as a metaphor for Grant, the scene of victory was the highlight: Nakamura Sōjūrō's flamboyant shout of "Appare Gen-ke no Daitōryō!" (Hurray for the Great Head of the Minamoto Family), honoring the bravery and wisdom of the courageous general ("daitōryō" being a homonym for "great head" of a family and "president" of a country) resounded through the theater to a thunderous applause from the audience.

For the finale, the top actors of the evening appeared in frock coats and formal kimono attire, and on behalf of the welcoming committee took turns with speeches declaiming the virtues of General Grant, expressing gratitude for the American friendship with Japan, and hoping for continued goodwill between Japan and the United States. Then, lastly it was announced that there would be a dance presented by a group of women offered as diversion for the travel-worn visitors. The dance was performed by about 100 of the top geisha of the Shimbashi and Yanagibashi pleasure quarters. Before gaily dressed members of the *nagauta* shamisen and drum ensemble appeared a colorful group of geisha in red and white striped kimono. They slipped off the right shoulder of their kimono revealing the sleeve of under-kimono dyed flesh color with a pattern of white stars – their costumes were the "stars and stripes" through and through. The round fans they held in their hands, too, were patterned with one side showing the *hinomaru* (rising sun) Japanese national flag, and the other the stars and stripes of the American flag. The dance was something like a combination of the well-known "Genroku hanami odori" and "Ise ondo" with the lyrics rewritten with lines about friendship between Japan and the United States.

A product of the height of Japan's Westernization campaign, this approach to entertaining visitors from afar with a colorful cross between Japanese and Western cultures was something that Japanese were particularly good at. Dauntlessly breaking away from tradition, they nevertheless used its good parts to even better effect than usual. The very same approach, to which we are now well accustomed, was used at the time of the Tokyo Olympics of 1964 and the Osaka Expo in 1970. It is worth noting that only a decade or so after the country had cracked open the shell of its long-isolated feudal era, Japanese already had this kind of outstanding skill for appealing to the outside world.

The curtain that closed the Shintomi performance that day was bright scarlet with a white circle in the center emblazoned with the characters "Tai Hei" (great peace), and next to that six characters stitched on reading "from Grant" with gold thread carefully sewn around the edges of each character. [28]

HOME HOSPITALITY FOR THE GRANT PARTY

On the evening of August 5 Eiichi returned to his newly completed second home in Ōji Asukayama in a much more agitated state than usual, and immediately told the family members who met him at the entrance, "We're going to be very busy. It turns out that day after tomorrow we will have a state guest come to visit. The house has just been finished and it may be tough on such short notice, but I hope everyone will help out by all means."

In other countries, it was the practice to invite foreign guests to visit private homes, and the committee to welcome Grant had argued that Japan should do the same. No suitable house had been found, so nothing had been decided. Then it was learned that Eiichi had just finished building a new, second house with quite a large

---

[28] See article at Kazunobu Minami Lab, "Hōru no donchō no seisaku" (On the Production of the New Stage Curtain for the Hall) at http://www.minami.arc.shibaura-it.ac.jp/work/aomori/book/54–57.pdf (in Japanese). Accessed 8-26-17.

Figure 11
Eiichi's first wife, Chiyo (1841–
1882), probably as she looked when
Grant visited. Photo: Shibusawa
Memorial Museum.

number of rooms. The welcoming committee had been planning
to show General Grant the Ōji Paper Mill that had been completed
four years earlier not far from the new house at nearby Asukayama
hill. So someone suggested that it would be ideal if the general
could be invited to visit on the way home. Eiichi being the head of
the welcoming committee, the matter was suddenly decided.

Eiichi's wife Chiyo was a most punctilious person and tended
to be cautious and not one to favor anything new, but she surprised her husband this time by saying, "My, what a great honor
that will be. We'll do whatever we can to prepare, and be happy to
see them." Eiichi must have been relieved.

It was the era before telephones and automobiles. The whole
household was mobilized to run errands, obtain needed supplies,
and make necessary contacts, and those involved worked day and
literally through the nights to expedite the preparations. Carpets
were spread over all the tatami floors. Armchairs and sofas were

borrowed from the foreign affairs ministry and arranged in the rooms. Trees were planted in the garden, gravel spread in the drive-way, and every corner of the house decorated with artwork and antiques, flower vases and other items. The famous Seiyōken res-taurant in Ueno was hired to prepare the meal and a huge supply of ingredients brought in with which the chefs would serve a feast.

In fact, Eiichi had built the Asukayama house expressly for entertaining guests, and it fulfilled its mission for more than fifty years thereafter as the focal point of his efforts in private-sector diplomacy. Well over 1,000 guests from overseas were entertained there, including Indian poet Rabindranath Tagore, China's Chi-ang Kai-shek, American secretary of state Philander Knox, and delegates from the Associated Chambers of Commerce of the Pacific Coast in the United States.

Today, Tokyo's urban sprawl surrounds the wooded landscape of Asukayama Park, but in 1879 (Meiji 12), except for the Ōji Paper Mill, the scene from the hill was completely rural and the view

FIGURE 12   The Shibusawa Asukayama residence (1879–1945), which served as an important stage for Eiichi's personal international exchange endeavors for over 50 years. Photo: Shibusawa Memorial Museum.

from the back of the house stretched endlessly across the Kantō plain with the Tsukuba mountains in the distance to the east.

The guests arrived around 2:30 in the afternoon and after a luncheon, from beneath a tent that had been put up in the garden, enjoyed demonstrations of judo and sumo.

As it happened, Mrs. Grant was not present that day. Victim of a typically Japanese summer phenomenon, one of her feet had swelled up after suffering from mosquito bites, making it difficult to put on her shoes, and she had not joined the party. That meant all the guests were men, so Chiyo and Utako greeted the guests and then withdrew, eating their meal in the living room.

The "yellow mound" that Utako had seen at the ball at the imperial college was served again at the luncheon and Utako learned for the first time that this was called "ice cream."

"Taking a teaspoon to taste, I found it the most deliciously sweet and cold dish I had ever eaten – there could hardly be anything more delicious in this world. At the recent dinner party I had not even tried it, thinking it was something out of place, but now that I know it was ice cream, I realized how silly I had been to refuse to eat it. Everyone had a big laugh at that."[29]

THE GRAND PAGEANT AT UENO PARK

The climax of the welcome for Grant was held on August 25th, with a pageant hosted by the people of Tokyo and attended by the Emperor Meiji and General Grant and his party. The venue was Ueno Park and the program, following the custom of pageants held for the entertainment of the shogun from olden times, featured *yabusame* (archery on horseback) and *inuoumono* ("dog shooting").[30] The ideas for the pageant were innovative and flamboyant and everything was done on a grand scale.

---

[29] *Ryūmon zasshi*, February 1931, p. 49.
[30] Translator's note: The *inuoumono* is a form of archery practice and sport for the samurai and nobility from the Kamakura period. The rules were very exacting and refined; as the sport developed, the arrows were designed so as not to harm the dogs. Except for this event in 1879, it was more or less extinct from the sixteenth century.

FIGURE 13   Hashimoto Chikanobu, *Entertaining Grant at Ueno Park*, 1879.
Shibusawa Memorial Museum.

The thinking behind this event was based on the belief that the emperor should no longer be thought of as a divine being. Now that the country had been opened to commerce and interchange with the world, it had moved beyond the backward times when people thought the emperor was a god. The planners saw the emperor as loving his people and the people as devoted to the human being who was their sovereign. It was important, they argued, to make this idea of the harmony between sovereign and subjects in Japan widely known among educated people in the world. It was a healthy way of thinking, but unfortunately such liberal ideas were soon overshadowed; the notion of the emperor as "divine" once more reared its head, propelling Japan down a most unfortunate path.

Some people were opposed to these ideas. Since welcome committee member Fukuchi was president of the *Tokyo Nichinichi shinbun* newspaper, the *Hōchi shinbun* and other papers competing with the *Nichinichi* announced their opposition to the pageant plans. Their reason was that it was an insult to the emperor to involve him in a diplomatic event. If the people of Tokyo wanted to entertain the emperor, moreover, they should avoid the hottest time of month (August) and hold it some time in the fall. A heated debate followed.

The politician and journalist Numa Morikazu (1844–1890) declared it absurd that Shibusawa and Fukuchi should call them-

selves representatives of the people of Tokyo. He made speeches
at various places saying that it was all very well to invite the
emperor to events, but not healthy to act as representatives of
800,000 Tokyo citizens without legitimate authority.

When it comes to the subject of the emperor, especially when
relations with other countries are concerned, the tendency for
discussion to acquire emotional heat in Japan seems to be typical, not only today but in the past. Moreover, as it happened
there had been some cases of cholera in Tokyo about this time,
and the question of whether or not the emperor should venture
out at all in these circumstances became an issue at the imperial
court. Minister of the Right Iwakura and others were rumored to
be unwilling to come out firmly in favor of the matter. At a time
when a dangerous epidemic was raging, argued the fierce opponents of the plan, the welcome committee members would be
traitors to the emperor if they did not cancel the emperor's attendance; the households of both Fukuchi and Shibusawa received
quite vicious letters of intimidation that made the young Utako
record that she became so fearful for her father's life that she
could not sleep at night.

Facing such criticisms, the welcome committee immediately
gathered at the Tokyo prefectural assembly hall to discuss the
matter. There Eiichi presented his perennial commitment to
the importance of improving Japan-U.S. relations, and argued
earnestly that if, despite the tremendous preparations that had
been made, the emperor were not to attend, the good faith
not only of the planners but the hundreds of thousands of
citizens would be betrayed.[31] Prefectural Governor Kusumoto
was deeply moved by Eiichi's passionate defense and declared
that he would put his job on the line in the effort to make the
imperial attendance at the pageant possible. And ultimately the
decision was made that it would take place. Here again, we
can detect Eiichi's personal sense of mission in the planning of
these events and the passion with which he argued in support
of them, effectively persuading others.

---

[31] *Ryūmon zasshi* 474, pp. 1–5; *Shibusawa denki shiryō*, vol. 25, pp. 524–
26 ff.

August 25th generally falls in the hottest time of the Japanese summer, but in 1879, the day dawned clear and even slightly cool. Utako describes how she, with her mother Chiyo, sister Kotoko, and brother Tokuji, all wearing brand new formal attire, set out by horse and carriage for the venue of the pageant. As they drove through the countryside on the outskirts of the city of Tokyo, the national flag was flying at the front of every house.

> As we neared Ueno the houses alternated Japanese and American flags. I have never again since then seen such a beautiful scene of national flags along the streets. The opponents of the plan were saying that the welcome committee could not possibly represent the citizens of Tokyo, that no one supported this plan, and that it was a case of abuse of authority to do something in the name of Tokyo citizens when none of the citizens individually entrusted the plan to Shibusawa and the others. It was probably in reaction to those vexing protests that I thought to myself: And now look! I'd like to show them how everyone was rejoicing in the occasion by putting up the flag! I was filled with the desire to stop our coach and go door to door, thanking everyone for their signal of support for the plan of Father and his fellows.[32]

Only twelve years after the beginning of the Meiji era in 1868, the fact that a young woman like Utako had this kind of response to the trends of public opinion is a good indication of how rapidly Japanese society was shedding all that was "backward." British minister Parkes, who had sneered that there was no such thing as "public opinion in Japan," was eventually forced to revise his opinion, for changes that would soon force the Western powers to revise the unequal treaties were steadily being put in place.

The area around Ueno, except for the path the imperial procession would follow, was packed with people. At the entrance to the park a great arch made of green foliage was erected to welcome the Grants and the imperial procession. The pageant

---

[32] *Ryūmon zasshi* 509 (February 1931), pp. 50–58; "Guranto Shōgun kangei no omoide (Hozumi Utako)" [Memories of the General Grant Welcome by Hozumi Utako], *Shibusawa denki shiryō*, vol. 25, pp. 532–33.

was presumably held at the large open space before the present-day Tokyo National Museum at the north end of the park. Red-and-white striped bunting was hung around the many spectator boxes set up for invited guests.

Around 3:00 p.m. the emperor arrived and presented greetings to General Grant and his party. The idea of an invitation from Tokyo citizens apparently pleased the young monarch immensely, and he is said to have described the occasion as "the greatest pleasure outing I have had since I was born."

The program of events began with demonstrations of kendo fencing and spearsmanship (*sōjutsu*) before the guests of honor. At that time there were still many masters of the old samurai martial arts passed down through the Tokugawa period (1603–1867) and they competed with various secret techniques. Next came the *yabusame* archery, in which warriors drew their arrows and took aim at the targets from the back of a galloping horse. The art of *yabusame* had died out at one time, but had been revived in the eighteenth century during the time of eighth shogun Tokugawa Yoshimune (r. 1716–1745).

Three targets had been set up along the course the horses would follow. The targets consisted of a lightweight board with a black circle painted in the center attached to the top of a six-*shaku* (1.82-meter) post. The horsemen appeared one at a time at the sounding of a *taiko* drum, and all were decked out in traditional hunting finery of Edo-period samurai. Shibusawa Utako's account records the scene as follows:

> The archers appeared, wearing traditional *ayaigasa* hunting hats made of woven rush to secure the samurai's topnot, silk Heian-style *suikan* garb, leather leggings (*mukabaki*), and with a quiver of arrows slung on their backs. The saddles were lacquered with gold inlaid designs. The riders were dressed in bright colors – dark green (*tokusa*), saffron (*ukon*), pink (*usubeni*), indigo blue (*kachiiro*), and purple (*fuji*). The *mukabaki* were made of deerskin or bear hide and the gloves were red, green and purple silk or gold brocade, making a truly beautiful sight. I heard that the archers' attire came from the collection of the old Maeda daimyo family residing in Hongō. Already by this time, the number of people who knew how to perform these arts of

archery had diminished considerably, and only by advertising widely had the organizers managed to gather twenty or thirty skilled enough in horseback archery to perform for the pageant.

As we watched, the horse galloped forth, with the horseman affixing his arrow and taking aim, and, just after passing the target, turning back and letting fly his arrow. When the arrow hit home on target, the wooden board shattered with a crack, the pieces falling to earth. Immediately the archer took aim at the second and then the third targets. The archers appeared one after another, their colorful costumes making a striking contrast with dapple-gray, chestnut-colored, fawn-colored horses – it is a most beautiful martial art.[33]

The *inuoumono* "dog-shooting" event, by contrast, was a failure.

The five or six archers were attired the same as those of the *yabusame* event. As they waited at one end of the arena, six or seven big dogs released at the other end began to run around. They were fine-looking dogs – some black, some spotted – but they were all mongrel types with drooping ears, as there were no longer any pure-bred Japanese dogs, with their erect ears and spiral tails, in the Tokyo area for use in the event.

Chased by the archers on horseback, the dogs circled the arena once or twice but before long they had all taken refuge in the lee of a bamboo fence there and here under the box seats, and despite the attendants' trying to chase them out with whips into the arena again, they only sought any opening to escape into, making a pitiful sight that brought the event to an end.

The failure of the *inuoumono* seeming to have been more-or-less expected, the program moved on quickly to the next event, *horobiki*, in which horsemen performed equestrian arts carrying on their backs long, cylindrical streamers called *horo*. The horsemen were two acknowledged experts named Kusakari and Ijūin. The two galloped their horses in a large circle around the arena, creating a whirlwind that raised the ends of the red-and-white streamers – which must have been eight or nine meters long – high in the air. They rode with great aplomb, and each time they passed the imperial box, they performed a deep bow on horseback. It made a truly splendid sight."[34]

---

[33] *Ryūmon zasshi* 509 (February 1931), pp. 55–56.
[34] Ibid.

The grand ceremonies finally over around six o'clock, Utako, her mother, sister, and brother left the Ueno Park venue and rested at the then famous Matsugen restaurant in Hirokōji, in a tatami room overlooking Shinobazu Pond. After sunset, the fireworks, which had been set up on the banks of the pond since earlier in the day, made a beautiful and colorful scene, rising incessantly. Utako noted the beauty of the paper lanterns, made like the orange "Chinese-lantern" plant shells that decorated the Park entrance, the streets of Hirokōji and elsewhere.

That day, the Grants had participated in a tree-planting ceremony in Ueno Park. People of the time called the trees they planted that day the "Grant Cypress" and the "Grant Magnolia," and the trees always seemed to visitors to the park to exhibit the air of those eminent visitors from afar.

The events of that day apparently made a deep impression. The ambassadors of various countries were lavish with praise, saying they had never seen anything so splendid, and an English-woman on a pleasure trip around the world recorded her amazement, saying that a country like Japan in East Asia put the civilization of the West to shame and that even the English people were incapable of putting on such a well-organized event.

On the day of the pageant, hawkers circulated in the crowds, selling programs of the events. They wore *hanten* jackets and buttoned-up knickers (*momohiki*) and advertised their wares by calling out "Tennō-sama omatsuri! banzuke" (Get your program for the Emperor's Festival!).

From beginning to end, the entire Grant visit had acquired the atmosphere of the typical evening festivals of summer held throughout the country in August. It was indeed the forerunner of private-sector diplomacy but emphasis was placed more on the atmosphere than on the content. The welcoming side did have a tendency to be one-sidedly excited, but on the other hand, in the sense that a very large number of citizens were involved in putting on this kind of "festival," it offers an interesting occasion for observing how Japan was in the process of growing.

Following his trip, General Grant purchased a house in upstate New York and settled down. He invested the modest wealth he had accumulated from his army career and from his duties as president of the United States in the bank where his son worked and was planning to lead a quiet life in retirement.

All would have been well if things had gone according to plan, but Grant's curious destiny, in which happiness and unhappiness always seemed to be back-to-back, haunted his life to the very end. In 1884, as a result of fraud by a member of the staff of his son's bank, the bank went out of business. His savings lost, the family was instantly reduced to penury. Poverty was not a stranger to Grant, who had risen from poor beginnings, but impoverishment in old age must have been hard to bear. The Grants were forced to sell the New York house and moved to Saratoga, but Grant's health quickly declined.

Around that time he was asked to write his memoirs, for publication in the *Century* magazine, and he began writing as a source of income. Five days after finally completing the manuscript about half a year later, Grant passed away at the age of 63. It was July 23,1885.

On June 15, 1902, in the course of his journey across the United States and Europe (see chapter 3), Eiichi visited Grant's grave in the center of New York City. He found the grave in a beautiful setting on the bank of the Hudson River; a grand and solemn tomb had been erected there, with donations from supporters of $2.5 million dollars.

CHAPTER 3

WORLD TOUR BEFORE THE STORM

છ

ON MAY 15, 1902, Eiichi got up at 6:00 a.m., and as usual, took a morning bath and strolled in the garden. He wrote a poem:

> *Midori koki / wakaba ni yuku te / okurarete / momiji no nishiki /*
> *iezuto ni semu*
> Setting forth from the depths of spring greenery,
> I'll return to the bright brocades of autumn.

It was the day of his departure on a tour in the United States and Europe. With the backing of the Tokyo Chamber of Commerce, he left Yokohama aboard the Toyo Kisen ship *Amerikamaru*, crossing to San Francisco, visiting San Francisco, Chicago, Washington, and New York among other cities. After stays in England, France, Germany, and elsewhere, he planned to take the route via the Suez Canal back to Japan, returning home in late October as the autumn colors were at their height.

It had been 23 years since he had welcomed General Ulysses S. Grant in Tokyo as head of the spanking new Tokyo Chamber of Commercial Law and as representative of the citizens of Tokyo prefecture in 1879. He had continued to lead the Chamber after its renaming as the Tokyo Chamber of Commerce.

This was the most fulfilling time of Eiichi's life. Compared to 1879, when the sole symbol of Japan's modernity was some small newborn banks, in less than two and a half decades Japan's industry had grown immeasurably. Now production was vigorously growing in the manufacture of paper, textiles, fertilizer, and cement as well as in all manner of fields – mining, shipbuilding, maritime transport, railroads, trade, insurance, and so forth. With astonishing energy and stamina, Eiichi had a hand in almost everything that was going on, belying his well-advanced age of 62. His idea of *gapponshugi* (ethical capitalism),[35] his primary weapon for creating and growing industry, had become firmly established as the conventional way of doing things, and using the joint-stock company approach to enterprise, the wealth of more and more people was being circulated in society, increased, and re-invested, stoking the engines of the country's growth.

Japan's position in the world, too, through revision of the unequal treaties it had concluded with the Western powers in the mid-nineteenth century and victory in the Sino-Japanese War of 1894–1895, had completely changed. Until then, Japan had only had to devote itself to modernizing the country as quickly as possible and pursuing its goal of "increasing the wealth of the nation and the strength of its arms" (*fukoku kyōhei*). Only through these means could it defend its independence as a nation and attain some parity among the powerful countries of international society. To slack off in these efforts even in the slightest would have left it vulnerable to the incursions of outside enemies. People in Japan were very cognizant of the situation in the world at that time when East Asia's wealth, passed down over centuries from the past, was vulnerable prey before hungry wolves.

Industry was already well advanced in Europe and transportation and communications were advancing rapidly. Japan's victory in 1895, showing that China was not simply a "sleeping lion" but an "ailing lion," whetted the European powers' imperialist appetites, igniting a frenzy of activity as they competed for rights to build railway lines and develop mines, establishing the famous "spheres of influence."

With its victory in the war against China, Japan soon found itself participating as a sort of junior partner in the "imperialist system" of Asia of the time. This was a totally new stage to perform on for Japan. No one knew how to dress for the

---

[35] See Fridenson and Kikkawa, *Ethical Capitalism.*

part or how to behave. The opportunity to extend the country's power was electrifying, but what perils lay ahead were completely unknown.

In the backdrop to Eiichi's plan for this 1902 trip was his urge to observe and think about the rapidly changing world situation after seeing it for himself. He was especially eager to tour the United States, which he had not visited before. "I knew from the newspapers, and accounts of friends, that it was a thriving country; I heard that it was in the process of tremendous progress," and he wanted to see it first hand "while I am still in good health."

Eiichi had gone to Europe in 1867 as part of the entourage of Tokugawa Akitake under the previous regime, but after the passing of 36 years, that journey was "like a dream from the previous century," he wrote, and he was eager to retrace the path that he had formerly traveled.

This time, Eiichi was accompanied by his second wife, Kaneko. His first wife, Chiyo, who was a cousin, younger by one year, from the same village where he was born, had supported him since their marriage in 1858 through the tumultuous years at the end of the Tokugawa shogunate. She was known as a wise and stead-

FIGURE 14   Shibusawa Eiichi during his 1902 tour in the United States and Europe; at the Waltham Watch Company, Massachusetts. Photo: Shibusawa Memorial Museum.

Figure 15
Eiichi's second wife,
Kaneko (1852–1934).
Photo: Shibusawa
Memorial Museum.

fast woman who maintained his household on her own during the long stretches when Eiichi's duties kept him away from home. In July 1882, however, she sadly succumbed to cholera. In 1883, Eiichi had remarried.

At 7:00 a.m. the carriage set out from the house in Asukayama, Ōji, in the northern suburbs of Tokyo and dropped by the Shibusawa office in Kabutochō in central Tokyo where he said goodbye to his staff there. When the carriage arrived at Shimbashi at 9:00 a.m., the station was overflowing with a crowd of people who had come to see him off on his journey.

Throughout his life, Eiichi enjoyed a curious popularity. Whenever he would depart on a trip overseas or elsewhere, an extraordinary crowd would assemble to see him off. In May 1902, too, the well-wishers thronging to wish him well on his trip included foreign minister Komura Jutarō, justice minister Kiyoura Keigo, finance minister Sone Arasuke, agriculture and commerce minister Hirata Tōsuke, communications minister Yoshikawa Akimasa, the governor of Tokyo Prefecture, the mayor of Tokyo City, and the ambassadors of the United States and Great Britain. Leaders from the business world on hand included Bank of Japan governor Yamamoto Tatsu, along with the presidents of the Industrial Bank of Japan and the Dai-ichi Kangyō Bank. Also there were top-flight industrialists of the day like Kondō Renpei, Asano Sōichirō, Yasuda Zenjirō, Ōkura Kihachirō, Masuda Takashi, Shōda Heigorō, Toyokawa Ryōhei, and Umakoshi Kyōhei. The newspapers the following day reported that the crowd to see off Eiichi had been over 1,500 strong.

Eiichi was indeed a man of great influence in the financial world. This was before he had been dubbed *ōgosho*, the doyen of Japanese business, but his general image was shaped by a reputation for being a person without whose support a business, in those early days of the modern economy, would not get off the ground.

There was surely a deeper secret in Eiichi's popularity. He possessed a quality of authority not found in others in the financial world – it could be called a kind of moral authority. In a sense he was viewed on the same level as the top political leaders of the time – known as *genkun* – such as Yamagata Aritomo, Itō Hirobumi, Inoue Kaoru, and so on. It was an era when everyone wanted to gain access to power and influence. The *genkun*, originally from pre-Meiji-era Satsuma and Choshū domains that had played the central role in toppling the Tokugawa shogunate, reigned supreme over Meiji society. All the ministers of state and generals, not to mention the businessmen and industrialists who had so recently been small-scale merchants under the old feudal system, cowered before them.

Eiichi, however, had no reason to feel intimidated. There was, of course, the fact that in the early days of the Meiji era, he had worked closely with Itō and Inoue at the fledgling finance ministry. But that was not the only reason. Since Eiichi had resigned his government post in 1873 – putting aside the assured prospect of the highest status and honor to be attained in the country – to work in the private sector, he had dedicated his life single-mindedly to the growth of modern Japan. He was not in the least concerned with personal aggrandizement. His decision was extraordinary in a culture where people were deeply imbued with the tradition in which officialdom was the focus of unquestioned respect and the private sector tended to be disdained (*kanson minpi*). At the time, to get involved in work of such uncertain prospects as founding a "bank" was tantamount to casting aside all earthly desires to take a monk's tonsure.

Eiichi had due respect for the *genkun*, the "founding fathers" of Meiji Japan, and for their positions at the pinnacle of power in Meiji society and their capacity for serving in those positions. He did not, however, have any reason to grovel before them. Just as they were pioneers devoting their lives to the future of their country, he, too, was working for all he was worth. Eiichi believed he was no different from them as a citizen and as a human being, and he lived according to that rule.

If the *genkun* statesmen recognized that Eiichi was in a class all his own, it was because Eiichi possessed abilities and knowledge that they had no choice but to recognize. He might be working among the part of society that was still sometimes dismissed – reflecting the lingering associations of the era when merchants and manufacturers were nearly at the bottom of the social ladder – as mere "townspeople," but he exhibited a way of thinking and working that was on a scale similar to that of their own endeavors. They were also smart enough to realize how important the economy was to a modern state and also how difficult it was to find people of caliber to take the lead in the business world. As a person doing work that they themselves could not do, they held him in very high regard.

A little-known anecdote of their esteem for Eiichi had played out in the autumn of the previous year, 1901, following the resignation of the Saionji Kinmochi cabinet. Negotiations had begun toward forming a cabinet led by Inoue Kaoru, and Itō Hirobumi, Yamagata Aritomo, and other fellow former-Chōshū domain members of the government were gung-ho to back

Inoue for his first chance at the prime-ministership. Inoue could not resist the allure of the post, and responded that he would consider accepting the post if someone with real talent for public finance – like Shibusawa Eiichi – would agree to be finance minister.

Eiichi received a stream of visitors – other men slated to join the proposed Inoue cabinet, including Kusumoto Masataka, who had been governor of Tokyo Prefecture at the time of the Grant visit, and Yoshikawa Akimasa – seeking to persuade him to join them. *Genkun* Yamagata invited Eiichi to his luxurious residence in Fujimi-chō where, along with Saigō Tsugumichi, the younger brother of the Meiji Restoration hero Saigō Takamori, they tried to make him an offer he couldn't refuse. Itō, too, pressed him, stressing Eiichi's close association with Inoue from the time of the Restoration onward. But Eiichi remained true to his original aspirations and managed to decline. As a result, the idea for an

Figure 16
Inoue Kaoru (1836–1915), member of the Meiji oligarchy who served as foreign minister and other posts. Photo: National Diet Library, Japan.

Inoue cabinet fizzled out and later a cabinet was formed under Katsura Tarō.

Later, it is said, Inoue remarked to Eiichi, "If I had formed a cabinet at that time I would probably have failed. That would have damaged my reputation for the rest of my life. I am glad you did not come on board." Inoue is said to have held a private party to celebrate the abortion of the cabinet idea.[36]

Surrounded by such illustrious people who genuinely respected him, Eiichi boarded the train that left Shimbashi at 9:25 and arrived in Yokohama at 10:00. At 11:00 he went aboard the *Amerika-maru*, and again a crowd of several hundred well-wishers had gathered, including the governor of Kanagawa Prefecture, the mayor of Yokohama, friends and relatives, whose attempts to see him off created congestion on the ship.

At 12:25 P.M., the ship lifted anchor and the voyage began. It had begun to rain as they departed and by the time they passed the point at Kannonzaki (near the mouth of Tokyo Bay), the deluge had increased and the ship had begun to roll in the strong winds.

The storm kept up for two days and two nights, and not only Eiichi and Kaneko but many of the ship's other passengers suffered greatly from seasickness. "All we could stomach through the entire day was a few pieces of fruit. We could only moan in our beds praying for the wind and the waves to die down." That experience seemed to have left an indelible mark on Eiichi, as whenever the subject of an ocean voyage came up, he would try to distance himself from the idea, saying that he was vulnerable to seasickness.

On May 23rd, the *Amerika-maru* entered the port at Honolulu. Only four years earlier, in 1898, Hawai'i had been virtually forced to accept annexation by the United States. Queen Liliuokalani, who had insisted on "Hawai'i for the Hawai'ians," was forced to abdicate and was much distressed by the whole matter.

Eiichi had been acquainted with Liliuokalani's elder brother, former King Kalakaua (1836–1891). In 1882, Kalakaua had

---

[36] *Shibusawa denki shiryō*, vol. 27, p. 594.

stopped by Japan during a trip around the world and had been entertained as a state guest. Eiichi had invited him to his home in Asukayama. A man of merry disposition, the king loved to drink, and by preference wore Japanese-style haori and hakama attire when attending banquets in Japan.

In those days, white people – Europeans and Americans – behaved with great arrogance and exceptionalism almost everywhere in the world except in Japan and a few other countries. King Kalakaua, apparently feeling unusually relaxed at a party attended only by Japanese and other people of color, remarked that he had not enjoyed himself so much for a long time – he would never forget the occasion. Yet indignation at the arrogant treatment of his people by the Americans, who were already treating Hawai'i as if they owned it, spilled out in both his words and behavior. He reproached his hosts, demanding to know why, despite Japanese having such handsome traditional attire as haori and hakama, they insisted on dressing in Western clothing. The message of the king's protest probably did not get across to the Japanese at the time, however, intent as they were on westernizing everything about their country.

Perhaps thinking to counter-balance the influence of the United States in Hawai'i that was growing day by day in his time, King Kalakaua called on the Japanese government to send immigrants to Hawai'i. In response to his call, in 1886, a travel treaty was signed between the governments of Japan and Hawai'i under which many Japanese began to migrate to the islands.

According to a census in 1900, of the total population of approximately 150,000 in Hawai'i Japanese accounted for more than 60,000 or 40 percent. There were some 30,000 native Hawai'ians, 29,000 Europeans and Americans, 24,000 Chinese, and the rest people of mixed background, so Japanese made up by far the largest proportion.

The majority of Japanese who migrated to Hawai'i became laborers on the pineapple, sugarcane, and other plantations but some were in business and they also included representatives of banks and trading companies from Japan. It was a group of these people in business called the Shōnin Dōshikai (Businessmen's

Society) who arranged a welcome for Shibusawa Eiichi. The venue was the residence of head of the Yokohama Specie Bank's Hawai'i branch Imanishi Kenji, located at the foot of Diamond Head. As Eiichi and his party moved by horse and carriage across the Waikiki bridge, a barrage of fireworks went off, and as they pulled up at the Imanishi house, too, more fireworks lit up the garden attached to the house, while a Hawai'ian ensemble of musicians welcomed them with local music.

Calling on the local businessmen to cooperate among themselves, Eiichi acknowledged the warm welcome he received and expressed his hope that the migrants from Japan would not long remain as contract workers but "strive to purchase land of their own, rise to the position of managers themselves, and advance and develop themselves to the point where they could provide capital for sugar manufacturing and other businesses as entrepreneurs themselves."

The Shibusawas' trip from Hawai'i to the U.S. mainland was uneventful, although the captain sponsored a costume ball for the amusement of the passengers. In addition to Eiichi and his party, those on board the ship included the talented chemist Takamine Jōkichi and his American wife, Caroline Hitch. Takamine, who eventually emigrated to the United States, is known for having isolated the enzyme *takadiastase*, and he and Eiichi had quite a close relationship involving the founding of a company to manufacture artificial fertilizer. On May 30, the ship arrived safely in San Francisco.

Some years later, the *San Francisco Chronicle* was to become the source of much anguish to Eiichi and his countrymen for a long time over the issue of Japanese immigration to the United States, but in 1902, it greeted Eiichi's arrival with headlines introducing him as the "Industrial Leader of Japan," [37] and describing him as not objecting to being known as "the Pierpont Morgan of far Nippon." Citing the banks and several dozen companies with which he was affiliated, it estimated his wealth as $100,000,000. The *San Francisco Examiner*, too, introduced

---

[37] *San Francisco Chronicle*, May 31, 1902.

him with the headline "Baron Shibusawa has $100,000,000." Despite his rather short stature (he was 154.5 cm tall), it described him as "tall, dignified."[38] Interestingly enough, the article notes that "The Baron thinks the American press has given undue prominence to the Japanese war spirit against Russia. . . 'I am for peace,' he says. 'The Anglo-Japanese alliance means peace. American influence in the Orient is strong and good. Russia and Japan can and will be friends, and in a commercial way benefit each other."

On June 2nd, Eiichi was given a tour of the Union Iron Works[39] shipyard. Since 1884, it had produced some 74 naval and mercantile ships. Eiichi's diary noted that "the shipyard covers some 30,000 *tsubo* (24.5 acres) and has 4,000 workers, I am told. Has well-equipped workshops for engine construction, tube manufacturing, casting, woodworking, electricity, and wood-molding. The dock is a hydraulic-pressure floating dock. Built at a cost of $500,000. They do some $45,000,000 dollars' worth of business annually. Worker's wages are 6 dollars a day at the highest; even the lowest wage is as high as 2 dollars a day – averaging 3 dollars a day." That day, 11 new warships were being fitted out in their berths, including the following cruisers:

Name	Size	Speed
California	13,400 tons	22 knots
South Dakota	13,400 tons	22 knots
Milwaukee	13,400 tons	22 knots
Ohio	12,280 tons	19 knots
Tacoma	3,400 tons	16.5 knots
Wyoming	3,000 tons	11.5 knots

These warships were symbols of the United States then emerging as a world power – the twentieth-century United States. In 1898, as the upshot of the Spanish-American War, American policy tilted decisively toward expansionism and imperialism.

---

[38] *San Francisco Examiner*, May 31, 1902.
[39] http://en.wikipedia.org/wiki/Union_Iron_Works

The establishment of American territorial rights to Puerto Rico, Guam, and the Philippines incorporated the United States firmly into the imperialist system and had a tremendous impact on its subsequent foreign policy. Quite unexpectedly, the United States and Japan both became members of the imperialist club at almost exactly the same time.

Up until just before Eiichi and his party disembarked at San Francisco, a force of nearly 100,000 regular U.S. troops had been engaged far across the Pacific Ocean in an intense battle with Philippine forces under Emilio Aguinaldo. The completely guerrilla-style war that had begun three years earlier claimed 250,000 lives on both sides and was equivalent in intransigence, cruelty, and scale to the Vietnam War of the 1960s and 1970s.

It was Theodore Roosevelt who was president of this new and expansionist United States. Backed by a lust for overseas expansion growing among the people driven by industrial development, the Roosevelt administration launched a forceful diplomacy toward the whole world backed by powerful military, particularly naval, forces. It was that policy that Japan, China, and other countries far across the Pacific Ocean would be destined to confront in the decades to come.

FROM WEST TO EAST

On June 3rd, Eiichi and his party left San Francisco, heading east over the Sierra Nevada mountains where snow still lingered, and crossing the arid and desolate expanses of Nevada until they reached Salt Lake City, Utah, on the morning of the 5th.

Nowhere does the immensity of the United States impress itself more deeply than in the landscape of these Western states. In the summer of 1968, I took the same route, though in the opposite direction, traveling by car, from Salt Lake City to San Francisco. The sight of the vast briny waters of Salt Lake and the cold, white, and salt-encrusted desert stretching as far as the eye can see has a not-of-this-world beauty that freshly struck me with the scale of the country.

In the Tabernacle of the Mormon Church, Eiichi listened to a performance of the famous organ and then continued his journey, crossing the Rocky Mountains, passing through the city of Denver, and crossing through the grain-raising regions of Nebraska, Iowa and Illinois, and finally arriving in Chicago.

> The vastness of the United States is extraordinary. We saw just part of it from the windows of the train, and while there may be some desolate parts as we saw in Nevada, it is all boundless uncultivated fields for as far as the eye can see, and from what I could see, the soil, moreover, is rich. I was born in a farming family, so I can tell at a glance whether land is fertile or not, and it was obvious from the way the weeds were flourishing that the condition of the soil is good. Moreover, there are few ups and downs in the land; it stretches out in vast plains as far as the eye can see with nothing in any direction to obstruct the view. (November 1, 1902, *Chūgai shōgyō shinpō*)

As they neared Chicago, they began to see ranches, where countless cattle and pigs dotted pastures that extended into the distance on a scale that defied imagination.

In Chicago, the group had a tour of the slaughterhouse and meat-processing factory operated by the famous Swift & Company, known at the time for its corned beef. They learned that some 60,000 animals were processed through the plant each week using a mechanized assembly line system. Some 250 cattle and 750 pigs were slaughtered per hour. A glimpse of some of them being slaughtered made members of the party shudder, and the sight of the meat of all those animals being efficiently and rapidly processed and packed in cans for market was quite overwhelming. Today, such automation and efficient production methods are taken for granted, but at the time mechanization and labor-saving technologies were virtually unknown in Japan.

> We have been hearing for some time that increasingly precision machines have been invented in the United States as labor-saving devices, but if we were to assume that the use of machines belonged to the agricultural and manufacturing industries alone

and were not used in other areas, that would be a gross mistake. In every aspect of daily life, they follow the policy of avoiding the use of human labor [wherever possible], and their skill at getting things done speedily is indeed admirable; it even inspires one with a sense of fear.

. . .

I observed several times the method they have of loading and unloading products like grain onto and from railroad cars using an air-pressure device. These inventions are closely involved with agricultural production and the sheer scale of all such equipment is beyond anything one can imagine without seeing it for oneself. (November 9, 1902, *Jiji shinpō*)

The party moved on from Chicago to Pittsburgh, where they toured the famous Homestead Steel Works. The mill had been one of the main centers of production of the Carnegie Steel Company until the previous year (1901) when it became part of U.S. Steel, known as the first billion-dollar trust. U.S. Steel was a kind of holding company created by J. P. Morgan by buying up not only Carnegie's Homestead mill but most of the other steelworks in the United States, and represented the pinnacle of the consolidation and monopoly in industry that had been pursued since the nineteenth century. After selling the steel mill, the then 64-year-old Carnegie retired from the world of business and devoted his life to donating his vast wealth to schools, social projects, and cultural organizations before dying in 1913.

The mill when Eiichi toured it was "220,000 *tsubo*" (54 acres) with railroads running its length and breadth. Observing the operations, from the dumping of the iron ore into the blast furnace to the emergence of steel plates, bars and other products from its rollers all operated by machines, Eiichi recalled,

The equipment was huge – enormous. The sheer scale of the mill left us all speechless with amazement. The machines are all operated with the latest electrically powered equipment, which I wouldn't even dare to try to explain. Suffice it to say that it was awe-inspiring. (November 9, 1902, *Jiji shinpō*)

MEETING WITH TOP LEADERS

On June 15th, Eiichi and his party arrived in Washington, D.C. where he met with various top leaders of the U.S. government. Forty-four-year-old president Theodore Roosevelt headed the administration in Washington at that time. Under him, the government had put aside the passive, non-interventionist tendencies of the late nineteenth century, embracing its position as the head of the country and actively spearheading a number of aggressive policies. George Washington may have presided over the creation of the United States of America; Abraham Lincoln may have prevented the union from breaking apart, but it was Theodore Roosevelt who really launched its aggressive policies in Asia.

Born in 1858 to a distinguished New York family, Roosevelt graduated from Harvard University in 1880. At a time when politicians were often considered shysters of a sort, Roosevelt dauntlessly chose the path of politics and signed up as a member of the Republican Party. He was a man of tremendous versatility. When not in the thick of the political fray, he devoted his time to study and writing – biographies, travelogues, histories, commentary on current affairs, and the like. He was also a mountain-climber and a top-notch scientist. The Smithsonian Institution is home to many specimens of plant and animal life that he brought back with him from his travels in Africa. A famous anecdote tells of Roosevelt's immense knowledge of birds. Out walking in London's New Forest with foreign secretary Sir Edward Grey, he amazed his British host by the depth of his knowledge of songbirds.[40]

Endowed with keen diplomatic instincts and deep insight into human nature, Roosevelt mobilized his political acumen and inimitable realism to further the Panama Canal construction project, pushing forcefully to get construction going. He skillfully contained Germany and other European powers on the North and South American continents, enhancing the prestige of the United States, and even managing to win the Nobel Prize

---

[40] See Thompson, *Theodore Roosevelt Abroad.*

for his role in mediating the end of the Russo-Japanese War. The United States when he took up the reins had barely gotten its feet wet in the waters of world affairs, but by the time he left office his country was literally a first-rate international power – one that was feared and respected around the globe, its support and protection sought after and its citizens respected as citizens of the world.

In the realm of domestic policy, Roosevelt's achievements were reformist in nature. He established the departments of Commerce and Labor, working for improvement of the lives of workers. While pushing forward anti-monopoly policies, he criticized the Standard Oil Trust and J. P. Morgan's railroad trust.

It would probably be an exaggeration to say that Roosevelt was a militarist, but he clearly understood the importance of power in international relations. In a speech delivered to the Naval War College in 1897, he said,

> All the great masterful races have been fighting races, and the minute that a race loses the hard fighting virtues, then, no matter what else it may retain, no matter how skilled in commerce and finance, in science or art, it has lost its proud right to stand as the equal of the best. . . . No nation should ever wage war wantonly, but no nation should ever avoid it at the cost of the loss of national honor. A nation should never fight unless forced to; but it should always be ready to fight.[41]

It was Roosevelt who as assistant secretary of the navy persuaded his superiors to build warships one after another and send a squadron to the western Pacific in preparation for the occupation of the Philippines.

Such being Roosevelt's proclivities, he had been deeply impressed by the capacity shown by the Japanese armed forces in the Sino-Japanese War of 1894–1895, and was quick to bring up the subject during his meeting with Eiichi. He said that he had been hearing much about Japan's recent progress. Japan's arts had long enjoyed great admiration around the world, but

---

[41] See Naval War College address, June 2, 1897.

recently it was the Japanese military that was the subject of great praise. According to a U.S. army general who had been stationed in Beijing at the time of the Boxer Rebellion (1900), the Russian, French, German, and British had all had great praise for the valor of the Japanese troops. Their discipline in particular was admirable, and ought to be a model for the soldiers of his own country, Roosevelt said.

To this Eiichi responded immediately with his own gesture of modesty, saying, "I am happy to hear kind words about Japan's arts and military, but I am a man of the business world. Regretfully, business in Japan is still undeveloped by comparison with its arts and military. But I am determined that I and my countrymen will study trade and industry diligently so that its industry will be just as worthy of praise the next time we might meet."[42]

The interview took place on the third floor of the White House in the presidential sitting room and lasted for about 40 minutes. Those present on the Japanese side included then Ambassador Takahira Kogorō (1854–1926) and a member of Eiichi's party named Ichihara Morihiro, who later became president of the Bank of Korea, serving as interpreter.

Ambassador Takahira was the diplomat who would exchange notes with U.S. diplomats resulting in the Root-Takahira Agreement of 1908 in which the two countries agreed to maintain each other's rights and interests in the Pacific. Roosevelt greatly praised Takahira in front of Eiichi and said that Mrs. Takahira was held in very high regard in Washington society, telling Eiichi to be sure to report these things to the Japanese government.

Possibly to compensate for the social faux pas of talking about military affairs to a businessman like Eiichi, Roosevelt said he had great praise for Eiichi's efforts in the business world, declaring that he would do whatever he could to cooperate with Eiichi, and asking his guest whether he had met the president of the New York Chamber of Commerce yet.

"No, not yet," Eiichi said. "I have received an introduction to him from the U.S. ambassador in Japan and so am planning to

---

[42] See *Shibusawa denki shiryō*, vol. 25, pp. 186–87.

see him when I go to New York." Thereupon Roosevelt offered to have his secretary of state contact the Chamber president and do whatever he could to facilitate the meeting and help Eiichi achieve the aims of his trip.

Eiichi spent only one day and two nights in Washington, but in addition to the president, he met secretary of the treasury Leslie M. Shaw and secretary of state John Hay. John Hay was the author of the famous open-door policy, which was to establish the pattern of U.S. foreign policy for the next 50 years and was to have a great impact on U.S. relations especially with Japan and China.[43]

At the time of Eiichi's visit, Elihu Root, who would later be the U.S. counterpart in the signing of the Root-Takahira Agreement, was secretary of defense. As the main instigator of the sudden appearance of the U.S. military in overseas affairs, he had his fingers in many matters including the Spanish-American War, the war with rebels in the Philippines, and the dispatch of U.S. troops to China at the time of the Boxer Rebellion.

William Howard Taft, who would succeed Roosevelt as president and whom Eiichi later came to know quite well, was then in the Philippines, where he was serving as governor-general and attempting to wipe out the nationalist army and pacify the people.

Eiichi and his party had a fulfilling day in Washington, sitting in on a session of Congress and visiting George Washington's former residence, Mount Vernon. The session of Congress they visited was engaged in discussion of the construction plans for the Panama Canal and ruling party members were giving speeches supporting the plan. Roosevelt promptly fulfilled his promise to Eiichi, and a letter of introduction, dated June 17th, to New York Chamber of Commerce Morris K. Jesup, was delivered to Eiichi.

MEETING THE MOVERS AND SHAKERS OF U.S. INDUSTRY

New York is a city of business, and Eiichi made many friends there. The U.S. economy at that time was incomparably larger than that of Japan and the people who controlled it were top-notch.

---

[43] Kennan, *American Diplomacy*, pp. 41–58. See also Chapter 1 of this volume, pp. 22–23

The first person he met was Anthony N. Brady, then the president of the Consolidated Gas Company. At the time, the Tokyo Gas Company, with which Eiichi was affiliated, was planning to increase its capital and expand its plant and equipment to respond to the rapid rise in gas demand following the Sino-Japanese War. Tokyo Gas was capitalized at 4.2 million yen and planned to double that amount to 8.4 million yen. The company decided to look for financial backing in New York and they had asked Eiichi to negotiate on their behalf.

Brady visited Eiichi at the Majestic Hotel where Shibusawa and his party were staying and he appeared to take an interest in the scheme; negotiations seemed to be going smoothly, so Eiichi sent a telegram to Tokyo saying, "the outlook looks good." He wrote in his diary on June 17th, "Negotiation on capital increase, payment of premium, and other items has been settled."

Then, on the 23rd, Brady said there were problems with the calculations of the method for increasing the capital. Eiichi did his best to explain, but could not obtain Brady's understanding, so no agreement was reached. Nevertheless, that evening Brady hosted a luxurious banquet at the Hoffman House restaurant in honor of Eiichi and his party. Brady had reserved the entire rooftop garden dining room on the 12th floor of the building for the gathering and the tables were surrounded with flower decorations and colored illumination lighting up a sign reading "In Honor of Baron Shibusawa." The food consisted of the finest dishes and was said to have cost no less than $150.00 per person in the prices of the day.

The other guests included President James Stillman of the National City Bank, Levi P. Morton of Morton Trust Company, Anthony Brady, also director of the American Tobacco Company, James B. Duke of the Consolidated Tobacco Company, and George O. Knapp of the Peoples Gas company in Chicago; the net worth of each of them was described as more than 50 million dollars, making them among the wealthiest Americans. This was around the time that Japan's Dai-ichi Bank, of which Eiichi was founder, had just increased its capital to 10 million yen (approximately 5 million dollars). These figures are very sketchy, but suffice it to say that Japan's wealth could not even compare to that of the United States at the turn of the twentieth century.

The American company Consolidated Tobacco had set up business in Japan and established a tie-up with Murai Brothers Shōkai. Its president, James B. Duke, told Eiichi that his company had struck up the deal not so much to make a profit as to benefit Japan as well and that he wanted to make it successful as the first joint venture business in Japan.

Roosevelt's letter of introduction had apparently been well timed and on June 24th, the New York Chamber of Commerce held a formal evening banquet to welcome Eiichi. The many businessmen attending included Lyman J. Gage, who had served as secretary of the treasury in the McKinley administration, former secretary of the interior Cornelius N. Bliss, Hanover National Bank president James Woodward and American Trust Company president John A. Stewart. New York Mayor Seth Low, also present, gave a speech. Formerly president of Columbia University, Low had come to office after a series of cases of corruption and fraud at city hall and was in the midst of industrious efforts to clean up the city government.

On the morning of June 25th, a young businessman named Frank A. Vanderlip visited Eiichi at his hotel. He was vice president of the National City Bank. He told Eiichi that President Stillman had invited Eiichi to his home for dinner that night and so he had come to introduce himself and speak with him about the arrangements.

Vanderlip was to establish a close friendship with Eiichi in later years, but at the time he was still a young 38-year-old banker. Born in Chicago, he had become a journalist specializing on the economy and had established his reputation with his articles on the economy published in the *Chicago Tribune* newspaper and the journal the *Economist*. Scouted by then secretary of the treasury Lyman Gage, he had become undersecretary of the treasury at the young age of 33. He had moved to the financial world in 1901 and been made vice-president of National City Bank. He became president of the bank in 1909 and played a leading role in the U.S. financial world for a long time. Although 24 years

Eiichi's junior, the two seem to have established a rapport from the beginning, and at Eiichi's invitation he came to Japan accompanying a group of businessmen in 1920.

The Stillman residence was a luxury home overlooking Central Park, and the dinner was an intimate family-like gathering of six, including the hosts, prepared with care and hospitality. The other guests included Vanderlip, Lyman Gage, along with William Rockefeller II, who was Stillman's son-in-law. Eiichi respected Stillman, but above all Stillman was the kind of businessman who suited his tastes the best. His diary is filled with praise for the American as "a most pleasant person with whom one feels not the least distance," "a man who can see the future of the U.S. economy," "he has a talent that embraces others and is tremendously popular," "most reasonable in both appearance and manner, as you would expect of a truly magnanimous person."

Seeing the way Brady and other top-level business leaders treated Stillman, Eiichi seems to have been very impressed that, "They hold his experience and knowledge in high esteem, not only in terms of money and politics, but almost as if they were his disciples, and consult him in everything."[44] In other words, the image of Stillman that Eiichi portrayed was of a personage much like Eiichi himself in position, dignity, and stature in Japan. Perhaps it was no wonder he was thus so impressed by Stillman.

After the meal, Stillman took the lead and showed Eiichi around the other rooms of the house. All the furnishings were splendid and extremely valuable, but what Eiichi appears to have noted, when shown into Stillman's bedroom, was that he had a chart of daily performance figures for the National City Bank hanging by his bedside. He was told that new figures for the chart were delivered every day, and the balance of accounts for that day showed that the deposits for the Rockefeller family totaled $900,000 and for the Standard Oil company $3,900,000, with the total deposits at the bank coming to $700 million. While

---

[44] *Shibusawa denki shiryō*, vol. 25, p. 245; *Ryūmon zasshi* 353, pp. 60–65.

Japan had made progress in its banking system, at the time, the total deposits at its largest bank, the Dai-ichi Bank, were only around 50 million yen (approximately 25 million dollars). But aside from the scale of the figures, what impressed Eiichi was the speed with which the accounting data was updated.

In the afternoon of that day, Eiichi had met with the famous king of railroads Edward Harriman. In 1898, Harriman had bought up the Union Pacific Railroad, which had ceased to run a profit, and in no time rebuilt it into a top-performing company. He went on in 1901 to purchase the Southern Pacific Railroad. His attempt to acquire the Northern Pacific Railroad, by quietly beginning to buy shares in the Northern Pacific when it was owned by his rival the railway magnate James Hill, set off a tumult on Wall Street such as not seen since the stock market had been founded. Harriman was an aggressive entrepreneur who specialized in "hard bargaining," and Eiichi described him as "a relatively short-statured man by American standards, but every part of his five-foot frame bursting with daring and drive."[45]

It was Harriman who would visit Japan soon after the Russo-Japanese War ended in 1905 in order to lay the groundwork for acquiring the rights to railways in Manchuria. Then Prime Minister Katsura Tarō, Inoue Kaoru, and other Japanese leaders were among those who were so impressed by his eloquence and intelligence that they entered into an agreement officially offering him the rights. Just at that juncture, however, foreign affairs minister Komura Jutarō returned to Tokyo from the conference held in Portsmouth, New Hampshire, where the peace treaty with Russia had just been concluded. He argued that the agreement was inconsistent with the terms of the treaty, and ultimately Harriman's plans were abandoned. Until his death Harriman clung to his grand dream of acquiring a railroad extending from Manchuria across Siberia all the way to Europe.

In those days, at the height of American's golden age of monopolist capital, ambitious and undaunted leaders like Harriman were active throughout U.S. industry. With what seemed

---

[45] *Shibusawa denki shiryō*, vol. 25, p. 664.

then to be limitless domestic resources against the backdrop of an economy that was growing by leaps and bounds, the power of such capitalist leaders posed a threat even to the federal government itself, causing President Roosevelt to invoke the Sherman Antitrust Act (1890) many times in order to protect the powers of government.

On June 13th, in Philadelphia, Eiichi visited Girard College, the famous school that had been established in 1833 according to the will of banker and financier Stephen Girard specifically for the education of orphans. He had a special interest in Girard College because of his active and committed engagement in charitable activities of all kinds. Eiichi had been involved since around 1874 in the management of the Tokyo Yōikuin, which was an institution run by the city of Tokyo for underprivileged citizens, including orphans, the sick, and the elderly, and he remained its president until his death at 91.

He found Girard College quite different from his own image of an "orphanage." It had classrooms, laboratories, workshops, dormitories, and a dining hall, all provided in splendid buildings on a broad 40-acre campus. The some-2,000 inhabitants of the campus – 1,600 students and 400 teachers – lived as if in a kind of independent society.

Girard was a most unusual individual. Born in 1750 in France, he had followed in the footsteps of his father in becoming a sailor. In the process of working in mercantile transport on the East Coast of the United States, he settled in Philadelphia and married, and with the assistance of his wife's family became the owner of a fleet of commercial transport ships. Perhaps reflecting his interest in literature, he named his ships after French writers – Rousseau, Montesquieu, Voltaire.

In 1812 he founded the Stephen Girard Bank. He had no children and when he died in 1831 he left his entire fortune, totaling some $7.5 million, to the city of Philadelphia, stipulating that it be used for charitable activities. His will set down in great detail how the money should be used, dictating the style of architecture to be built at the college – down to the shapes of the buildings' windows and the color of their walls. Interestingly enough, he also stipulated firmly that no ecclesiastic or missionary of any sect be a director, teacher, or staff member.

Although it had taken 70 years from the time Girard died, the city faithfully carried out his will, and by investing – according to his will – the funds remaining after the buildings were completed, the endowment had reached as much as $35 million by the time Eiichi visited in 1902. Eiichi was impressed by Stephen Girard as an ideal example of the tremendous variety and abundance he found in the United States, and he was all in favor of banning the intervention of religion in the running of the school.

Eiichi had heard that the United States was a money-worshipping country where monopolist capital was paramount, So he was delighted to see philanthropic projects such as Girard College standing proudly in its cities. That day he had also visited Bryn Mawr College, the highly respected college for women in Philadelphia's suburbs, where he was shown around a beautiful building that had just been completed thanks to a $250,000 gift from the Rockefeller family.

Eiichi would often say, "The United States has many businessmen inspired by the spirit of benevolence," and he believed that the way to foster healthy ties between Japan and the United States was to assiduously nurture ties with people of that spirit. That conviction was to provide the warp upon which he wove the fabric of his private diplomacy in his later years.

TO EUROPE

On July 2nd, Eiichi and his party set sail from New York for Europe on board the *SS Majestic*, a White Star Line luxury passenger steamship of 10,100 tons gross weight. It left at noon under clear and sunny skies. The sea was quiet and the ship hardly rocked with its movement. After more than 10 days in the heat and congestion of New York City, with every moment of his schedule packed with visits, banquets and the like, Eiichi wrote in his diary that "today I feel I have found serenity for mind and body to carry out this journey with calm and order."[46]

---

[46] *Shibusawa denki shiryō*, vol. 25, p. 249.

As they neared Europe the temperatures dropped and more days were darkened by fog and rain, but the Atlantic Ocean in summer was calm and they did not suffer from seasickness.

On the evening of July 8th, the passengers participated in an evening of entertainment on the ship and Eiichi's wife, Kaneko, who was a skilled player of the shamisen and a good singer of *nagauta* (traditional lyrical songs), played "Echigo shishi" (Echigo Lion Dance). Her performance was so popular that the applause did not die down, and she then did an encore, singing "Yoshiwara suzume" (Sparrow of Yoshiwara).

On July 10th the ship reached Liverpool. The party was met by a large group of local staff of Shibusawa-related companies and boarded a train for London. It was a bright summer day and the greenery of the landscape along the train line was beautiful. It grew quite warm.

After the vast, unmarked landscapes he had seen in the United States, the farms and pastures of England struck Eiichi as very self-contained and obviously tended with great care. He noted that the way the railroad carriages were made and the setting of the track was extremely solid – to him these were telling signs of the national differences between the two countries.

England was a country with a unique tempo of life. Not just the way people lived, but their work and ways of doing things, even the appearance of the landscape, were all extremely sedate and settled, and Eiichi was impressed at how everything was governed by rules and order. There seemed to be no hurry-and-flurry, no impatience or haste to get things done in the shortest time possible. Everything appeared to take place in accordance with fixed manners, moving steadily forward. The sense of history one felt was not like the dreamlike quality that imbued the backdrop of old parts of Japan like Kyoto or Nara; rather, history and tradition inexorably penetrated every aspect of daily life. The way people drank tea, went for walks in the park, the way they dressed – all were governed by tradition, and violations were met by silently expressed social pressure to conform.

One of the things about England that always surprises Japanese is how little the landscape changes. Eiichi's eldest son,

Tokuji, was quite a good photographer, and my father, Shibu-sawa Keizō, compiled and edited an unusual collection of 550 of Tokuji's photographs taken between 1893 and 1910 enti-tled *Shunkan no ruiseki* (Accumulated Moments). The numer-ous snapshots include quite a few extremely expressive works of art. Among them are 114 photographs that were taken in Europe and the United States in 1899, three years before Eiichi's trip there. If you compare those photos to ones from the post-World War II period, it is startling to see how little had changed in six or seven decades. Any photos of Japan – places such as the Sumida River, Ginza, Meguro, or the coastal resort town of Ōiso – taken around the turn of the century would lead you to think you were looking at scenes in a com-pletely different country.

Japan is a place where things are constantly in flux and people actually appear to take pleasure in seeing things change before their very eyes. Perhaps because of this trait, few Japanese find England suits their personalities in the long run. Indeed, this was true of Eiichi. Having seen the tremendous vitality of daily life and impatience for progress that characterized the United States, he could only think of the sedate and unexcited tone of life in England as a sign of stagnation. While America was gal-loping off hell-bent into the future, England was strolling along at the sedate pace of an ox. He fully appreciated the wisdom and steadiness that were such English strengths. Still, much seemed old-fashioned, with people stubbornly clinging to time-honored ways with no attempt to change; Eiichi found it unfathomable that they should be so sure that only their way of doing things was right. Most of those who insisted on preserving traditions were already tottering with age. Such people would be incapable, he realized, of pursuing the kind of astonishing activity he had seen on the other side of the Atlantic Ocean.

The treatment Eiichi received in England, too, was as different from that in the United States as night and day. In the United States, upon learning about Eiichi's achievements and influence from a report provided by the American ambassador in Tokyo, the U.S. president met with Eiichi and talked about current affairs with him – not just that, but even went to the trouble to give him introductions to leaders of the business world.

Partly as a result, maybe, the businessmen he met in New York took a keen interest in Eiichi not only as presenting them with opportunities to do business, but to get to know him as a person and gauge his potential. They were quick to extend him invitations and introduce him to their associates. His itinerary for the two weeks in New York had thus been packed from morning to night with visitors, banquets, and other events.

In England, by contrast, Eiichi and his party found a society deeply influenced by class hierarchies and formalities in human relations, and they had more difficulty meeting with individuals and talking openly about business. He had no meeting with the prime minister or audience with the king. On the 23rd of July, foreign secretary Lord Lansdowne finally agreed to meet with Eiichi, but merely out of duty, and they did not talk in much depth. The first Anglo-Japanese Alliance had just been signed and England at the time had more interests in Japan and the Far East than did the United States. The Anglo-Japanese Alliance was supposedly an important card England was playing in order to check the rapid southward advances of Russia into Manchuria and to contain the movements of Germany, its rival in Europe.

Two weeks after their arrival, on the 25th, a meeting was finally arranged for Eiichi at the Chamber of Commerce through the good offices of a member of parliament J. J. Keswick, chairman of the Jardine Matheson & Company, which was notorious for its role in the Opium War and as the chief agent of Britain's Far Eastern policies. The interview began at 2:30 in the afternoon with about 30 businessmen attending and lasted only about an hour.

Eiichi as usual explained with great sincerity his hopes for interchange between Japanese and British businessmen. Those attending listened courteously, but there were none of the active and eager questions he had received in the United States. Indeed, a few of the businessmen present brought up cases of embezzlement by Japanese merchants and even challenged Eiichi, declaring that Japanese businessmen often violated their contracts.

When the Americans saw an influential Japanese, they latched onto him and made the most of the acquaintance, entertaining him with much attention and trying to learn whatever they could about Japan. The attitude of the British, by contrast, was generally disdain, suggesting that they thought they had no need to hear what a Japanese might have to say.

Eiichi had been invited to attend a formal-dress banquet held on the evening of the 25th, at Mansion House, the home and office of the mayor of London. The banquets were famous for their preservation of the pageantry of olden times with the mayor, judges, high-ranking prelates, and city officials decked out in the wigs and robes of old and the showing of the mayorial insignia (sword, mace, etc.). These banquets followed traditions of the time when the mayor of London as the representative of the London citizenry had almost rivaled the authority of the king, but to outsiders they were puzzling occasions of pomp and circumstance. Eiichi wrote in his diary: "I was told that 318 people were invited to the banquet. The mayor, the guests, and the procedures of the event, down to the method of exchanging cups amid the meal, was all very old-fashioned. The food was extremely fine."

The *Daily Mail* newspaper announced Eiichi's presence with headlines similar to those in the United States, "Japan's Pierpont Morgan: Great Oriental Financier Now in London," but Eiichi's response to reporters' questions was critical:

> America seems to me like the young man of twenty-five, full of impetuous vigour, in the first flush of his strength, who thinks nothing too great or too high for him to tackle. In England, on the contrary, I find the middle-aged man. His activity, his readiness to rush into every concern, may not be so great, but possibly there is a maturity of judgment and a wisdom about the ripened life of your nation which the younger lacks. . . . But your most dangerous competitor is Germany. The German trader gains continually over the English or American because he takes the trouble to learn the native tongue, while you do not. ...The consequence is that if English traders do not take care they will find in a few years that the Germans have taken a large part of their business from them.[47]

---

[47] *Daily Mail* (London, England), July 12, 1902, p. 3.

Summer in England was beautiful. Without any pressing invitations or requests for their time, Eiichi and his party spent time in pleasure boating on the upper reaches of the Thames, enjoying the landscape of Richmond and Kew Gardens. They attended the theater and saw Shakespeare's *Merchant of Venice* and enjoyed the opera *Aida*, and were impressed with the performances despite not understanding a word that was said.

Eiichi took one day for a detailed tour of the port facilities of London. At the time, ships were rapidly growing in size and the port equipment was fast becoming obsolete. Eiichi could not help wondering why there seemed to be no effort to update the equipment. He also toured the conventional sights of the Tower of London and London Bridge (completed in 1831). That bridge was famous as a symbol of London, but Eiichi could see that it was not of a very practical design. Indeed, that bridge was much later bought up by an American and moved to a location in Arizona near the Hoover Dam, where it became a well-known tourist attraction.

When traveling back and forth across the city of London, Eiichi and his party often used the Tube. The underground railways crisscrossing the city in tunnels several dozen meters underground were impressive. He had nothing but praise for their wise design and thoughtful and courteous service. That very same underground transit service continues to operate today, carrying rush hour traffic with great efficiency.

He learned, however, that the underground had been built by introducing capital and technology from the United Sates. Some people, observing such active overseas expansion by U.S. capital, began to gossip that the center of world finance would soon shift from London to New York. Eiichi, however, did not take that view. The United States was in the midst of a fever of progress and development. It did have tremendous power. But with the vast expanses of its territory still to develop, establishing new industry would require an almost infinite amount of capital over the decades to come. On the other hand, England had no such demand for capital. Even where its equipment was growing obsolete, little effort was made to replace or augment it. So the

British had money; if Japan wanted to obtain foreign capital, thought Eiichi, it ought to come to England.

In those days, czarist Russia held rights and interests in Manchuria centering on the South Manchurian Railway and the port at Dalian and it was gradually pushing further south toward the Korean peninsula. Japan had incorporated Korea into its sphere of interest and could not allow it to be taken over by Russia. Not only military force but all manner of means must be used to keep Korea away from Russia. Economic assistance would be provided and railways in particular were needed. Railways were vital not only for development; should there be war with Russia, the presence or not of a railway would be the critical factor in victory or defeat.

Such concerns were behind Eiichi's efforts, begun in 1896, to found the Keifu (Seoul-Pusan) Railway Company for the purpose of building a railroad built between Seoul and Busan (Pusan), and among those supporting him were politician-businessmen like Ōe Taku and Takeuchi Tsuna (father of later prime minister Yoshida Shigeru). Japan had had some success in its modernization, but it was still quite a poor country. Such a major project of overseas investment would not be easy. It ought to have been spearheaded with government capital but the government was reluctant to provide funding, knowing that such open support would arouse the ire of Russia. Even his old friend Inoue Kaoru was forced to turn a cold shoulder to Eiichi's fund-raising difficulties.

This had led Eiichi to consider introducing foreign capital. He had chosen England's Samuel trading company. Its owner, Marcus Samuel, was an immensely wealthy man who later became mayor of London.

On July 27th, the Samuel family invited Eiichi and his wife to their villa in the suburbs of London. More than a villa, it was really a vast country estate. Perhaps because the rate of land utilization was low, the villas of England's wealthy families were of an awesomely large scale. In his diary, Eiichi wrote:

> The villa was on a grand scale and the size of the garden astounding. They told us it covered an area of 600 acres. It had trees of all kinds

and the large lake was said to be stocked with many kinds of fish. Several hundred cows, horses, deer, and sheep graze among the trees. The furnishings and decorations of the rooms are antique and they maintain a number of carriages and teams in the carriage house. We were amazed at the gorgeousness and scale of everything. We were entertained by the Samuel family including their young children. We had luncheon at 2:00 in the afternoon and took the train back at 4:15.

The day at the villa was all very fine, but Samuel insisted on a commission fee of 7.5 percent or over for purchase of a corporate bond of the Keifu Railway Company and would not budge, so Eiichi decided to try negotiating with Samuel's branch office in Yokohama after getting back to Japan and left the matter undecided there in England.

After Eiichi returned to Japan, the government's policy changed. Although following the end of the Sino-Japanese War of 1894–1895 Japan had endeavored to avoid anything that would provoke Russia, the government finally gave up its policy of amity and switched to preparing for the inevitable confrontation with Russia. It was around this time that the powerful leaders Yamagata, Itō, Katsura, and Komura had their famous meeting at Yamagata's Murin'an villa in Kyoto and resolved "Never to let go of Korea, no matter what difficulties might arise."

Inoue Kaoru's indifference regarding the Seoul-Pusan railway project suddenly about-faced to active support in 1903. Eiichi could not help being irritated when Inoue began to ask insistently why construction wasn't yet finished. The story goes that Eiichi chided Inoue for his inconsistency, doing nothing to help all along and then suddenly demanding that the job be quickly finished. "You are asking the impossible," Eiichi said. "I will handle the matter in my own way."

Inoue was nonplussed, but in the end he arranged for the Bank of Japan 5 million yen loan that was needed for the time being.

On August 8th, Eiichi and his party left England after a stay of a little more than a month. In Paris, he wrote a classical Chinese-style poem, which might be translated as follows:

Each and every flower and blade of grass fills me with emotion
All those hills and rivers are old friends
Ah! No differences at all between the past and the present
My reveries and me, carried into Paris on the autumn breeze.

For Eiichi, Paris held many memories. His first visit there had been in 1867, when he served as an aide to Tokugawa Akitake, who went to represent Japan at the Paris international exposition at the invitation of Napoleon III. (Akitake, younger brother of the last shogun Tokugawa Yoshinobu, was then in his early teens.) European civilization was at its height in those days, and Paris in particular was flourishing like a flower in full bloom. Napoleon III held splendid parades down Paris's main streets, attended the exposition, and in the presence of representatives from all over the world, presented his appeal for cultural harmony and progress. For Eiichi, that experience had been an extravagant pageant such as one does not see even in one's dreams and the Emperor's speech had sounded to him like nothing more than braggadocio aimed at the whole world.

Just as is the case with international expositions today, there were pavilions for the displays of each country set up around the grounds, and among them there was a Japanese shop selling tea. It was made entirely of *hinoki* cypress and consisted of a six-tatami-mat room with an accompanying earthen floor. On the tatami were three young girls named Kane, Sumi, and Sato, their hair done in traditional *momoware* style, who would serve tea or sake to visitors to the shop.

After the exposition (March–August) was over, Akitake and his entourage had spent almost all the rest of 1867 traveling. They had toured Switzerland, Holland, and Belgium, and then to Italy and finally England. The situation in Japan had begun to undergo rapid changes from the beginning of 1868 with the battle of Toba-Fushimi, in which forces representing the emperor faced off against those of the now defunct Tokugawa shogunate (1603–1867). Akitake's elder brother and former shogun Tokugawa Yoshinobu swore absolute allegiance to the throne and confined himself to his home in Shizuoka, and the emperor took control of sovereign power, opening the curtain on the Meiji era. Akitake had remained in Paris to study, and it was finally on December 16, 1868 that he and his entourage returned to Japan. So it happened that Eiichi was far away in Paris during the tumultuous events that shook Japan in 1867 and 1868.

That time spent in Europe was a very important experience in Eiichi's life and also a turning point for him, for it was there that he discovered the secret that his country most needed for its modernization. Many of the ideas that became the themes of Eiichi's life – *gapponshugi* ("ethical capitalism"), democracy, and rejection of *kanson minpi* (worship of officialdom and scorn for the private sector) – first began to bud in his mind during his experiences while he was in Paris.

Eiichi had been in Paris earlier as a low-ranking member of the entourage of a feudal-era samurai. In the more than three decades since then, Eiichi had worked assiduously to plant ideas he had learned abroad in the soil of his own country. He tried anything that he thought was good and right. He did sometimes fail, but he also achieved great success. And now he was back in Paris, having risen to the stature of most respected leader of industry in a country that had managed to become a modern state.

One of the people who welcomed Eiichi back to Paris was an old friend from those days, a retired soldier named Villette who had turned 80 years of age. He lived near Versailles and invited the Shibusawas to his house. He gathered his family and they entertained the couple with great warmth.

Thirty-five years earlier, at the order of Napoleon III, Villette, then an army colonel,[48] had been part of Akitake's entourage to entertain as well as advise the group. He had been a mid-career officer in his mid-40s at the time, and Eiichi remembered him as a fearsomely confident fellow. He had been quite overbearing most of the time, boasting of himself working under Napoleon, and ordering the then young Eiichi this way and that at his whim. Eiichi had been so incensed at such treatment that he had once been just one step short of challenging him to a duel.

---

[48] *Shibusawa denki shiryō*, vol. 2, p. 59.

The 80-year-old Villette, however, had greatly mellowed, and he was genuinely delighted to be reunited with Eiichi, who had achieved so much by the age of 62, and the two old fellows fell to reminiscing, forgetting the passage of time.

One of the other Frenchmen who had been assigned to Akitake's entourage as an advisor was a banker named Paul Fleury-Hérard. At the time, Eiichi had been astonished at the relationship between these two men. While Villette had acted with great arrogance toward the Japanese group, he never seemed to assert himself toward Fleury-Hérard, and clearly sought to consult and honor him in all things.

The experience opened Eiichi's eyes, because in Japan the traditions of the feudal era meant that even the lowest official of the government – lowest-ranking samurai – could call in a respected merchant and then order him around in whatever way he pleased, speaking to him as an inferior. Eiichi realized what shameful behavior it was. It was wrong to discriminate among human beings on the basis of occupation or status. If a society allowed such behavior, he thought, it would be impossible to mobilize the strengths of the people as a whole. It was the beginning of his understanding of the relationship between democracy in the West and the strength of its nations.

But what Japan most needed at that time was the strengthening and development of its economy. Once he had seen Europe, Eiichi began to feel guilty about wasting even one day in the task of repairing the poverty and backwardness of his own country. It was wrong that the merchants and artisans who were most important forces in the economy should be oppressed by a senseless social status system, and that their freedom of activity, and even thought, was restricted. A country's economy could never grow under such circumstances. That outmoded system had to be abolished; the evil custom of worshipping officialdom and despising the people had to be cast aside and the status of those engaged in commerce and industry raised – these would be the consistent themes of Eiichi's endeavors for the rest of his career.

Touring the Champs d'Élysées, the Louvre, the Bois de Boulogne park, and other sights, Eiichi made the rounds of the places he had visited on his first trip. The only new attraction was the Eiffel Tower, built in 1900. Paris was as serene and beautiful as it had been 35 years earlier. It was all very nostalgic, but he found himself not quite as moved as he had anticipated. It troubled him, rather, that there were so few signs of further progress since that time.

"It is a most beautiful city – perhaps it is the most beautiful city in the world. But, that is all," he wrote candidly. Eiichi had a talent for writing and he was a good speaker; he was sensitive to the feelings of others and warm-hearted enough to really care about others. But he was not overly sentimental; he had almost nothing to do with the kind of literary taste for dwelling on or reveling in his own feelings. That was partly because of his personality, but also because he led a life of extraordinary activity that did not really allow for such leisure. Every day he was called upon to make decisions and solve problems for projects and the people related to them. He may have decided that he just could not afford to use his time and mental energy on anything but what was really necessary. In that respect, Eiichi was a pragmatist, and every minute, every second of his life was devoted to some specific purpose.

In 1902, France was an ally of Russia. Russia had issued a huge quantity of foreign bonds in order to build the railroad across Siberia and to fund the administration of Manchuria, and France had purchased the great bulk of them. Thus France was greatly opposed to the policies of Japan, which was allied with Britain and harbored enmity toward Russia. Should the rivalry over Manchuria provoke war between Japan and Russia, it was clear that, regardless of which side won or lost, collecting on the bills from Russia would be very difficult.

An executive of the Crédit Lyonnais, a major bank in Paris, whom Eiichi met, openly criticized Japan for having so quickly used up the entire 500 million yen in reparations paid to it by China following the end of the Sino-Japanese War. Japan's economic growth was certainly remarkable, but wasn't it fiscally irresponsible to spend such a huge amount of money in such a short period of time? It was simply unthinkable that an advanced nation would do such a thing, the banker declared. He had heard that relations between Japan and Russia might be broken off, but he also warned that should Japan commit reckless acts like war it would lose the trust of the other big powers and would quickly find it could not sell any foreign bonds.

Eiichi was by nature opposed to war. He believed that war interfered with economic growth. He argued consistently that peace should be maintained and the strength of the people increased, but he was not much impressed by such assertions from the viewpoint of the French side. Whatever the French might say, Japan had to try even harder. Observing the progress achieved in the United States and Europe on his tour, Eiichi renewed his resolve that Japan should increase its national wealth even further and make itself into a country that was the peer of any of the nations of the West.

Whatever his resolve, the work of the Crédit Lyonnais bank in statistical research was outstanding and Eiichi took a keen interest in it. The bank gathered a huge amount of data with everything from information about the fiscal and economic situation of each country to the credit level of each company, and it used the information in drawing up the bank's management policies and also provided it to its customers for reference use.

Leaving France, Eiichi and his party traveled around Germany, Belgium, and Italy, and on September 20th boarded the *Kanagawa-maru* at Port Said to sail back to Japan. Thirty-five years earlier, he had changed trains at Suez and passed along the strait covered with dust, but this time the Suez Canal had been completed and he was able to relax on the ship's deck, gazing out at the desert on both sides of the canal and the sight of travelers as they made their way on camelback through the landscape. In no time they had emerged into the Red Sea.

On the ship, Eiichi was in illustrious company. Also returning to Japan were Minobe Tatsukichi, scholar of law who propounded the theory of the emperor as an organ of the state and was later persecuted by the military, and international authority on insects Matsumura Shōnen, as well as writer Iwaya Sueo (known as Sazanami). Iwaya would be with Shibusawa again on his trip to the United States in 1909.

Eiichi and his party reached Singapore on October 16. Being Britain's forward base in the East, Singapore's architecture, place names, and even the look of the townscape reminded him of London. They found Japanese trading companies doing a brisk business and numerous Japanese residents, making them feel they were coming close to home. Sixty to 70 percent of the coal coming and going in the port was from Japan, and they were told it was coal from the Miike mines handled by Mitsui Trading Company. The Mitsui company opened its company club in Singapore to the Eiichi group and entertained them there.

Eiichi was surprised to hear that there were more than a thousand Japanese residing in Singapore, but later he was surprised again to find that more than 800 of them were prostitutes. He wondered what connections they had used to come over there. These were women from inside and outside Japan proper who had ended up there. There were also quite a number of gamblers who were there to prey on the money the women made. Japan may have won the Sino-Japanese War and its economy may have grown, but the stresses that gripped daily life in the home islands were still severe. Eiichi could see that Japan's emigration policy, sending out "special migrants" like these all over the world, would eventually lead to censure in the receiving countries.

In Singapore, another illustrious passenger boarded the ship: Okakura Kakuzō (Tenshin; 1862–1913). He was on his way back to Japan after a trip to India to survey its ancient arts. Okakura was accompanied by a handsome young man who was the son of a wealthy merchant of Calcutta who wanted to see Japan. This is most likely the prominent supporter of the Indian Independence movement Subodh Chandra Mallik (1879–1920), who was the son of a wealthy Bengali landowner, or a member of his family. Okakura had become acquainted with Subodh Chandra Mallik during a trip to India in 1901–1902. At that time, Okakura became involved with revolutionary leaders in Bengal, going so far as to offer inspiration and encouragement to those plotting to assassinate officials and supporters of the British Raj.[49] Okakura's well-known work *Ideals of the East*, which begins with the famous line "Asia is one," was published in London in this year.

On October 30th, Eiichi and his party landed safely at the port in Kobe.

---

[49] Thanks to Phyllis Birnbaum for this information, August 2017.

CHAPTER 4

FLATTERY WITHOUT SCRUPLE

℘

IN 1903, NEGOTIATIONS with Russia had become increasingly difficult. On October 17, Eiichi was working in his office in Kabutochō as usual when he received a high-ranking and unannounced visitor: Vice-Chief of the General Staff General Kodama Gentarō. Kodama was known as a brilliant military strategist.

Among men in the military, Kodama was even-tempered and rather taciturn. He chose his words carefully and had the ability to quickly and unerringly communicate complex issues. Eiichi was not well acquainted with Kodama but thought he did not have the offensive quality of a schemer, as smart people sometimes tend to be. Eiichi saw that Kodama was intelligent and reliable, and he believed that the general did not disdain him for being a businessman, as was still the tendency in those times.

Kodama opened the conversation by saying, "I came today to discuss an important matter. Do you have time now to hear me out?" Eiichi replied in the affirmative. Even if his visitor had not been as eminent as Kodama, he believed in giving his full attention to whoever was before him at a particular moment. No matter what their status or occupation, Eiichi made a point of meeting with everyone who called on him, listening carefully to what they had to say, giving thoughtful answers to their questions, and offering appropriate advice. Therefore, he spent a lot of time with visitors, and given how busy he was, his workdays stretched even longer. Kindness and sincerity were part and par-

Figure 17
Kodama Gentarō (1852–1906), Imperial Army General. Photo: National Diet Library, Japan.

cel of Eiichi's character, and these qualities were also the source of his unparalleled popularity.

Kodama told Eiichi that relations between Japan and Russia had reached a new low. Things having come to this pass, he said, he wanted Japan's business world to be prepared for war. He said he knew that Eiichi was an advocate of peace and respected him for his stance but that those calling for war should no longer be confined only to the military. If business and industry were to lean in favor of war, Russia would see that Japan was strong and presented a united front, and depending on how things panned out, there might be a final chance to attain peace. He gave Eiichi a candid account of recent negotiations, saying that as long as Russia thought Japan was trying to avoid war, it would continue escalating its demands. He hoped that Eiichi would be willing to tactfully circulate these realities of the situation and round up support among his business associates.

Figure 18
Ōkubo Toshimichi
(1830–1878), leader of
the Meiji government.
Photo: National Diet
Library, Japan.

The fact that Kodama went to the trouble of visiting Shibusawa suggests the sense of urgency he felt about dealing with Russia. He must have thought he had to get Japan's leading industrialist on board as quickly as possible. Eiichi's belief in the importance of peace and his opposition to war was long-standing, dating back to 1871 when he had served as *daijō*, or bureau head, in the Ministry of Finance. At the time, he had attended a meeting on behalf of his superior, Inoue Kaoru. He was asked to speak by *sangi* councilor and Minister of Finance Ōkubo Toshimichi (1830–1878), who had just returned from a cabinet meeting. Ōkubo held the title of finance minister, but Inoue was the de facto head of the ministry.

Ōkubo said that the work of abolishing domains and establishing prefectures had finally gotten started but that the army had to be well prepared in order to deal with expected opposition to the change. At the cabinet meeting, he said, the army had requested 8 million yen. He had intended to sound out Inoue about the matter before giving his approval but felt that the sum was manageable. Therefore, he had given his approval to the army then and there and wanted the ministry to follow through.

This brought an immediate objection from Eiichi, who said, "I could understand if you were spending this money because there was sufficient income, but simply deciding to spend money without considering how much money is available is not sound fiscal practice. As things stand now, allocating 8 million yen to the army is simply the minister's unfounded personal estimation, and I cannot agree to this."

This angered Ōkubo, who replied, "Very well, then, does that mean you do not care what happens to the army and the navy, or to the country?"

At the time, Eiichi was still only 31. Despite this, and because he was quite fed up with the high-handed ways of the faction within the new government of people from the Chōshū and Satsuma domains at the time – Ōkubo was from Satsuma – Eiichi refused to give an inch.

"In finance, the ironclad rule is to balance income and expenditure. What kind of country decides to spend first, without knowing where the money is coming from?"

"Be quiet! I didn't come here today to be lectured by you. No matter how important finance is, we cannot ignore the army and the navy."

After this tit-for-tat exchange, Eiichi said, "Then do as you please. I resign!" and indignantly left the room. Inoue later prevailed upon him to remain in his post, but the experience left him a bitter critic of the military's overbearing behavior in the area of finance for the next sixty years.

Partly because of the long-entrenched tradition of respect for officialdom and disdain for the private sector (*kanson minpi*), when it came to spending on the military, there was a tendency to dispense funds liberally without much scruple. The attitude, moreover, that anyone who raised the issue of finances was unpatriotic would later lead the country down a very bitter path indeed.

In addition to the finance issue, Eiichi was uncomfortable with the national traits of his countrymen. He believed they had a penchant for getting excited and showing off, and were quick to grow overconfident and headstrong. For the government to take advantage of these traits and stir people up, encouraging the clamor for war and calling it "public opinion," was just absurd. As he had seen at the time of the Sino-Japanese War (1894–1895), when the country did go to war and win, the victory would only encourage those tendencies, giving other countries the impression that Japan was a warlike country. Such a reputation would never be to Japan's advantage.[50] Eiichi's perception, or premonition, of what would happen was to be fulfilled in almost every respect from the end of the Russo-Japanese War onward, leading to grave difficulties and calamity in Japan's future.

Surely General Kodama, sitting with Eiichi in his office in 1903, knew his host's views. Kodama went on to explain that Russia was bent on extending its sphere of influence over the entire Korean peninsula. This, too, came as a surprise to Eiichi. It was general knowledge at the time that negotiations were going on toward drawing a line somewhere around the 38th parallel, in effect partitioning the Korean peninsula, but Kodama said that reaching an agreement on that was proving difficult. If what Kodama said was indeed true, Russia's sphere of influence would extend down to the Tsushima Strait – immediately facing Japan's coast. That would not only undermine Japan's defenses but also negate everything that Japan had worked so hard to achieve since the opening of the country. Japan could not allow that to happen. Eiichi replied, "I understand. If that is the situation, I will do my best."

Even so, he reflected, it would be unnatural for businessmen to come out and make overtly warlike pronouncements; doing so might even backfire. After pondering the matter, Eiichi offered Kodama a suggestion. If war did break out, military transport would naturally be a problem. Whereupon Eiichi proposed that Nippon Yūsen (the NYK Line) be asked to indicate its

---

[50] For Eiichi's recollections about the Kodama visit and remarks about the character of Japanese, see *Shibusawa denki shiryō*, vol. 28, p. 475.

intention to offer all its ships to provide military transport in case of war; this would signal to business circles just how dire the situation was and help them prepare for the worst. This sophisticated, innovative idea was typical of Eiichi's serious-minded personality and ingenuity at coming up with approaches suited to particular circumstances. Kodama, who was also known for coming up with good ideas, was suitably impressed and asked Eiichi to start implementing his plan immediately.

Eiichi had been linked with NYK since the company's earliest days and was at the time a board member. He went to Nippon Yūsen the very next day to present his idea to company president Kondō Renpei (1848–1921), who readily agreed to put into action the plan that Eiichi had discussed with Kodama. The plan was to prepare a notice to be issued in the name of the board members of NYK and sent to not only shippers but also banks, government offices, and others, announcing that in the event of sudden developments (outbreak of hostilities), NYK reserved the right to refuse civilian freight at any time and would put all their ships at the government's disposal for military transport.

ILL AGAIN AS WAR RAGES

Soon after the meeting with Kodama, on November 21, Eiichi contracted influenza and later an acute ear infection that confined him to his sickbed for six months. During that time, the war with Russia began, in February 1904. Eiichi's doctors included Takaki Kanehiro, a prominent physician and later the founder of the forerunner to Jikei University School of Medicine, and Dr. Erwin (von) Bälz, inventor of Bälz Water – a mixture of glycerin and water used to soothe chapped skin. On December 1, minor surgery was performed on his ear and the ear condition rapidly improved, but he remained in poor health for quite some time.

The strange thing is that Eiichi seemed to succumb to illness during the times Japan was at war. In 1894, at the time of the first Sino-Japanese War, he had developed pain in his mouth that was later determined to be cancer, and remained out of circulation for some time. On November 18 of that year, he was operated on by foreign surgeon Julius Scriba, with Drs. Takaki and Hashimoto Tsunatsune, another prominent Japanese doctor, in attendance. The operation left a scar on Eiichi's cheek, which foreign newspapers thought might be the result of a sword wound suffered during fighting at the time of the Meiji Restoration. The reality was less heroic, as Eiichi ruefully recorded in a Chinese-style poem (*kanshi*) he composed at the time of his operation:

A storm of youthful valor and strength
Eager to back a million troops with a single sword
Alas! All heroic passions vanquished,
By illness, leaving only a lean face and the scar of the knife.

Being younger at the time, Eiichi had recovered more quickly and by March 1895 was able to return from the countryside and resume working as usual. In 1904, Eiichi was 64 years old, and long years of hard work had taken their toll. In March and April, he moved to Kōzu in what is now the city of Odawara to convalesce. He did not work and received no visitors, but he failed to achieve complete recovery. He often felt as though he was coming down with a cold, and even the slightest overexertion could bring on a fever. All he could do was to cloister himself in his lodgings, composing poetry, including *waka*.

When the weather began to warm up, he returned to Tokyo on April 24, 1904. But on the 27th, he developed a fever again and was diagnosed with pneumonia. That was in the days before sulfa drugs or antibiotics. He continued to have a high fever and developed a severe cough and heavy phlegm. The fever sapped his appetite, and for several days he could only tolerate a liquid diet.

Alarmed at his haggard appearance, his secretary Yasoshima Chikanori attempted to cheer him up by saying, "Sir, you've been ill for quite a while, but you have not wasted away a bit. That is proof of your inner strength." To which Eiichi, smiling wanly, replied in a weak voice, "You may well say that, but remember that pigs are roly-poly until the day they die."

In mid-May, Eiichi still had a fever, and his cough and phlegm had developed an unpleasant smell. His doctors determined that he was in the early stages of pulmonary gangrene. Takaki, Bälz and young doctors on the medical staff at Tokyo Imperial University looked after Eiichi around the clock, assisted by four nurses, and there was an ominous air about Eiichi's Asukayama residence.

Eiichi, weakened physically and psychologically by the fever, started to feel that he might be at death's door. He had always said that when he died, he wanted to die quietly, without complaining or causing anyone any trouble. But as death loomed before him, he began to fuss over things around him that he had never paid attention to before, and suddenly became quite cantankerous, as even he himself realized.

May 18. It had been raining since morning, and Eiichi had had a fever over 38°C since before dawn, was coughing up bloody sputum, and was in a generally weakened state. Summoning his eldest son Tokuji and secretary Yasoshima to his bedside, he told them of his wishes concerning the future of the Dai-ichi Bank among other matters of concern. He told them to ask Sasaki Yunosuke to succeed him as bank president and said that in the event of his death he hoped that everyone in the company would band together, since rivals would be sure to zero in on his business. In a thin, reedy voice, he continued, touching on how to manage the Korean economy, and how to run the Shibusawa business and dispose of his estate. Illness makes the sufferer feel powerless; Eiichi's emotions were stirred and he shed tears several times as he spoke.

One day, former shogun Tokugawa Yoshinobu himself came for a bedside visit. He held Eiichi's hand, spilling tears as well. Sharing a curious fate since the last years of the shogunate, these two men, once master and subordinate, had a relationship that others could never fathom. On June 9, Eiichi received a convalescence gift of sweets from Emperor Meiji. Eiichi was deeply touched and composed a *waka* poem to express his feelings.

Fuseya moru / umeki no koe no / omoiki ya / kumo no ue made / kikoyu beshi to wa

As I lay groaning on my sickbed, little did I know that my suffering
had reached the ears of His Majesty

In a preface to the poem, Eiichi wrote how blessed and honored
he felt, as a "humble subject" – a person not even a member of
the government, but of the private sector – to have received such
a thoughtful gift from the country's sovereign. He thought that
the gift must be an indication of the emperor's constant concern for the progress of the nation's economy, just part of it spilling over for this "humble subject." The fact that even at times
like that, Eiichi would interpret the imperial gift not as care for
himself personally but as the emperor's attention to the business
world as a whole was typical of how dedicated Eiichi was to his
mission to enhance the status of the business world.[51]

The emperor's gift was sweets consisting of *konpeitō* sugar
candy and *yōkan*, a gelled sweet bean paste. My father Keizō
(Eiichi's grandson) was born in 1896, so he would have been
eight years old at the time. Taken to pay a visit to his grandfather,
he was shown the sweets and later clearly recollected his childish
wonder at the beauty of the square confections, which were fash-
ioned of a clear gel with two goldfish made of *yōkan* floating in it.

Although he himself and those around him had begun thinking he was so seriously ill that he would never recover, his inner
strength must have kept him going, for it was around this time
that Eiichi's condition gradually started improving. All the while,
the war on which Japan had staked its fate was proceeding. Eiichi
had a map of the battlefields in Manchuria affixed to a fold-
ing screen in his room and followed the developments from his
sickbed. Kodama was the de facto commander of land combat
operations and was devoting all his energies to the fighting on
the Manchurian plains. As Eiichi gradually recovered, he also
contributed to the war effort. Early in 1905, he attended a public
meeting on the war situation held at the Kabukiza Theater and
gave a long speech on the theme of war and the economy, where

---

[51] "Shibusawa Eiichi ten'on ni kankyusu" [Shibusawa Eiichi Weeps at the
Favor Shown by the Emperor] *Jitsugyo no Nihon* 7:14 (July 1, 1904),
quoted in *Shibusawa denki shiryō*, vol. 29, p. 151.

he spoke of the moral obligations and patriotism of people in business and industry.[52]

ENDING ONE WAR AND PREVENTING THE NEXT

For Japan, it was a long and painful war. Russia at the time was facing many difficulties in its internal political situation and could not fight at full strength, but it was nevertheless a world power, and Japan was fighting against Europeans and European civilization for the first time in its history. As evidenced from the offense and defense at Port Arthur (now part of the city of Dalian), the battlefield tactics and the weapons Japan faced were completely different and much more destructive than ten years earlier when it had waged war against China.

Everyone in Japan, from the emperor on down, dug in and held fast against the enemy for more than a year. Bloodied and beaten, weakened to the point it could barely keep going, the country kept fighting through willpower alone. On the verge of exhaustion, it was only the almost miraculous victories at Mukden in Manchuria and the Sea of Japan naval battle (the Battle of Tsushima) that saved the day, and Japan managed to get itself to the point of peace negotiations. Japanese diplomatic maneuvering, which had been initiated even before the war, principally with U.S. President Theodore Roosevelt, finally bore fruit, saving the country from ruin.[53]

On July 8, 1905, Japanese foreign minister Komura Jutarō left Japan, invested with full powers to negotiate on Japan's behalf at the peace conference ending the hostilities. Arranged by Roosevelt, the conference was to be held from August 10 in Portsmouth, New Hampshire. July 8 was a Saturday, and unusual for July, a cool wind was blowing. His health by then recouped, Eiichi made his way to Shimbashi Station and saw the foreign minister off at 2 p.m. For Japan, it was vital to win a favorable outcome at the peace conference. We can imagine that the mood

---

[52] *Shibusawa denki shiryō*, vol. 28, pp. 478–85.
[53] For details on the war see Ian Nish, *The Origins of the Russo-Japanese War* and Dennis Ashton Warner and Peggy Warner, *The Tide at Sunrise: A History of the Russo-Japanese War, 1904–1905.*

FIGURE 19
William Howard Taft
(1857–1930), U.S.
Secretary of War; later
27th president. Photo:
Shibusawa Memorial
Museum.

of the foreign minister and all those who surrounded him to see
him off must have been quite sober and filled with worry.[54]

Immediately after Komura left Japan, U.S. Secretary of War
William Howard Taft, who would later succeed Roosevelt as the
27th president of the United States, arrived in Tokyo, on his way
to the Philippines with an entourage including many congressmen and senators as well as Roosevelt's eldest daughter. Eiichi,
representing 28 leading industrialists from the Tokyo-Yokohama
area, hosted a reception for the party at the Kōyōkan, a high-class,
members-only traditional restaurant in Shiba Park, on July 27.

Until the previous year (1904), Taft had been governor-general of the Philippines, overseeing its administration as a U.S.
protectorate, and he was considered a "Far East hand" in the

---

[54] For a profile of Komura, including his crucial role in the negotiations
which led to the Treaty of Portsmouth, see Ian Nish, *Japanese Foreign
Policy, 1869–1942: Kasumigaseki to Miyakezaka*, pp. 59–82.

Roosevelt administration. The ostensible purpose of Taft's trip was an inspection tour of the Philippines, but he was rumored to be in Tokyo to craft the framework for future U.S.-Japan relations with Japanese political leaders.

Eiichi met Taft a total of four times in his life and considered him "an affable, kind man and a talented politician who makes a positive impression on all who meet him."[55] The Americans had requested that the reception be Japanese-style, which is why it was held at the Kōyōkan. Their party, however, consisted of more than 80 people, including members of the entourage and embassy personnel. The Japanese side was headed by former prime minister Itō Hirobumi, and including accompanying guests, cabinet ministers and other leaders, the total was nearly 150-strong. No room was large enough to hold everyone, so the men were seated on the second floor and the women on the first floor, with the rooms opened up to form one large space on each of the floors and everyone seated on *zabuton* cushions to partake of a meal served on individual trays. The menu and information about the entertainment had been translated into English and, the season being summer, printed on the back of flat *uchiwa* fans distributed to all the guests.[56]

After the meal, everyone was directed to the first floor and seated on chairs to watch the entertainment. Eiichi gave a short but flattering address welcoming the guests, alluding to the close relations that had developed between Japan and the United States since the arrival of Commodore Perry and his ships, and thanking the U.S. for its role in helping Japan modernize its institutions.

Following remarks by Taft and senators and congressmen, there was entertainment. It featured traditional dances, a play, and a *kappore* comic dance by a troupe of geisha, all of which were greeted with enthusiastic applause. The well-fed and entertained

---

[55] "Beikoku jū daijitsugyōka no inshō (shōzen)" (Impressions of Ten Major American Entrepreneurs (Continued)), *Jitsugyō no sekai* 18:12 (Dec. 1, 1921).

[56] *Shibusawa Eiichi nikki*, quoted in *Shibusawa denki shiryō*, vol. 25, p. 561.

guests began heading for home around midnight. Eiichi was also preparing to go home when he was collared by Itō Hirobumi, who was in a jovial mood after drinking, and invited him to have "one for the road." The two men headed back inside, where Itō waxed prolific about the state of the country and the government; it was after 2 a.m. before Eiichi could finally get away.[57]

Two days later, on July 29, Taft and Prime Minister Katsura Tarō exchanged a secret document known as the Katsura-Taft Memorandum, the gist of which was that the United States acknowledged Japan's sovereignty over the Korean peninsula whereas Japan would forbear from any aggressive intent toward the Philippines.

In a letter to Taft, Roosevelt said, "The Philippines Islands form our heel of Achilles," for without adequate fortification and a "great fleet" this territory would be "vulnerable" and remain a "temptation" to Japan.[58] In other words, Roosevelt's basic diplomatic approach to ensuring the security of U.S. interests in the Philippines was to curry favor with Japan and compromise his own country's policy on the continent as far as Japan's presence there was concerned. Taking advantage of this position, Japan's first step after the Russo-Japanese War was a steady, forceful movement towards the annexation of Korea.

Yet, despite the compromises made on both sides, relations between Japan and the United States grew progressively worse. In negotiations at the peace conference, Japan was forced to give up its demand for reparations. This greatly disturbed the Japanese public, which suspected that this was Roosevelt's doing, and stirred up much anti-American sentiment.

Eiichi made the following entry in his diary on September 5: "A rally took place in Hibiya Park and the whole city is stirred up. People are upset at the terms of the peace treaty and have begun demonstrating. In the evening, they stormed the home minister's official residence and set fire to several police stations. Unrest is rife throughout the city."

---

[57] Ibid.
[58] Roosevelt to Taft, 21 August 1907, in Roosevelt, *Letters*, vol. 5, pp. 761–62.

Meanwhile, a menacing letter addressed to "that traitor Shibusawa" arrived at Eiichi's Fukagawa residence, threatening to "cut his head off." Thinking it best to take precautions when going to his office in Kabutochō, Eiichi had to avoid the main roads and go by rickshaw via Yanaka and Nezu-dōri for quite some time.

Another diary entry, on September 7: "Cloudy, hot and humid. The unrest continues, and the government has had to proclaim martial law, which pains me greatly. Little did I think the capital of the empire of Japan, despite successive victories [with China and Russia], would be in a warlike chaos like this even without any enemy soldiers present."

MITIGATING MIGRATION MATTERS

Coincidentally, the movement in the United States to exclude Japanese migrants was building up and becoming a major diplomatic issue. After the Chinese Exclusion Act was passed in 1882, emigration to the United States from Japan became quite substantial. Since this law stopped Chinese from entering the United States, Japanese workers were welcomed everywhere, as they helped alleviate labor shortages. California farmers and fruit growers vied to hire Japanese workers, because they were skilled yet worked for low wages.

Nishiyama Gen was one of the first Japanese to emigrate to the United States.[59] Based in Salt Lake City, he supplied Japanese laborers to the coal mines throughout Utah. He was a man of good character and popular with the workers, and it is said that he was the first labor broker to win working conditions for Japanese miners on a par with those offered to Caucasians.

Other Japanese were active in a similar role in other areas, supplying Japanese labor to railroad or coal mine operators. Since the pay and working conditions were much better than in

---

[59] In July 1969, his son, Nishiyama Sen, was the simultaneous interpreter in charge of interpreting the Apollo moon landing into Japanese, mightily impressing the Japanese public with his fluent and accurate rendition of the event.

Japan, emigration from Japan increased with each passing year. By 1897, there were 13,000 Japanese in the United States.

Naturally enough, this situation touched off dissatisfaction in the labor market. At its annual meeting in 1897 in Salt Lake City, the Western Labor Union, a federation of 58 labor unions in the western states and western Canada, passed a resolution opposing emigration by Japanese workers, marking the first time that an emigration issue was taken up as a labor issue.

The immigrants included groups of less desirable individuals, such as prostitutes and gamblers, and the inflow of people became more and more frequently cited as having a negative effect on American society. Acting on reports on this worrisome situation from its diplomatic corps, the Japanese government took steps to restrict emigration, but it was too late, and the number of Japanese heading for the United States continued to climb.

According to data from United States government sources, the number of Japanese entering the country was as follows (numbers for each year are those entering the U.S. in the last one year up to and including June of the year in question):

1897	1,526
1898	2,230
1899	3,396
1900	12,626
1901	4,908
1902	5,325
1903	6,990
1904	7,771
1905	4,319
1906	5,178
1907	9,948
1908	7,250
1909	1,590

Source: Japanese Ministry of Foreign Affairs, ed., *Tai-Bei imin mondai narabini Kashū hai-Nichi undō no enkaku* (History of the Issue of Immigration to the United States and the Anti-Japanese Movement in California), Tokyo, 1920.

Especially as demonstrated through the victory in the Russo-Japanese War, Japan's rapid progress in becoming a modern country set off a kind of "yellow peril" alarm, typified by the formation in San Francisco of the Japanese Exclusion League in May 1905. Its membership rapidly grew into the thousands, with chapters in many locations, and the league directed its members to boycott Japanese-owned stores, making it a force that could not be disregarded. The *San Francisco Chronicle* featured a series of sensational articles, further fanning anti-Japanese sentiment.

"Crime and Poverty Go Hand in Hand with Asiatic Labor"
"Japanese Men a Menace to American Women"
"Brown Men Are an Evil in the Public Schools"
"Brown Artisans Steal Brains of Whites"[60]

Local politicians, sensitive to trends in public opinion, soon got on the bandwagon to mount anti-Japanese campaigns or submit bills to expel Japanese.

For example, the San Francisco Board of Education announced a resolution favoring separate schools for Japanese children. The Board's statement said that the reason for the plan was that "our children should not be placed in any position where their youthful impression may be affected by association with pupils of the Mongolian race."[61]

Earlier, when the United States had discriminated against Chinese and excluded them, it had been able to exploit their weaknesses and make unreasonable demands. But Roosevelt knew very well that this would not be possible where Japanese were concerned. In a June 1905 letter to his close friend Henry Cabot Lodge, Roosevelt wrote that people on the Pacific Coast were insulting, provocative and trying to exclude Japanese "on the ground that they are an immoral, degraded and worthless race." He warned that Japan was in fact a "formidable new power – a power jealous, sensitive and warlike," and that if Japan decided

---

[60] *San Francisco Chronicle*, February 13–March 13, 1905. See also Roger Daniels, *Asian America*, p. 116.
[61] See Wollenberg, "'Yellow Peril' in the Schools (II)," p. 15.

to establish naval supremacy in the Pacific, it would be capable of wresting the Philippines and Hawai'i from U.S. hands. He argued that efforts must be made to persuade people in California to be civil, just, and generous to Japanese and at the same time to strengthen and modernize the U.S. naval fleet (in case a Japanese attack were to occur).[62]

Even as ominous clouds gathered, the two countries' governments continued to gloss over the situation and keep up a diplomacy of mutual flattery through which they thought they were maintaining order in the Pacific.

On April 18, 1906, San Francisco was struck by a devastating earthquake. Strong tremors shook the city at 5:15 a.m., followed by several strong aftershocks that plunged the city into panic. Fires broke out, and fanned by strong winds, spread over a wide area. Several splendid buildings along the main streets, including the Palace Hotel and the offices of the *San Francisco Examiner*, were consumed by the flames, as were the Japanese consulate, Chinatown, and the area where the Japanese community resided. The strong winds, continually changing direction, and the lack of water pressure complicating firefighting efforts, made the fire spread further and further; it burned for three days and nights until April 21st. The "great calamity" left 295 people dead and 593 injured and an estimated 400 million dollars in damage.

In Japan, the Red Cross Society sprang into action, leading efforts to collect relief donations. Japanese government officials and representatives of business and other circles met at the foreign minister's official residence on April 29 to discuss how to raise the donations. It was announced there that the imperial family would donate 200,000 yen, and the Bank of Japan, Mitsui, Mitsubishi, Nippon Yūsen (NYK), Dai-ichi Bank and other leading concerns pledged 170,000 yen.

San Francisco was the center of the movement to expel Japanese immigrants and its most prominent hotspot. Precisely because of that, Eiichi believed it was important to collect as much

---

[62] Roosevelt to Lodge, 5 June 1905, in Roosevelt, *Letters*, vol. 4, pp. 1,202–1,206; Kennedy, *The American Spirit*, p. 512.

money as possible, so as to demonstrate Japan's sincere concern in such a way that it might soften anti-Japanese sentiment. He devoted great energy to the task, writing letters and visiting dozens of acquaintances in various sectors of industry to request donations for San Francisco. Some companies believed that it went against their foundational principles as money-making enterprises to donate to a cause unrelated to their business. But Eiichi saw the matter in a larger context, asserting that the anti-Japanese movement could be critical to his country's fate. He believed Japanese businessmen should as a matter of course give generously in order to influence American thinking and counter their discriminatory images of Japanese.

Thanks to the efforts of Eiichi and others, Japan donated over 250,000 dollars, a sum that exceeded the total of donations from all other countries. Ueno Suesaburō, the Japanese consul in San Francisco, wrote to Eiichi to thank him for his efforts and said that the citizens of the city were very grateful for the assistance.

Despite the sincerity of these gestures, the reports of anti-Japanese behavior continued: a Japanese scientist walking along the street in San Francisco had had rocks thrown at him, and a Japanese-operated restaurant was boycotted. On October 11 of the same year, the Board of Education decided to go ahead with its discriminatory policy excluding Japanese children from public schools.

The Japanese government lodged a protest on October 25, saying that "whatever the reason, discriminating against Japanese children and preventing them from attending public schools means that Japanese bear the brunt of racial discrimination: this cannot be overlooked." In light of the historically friendly relations between the two countries and from the perspective of justice and humanity, Japan demanded that the American government take the appropriate steps in response.

Roosevelt saw this development as the biggest threat to his brand of diplomacy and dispatched his secretary of commerce and labor, Victor H. Metcalf, to California the next day to study the situation, while at the same time ordering Charles J. Bonaparte, the secretary of the navy, to compare the relative strengths of Japanese and American naval forces, in order to prepare for the possibility of war.

In a letter to Senator Eugene Hale on the 27th, Roosevelt touched on the possibility of war with Japan. He wrote that "the Japanese are proud, sensitive and warlike, are flushed with the glory of their recent triumph, and are in my opinion bent upon establishing themselves as the leading power in the Pacific." If "sufficiently irritated and humiliated," Japan would come to see the United States not Russia as "the national enemy whom she will ultimately have to fight." Consequently, it was necessary to keep the U.S. navy "in such shape as to make it a risky thing for Japan to go to war with us." In a letter to his son Kermit the same day, he decried the "infernal fools" in California, especially San Francisco, for their rude and insulting treatment of Japanese, saying that if war ever broke out, it would be all of the United States that would "pay the consequences."[63]

In December, after reading Metcalf's report, in his annual message to Congress, Roosevelt called special attention to the Japanese immigration issue. He complimented Japan's civilization and praised the country for its progress in modernizing and touched on the heartfelt sympathies and generous monetary assistance proffered after the San Francisco earthquake. He also emphasized the importance of the economic ties between Japan and the United States and branded discriminatory practices against the Japanese as "wicked absurdity."[64] Finally, he indicated that, if necessary, he would send the U.S. Army to protect Japanese in California.

---

[63] Roosevelt to Hale, 27 October 1906, and Roosevelt to Kermit Roosevelt, 27 October 1906, in Roosevelt, *Letters*, vol. 5, pp. 473–76. In the opinion of Charles E. Neu, in *An Uncertain Friendship: Theodore Roosevelt and Japan, 1906–1909*, pp. 95–96, Roosevelt may have exaggerated somewhat in order to "frighten" Hale, and therefore Congress, into agreeing to the construction of a new dreadnought-type battleship. But, as shown in the letter to his son, Roosevelt's exasperation with the anti-Japanese agitation in California was certainly real.

[64] See Robert C. Kennedy, "On This Day," http://www.nytimes.com/learning/general/onthisday/harp/1110.html.

Roosevelt's flattering gesture was very well received in Japan. Diplomat and friend of America Kaneko Kentarō declared, "Roosevelt's comments are the greatest by an American president since George Washington's farewell address." But in California, Roosevelt's threat to send federal troops to "do police duty" was taken as "an insult." In an editorial, the *San Francisco Chronicle* declared that "Feeling in this State is not now against the Japanese but against an unpatriotic President."[65]

Caught between the two sides, a vexed Roosevelt tried to find middle ground. The result was an announcement by the Japanese foreign minister on February 14, 1907 that restrictions would be placed on Japanese emigration. This became the "Gentlemen's Agreement" between the two countries with which Roosevelt was able to calm down the California State Legislature. He even invited all the members of the San Francisco Board of Education to the White House and lavished them with presidential hospitality. Roosevelt's great efforts to defuse the situation paid off when the Board of Education rescinded its discriminatory order against Japanese schoolchildren on March 13, 1907.

ENTERTAINING TAFT

The tensions between the United States and Japan over the treatment of Japanese may have been behind the return of Taft and his family to Japan in September 1907. At the time, Taft was expected to run as Roosevelt's successor in the presidential election the following year, so Japan was welcoming the de facto next president of the United States. Emperor Meiji offered Taft and his party accommodation at the Shiba Detached Palace, and Taft was welcomed and entertained by both the government and the private sector.

On September 30, Eiichi, together with Ozaki Yukio, mayor of the city of Tokyo, and Nakano Buei, head of the Tokyo Chamber of Commerce, hosted a grand reception at the Imperial Hotel where the men were expected to dress in white tie and tails and the women in formal floor-length gowns or kimono.

---

[65] *San Francisco Chronicle*, December 21, 1906.

An elaborate full-course meal was served, and the orchestra played numbers including "The Stars and Stripes Forever," the overtures from "Carmen" and "Faust," and "The Blue Danube." The guests of honor were Taft and his wife and the new American ambassador to Japan Thomas J. O'Brien, and the guest list included Prime Minister Saionji Kinmochi and his Cabinet, elder statesmen (*genrō*) Matsukata Masayoshi, Inoue Kaoru, Ōkuma Shigenobu, and Itagaki Taisuke, and Russo-Japanese War heroes Ōyama Iwao, Nogi Maresuke, Tōgō Heihachirō and other notables, all accompanied by their spouses.

Eiichi offered welcoming remarks even more flattering than those he had made at Kōyōkan two years earlier. He made several references to the historic friendship between Japan and the United States and said in an impassioned tone, "We think of the people of the United States as we do of our own people... (applause) and we respectfully request that after your return to the United States Your Excellency Secretary Taft make it known to everyone there, in and outside government, that we hope they too will think of us as they do of their own people (applause)."[66]

Following this address, Taft launched into very interesting remarks of his own, a frank recounting of the two countries' various shady dealings and compromises based entirely on pragmatic considerations at the time. Almost from the start, Taft touched on the move by San Francisco to exclude Japanese immigrants, saying that this was unfair and wrong, and that the government and responsible politicians would surely take steps to find a solution. He urged Japan not to think, even for an instant, of going to war with the United States, saying that this would be wrong and a crime against civilization. His remarks sounded like an entreaty to avoid even mentioning the very idea.

As a reward for not going to war against the United States, he made sure to promise Korea to Japan. Taft must have thought that Japan could change Korea, which he apparently believed had been "misgoverned" for 1,500 years, and said that Japan had a duty to change that country. He lauded the efforts of the well-respected Itō

---

[66] *Shibusawa denki shiryō*, vol. 25, pp. 572.

Hirobumi, who was at that very moment doing his best as resident-general in Korea. Taft said that although Japan's de facto occupation of Korea was being discussed pro and con around the world and that news reports and commentaries cast Japan in a negative light, Japan's Korea policy had the full support of the United States.

In Taft's words, "We are living in an age when the intervention of a stronger nation in the affairs of a people unable to maintain a Government of law and order, to assist the latter to better government becomes a national duty and works for the progress of the world."[67]

He continued that similarly, the United States accepted responsibility for governing the Philippines despite the fact that it was a complicated undertaking requiring much time and effort. He said that the United States had no time to think of going to war with Japan, and that therefore, the two countries, being in similar circumstances, must uphold peace at any cost. He concluded by saying that the majority of Americans were well disposed toward Japanese and that he himself was convinced that peace between Japan and the United States would prevail for many years.

In other words, Taft gave Japan the green light to do whatever it wished in Korea and in return for the United States turning a blind eye to Japan's actions in Korea, Japan should leave the Philippines to the United States. It was almost like gangland bosses divvying up territory. Nothing could have been more upsetting to Koreans trembling at the ever-increasing pressure from Japan, or Filipinos, who had lost their war for independence. Here were worthies from the United States and Japan, clad in white tie and tails, enjoying good food and pleasant music, applauding self-serving orations, and raising their glasses in a toast to friendship between Japan and the United States, but at untold cost to millions of Asians.

On October 18, Taft sent Roosevelt a telegram assuring him that the Japanese government was very enthusiastic about avoiding war with the United States.

---

[67] Quoted from original English record of the speech in *Shibusawa denki shiryō*, vol. 25, p. 574.

ENTERTAINING THE GREAT WHITE FLEET

On October 22, 1908, Eiichi stood on stage at the Kabukiza Theater to give a welcome address in the name of the Tokyo Bankers' Club, the Tokyo Clearing House, and the Tokyo Bankers' Association to officers and men of the United States Atlantic Fleet (the "Great White Fleet") visiting Japan. The theater had been reserved for the occasion – bars were set up on each floor and everyone helped themselves to the lavish buffet provided. Plays and dances were performed on the stage but few of the seamen paid attention, so busy were they eating, drinking, and singing loudly everywhere.

The Atlantic Fleet consisted of a convoy of 16 warships led by the flagship *Connecticut*. One of the ships, the *Ohio*, had been under construction at San Francisco's Union Iron Works when Eiichi toured the facility in 1902. Having the fleet of the United States Navy circumnavigate the globe on a nearly two-year long voyage was a typically grand and extravagant gesture of the kind that Roosevelt liked.[68]

Roosevelt espoused the beliefs of Alfred T. Mahan in the importance of sea power for great countries and devoted passionate energy to the idea of building up a strong navy. By having the fleet circle the globe, he intended to fulfill several aims, such as displaying U.S. might to the world (at the time, the American Navy ranked second in the world after Britain's, while Japan's was the fifth largest), boosting the popularity of the navy within the United States, and highlighting the vital importance of the Panama Canal, then under construction, to the country's defense.

In fact, countries like Canada or Australia, which saw a threat in the rapid expansion of Japan's navy, welcomed the great American fleet as symbolizing an effective deterrent against war, and the arrival of the fleet in Japan was calculated to highlight the power of the United States to "potential" enemies such as Japan

---

[68] See Reckner, *Teddy Roosevelt's Great White Fleet*. Although Roosevelt wrote to Taft in July 1907 that sending the fleet "would practically be a practice voyage," he clearly saw other advantages to the mission. Roosevelt to Taft, 10 July 1907, in Roosevelt, *Letters*, vol. 5. p. 709.

itself. As far as that was concerned, Roosevelt's freewheeling approach was quite different from mainstream thought at the time and foreshadowed American thinking on defense.

As far as Japan was concerned, however, and unlike what many in the world suspected, no one, in the political sphere at least, was thinking of going to war against the United States. At this point in time, in fact, Japan was taking great pains to convey its peaceful intentions and win the favor of the United States. It was rumored that its lavish reception, which far exceeded anything the fleet had experienced in its nearly two years of sailing over the seven seas, instantly converted not only navy officials but also reporters accompanying the tour into fervent Japanophiles.

During the week that the fleet was moored at Yokohama, Rear Admiral Charles S. Sperry and other high-ranking officers stayed at the Hama Detached Palace, and all the other officers were given rooms at the Imperial Hotel. The party were feted at reception after reception hosted by noted politicians and industrialists – Prime Minister Katsura Tarō, foreign minister Komura Jutarō, admiral Tōgō Heihachirō, head of the Mitsui *zaibatsu* Mitsui Hachirōemon, head of the Mitsubishi *zaibatsu* Iwasaki Hisaya, leading bankers – as well as by the cities of Tokyo and Yokohama. Waseda University and Keio University invited the officers and men to their baseball game. The Japanese navy held a fancy party aboard the *Mikasa*, the Imperial Japanese Navy flagship made famous by the Battle of Tsushima, where Sperry and Tōgō, hero of the Battle of Tsushima, were tossed into the air three times each by Japanese officers for Sperry and American officers for Tōgō. A young officer named William Halsey, who as commander of the Pacific Fleet would later harry the Imperial Japanese Navy in World War II, was among those present.

On November 30 of the same year, 1908, Japanese ambassador to the United States Takahira Kogorō and U.S. secretary of state Elihu Root concluded the Root-Takahira Agreement, which expanded the scope of the secret Katsura-Taft Memorandum. In the Agreement, Japan acknowledged the United States' occupation of the Philippines, while the United States recognized Japan's influence in Manchuria.

Roosevelt was a realist who did not believe in bluffing. Facing the realities of defending the Philippines and the expulsion of Japanese immigrants from the United States, he knew that to ingratiate itself with Japan, the United States would have to bend its traditional policy stance toward the Far East – the open door policy and affirmation of the territorial integrity of China – and compromise with Japan on the Korean peninsula and Manchuria.

There would be no point in arguing forcefully for China's territorial integrity unless the United States were prepared to take meaningful action, even go to war if necessary. If the United States objected to Japan's ambitions in Manchuria and went to war over the issue, it would need a stronger navy than Britain's and a more powerful army than Germany's. These it did not have. Therefore, Roosevelt opted to compromise over China in order to buy the safety of its occupation of the Philippines.

Japan also understood and accepted this sort of realistic bargaining. Given the negative sentiment toward Japanese immigrants in the United States and other problems which might flare up at any moment, Japan and the United States flattered each other as much as possible and succeeded, on the surface, in papering over their differences. The Root-Takahira Agreement, which was very favorable to Japan, was the culmination of these maneuvers.

The Agreement had one weakness, however: it was simply an agreement between the governments of the two countries and not a treaty that needed to be ratified by parliaments. It was only binding on the Roosevelt administration, a type of arrangement that bedevils diplomacy with the United States to this day. The Agreement was signed just four months before the end of Roosevelt's term. This worried the Japanese government, which repeatedly sought confirmation from ambassador Takahira. The ambassador replied that everything would be fine, given that Roosevelt's successor Taft was friendly toward Japan, as the Japanese government well knew, and that he would no doubt continue upholding Roosevelt's foreign policy.

But Taft changed his position the moment he assumed the presidency, shifting the emphasis of United States policy in the Far East once again to protecting China's territorial integrity. The racial discrimination against Japanese in California had stirred a near-hysteria in Japan, where since the mid-nineteenth century people had worked themselves into a frenzy in the aspiration to "join the West and dissociate from Asia." Their efforts had staved off colonization by Western powers, but victory in the wars with China and Russia had convinced them of their superiority over other parts of Asia, and the flattery of American diplomacy further pulled the wool over their eyes. Even Eiichi did not seem to realize how blinded and even immoral that attitude was, and in his own realm of private diplomacy willingly played the game of flattery as well. Thus ended the season of diplomacy by flattery and began a period of infinitely more difficult relations between Japan and the United States.

CHAPTER 5

PROMOTING GOODWILL
IN THE UNITED STATES

ຂວ

TOWARD THE END of 1907, around the time of the Gentlemen's Agreement regarding Japanese emigration to the United States, one of Japan's most senior diplomats, who was soon to be reappointed as foreign minister, Komura Jutarō, invited Shibusawa Eiichi and his fellow members from the Tokyo Chamber of Commerce to consult about the situation between Japan and the United States. By that time, the discord triggered by the San Francisco School Board's expulsion of Japanese students from public schools had been more or less calmed under the exchange of notes known as the Gentlemen's Agreement. Even though the issue of discrimination against Japanese had been resolved for the time being, said Komura, the United States was still a land of public opinion. The incident demonstrated how each American state functions like an individual country with its own laws. In order to sustain peace with the United States, Japan should not only negotiate with Washington but also develop close relations between the Japanese and American people. Since there were chambers of commerce in American as well as Japanese cities, could Eiichi and his colleagues, Komura wondered, find some way to use these organizations to promote goodwill?[69]

At that meeting, Eiichi seems to have grasped the importance of people-to-people diplomacy, and from that time onward he began to act with a consistent plan and a strong sense of

---

[69] *Shibusawa denki shiryō*, vol. 25, pp. 628–29.

Figure 20
Komura Jutarō
(1855–1911), statesman
and diplomat. Photo:
National Diet Library,
Japan.

duty to contribute to fostering international goodwill. From the founding of the Tokyo Chamber of Commerce in 1878, Eiichi had served continuously as its president, working assiduously to develop commerce and industry in Japan. He was determined, in the face of a long tradition of disdain for business, to elevate the status of people in commerce and industry. After he became gravely ill in 1904, however, he expressed his wish to resign from the position for health reasons. His resignation was finally acknowledged at the spring general meeting of 1905, and Nakano Buei (then president of the Tokyo Stock Exchange) succeeded him. Although Eiichi was then no longer in a position of direct responsibility, the strong urging of Komura and Nakano and his own deep awareness of the importance of the Japan-U.S. relationship drove him to use his still-powerful influence in the chamber to launch private-sector efforts aimed at improving relations.

At Eiichi's instigation, members of the chambers of commerce in Tokyo, Osaka, Kobe, Nagoya, Yokohama, and Kyoto were immediately gathered together, and the first thing they agreed upon was a plan to invite a delegation of chambers of commerce members from cities on the U.S. West Coast to Japan. Formal invitations were sent in July of 1908, and over 50 representatives from San Francisco, Los Angeles, Seattle, Tacoma, Portland, San Diego, Honolulu, and other cities took up the invitation. They arrived on October 12 – around the time Japan welcomed at the port in Yokohama the U.S. Atlantic Fleet, then on its historic world cruise – and stayed until November 4.

Today, in our modern age of air travel, having large groups of people come to Japan for international meetings and tours is nothing out of the ordinary, but a century ago the country had never seen such a large group of people from abroad visit Japan solely on a civilian initiative. It was a fitting launch for fully fledged civilian diplomacy.

Various welcoming events were held for the guests, including a banquet held at the elegant Kōyōkan restaurant in Shiba Park, and tours of various important sites. On October 16, Eiichi personally invited the guests to his home at Oji Asukayama in the northern part of Tokyo.

It was an occasion of much anticipation. When Eiichi awoke at six o'clock and stepped outside, he found the garden shrouded in the rain that had been falling since the previous evening, leaving the trees and the lawn drenched. They had no choice but to entertain the guests indoors, but, as he was preparing for his welcoming speech, around eleven o'clock the rain cleared, and bright rays of autumn sunshine broke through the clouds, lighting up the garden.

The guests began to arrive around noon and enjoyed a Western-style luncheon in a makeshift dining room. There were over one hundred guests, including the fifty or so visitors from the United States, many Japanese business leaders, and the ambassador of the United States and his wife. After lunch, Eiichi gave a short but sincere welcoming speech,[70] and the guests afterwards

---

[70] As recorded in *Ryūmon zasshi*, No. 245, pp. 1–5, in *Shibusawa denki shiryō*, vol. 25, pp. 621–23.

enjoyed his hospitality – some took walks in the garden, sat briefly in the tearoom, and rested in the "moon-viewing" arbor in the garden. Some also enjoyed dances and other artistic entertainments provided by geisha in the tatami room.

The autumn garden sparkled after the rain; the guests relaxed among the bright autumn foliage illuminated in the evening sun. Eiichi was especially charming; he attracted everyone's attention with his warm smile, extending hospitality and sincerity to all of the guests equally. At six thirty, before the guests dispersed, delegation leader F. W. Dorman gave a speech expressing his gratitude to Eiichi, and asked for a copy of the speech Eiichi had delivered that day. He said that it expressed the true sentiments of the Japanese, and he wished to make its words known in all the cities along the West Coast via their chambers of commerce in order to deepen understanding of Japan.

Until his death Eiichi enjoyed singular popularity among Americans, who appeared to think that he was somehow the representative of all the good qualities of Japanese. It seems to have been from around the time of this U.S. business delegation's visit to Japan that his name began to be remembered overseas. Eiichi possessed a quality that inspired Americans' sense of affinity and respect. Unlike most Japanese of the time, who were more submissive to the constraining rules and responsibilities of a collective society, Eiichi followed a path he himself had set forth, dauntlessly holding to his own standards. His achievements in the modernization of Japan – the "wonder of the world" about which there was so much discussion worldwide – spoke for themselves. An aura befitting that achievement had developed around him over the years, adding luster to his character. His modest, cheerful attitude, full of sincerity and affection, left a strong impression on anyone who met him or observed him in action.

Although Eiichi had been educated in Confucian and East Asian values that then must have seemed curious to the American people, his solid and independent lifestyle was certainly familiar and even appealing to them. Eiichi thus received unprecedented respect and recognition among many Americans as a man apart from the usual stiffness and reserve of conventional Japanese society. That respect formed the groundwork upon which Eiichi conducted his private diplomacy.

RETIRING FROM BUSINESS

In June of 1909, Eiichi resolved to finally retire from business and to resign from his positions in many companies and organizations. He had always felt that he had too many jobs for a man aged nearly seventy; he realized that the burdens were too much for his health. Even Sasaki Yūnosuke, a man he had worked with at the Dai-ichi Bank for more than thirty years, strongly recommended that Eiichi relieve himself of everything, keeping only the Dai-ichi Bank as his primary position.

Some newspapers had begun to criticize Eiichi for holding too many executive posts, arguing that trying to do everything himself could only have a negative effect on the Japanese business world. Eiichi himself believed that a person should not try to be a jack-of-all-trades but specialize in a particular field. Still, he had begun his career at the dawn of modern Japanese private enterprise, and it had meant he had to stand in the forefront, come up with original ideas, and engage in negotiations personally for whatever it might be – whether it was making paper, laying railroad track, making fertilizer, or promoting the shipping and insurance industries. But much progress had been made, and there were many talented people managing their enterprises with outstanding results, convincing him that this was an opportune time to withdraw from the frontlines.

Sunday, June 6, a rainy day in the early summer wet season. At ten o'clock, Eiichi summoned twenty-three executives of top corporations to his office in Kabutochō, and announced his resolve to retire. He first gave his sincere apology for asking them to come forth to listen to him talk about something so personal, and then proceeded to give a detailed explanation of his decision.

I cannot simply reduce my duties one by one. If I am going to resign, I need to do so across the board. There are some duties I took on for one special reason or other, but worrying about such things would only lead me back to where I started. That would mean I couldn't retire until I die! . . .

Confucius said, "at forty I had no delusions, at fifty I learned the mandate of heaven, at sixty my ears were attentive to the truth, at seventy I followed my desires without overstepping ethical boundaries." I am not sure whether I am today overstepping those boundaries or not, but I am not going to let what others might say change my mind. This is not a matter of continuing to work because others praise me or quitting because I am criticized.

After I became ill some years ago, I tried to cut down on my workload, but whenever people asked me to do something, I always ended up accepting. Of course, always ending up that way is partly my responsibility, but all of that is something that had already happened, so I would not complain to anyone or make excuses. I must ask you to give your consent to my resignation, as I have explained it today. No matter what you may have to say, I am resolved on this matter and must, by all means, receive your consent.

This announcement came as a great shock to all present, as they had wondered what could be afoot that Eiichi would summon them to meet on a holiday. They tried their best to convince him otherwise, as Eiichi still held great influence in the business world and he continued to be a vital source of ideas, an advisor on personnel matters, one who instinctively understood the delicate inner workings of companies, and also a pipeline for interchange between statesmen and government officials and the business world. Many managers of businesses had taken up their positions because Eiichi had asked them to or with his strong backing. Nishino Keinosuke, a senior managing director of the Imperial Theater (Teikoku Gekijo), was vehement: "I began this work under the agreement that you would guide and supervise the theater, which means you are the driving force in the running of this enterprise. If you say that you must leave, then I must also leave, too."

"That is nonsense!" countered Eiichi, "What would you do if I die?"

Nishino's reply was, "Death is a different story. As long as you are alive, I will say what I have to say." He refused to give his approval.

Lunch was served in the office and they continued talking until three o'clock, but the discussion was not concluded. But now that Eiichi had presented his position, he knew that if he backed down he would be forced back to where he had started, so on this day he politely but clearly emphasized his intention to resign, and asked for everyone's understanding.[71]

And, as good as his word, Eiichi resigned from sixty-one enterprises. The positions he remained in were as follows: president of the Dai-ichi Bank, chairman of the Tokyo Savings Bank, director of the Imperial Theater, chairman of the Tokyo Credit Manager, committee member of the Tokyo Clearing House, chairman of the Banker's Association, and committee chair of the Banker's Club. He had also been in responsible positions of thirty social welfare, charitable, and educational institutions, and he resigned from thirteen of those posts, while staying with the remaining seventeen, including the Japanese Foundation for Cancer Research, Tokyo Yōikuin (relief institution for underprivileged residents of Tokyo), and Japan Women's University. He further explained:

> My reason for retirement is not simply old age, and I am not completely abandoning the business world. . . . In some cases, I will be glad to give advice. But I believe it is unwise for me to continue my involvement in such a large number of organizations for the rest of my life . . . It is my deepest wish to be freed from these positions of responsibility.

Ever since his illness and surgery during the Russo-Japanese War, he was not as confident of quick recovery as before, but he did not look particularly frail either. He was fully willing to do whatever he could to help society as a free individual outside of the world of business, as a citizen of Japan and as a citizen of the world. His wish was to be separated from severe time constraints and responsibilities associated with commercial enterprises, and devote his time, energy, and spirit to what he believed was necessary for his country and society.

---

[71] Shibusawa, "Rōgo no omoide," *Seien hyakuwa*, p. 255.

One project he sought to complete was the biography of Tokugawa Yoshinobu. The compilation and research had been going on for fifteen years, and was still unfinished. He wished to restore his lord's honor and status in society, and also set down a fair portrayal of the role Yoshinobu had played in those turbulent years from the end of the Tokugawa shogunate to the Meiji Restoration. Several outstanding editors were spearheading the project, including Dr. Hagino Yoshiyuki of Tokyo Imperial University. The project was proceeding well, but Yoshinobu was already seventy-three years old, and Eiichi himself was seventy. Eiichi was determined to complete the project while Yoshinobu was still alive.

Eiichi also wanted to devote more time to projects for the advancement of society. He had been working with the Tokyo Yōikuin since 1874 and providing support for many other public benefit projects. He was fully willing to go on supporting these causes, but he had begun to want to do more to tackle the problems of society. He saw that, as the economy advanced and society progressed, many people were becoming more affluent, but at the same time, the strains and disparities within society were also growing. These were new stresses that could not be resolved just by following the "enrich the country, strengthen the military" slogan that had carried the country forward for several decades. They could be seen as related to the surfacing around this time of leftwing ideologies and the labor movement. The remedies, he thought, had to be found not only to economic issues but to matters closely associated with people's lives.

DELEGATION TO VISIT THE UNITED STATES

The Japan-U.S. relationship was among the issues that particularly interested Eiichi. Also in 1909, word came from the United States that, in return for the hospitality in Japan they had enjoyed in 1908, members of chambers of commerce in the American West Coast wanted to invite about thirty Japanese business leaders to visit the United States and show them around the country, in order to promote better understanding among businessmen of the two countries and contribute to international goodwill. Japan and the United States were facing many diplomatic difficulties at the time, so Eiichi himself was eager to see the plan realized. As soon as the official invitation arrived in May of 1909, the chambers of commerce of Tokyo and other cities all over Japan began the process of choosing members of the delegation.

The government was much pleased by this initiative in what would be known as private diplomacy. Foreign Minister Komura and elder statesmen such as Katsura Tarō and Inoue Kaoru understood the potential value of the tour, and took every opportunity to express their support. Eiichi had been a favorite to serve as the head of the delegation from the outset, but he was reluctant to encourage the idea. Seventy was at the time considered quite an advanced age, the equivalent today, perhaps, of ninety. He was not very good at English and was prone to seasickness; his health had not been as robust as it was before his 1905 illness. This tour, crossing the Pacific Ocean by ship, would be no leisure holiday; the group would visit fifty or so cities across the United States according to the schedule proposed by their hosts. Eiichi had traveled across the United States before (in 1902) and he knew quite well how physically exhausting the journey would be.

On the other hand, members of the welcoming committee in the United States had left Japan the previous year with a strong impression of Eiichi's hospitality. They sent a telegraph to the Tokyo Chamber of Commerce saying that his attendance would surely raise the caliber of the delegation, and they were most eager for him to join it if possible. Foreign Minister Komura and others said they were well aware of Eiichi's advanced age, but urged him to participate if health would allow. Finally, on June 21, the chamber's executives met and came to the conclusion that Eiichi must by all means be included in the delegation. Senge Takatomi, Takahashi Korekiyo, and Nakano Buei visited Eiichi's office in Kabutochō and presented their formal request.

Their visit came soon after he had resigned most of his executive positions as mentioned earlier, and at first he declined, declaring that such a great undertaking could be too strenuous for him, but the idea was also tremendously exciting and offered a chance to greatly serve his country. Later, remembering his decision, he reflected that he had been born long ago during the Edo period, yet never became a soldier in his youth. He realized that, at the age of seventy he had been "conscripted" for the first time. He had accepted the post of leader of the delegation, telling himself "the term of service is only three months, . . . so I shall go, even if it means I don't come back alive."[72]

The delegation was named "Tobei Jitsugyodan" in Japanese, in English, "Honorary Commercial Commissioners of Japan to the United States of America." After many twists and turns in the process of selecting its members, about thirty chamber of commerce members were chosen as official representatives, and partly in response to a request from the United States, professionals in sericulture, agriculture, education, and trade, along with doctors, members of the press, and supporting staff were also included, forming a delegation of well over fifty.[73]

The four chambers of commerce in Seattle, Tacoma, Portland, and Spokane engaged in the preparations with great enthusiasm. After sending off the official invitation to Japan on March 26, they immediately selected three representatives – two of whom had visited Japan in the previous year – to visit the American cities the delegation would tour and discuss the details of their itinerary.

First, they discussed arrangements and fares for the special train to carry the group with James Hill of the Great Northern Railway, Howard Elliot of Northern Pacific, William C. Brown of New York Central, and Edward Harriman of Union Pacific, who was an old friend of Eiichi's and had other close ties with people in East Asia. The planners won full support from these influential men in the railway industry. They then met with

---

[72] Speech given on August 4, 1909 at a farewell party given by the Tōkyō Ginkō Shūkaijo and other organizations. See *Shibusawa Eiichi denki shiryō*, vol. 32, p. 51.

[73] According to Kimura Masato, this business mission "was the largest-scale such effort Japan ever undertook." See "Shibusawa Eiichi's View of Business Morality in Global Society," in Fridenson and Kikkawa, *Ethical Capitalism*, p. 133.

U.S. secretary of state Philander C. Knox and other government officials in Washington to prepare for official support in various parts of the country. They also negotiated with the leading enterprises of the regions through which the party would travel – such as the Parke-Davis pharmaceutical company in Detroit, the General Electric company in Schenectady, New York, U.S. Steel in Cleveland, and J. P. Morgan in New York – and determined the dates and other details for the Japanese delegation's visits to their plants and for the holding of banquets. Gradually, the outlines of a grand tour took shape.

With anti-Japanese sentiment rising in California, the chambers of San Francisco and other cities there had at first turned a cold shoulder to the idea of the tour, and the chambers of Washington state and Oregon had decided that if necessary, California would be excluded from the itinerary. But as anticipation of the visit began to build, and with the intercession of secretary of state Knox, California eventually decided to participate, and on June 16, the chambers of commerce of San Francisco, Oakland, Los Angeles, and San Diego sent their joint invitation to Japan via telegraph.

TOUR OF THE UNITED STATES

As the delegation's departure from Japan neared, the members faced the customary wave of sending-off parties. On August 17, an elegant luncheon was held at Shiba Detached Palace in the name of Emperor Meiji. The emperor himself did not attend, but the hosts were the minister of the Imperial Household as his representative, along with the prime minister and other cabinet ministers, and their presence went far in boosting the prestige of the delegation.

Foreign minister Komura had been enthusiastic from the early stage of its planning. The Ministry of Foreign Affairs issued a statement saying, "American people's attitudes have turned favorably toward Japan since 1908 not only because of the port call of the American Atlantic fleet but as a result of the American businessmen's visit to our country." The ministry then expressed its decision that "the imperial government shall consider the visit to the United States by our businessmen not as simply a private affair but will extend it special support," and designated Japanese consul general in New York Mizuno Kōkichi and his wife to accompany the group throughout its tour.[74]

Accompanied by much fanfare, the group boarded the U.S. ship *Minnesota* and departed from Yokohama on August 19, 1909. Management of such a large group made up of leading figures in their respective fields would not be easy. Eiichi immediately used his spare time on board the ship to hold gatherings and committee meetings, where he set up an internal structure for the members, rules to be observed during the visit, and duties for each representative such as liaison, recorder, publicity, and general affairs. Takaishi Shingorō, who would later join the staff of the *Mainichi Shimbun* newspaper and become a member of the International Olympic Committee, was assigned to press-related tasks, and Iwaya Sueo (Sazanami), who later became a famous fiction writer, was assigned as record keeper.

Most of the group members had never visited a foreign country before, so Eiichi occasionally gathered everyone together to instruct them on ways to avoid disgraceful behavior. He had them read aloud to one another from books such as Katō Tsunetada's *Haikara-buri* (Modern Style) and Sonoda Kōkichi's *Sekishin ippen* (Thoughts on Sincerity), both of which were popular traveler's guidebooks of the time.

Eiichi had always cared deeply about his country and his ideas and visions were often on a grand scale, but at the same time he had since he was young always been attentive to the niceties of comportment and manners. He had formed the habit in his youth of attending even to the smallest matter and preparing for all possibilities from the outset, and this became his natural working style. One of the reasons for being able to manage each of the businesses he was involved in without much trouble and with ultimate success was because of this meticulous way of handling things.

On the day before they arrived in the United States, Eiichi organized a general meeting at which he produced a list of behests

---

[74] *Shibusawa denki shiryō*, vol. 32, p. 29.

for the group entitled "Memoranda for the Commission." It called on members to "follow the orders of the commission head" and "restrain yourselves in deed and speech, strive to cultivate friendly relations between Japan and the United States, and take steps to enhance commercial ties."[75] And thus the delegation readied itself for arrival in the United States the following day.

Starting on August 31, the delegation visited about sixty locations in ninety days, and received overwhelming hospitality in each city. That they were able to have such a long and marvelous journey is a testimony to the organizational attention of their American hosts all across the country and the comforts of travel that were available even in an era where there were no airplanes or interstate highways. Their itinerary (see appendix, end of this chapter) shows the places they passed through, just some of the sights they toured, and the cross-section of American life they observed. Just one week gives a sense of the atmosphere of the tour.

> October 22, sunny: Arrived New Haven at 4:00 A.M. Visited factories and Yale University. Arrived Providence at 1:50 P.M. Slept on the train.
>
> October 23, cloudy: Arrived Boston at 8:00 A.M. Visited the Waltham Clock Company and Harvard University. Hotel lodgings.
>
> October 24 (Sunday), rainy: Day trip to Newport, visited the grave of Commodore Matthew C. Perry. Hotel lodgings.
>
> October 25, cloudy: Visited various factories. Slept on the train.
>
> October 26, sunny: Arrived Wooster at 8:00 A.M. Visited the sewage purification plant. Arrived Springfield 2:00 P.M. Received official telegram informing us about the assassination of Itō Hirobumi. Slept on the train.
>
> October 27, sunny: Arrived Newark at 9:00 A.M. Met with Thomas Edison. Attended welcome party. Arrived Reading (Pennsylvania) at 9:00 P.M. Slept on the train.
>
> October 28, cloudy: Arrived South Mount at 8:00 a.m. Attended welcome party. Returned to Reading at 10:00 a.m. and attended their great welcome party. Arrived at Philadelphia at 6:30 p.m. Stayed at Bellevue Stratford Hotel.[76]

---

[75] *Shibusawa denki shiryō*, vol. 32, pp. 75–76.

[76] *Tobei Jitsugyōdan shi* [A Record of the Honorary Commercial Commissioners of Japan to the United States of America].

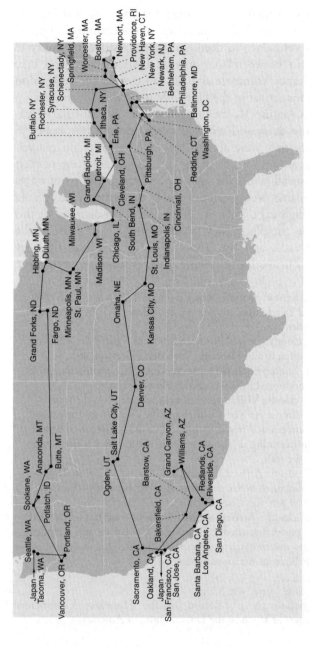

FIGURE 21   Map of the itinerary of the 1909 business delegation to the United States. © Shibusawa Memorial Museum.

FIGURE 22   The honorary commissioners after visiting the Edison Electric Company
in Chicago, Illinois. (Eiichi, is seventh from right in the front row). Photo:
Shibusawa Memorial Museum.

What made this great journey possible in such a short amount
of time was the "Million Dollar Train," a special train provided
by American enterprises for the delegation. It consisted of two
locomotives, two cargo cars, one dining car, seven sleeping cars,
and an observatory car at the end. The fact that different railroad companies, some of them competitors, gathered together
to jointly put this train into the service of the delegation and
managed this hectic 90-day schedule without any major mis-
haps, deserves special mention. As quoted by Shiraishi Kitarō,
Eiichi recalled:

> It may be hard to picture this while envisioning Japanese trains, but
> the sleeping cars are much bigger than those of Japan. The compart-
> ments may be small but are separate, each room with a door. And
> on this train the entire party boarded; there were fifty-odd of us, ten
> or so more people who came with us when we arrived in the United
> States, the crew of the train, conductors, and so on. The number of
> people on the train totaled almost one hundred and twenty, thirty,
> or even fifty. The train was truly designed as our residence, and
> nobody else was on board the sleepers except for us. Because I was

the leader of the delegation, they gave me three rooms – granted I had my staff accompanying me. These rooms were then my home throughout the tour.

When the train arrived at a destination, forty or fifty automobiles would be parked at the station. If the promise was to come at nine o'clock, they would be there around seven. We had our breakfast on the train, and when we finished the men from the welcoming committee greeted us in their automobiles. We were then divided up and boarded the automobiles, and they would drive us around, and depending on the location they would take us to the city hall. At least a hundred people would greet us, and a welcoming speech would be given. No banquet or anything was served. They just came to us and said thank you for coming. Then our representative had to give a speech in reply. Then we would visit schools and parks and such – in many cases country clubs, where we would have a luncheon. When we visited these clubs, there would be a hundred, hundred and fifty, or three hundred people who had come to meet us, having received advance notice. Their luncheons were mostly informal, but some were extremely formal, and some were simple and brief. Everyone gathered to shake our hands, introducing themselves to everyone. Because I was the head of the delegation, many people came to me and shook my hand, and explained to me about the country, asking what we thought of the United States, what surprised us, or telling us there are such-and-such things in the United States, and that we would soon see them all.

We continued with our conversations for a while and moved to the dining room after the announcement that the meal was ready. When we finished our meal more speeches followed, and one or two of us were also expected to give speeches, but sometimes as many as five people stood up to speak, which meant the luncheon often ended at around three or four o'clock. Then they would take us to show us their local specialties such as the electric lamp and gas factories, and then we would return to our train in the evening and change our clothes – full formal dress, so to speak: tie and tails with medals attached – and go out again to attend another banquet. Many of these dinner receptions were held in magnificent hotels, or dining rooms specially set up for us. They would sometimes be held at someone's private house. These dinner receptions consisted of even more speeches than at the luncheons. They would end at around one o'clock in the morning at the earliest. Then we would immediately return to our train, which would start moving as we were changing into our bedclothes. The next morning would follow a similar schedule, and it is safe to say that the tour was like this every day.[77]

The weather was pleasant during the visit, allowing the delegation to enjoy magnificent autumn landscapes across the United States. The only days when the weather was bad were in Denver, Colorado, where they were snowed in for two days. Only a few days were rainy.

On one of those rare rainy days, Eiichi visited the grave of Matthew C. Perry at the naval base in Newport, Rhode Island. The group was in Boston on Sunday, October 24, and there were no plans for that day, so he had decided to take some of his close associates and go on a day trip to Newport.

Under two great oak trees wet in a cold autumn rain lay the grave of Commodore Perry. Eiichi placed a wreath he had brought with him from Boston and he and his companions held a moment of silence. His poem commemorating that moment goes as follows:

手向けつる	Tamuke tsuru
心の花の	kokoro no hana no
ひとえだに	hitoeda ni
なみだの雨も	Namida no ame mo
そへてけるかな	soete keru kana
（栄一）	–Eiichi[78]

(On the bouquet of flowers offered from my heart, tears and raindrops fall together – Eiichi)

Across Eiichi's mind must have raced vivid memories of the tumultuous historical events of U.S.-Japan relations that had taken place during his lifetime. The 1853 arrival of Commodore Perry's "black ships" off the Japanese coast signaled the beginning of Japanese modernization. When he thought of the United States, he always tried to recall the history that began with Com-

---

[77] Shiraishi, "Wajō no ie" (Home on Wheels). In *Shibusawa Eiichi-o* [The Life of Shibusawa Eiichi], pp. 517–519.

[78] *Shibusawa denki shiryō*, vol. 32, p. 252.

modore Perry and Consul Harris in the 1850s, and think of the present as its continuation.

"As the saying goes, 'there is no seed planted that does not grow,'" he later wrote, and "This delegation did not come into being by chance; if we trace its origin, we find it in quite a distant past."[79]

The origins of the delegation could be traced back to all of the diplomatic history between Japan and the United States that began with the arrival of Perry and efforts of Townsend Harris that followed. More recently planted "seeds" were the visits of the U.S. Atlantic fleet to Yokohama and the West Coast chambers of commerce delegation to Japan. These seeds sprouted and came to fruition in the Japanese businessmen's U.S. tour. These sprouts, Eiichi believed, "must be cultivated and blossom into beautiful flowers that will bear great fruit. This is the responsibility of Japanese business leaders."

Looking back into the past shows ways to better understand the present as well as to better prepare us for the future. This was the distinctive way of thinking that Eiichi had developed, based on his education emphasizing the importance of cause and effect in history.[80]

NEWS OF ITŌ HIROBUMI'S ASSASSINATION

Two days after the visit to Perry's grave, the group left Boston and headed via Worcester, Massachusetts to Springfield, Connecticut. The New England autumn was especially beautiful, the sky clear after the rain, the brilliant foliage shining in all its glory. As Eiichi was gazing at this autumn beauty from the train windows, the shocking news came that his old friend Itō Hirobumi had been assassinated by a Korean nationalist in Harbin, Manchuria.

---

[79] From "Tobei Jitsugyodan no yurai" [The Origin of the Japanese Commercial Commissioners to the United States], in *Tobei jitsugyodan-shi*, 1910.

[80] On October 20, Eiichi also visited the grave of Townsend Harris in New York. *Ryūmon zasshi* record of the journey for October 20; see *Shibusawa denki shiryō*, vol. 32, p. 227.

"It can't be! There must be some kind of a mistake." Eiichi at first did not want to believe this grievous news, trying to force-fully push it out of his mind. But when the train reached the next station, local news reporters rushed onto the train with details. It was true after all.

Pressed by the reporters for comment from the commission's leader, Eiichi slowly began talking about Itō and his achieve-ments, but his eyes misted over, and he could not contain his emotions. The observatory car suddenly became silent, and the regular clacking of the moving train echoed hollowly under the bright autumn sunlight.[81]

Later Eiichi composed a Chinese-style poem mourning the loss of his old friend.

異域先驚凶報伝
霊壇今日涙潜然
温容在目恍如夢
花落水流四十年

In a foreign land, I was stunned to hear sad news
Before your altar today my tears stream forth
Your countenance lingers vividly in my mind, a dream
Flowers fall, water flows, over our forty years[82]

Itō and Eiichi had known each other for forty years, since the beginning of the Meiji era when they had been colleagues in the Ministry of Finance. Itō was a talented man. He, along with Ōkuma Shigenobu, Inoue Kaoru, and Eiichi, had come up with the idea for the "First National Bank" (renamed Dai-ichi [First] Bank in 1896) based on the ideas for a national bank Ito had developed from his observations in the United States. In those very early days of the new era, Itō was not on good terms with the Satsuma-born founding statesman Ōkubo Toshimichi, which brought him such misfortunes as being shunted into a job at the Osaka Mint Office. From there he wrote to Eiichi, musing

---

[81] Account based on *Shibusawa denki shiryō*, vol. 32, pp. 253–54.
[82] *Shibusawa denki shiryō*, vol. 49, p. 450.

on how pitiful a man has become once his downfall begins. He complained that not even Inoue, also a Chōshū-native comrade since their youth, seemed to care about him. Later, Eiichi would joke about this letter with him, and Itō would tense up and say, "Please don't hold that letter over my head. I will give you one thousand yen to have it back!"[83]

Itō would eventually win Ōkubo's trust and climb to hold the highest posts of Japan's leadership. Not only was he gifted, but his stature grew both as a political leader and a human being, and Eiichi had liked what he saw. They did not work directly together in their careers, but Itō often sought out Eiichi for his advice and views.

Itō would often say to Eiichi, "You are the only one I know who puts himself aside when you work." There were many who tried to use influential persons for their own benefit, but even those who approached Itō without such ulterior motives were often so dazzled by the aura of power he exuded that they were unable to relate to him on ordinary terms. Ito felt the loneliness of a man of great power. Then there was Eiichi, who had already established his own world and had no need to fear others or fawn upon the powerful. He maintained a warm friendship with Itō, just as in the days before Itō rose to prominence, to the end. They were in a way comrades-in-arms, both devoted to their country, both shouldering heavy burdens and pressures from their daily labors. They understood each other's pain, and they comforted and encouraged each other. It was a surprisingly new sensation for Itō to have such a man by his side. Sometimes they would put aside their formal guise and go out drinking together. And when Eiichi was in trouble, Itō did not hesitate to provide his support.

About twenty years earlier, when Eiichi was anguishing over how to recoup the honor of Tokugawa Yoshinobu, he happened to meet Yamagata Aritomo – founder of Japan's modern army and, like Itō, a native of the former domain of Chōshū, which along with the Satsuma domain, played the central role in the

---

[83] *Shibusawa denki shiryō*, vol. 32, p. 644.

toppling of the Tokugawa shogunate. After listening to Eiichi's earnest explanation of what he was trying to do, Yamagata replied flatly: "That was how things happened. No matter how hard you may try to recover his status, I can't support you." Eiichi then discussed the problem with Inoue Kaoru, another Chōshū man. Inoue advised him to discuss it with Itō, confirming that Yamagata would be of no help. Indeed, the younger and more perceptive Itō promised to lend his full support. After many twists and turns, Yoshinobu's good name had been restored and in 1902 he was accorded the title of prince.

Over the years before his death, Itō had been much involved with Japan's ambitions in Korea. Before the end of the Russo-Japanese War he went to Korea and was instrumental in the conclusion of the 1905 Japan-Korea Protectorate Treaty under which Korea officially became a protectorate of Japan, and he worked diligently in the administration as its resident-general.

This was the first time since the country's founding that Japan had tried to administer colonial territories, and the task was full of trouble and turmoil. From the outset, it was naïve and absurd of Japan to think that the measure of wealth and military might it had recently acquired gave it the right to administer and exploit another country. Ultimately, however, the power vacuum in Korea created an opportunity that held an irresistible appeal to the vanity and greed of certain Japanese of that period.

After the Russo-Japanese War ended, Russia withdrew its military from the Korean peninsula area. The United States accepted Japan's free hand in Korea in exchange for U.S. control of the Philippines. Negotiations with Britain and France had been settled early on. This essentially meant that the Korean peninsula and Manchuria were simply waiting for Japan's invasion. The question was, how and when.

The continental expansion policy Japan was advocating risked bringing down upon Japan the wrath of the entire world, snuffing out ambitions of any sort. Keenly aware of this possibility, Itō had decided he would have to deal with the problem directly rather than leaving it to others. In a letter to Foreign Minister Hayashi Tadasu in November 1907, Itō wrote, "Most of the

FIGURE 23
Itō Hirobumi, who was first
governor-general of Korea under
Japanese colonial rule. Photo:
Shibusawa Memorial Museum.

world is determined to isolate Japan . . . If we adopt mistaken
policies or err in our actions, disaster will immediately follow."[84]

Eiichi also felt that danger. Continental policy would determine the fundamentals of Japan's foreign policy, thus determin-
ing the fate of the country. This was of course directly related to
the relationship between Japan and the United States with which
the commercial commission came face to face. Eiichi trusted
Itō's judgment and political abilities, and earnestly hoped that
he would lead the nation in the right direction at this difficult
time. Every time Itō came back to Japan on leave from his duties
in Korea, Eiichi took upon himself as a private citizen to give a
grand banquet in Itō's honor, applauding him for his labors.

And now this kingpin had suddenly departed the scene. As
he journeyed across the United States by train, Eiichi must have

---

[84] Iriye, *Nihon no gaikō*, pp. 9–10.

seen black clouds growing in the East Asian skies, casting an eerie shadow over the region. When the business delegation arrived at Springfield that evening, they politely declined to attend the welcome party, and returned to their train rooms to mourn Ito's death, sharing a moment of silence and sending telegrams of condolence.

EIICHI'S APPRAISAL OF AMERICA

Compared to the country he had seen seven years earlier, the United States in 1909 had undergone even further development. Active and progressive management policies seemed to extend into every aspect of the American people's lives. The people they met everywhere, whether deep in the mountains or out on their farms in the plains, were cheerful, friendly, frank, and casual, but possessed of a strong self-confidence. They might seem rough, but certainly they were not violent. They were unexpectedly serious.

Eiichi was surprised to observe the deep passion for learning and knowledge in the United States. The delegation visited a number of highly respected universities including Cornell, the University of Wisconsin, Harvard, the University of Chicago, Yale, and the University of Pennsylvania. They were surprised by their beautiful campuses and well-organized programs, but they were even more astonished to hear that they had all been built with private donations.

Eiichi was furthermore impressed to find that Americans were not addicted to knowledge for its own sake but understood that it should be used to its full potential. Everything from factories and farms to civil engineering and construction was designed for maximum efficiency and effectiveness by applying the latest knowledge. While Americans did sometimes seem a bit unrefined and overly bold, Eiichi felt that Japan could learn a lot from their attitude towards knowledge and learning and from their well-planned utilization of knowledge.

Eiichi was also strongly impressed by what he saw as a conservation of manpower. Perhaps it was because the land was so vast and there was still a shortage of labor, he thought, but even when visiting a dignified businessman's house, he observed how the host and his wife would operate the elevator and serve the guests, performing all of the duties that would have been left to servants in Japan. It was no wonder, he realized, that their mechanical technology improved. He felt, too, that the principle of human dignity would quickly become established.

Eiichi saw that the United States would only follow a path of further development. And when he imagined that one day such Americans might confront Japanese as economic rivals, a chill went down his spine. During their visits to the various chambers of commerce, he heard numerous times about U.S. business-men's determination to challenge Japan in trade competition – a peacetime sort of war.

He was both surprised and embarrassed to find that Ameri-cans seemed to greatly overrate Japan. They would often express admiration about how brave, chivalrous, and full of progressive spirit were the Japanese, to the point of hyperbole. They seemed to think of Japan as more than what it actually was.

"To be seen as greater than the reality may be something of an honor, but it is also frightening, because we must assume that they will be preparing to challenge us by obtaining a strength that will surpass their image of us."[85]

The above is an excerpt of Eiichi's impressions of the tour that he set down in the book *Seien hyakuwa* (One Hundred Essays by Seien [Shibusawa Eiichi]), published in 1912. The skillful dove-tailing of knowledge and practice in the United States would lead to the eventual emergence of the so-called Big Science aimed at developing everything from space science to genetic engineering, and the digital revolution, transforming people's lives across the globe. Almost all of the qualities of Americans that impressed Eiichi a century ago are still present.

At the time of Eiichi's visit some Americans had criticized the quality of Japanese products. Later they came to respect, even if they also feared, the economic dynamism and technological

---

[85] Shibusawa, *Seien hyakuwa*, p. 254.

prowess of postwar Japan as it rose rapidly to second place in global GNP rankings.

Eiichi returned to Japan convinced that his country must forge friendly relations with the United States no matter what the cost in order to remain on the path of harmony and prosperity. In the sense of improving the relationship between Japan and the United States "this tour was like a patient with a stomach ailment being sent off to get exercise rather than given medicine to cure his condition. It is thus difficult to give a clear list of the exact ways this tour has been beneficial."[86]

The fact of the matter was, however, that they visited a great number of locations across the United States, where they were greeted with sincerity and enthusiasm by the Americans, and "conversed with them in a friendly and open-hearted manner." Above all, Eiichi definitely confirmed with his own eyes that many Americans thought highly of Japan. Perhaps the discrimination against Japanese on the West Coast had been reported rather too emotionally. Such a matter should not obstruct the fellowship between the two countries. Eiichi felt that the focus from then on had to be to avoid conflict and work together.

It was a sunny day in eastern Japan on December 17, 1909. In those days when there was no such thing as smog, the snow-capped Mt. Fuji rose on the horizon under a cloudless winter sky. On this day, the *Chiyo Maru* sailed safely into the Yoko-hama port and was met by massive crowd that had been waiting to give the delegation a hearty welcome home. And thus their memorable journey came to an end.

---

[86] Shibusawa, *Seien hyakuwa*, p. 703.

CHAPTER 6

THE ROOTS OF THE
ANTI-JAPANESE MOVEMENT

∞

BEGINNING WITH KOREA and continuing into Manchuria, expansion of Japan's interests and sphere of influence on the continent was the theme that preoccupied Japan nonstop from the latter part of the nineteenth century through the first half of the twentieth. In the course of the bloody wars waged against China in 1894–1895 and against Russia in 1904–1905 Japanese acquired what was to become a deep-seated obsession that the very survival of the nation depended upon control of the Korean peninsula and that its sway over Korea would be in peril if Manchuria were not secured as well. The idea of invading and occupying Korea (known as "Seikanron") debated at the beginning of the new Meiji regime was no more than an expression of the naïve desire for survival of a still-weak and untried state just beginning to open its eyes to what was going on in the world. But as time went on, that idea of placing Korea – and Manchuria – under Japan's control became a strong demand of the people of what was now a world power. It became embedded in the minds of people of all political persuasions as the righteous claim won through the bloody toll of repeated wars and driven by intense patriotism.

The lives of countless men – the fathers, husbands, and sons of households – were lost in the pursuit of expansion into the continent. To support such wars waged with every passing decade, people put up with horrendous sacrifices and harsh austerities, well aware that they would have to endure those hardships for still more years to come, and determined to do so.

After the Sino-Japanese War, the Liaodong Peninsula Japan had won at the cost of much blood and sacrifice was snatched away due to what was seen as China's scheming and the intervention of Germany, France, and Russia. When the Western powers failed to stand behind Japan's right to territory it had won in battle, Japanese learned the folly of such trust. The experience of having won territory at great sacrifice only to have it taken away by the collusion of other powers became an unforgettable sore spot that would rankle in Japan's diplomatic relations from then on. It fed a national determination and commitment to vengeance. Japanese became convinced that anything they would attain could only be won by the strength of their own arms. Every battle during the war was a desperate struggle to the death. And whatever was acquired, they must cling to with desperate stubbornness. The only way to sustain Japan's status as a proud major power in the world was to endure the cruelest struggle. This behest was carved deeply into the psyches of everyone, old and young, men and women, even small children old enough to know what was going on around them.

For the imperialist powers of the West the Chinese mainland was far distant from home shores and mainly the object of investment for the sake of surplus profits. Russia, with its contiguous borders, was quite serious about its stake in East Asia, but its most valued territories were separated from potential Asian rivals by the vastness of the Siberian steppes. Its national interests were divided in two directions between Europe and Asia. The United States might parade the high ideals of the open door and equal opportunity, but the China trade was simply an accessory to its world-straddling commerce. With other countries enjoying the honey pot, America could not resist wanting to get a share for itself.

Japanese, however, had convinced themselves that a foothold on the continent was literally essential to national survival. In order for Japan to join the world powers in military and economic terms there had to be a guarantee that the Korean peninsula and Manchuria would not become anti-Japanese; the region had to be kept on Japan's side.

Since 1960, Japan's national security has rested mainly upon the existence of the Japan-U.S. security treaty, and the country has assumed that it will be defended in case of an emergency. During the Cold War era, the ideological equilibrium reached between the United States and the Soviet Union allowed Japan to concentrate fully on economic growth. Without the treaty, Japan could easily have been ignored when push came to shove between the two superpowers, leaving the archipelago vulnerable to attack or domination by one side or the other. It is highly unlikely that Japan would ever attempt another invasion on the continent, but in the changing regional security environment of today, espousing the naive pacifism Japan stood by for decades since the signing of the peace treaty ending World War II has become very difficult. Japan is expected to contribute more to the alliance.

In Eiichi's time in the late nineteenth century, however, Japan was on its own. In the survival-of-the-fittest world of those days, it had not a single ally. For a short period from the 1870s through to the mid-1890s, Japanese sensed that they might rely on a "sympathetic" United States, and this expectation remained at least partially in place into the Roosevelt era, but with the advent of the Taft administration in the spring of 1909 the United States suddenly changed its tune, and Japan realized that it would be entirely on its own in defending its interests.

When we look at the matter from a different perspective, of course, the notion that the Korean peninsula and Manchuria were Japan's "lifeline" – even if that was true geographically and militarily – was unrealistic, for they were, after all, inhabited by millions of people who were not Japanese. The idea that they could be made into pro-Japanese bastions in order to secure Japan's geopolitical survival was impossible and absurd. Each country has its own destiny, and each its own hopes, joys, and laments. The argument that such places could be made to fit into a certain scheme to suit the purposes of Japan's security and advancement was unsupportable.

If a country is convinced it cannot survive without sacrificing others, then the value of surviving in that particular way should be fundamentally reconsidered. And in fact, because Japan insisted in the 1930s and 1940s on running things entirely according to its own self-centered arguments, it placed itself upon the path of self-destruction.

If Japan could have detected beforehand – even faintly – how foolhardy, damaging, and agonizing would be the single-minded and self-centered – at times even hysterical – efforts it pursued from the end of the Russo-Japanese War to the end of World War II, the country's destiny might have been quite different. And world history, too, would no doubt have moved in some other direction. Instead of incurring the eternal hatred and hostility of Chinese, Koreans, and many others in Asia, it might have been able to work together with these peoples to make the first steps toward a better world order.

There were those who aspired to wiser choices at the time. At the end of the Russo-Japanese War, popular novelist Tokutomi Roka (Kenjirō; 1868–1927) declared that Japan should rouse itself from its obsession with the expansion of the state and seek instead to "spread justice through the four seas."[87] His elder brother, the well-known journalist Tokutomi Sohō, argued that the country's mission ought to be "introducing the civilizations of East and West to each other, harmonizing the relationship between the yellow and white races, and coalescing the whole of humanity so as to reach the ultimate goal of justice."[88]

However, these were but minority voices, drowned out in the mad celebrations of Japan's victory over Russia. The victory more successful than ever hoped-for gave rise to a bold arrogance in Japanese far greater than their actual stature in world affairs, even though such attitudes cast an even bleaker pall over the future of the country.

Japanese are by nature especially sensitive to what others think of them. As soon as they sense that they appear to be lesser or weaker or looked down upon by other countries, they feel even smaller than reality and lose confidence. Then they frantically

---

[87] Iriye, *Japan and the Wider World*, p. 33.
[88] Iriye, *Japan and the Wider World*, p. 34.

begin to work to remedy the situation. They will study feverishly, hardly taking time to sleep, striving ceaselessly to strengthen their country. When Japan won in the war against Russia, the way the world viewed them changed. This extremely self-centered and sensitive people quickly detected the change and reacted by growing haughty.

While Japanese knew their country was small by comparison with the Western powers both in military strength and wealth, they began to feel that there was no longer any need for them to be excessively deferential in international society. They developed a pride displayed as superiority – well-founded or unfounded – vis-à-vis Chinese, Koreans, and other Asians. As if giving vent to long pent-up frustration, they began to strut and swagger. This tendency had grown conspicuous among Japanese since the victory in the Sino-Japanese War, but after the Russo-Japanese War it went completely out of control. Japan may have attained some measure of success in modernization, but to boast of such success and despise and insult others who had not was extremely unpleasant. I am not sure whether this is a particular trait of Japanese or whether any other people in the same circumstances would conduct themselves in the same manner, but in any case, that mean and crude mentality was to bedevil Japanese history thereafter.

Itō Hirobumi, distinguished as he was as a statesman, was no exception. He had headed out for the post of governor-general of Korea apparently convinced of the naïve notion that Koreans would feel happy under Japanese protection; they might complain at the beginning but, if Japanese took the initiative in freeing them from the backwardness of their government and economy and brought them the blessings of modernity, he and others assumed, Koreans would certainly become devoted to Japan as a result.

Even Eiichi had not seen the gaping pitfall in this kind of thinking. On December 18, 1905, Eiichi had invited friends and associates in the world of business to a reception for Itō at the Imperial Hotel in Tokyo. It was immediately after the signing of the Japan-Korea Treaty (or Japan-Korea Protectorate Treaty) on November 11, according to which Korea was forced to hand over to Japan complete responsibility for its foreign affairs. In reply to Eiichi's gracious welcome to the reception, Itō stated proudly that when he had gone to see Korean Emperor Gojong just before returning to Japan, the emperor had told him "I trust Your Excellency more than my own ministers . . . I look forward to your return to Korea." Itō asked for the business leaders' support, saying that, "It is to our advantage to sympathize with him [the Emperor] and help him."

Ultimately, total lack of sensitivity toward Koreans on the part of Itō, not to mention the majority of Japanese at that time, was to become reason enough for his assassination by a Korean nationalist in Harbin. It is difficult to imagine any sovereign really saying he "trusts" the envoy who has just literally coerced that sovereign to make his country the protectorate of an outside power.

Anti-Japanese sentiment in Korea rapidly swelled in the wake of the treaty signing. The Korean prime minister, Ye Wanyong, who had been in favor of cooperation with the Japanese, was denounced as a traitor to the country and his residence burned to the ground. Rebellion spread throughout the country, and Itō had to mobilize the Japanese imperial army to suppress it.

Patriotic activity also arose among Koreans living overseas. Syngman Rhee, later South Korea's first president and at the time a young newspaper journalist working in the United States, appealed to the world for sympathy in Korea's plight. He secured an interview with President Theodore Roosevelt, hoping to obtain help in preserving the independence of his country, but unfortunately, at the time Roosevelt was in the midst of a policy of flattering Japan, and so Rhee's pleas fell on deaf ears. Emperor Gojong himself sent secret emissaries to the second international Hague Peace Convention in mid-1907 in hopes of getting the attention of other major powers. The Japanese government was infuriated by his subterfuge. It sent its foreign minister Hayashi Tadasu to Seoul and he and Itō personally confronted the emperor, intimidating him until they succeeded in making the incident the pretext for forcing him to abdicate the throne. Thus

Japan played the same trick on Korea that the imperialist powers of Europe had been playing against countries in Asia for several hundred years, and by tactics no less devious and self-serving. Nothing could be more ironic than the fact that the perpetrators were the very same Japanese who had gritted their teeth in fury at the news of Britain's duplicitous treatment of China in the Opium Wars (1840–1842, 1856–1860). The forced signing of the 1905 Japan-Korea Treaty was a decisive moment in the ill-fated history of the Meiji era.

Voices of indignation arose among foreigners residing in Korea at that time, declaring the "rape" of Korea. Ernest Bethell, the publisher of the *Korean Daily News*, an English-language newspaper, filled the pages of the paper with information about the Japanese takeover, appealing to the world to condemn Japan's unlawful behavior. At the behest of the Japanese resident-general, the British consular court arrested Bethell and sentenced him to three weeks in prison for going too far, but he would not give up and continued his anti-Japanese propaganda. Countless others, Americans, French, and so on, worked both directly and indirectly to push back against the implementation of Japan's policies.

One of the Americans was Willard Straight (1880–1918), who had been posted to Seoul as U.S. vice-consul. Then 24 years old, this young man would devote the rest of his life to obstructing the continental ambitions of Japan, and in that endeavor he left his imprint on history at centers of influence such as the U.S. Department of State and Wall Street. During the Russo-Japanese War, Straight volunteered to serve as a front-line war correspondent, and what he observed of the Japanese at that time only intensified his hatred and hostility toward them. In his diary, he wrote: "They all hate us, all of them, officers and men. They have been the underdog until now, they have been the scholars, we the masters, and now they're going to show us a thing or two if it can be done. They hate us. God knows the feeling is mutual."[89]

Straight was born in New York and had been orphaned at an early age, but was a bright student and attended Cornell

---

[89] Akira Iriye, *Across the Pacific*, pp. 103–104.

University. After graduation, he went to the Far East, working first in Customs in China and later in the U.S. Embassy
in Seoul. Ambitious and intelligent, he soon distinguished
himself in the diplomatic corps, and early on his talents were
noticed by top-level leaders like Edward Harriman and Theodore Roosevelt. When William H. Taft visited Japan in 1907,
he met Straight there and wrote of the strong impression the
young man made on him.[90]

At the end of 1905, when the United States closed its embassy
in Korea and left "like the stampede of rats from a sinking ship,"[91]
Straight went back to the United States, but the following June
(1906), he returned to the Far East as the first U.S. consul in
Mukden. Straight's hatred of Japanese and his intense reaction
against Japanese control of Korea and Manchuria was infused
not only with his sense of justice but with the emotions of racial
prejudice. Japanese of the time, Eiichi included, did not antici-
pate or understand how deeply these prejudices gripped Americans.

In Mukden, Straight recognized that the demise of Korea was
already established fact and nothing could be done about it, but
he was determined to thwart the advance of Japan into Manchuria and China. Until then, American policy had been concilia-
tory toward Japan as a means of defending U.S. interests in the
Philippines. One of the reasons for that stance, he thought, had
been that American investment in China was still very low. Reliable data on investments at this period is not available, but U.S.
investment in China in 1900 was estimated to amount to only
$19 million, while that in Japan was probably roughly equal, in
addition to which Americans had bought up $45 million of Jap-
anese public loans extended for the waging of the Russo-Japanese
War. In terms of trade as well, U.S. trade with Japan amounted

---

[90] O'Connor, *Pacific Destiny*, p. 348. The following discussion of Straight's
      role in U.S. policy-making towards Japan and China draws on Griswold,
      The Far Eastern Policy of the United States, pp. 137–43, O'Connor,
      pp. 348–51 as well as the Shibusawa archive.

[91] As quoted in Griswold, *The Far-Eastern Policy of the United States*,
      p. 136.

to nearly $100 million in 1908, while that with China was not even half that much. At that time, therefore, Japan was a much more important economic partner than China.[92]

During his assignment in Mukden, Straight poured his energies into finding ways to reverse those proportions of investment by increasing U.S. interests in China. The man who sponsored his efforts and conspired with him to that end was Southern Pacific Railways president Edward Harriman. Harriman had been interested in investing in railways in Manchuria from some time before, and it is thought that the assignment of Straight to the embassy in Mukden was arranged with Harriman's influence.

In September 1905, Harriman visited Japan, optimistically hoping to get the Japanese government to sell him the South Manchurian Railway. On the 12th, the very day that the streets of Tokyo were throbbing with protests against the terms of the peace treaty with Russia drawn up in Portsmouth, Harriman was visiting Eiichi at the Asukayama residence in Ōji. It was the second time they had met. Three years earlier, Eiichi had had an interview with Harriman in New York. Harriman arrived at Asukayama at about 3:00 p.m., bringing with him his two daughters and the wife of the American minister to Japan. They enjoyed chatting with Shiraishi Motojirō and his wife – who also were there as guests[93] – strolling around the garden, observing the tea ceremony being performed in the tea house, and drinking champagne and coffee in the gazebo. The party dispersed at around 6:00 in the evening.

Eiichi later recalled, "To be quite frank, he gave an impression of being quick-witted and sharp enough to catch the whole picture with the briefest suggestion, and moreover has very personal and thoroughgoing views on all the relevant issues. No wonder

---

[92] Ibid, p. 137.
[93] Shiraishi (1867–1945) had been hired after graduating from university by the Asano zaibatsu in 1892 and later married the second daughter of zaibatsu founder Asano Sōichirō. Shiraishi later became one of the top executives of the Asano group.

he holds extremely influential positions in the United States and plays a very important role in U.S. affairs."[94]

Regarding the South Manchurian Railway, rights to which Japan had just acquired as a result of the Russo-Japanese War, Harriman proposed that the Japanese government either sell it to him or cooperate in setting up a syndicate for its joint management. Japan was thirsting for capital after the draining costs of the war, and so the Japanese side was very receptive to the idea, going so far as to sign an agreement to that effect under the name of Prime Minister Katsura Tarō. The agreement was revoked, however, after foreign minister Komura Jutarō, who had represented Japan at the peace negotiations in Portsmouth ending the hostilities between Japan and Russia, returned to Japan and firmly opposed the sale. Komura argued that the railway was one of the few concessions Japan had won in the war, and that it did not make sense to involve foreigners in its management from the very outset. He also pointed out that, anyway, Japan could not dispose of the railway without first obtaining the approval of China.

The view of the government eventually shifted over to Komura's position, and it was decided to create a semiofficial company for implementing state policy, called the South Manchuria Railway Co., Ltd. (SMR; Mantetsu), to manage the railway. In July 1906, a founding committee was established by government decree, and the chairman of the committee was General Kodama Gentarō. Eiichi was a member of the committee, and he became especially involved, as chairman of a subcommittee, in drafting the by-laws of the organization. Kodama, however, had been severely overworked during the war and was much weakened both mentally and physically, and within 10 days of his appointment to the post he collapsed as if sapped of all his strength and died. Kodama was replaced by army minister Terauchi Masatake, and finally on November 26, the new company was officially established. The first president was Gotō Shinpei and the vice-

---

[94] Remarks printed in the *Jitsugyō no sekai* [The World of Business] magazine, December 1921. See *Shibusawa denki shiryō*, vol. 25, pp. 664–65.

president Nakamura Yoshikoto. Eiichi was called on to serve as a board member of the company several times, but it went against his principles to take such a semi-governmental position, and each time he politely declined.

Willard Straight did his best to egg on Harriman, endeavoring to reignite the railway magnate's ambitious plan. Straight was determined to find a way to either buy up the South Manchurian Railway (Mantetsu) and jointly manage it with Japan, or if that failed, to build a parallel railroad and do everything possible to compete with and hinder Japan's efforts to manage the Mantetsu. Harriman was all in favor of this policy and did everything he could to fulfill his own dream of building a transportation network, starting off with the Manchurian Railway, to stretch from the Pacific to the Atlantic Ocean and, linked by steamship lines across the oceans, encircle the globe. Unfortunately, business in New York took a turn for the worse in 1907 and he was forced to put his plans on hold.

Meanwhile, Mukden-based Straight created an organization called the Chinese-American Publicity Bureau within the consulate-general and put it in charge of propaganda activities and attraction of capital from the United States. It was not long before this publicity bureau had all the qualities of an anti-Japanese propaganda headquarters.

In 1908, Straight was called back to Washington and at the age of 28 appointed head of Far Eastern Affairs at the State Department. It was about that time that the United States and Japan signed the Takahira-Root Agreement, which he described in his diary, along with the U.S. withdrawal from the Korean peninsula, as a "terrible diplomatic blunder to be laid to the door of T.R."[95]

In March 1909, William Taft became president and Philander C. Knox was made secretary of state. Knox had served as attorney general since the time of the McKinley administration, was elected to the Senate representing Pennsylvania in 1904, and in 1908 had been rumored to be a candidate for president

---

[95] O'Connor, *Pacific Destiny*, p. 348.

as well, so he was less a diplomat than an expert on domestic politics. Like secretaries of state before him, Knox had started out in the legal profession, so he had a tendency to interpret foreign-relations issues in terms of legal principles. On that score he resembled Taft, who was also originally a lawyer. They formed quite a contrast to the innately political and nimble gamesman Theodore Roosevelt before them, and it seems that Japanese statesmen as well as Eiichi did not adequately appreciate the extent to which the legalistic tendencies of the Americans were coming to the fore.[96]

The Taft administration announced that it would maintain the previous administration's policy advocating the open door and protection of China's territorial integrity. No doubt influenced by the Far Eastern bureau where Straight was then working, Secretary of State Knox argued that American investment in Chinese railways ought to be encouraged, as it would give the United States an interest in Chinese affairs and some say in that country, contributing to the preservation of Chinese territory. The Taft-Knox "dollar diplomacy" was justified by the idea that the United States, which declared it had no territorial but only commercial ambitions, was the best qualified to protect China against outside (Japanese) incursions.[97]

At that time, American public opinion had gradually begun to coalesce around the idea that China had to be protected from the advance of Japan onto the continent. When called in by President Taft to advise him on China policy, bishop of the Methodist Episcopal Church in Beijing (Peking) Rev. J. W. Bashford expressed his view that if Japan were to appropriate Manchuria for itself, the Western powers were likely to be quick to partition the entire country of China. The United States should never allow such illegitimate action, he argued, for China was inherently the

---

[96] Griswold, *The Far Eastern Policy of the United States*, p. 134.

[97] The term "dollar diplomacy" was used by Taft in his final State of the Union address to Congress in 1912. Tosh Minohara, Shusuke Takahara and Ryota Murai, "The Great War and Shifting Relations, 1909–19," in Makoto Iokibe and Tosh Minohara, eds., *The History of US-Japan Relations: From Perry to Present*, p. 44.

larger and by far more commercially and industrially promising
object of interest than Japan. The United States should do whatever it could to protect China's territorial integrity and stand by
the principle of the open door. If Japan understood American
interests to be unselfish and unambitious, there would be no
war between the two countries, and he argued, "Moreover, if the
worst comes, a nation which is unwilling to stand for righteousness has no claim upon the Almighty for continued existence."[98]

Reflecting such views, the State Department exercised its
influence with New York-based investors to form a group to back
a loan to China. Straight was invited to be the Beijing representative to this group and ultimately he resigned from the State
Department once more to take on that role. The members of the
group included Edward Harriman as well as J. P. Morgan and
Company, Kuhn, Loeb & Co., the First National Bank, and the
National City Bank, run by Eiichi's old acquaintance James Stillman (see chapter 3). Straight travelled with Harriman to Russia
to participate in negotiations for the sale of the Chinese Eastern
Railway, a branch of the South Manchurian Railway, and devel-
oped the plan for a line to run parallel to the South Manchurian
Railway known as the Jinzhou-Aihui (Chinchow-Aigun) line,
but these projects, too, were frustrated by the untimely death of
Harriman in September 1909.

Knox remained enthusiastic about promotion of the China
investment policy and next came up with a proposal to neutralize all the railways in Manchuria. The U.S. State Department
then promptly called on Britain, Japan, France, Germany, and
Russia to agree to the plan. The idea was to create a syndicate
composed of the six countries including the United States which
would then buy up all the railways in Manchuria operated by
Russia and Japan. The syndicate would jointly operate the railways for commercial purposes, prohibiting their use for political
or military purposes. This wild and ill-considered proposition
completely ignored the historical context as well as the situation

---

[98] Griswold, *The Far Eastern Policy of the United States*, pp. 145–46.
Quoted from "Bashford to Taft, May 15, enclosing memorandum of
May 8, 1911. Knox papers."

in China, and its intention of countering the advance of Japanese interests was blatant. It was an example of what one might call ill-intentioned idealism.

Later, when the Conference of Concerned Japanese and Americans (Nichi-Bei Yūshi Kyōgikai) was convened in Tokyo in April 26, 1920, Eiichi remembered Knox's proposal and remarked as follows:

> The following year, then U.S. Secretary of State Knox proposed to make the South Manchurian Railroad neutral. When we heard of it, we could not help thinking that American politicians are certainly presumptuous and the idea really rather fantastic. Although this is mainly in relation to politics, it was an incident that made me think of how the people of the United States really lack consideration for Japan.[99]

Both Britain and Russia naturally rejected the proposal and Knox's strategy ultimately came to naught. Straight despaired and gave up his Manchuria investment promotion scheme. He married Dorothy Whitney, the daughter of a financier, and entered the business world as a partner in J. P. Morgan and Company at the age of 32. Among his achievements was the founding of *The New Republic* (then considered a liberal magazine) and the *Journal of the American Asiatic Association*, which later became *Asian Magazine*, a prominent journal of opinion. After World War I, he went to Europe and worked there for a time, but contracted the influenza that was then epidemic in France and died, age 40.

Straight was in the State Department for less than one year, but in that short time he got the American political and financial worlds involved in the maelstrom of Chinese political events, and his idea of celebrating the stance of the United States as the guardian angel of Chinese independence was to remain the basic theme of American Far Eastern policy until World War II, much to the continuing consternation of Japan.

In September 1912, Secretary of State Knox came to Japan, to attend the state funeral for Emperor Meiji. He boarded the cruiser

---

[99] *Shibusawa denki shiryō*, vol. 35, p. 363.

Maryland in Seattle, arrived at Yokohama on September 9, participated in the funeral on the 13th, visited the imperial Fushimi Momoyama-ryo grave in Kyoto, and on the 22nd left Japan to return to the United States via Hawai'i.

As he often did with visiting dignitaries, Eiichi invited Secretary Knox, his wife, and entourage to the Asukayama residence for luncheon. Carpets were spread over the tatami floors, a large dining table was placed in the center of the room, and bonsai and other decorations set around. The shoji panels were removed to fully open up the view of the garden on the eastern and southern sides of the room. Mrs. Knox was delighted with the arrangements, which she said reminded her of a country club in the United States. After lunch, they strolled in the garden, enjoyed the creations of an impromptu painter, and left after an enjoyable afternoon.

The other illustrious guests at this luncheon included Thomas J. O'Brien, the American ambassador to Japan at the time, foreign minister Uchida Kōsai, financial expert Takahashi Korekiyo, zaibatsu family head Mitsui Hachirōemon, and Dr. Nitobe Inazō and his wife, Mary Patterson Elkinton. Among the members of Knox's entourage listed as guests were head of the Far Eastern Bureau of the U.S. State Department R. S. Miller and a young U.S. Army officer named John Pershing. Miller had succeeded to the post held by Willard Straight, and Pershing was the future legendary World War I hero.

Considering that Knox's visit to Japan took place at a time when the cooling of American sentiments toward Japan was strongly felt as a result of the U.S. demand for the neutralization of the South Manchurian Railway, the tone of Japanese editorials on the subject was mixed, but there was general satisfaction with the fact that the serving U.S. secretary of state had attended the emperor's funeral and had returned directly home, despite a polite invitation from China to visit Beijing.

CALIFORNIA AS A HOTBED OF ANTI-JAPANESE SENTIMENT

One day in November 1908, Eiichi received a visit from a certain Watanabe Kinzō, who identified himself as a councilor of

Figure 24
Ushijima Kinji (George
Shima; 1864–1926),
first president of the
Japanese Association
of America. Photo:
Shibusawa Memorial
Museum.

the Japanese Association of America. Japanese volunteers had
founded the Association in the spring of that year in order to
cope with the rapidly intensifying anti-Japanese tendencies in
the Western part of the United States and to protect their liveli-
hood. Among the current aims of the Association at the time
were to promote the welfare of Japanese living in the United
States, work with pro-Japanese Americans to try to mitigate and
reduce anti-Japanese sentiment, and, when Japanese suffered
unfair treatment, hire American lawyers to fight back and defend
their interests.

The first to serve as president of the Association was Ushijima
Kinji (George Shima; 1864–1926). Born in Kurume, Fukuoka
prefecture, he had gone to the United States in 1888 and become
a farmer in the Stockton (California) area, eventually acquiring
a huge 60,000-acre farm in the San Joaquin area and earning a
reputation as the "king of potatoes" for his foremost product.

Watanabe had come to Japan on behalf of Ushijima to promote understanding in the parent country of the plight of Japanese in the United States and to request the material as well as moral support of interested persons in the homeland.

While talking with Watanabe, Eiichi recalled his experience several years earlier (1902) during his trip to the United States when he had toured the Golden Gate beach park and observed a sign saying "No Japanese allowed." He told Watanabe about what he had seen and warned him about it. He then indicated that he understood the situation very well, agreed with the importance of the Association's activities, and promised to do everything he could to help.

When he gathered together members of the business world who had close relations with the United States and long-standing interest in Japan-U.S. relations, and explained the situation to them, they immediately offered their help. Leader of the modern ceramics industry Morimura Ichizaemon pledged 5,000 yen and others including Ōkura Kihachirō, Takahashi Korekiyo, and Gotō Shinpei followed suit,[100] so that after adding 1,000 yen himself, Eiichi was able to present Watanabe with a total of over 20,000 yen in donations to the Association's cause. This was the beginning of Eiichi's more substantial involvement with the issues of the Japanese emigrants in the United States.

Although the 1906 California law ordering Japanese students to be segregated from white students had been rescinded in 1907 through the efforts of Theodore Roosevelt and others, the anti-Japanese mood was by no means eased, and there were boycotts of shops run by Japanese and continuing incidents of violence against Japanese immigrants. In the spring of 1909, some 16 anti-Japanese bills were lined up for deliberation in the

---

[100] Translator's note: Morimura Ichizaemon (VI; 1839–1919), founder of the Noritake ceramics company; Ōkura Kihachirō (1837–1928), self-made man, founder of the Ōkura zaibatsu, antique collector; Takahashi Korekiyo (1854–1936), politician, twentieth prime minister, head of Bank of Japan and Ministry of Finance; Gotō Shinpei (1857–1929), doctor, statesman and cabinet minister, first governor-general of Taiwan.

California State Legislature – many of them reflecting blatant racial prejudice – including bills prohibiting marriage between Japanese men and white women and a special per capita tax on Japanese. Reflecting the trend of the times, political organizations of various kinds as well as the state legislature adopted anti-Japanese resolutions and proposed bills of a similar nature.

In 1910, the California legislature ordered the head of the state government labor office, John D. MacKenzie, to conduct a survey of the lives of Japanese immigrants. Since the survey was intended from the outset to confirm the basis for further escalating anti-Japanese exclusionary legislation, it was believed that its findings would be skewed to support that end.

As it happened, however, MacKenzie was a man who believed in fairness, and the results of the survey were in fact extremely fair. The analysis recognized the efforts and achievements of Japanese immigrants in California and their difficulties in opening up new land in the state. It showed that Japanese farm workers were skilled and hardworking and that they supplied an inexpensive source of labor that could not be found among the white labor force. Without Japanese workers, there was no hope for the advancement of Californian agriculture. Regarding Japanese landowners, the survey pointed to the noteworthy cases in which Japanese had purchased land that had been abandoned by white farmers and turned it into fertile fields through intense effort and hard work; they were top-level farm managers.[101]

When the results were reported in the state legislature, however, the assembly erupted in fury, declaring that MacKenzie had ignored the will of the people of the state, handed him an official reprimand, and promptly rejected the report.[102]

As this incident illustrates, it seems that state politics at that time was not always a reflection of reality but had a tendency

---

[101] See Shurtleff and Aoyagi *How Japanese and Japanese-Americans Brought Soyfoods to the United States and the Hawaiian Islands: A History (1851–2011)*.

[102] Shurtleff and Aoyagi, *How Japanese and Japanese-Americans Brought Soyfoods*.

to be controlled by the whims of political bosses. There were rumors that Eugene Schmitz, who was San Francisco mayor from 1902 to 1907 and known as a prime promoter of the segregation of Japanese students in the schools, deliberately sensationalized the anti-Japanese movement in order to divert the attention of citizens from the suspicion of graft and abuse of his powers as mayor.[103]

Whatever the cause, anti-Japanese sentiment was clearly a predominant consensus in California at that time. Powerful local organizations like the Native Sons of the Golden West (an association then led by wealthy, influential, and exclusively white Californians), the California Grange (a kind of agricultural cooperative group), and the California Federation of Labor (representing the interests and benefits of white workers in the state) all waved the anti-Japanese banner. The members of these organizations were proud that they had moved to the West Coast early on and eager to protect their perogatives.

Antipathy toward immigrants from East Asia already had a long history. It was mainly the Working Men's Party (WMP) – made up of white workers – that was behind the boycotts, assaults, and burning of homes from which Chinese immigrant workers suffered in the 1870s. On the pretext of preventing jobs being taken away from white workers by Asian workers willing to work for cheap wages, the WMP invariably led the way in the exclusionist movement.

The San Francisco Labor Council sponsored a rally to protest Japanese immigration in 1900 featuring a special lecture in support of their cause. Stanford University sociologist Dr. Edward A. Ross used the podium to declare that Japanese were incapable of assimilating into American society, that their cheap wages threatened to undermine the living standards of American workers, and that Japanese could not be made to understand American political institutions. He advocated that they be denied permission to enter the country.[104]

---

[103] See Raymond Leslie Buell, "The Development of Anti-Japanese Agitation in the United States" (1922).
[104] O'Connor, *Pacific Destiny*, p. 332.

SHAPING AMERICAN ATTITUDES TOWARD THE FAR EAST:
LONDON, LODGE, LEA

Among advocates seeking to protect the prerogatives of white
workers, one of the most influential all over the United States was
prominent author Jack London. During a speech at the Socialist Party Convention in Oakland, California, London delivered
such an intense tirade against Japanese that the chairman had
tried to curb his remarks. But London would not be deterred
and, pounding the table, shouted "What the devil! I am first of
all a white man and only then a Socialist."[105]

London's writing is straightforward and easy to read. His *Call
of the Wild*, *The Sea-wolf*, *White Fang*, and other works are treasured by young readers all over the world. But there are places
in his works where his writing reveals an undisguised gruesome-
ness that sends shivers down one's spine. Perhaps the experiences
of poverty in his childhood and the irregular and uninhibited
course of his youth created sensitivities and impulses of a twisted
cruelty in his otherwise brilliant mind.

One story entitled "The Unparalleled Invasion" depicts a
China where the population burgeons year after year until it is
more than 1 billion. Then, launching a human-wave strategy,
it invades all the countries of Asia and sets out to take over the
rest of the world. The terror-struck West as a last resort devel-
ops a kind of bacteriological weapon and sends it into China.
The strategy works and the entire population of China is wiped
out; Asia becomes a continent of death. London wrote this long
before Mao Zedong's use of human-wave tactics and the invention of chemical and biological weapons.

In 1904, London observed the Russo-Japanese War as a reporter
for the Hearst-owned newspapers. He seems to have made contact
with Japanese in a way that would deliberately cultivate the worst
possible impression. In Japan he entered off-limits territory with a
camera and was arrested on suspicion of spying. In Korea he struck
the valet he had hired and was brought before a military tribunal
by the Japanese army. He managed to avoid punishment when

---

[105] O'Connor, *Pacific Destiny*, p. 339, see note 12, as quoted from *Jack
London: A Biography* (Boston: Little, Brown, 1964), pp. 220–21.

the U.S. government intervened and gained his release on the condition that he return immediately to the United States. So within a very short period of time and through some rather extraordinary experiences, London acquired a very "accurate" understanding of Japan and Japanese. Magazines like the *Atlantic Monthly*, the newspapers in the Hearst-owned media empire, and other influential mass media publications competed to publish his views, and in due course those views were absorbed in various ways as the basis of American thinking on East Asian issues.[106]

From the time of the Russo-Japanese War, London became disgusted with the way Westerners admired and praised the purity of Japanese patriotism. Their love of country was essentially different from that of Westerners. Their loyalty – what they called *yamato-damashi* – was blind, as toward an absolute idol, and he concluded it was something so dangerous that it threatened the very foundations of the Western value system.[107]

In 1905, London met and married a vibrant woman named Charmian Kittredge, but instead of settling down in a home, he purchased a boat and set out on a grand journey with his wife to the South Seas that involved many adventures. Next, he purchased a ranch in the Sonoma Valley outside of San Francisco and there built an extravagant house costing as much as $80,000. To support such luxuries, he chained himself to his desk and churned out one book and article after another.

Unfortunately, just before the luxurious mansion was about to be completed, a fire broke out – the cause of which was never known – and burned it to the ground. London was apparently undeterred and simply said he would rebuild it, but by that time his health was already failing. The combined toll of extreme hard work from a young age and too much adversity and adventure had sapped his health, and in 1916, at 40 – the same age as Willard Straight – he died of uremia and other ailments.

From the time of the Russo-Japanese War rumors of war between the United States and Japan were circulating with quite

---

[106] O'Connor, *Pacific Destiny*, p. 342.
[107] O'Connor, *Pacific Destiny*, p. 341.

a high degree of possibility, and fictionalized accounts were quick to be published in the United States. Such a possibility was seen as absurd in Japan, but the rumors did not die out in the United States, and would only later resurface to excite the public over and over. Of course, it was precisely because of the possibility of war that Roosevelt had pursued his strategy of flattery in order to forestall a Japanese Imperial Army attack on the Philippines, and it was understandable if the rumors of war kept on surfacing. The chairman of the military affairs committee declared in Congress that Japan was preparing to go to war over the Philippines.

In 1911, a rumor began to circulate that Mexico had signed a secret treaty with Japan[108] and that it planned to settle a large number of Japanese immigrants in the Magdalena river delta area. Tensions flared in the United States when people speculated that it was ostensibly a move to absorb immigration so that the Japanese army planned to use the area as a forward attack base, and things escalated to the point that Senator Henry Cabot Lodge condemned both countries in the Senate. Then-president of Mexico Porfirio Diaz denied the speculations, and the Japanese side, too, declared them completely unfounded in fact. Lodge was a follower of the thinking of Alfred Mahan and an advocate of a large navy, and he may have been quite happy to take advantage of even a rumor to obtain the funds for building more naval ships, but in any case, it also added new fuel to the fires of immigration problems in the western United States.

Before the Russo-Japanese War, Japanese immigrants had enjoyed a more favorable reputation in the United States than Chinese immigrants, and though there were people of anti-Japanese persuasion, their arguments tended to be either reflections of racial prejudice or competition for jobs. After Japan's victory over Russia, however, discussion of such issues became entangled with concerns about national defense. There were suspicions that the Japanese immigrants who so quietly cultivated

---

[108] No concrete evidence of such a "secret treaty" has been found. The only agreement concluded in 1910–1911 was between a Japanese whaling company and the Mexican government over fishing rights. Conroy et al., *West Across the Pacific*, p. 87.

their fields and trimmed white people's gardens by day were secretly at the beck and call of the Japanese army, acting as spies and passers of information. All Japanese immigrants were subject to the suspicion that if war broke out, they would rise up in support of Japan.[109]

The suspicion was especially intense in California, and it lurked beneath the surface all the way until 1941 when the United States declared war on Japan following the attack on Pearl Harbor. The completely unfounded impression of the loyalties of Japanese living throughout the state was behind the policy under which all Japanese nationals in the state were relocated to camps in Utah and other remote places for the duration of World War II.

Adding impetus to this anti-Japanese mood was a book published in 1909 that predicted a war between Japan and the United States. Comparing and examining the fighting strength of the two sides, it concluded that the United States would be defeated, and became a sudden best-seller. Titled *Valor of Ignorance*, it was written by a young man of 33 named Homer Lea.[110] Lea was a keen and incisive observer, who had researched the book by personally inspecting the coastline of California, and his predictions were based on his survey of the topography and conditions for defense of U.S. shores.

According to Lea, the Japanese military was already prepared for war, but the United States had grown psychologically slack and was completely lacking in preparedness. The American navy might have 24 battleships as opposed to Japan's 14, but the total number of guns mounted on them was fewer than the number carried by the Japanese ships. On top of that, because the U. S. navy was split between the Atlantic and the Pacific, he concluded that its total forces were nowhere near sufficient. The number of days it would take for ships in the Atlantic to reach the Pacific and otherwise prepare was greater than needed by the Japanese navy to cross the Pacific. (Supply lines would be key; in 1908, when the 16-ship "Great White Fleet" had sailed around the

---

[109] O'Connor, *Pacific Destiny*, p. 334.
[110] O'Connor, *Pacific Destiny*, pp. 316–22.

world, it had been accompanied by 29 chartered transport ships to keep it supplied with coal and provisions.)

Regarding the defense of coastlines, Lea's book pointed out that Alaska, the Philippines, and Hawai'i had virtually nothing in the way of military facilities. Along the coast of the mainland United States, there were 67 fortifications to guard 26 ports with some 268 cannon, but only 124 were in working order. In order to fully mobilize these coastal defenses, a total of 1,600 officers and 40,000 men would be needed, but in fact they were manned by only 350 officers and 10,000 enlisted men.

U.S. regular troops, too, were insufficient, having fallen 30 percent short of the strength required and reflecting the extremely low awareness of the people regarding defense and the higher priority they accorded to making money and protecting their wealth. The morale and fighting spirit of the American military, Lea declared, was extremely low, and of 60,000 soldiers, some 6,000 had deserted ranks. For the Japanese military, as had been said at the time of the Russo-Japanese War a few years earlier, the deserter rate was virtually zero.

The American people had become soft and sickly, the book declared, which would explain why in the war with Spain, there had been 13 deaths from illness for every American who died in action. Again, at the time of the Russo-Japanese War, the contrast with the Japanese army was stark, at one death from illness for every four who died in action. If such a ratio were to be sustained in the case of a Japanese-American war, the United States would be pushed to the limits of its fighting strength.

Lea also predicted that Japan's specific strategy would be to launch surprise attacks on the Philippines and Hawai'i prior to its declaration of war. In the case of the Philippines, it would start by landing via the Lingayen Gulf and march south to Manila, occupying it within three weeks. (In 1941, Lea's predictions were almost all played out when Japan did exactly that, except that it took five more days to take over Manila.)

Lea's prophecy went on to say that once the Japanese took the whole West Coast, it would be difficult for the U.S. army to retaliate. In the north, the Cascade Mountains and the Sierra

Nevada rose steeply, cutting off access to the West, and in the south, the Mojave Desert and Death Valley made traverse from east to west difficult. The only path might be the Imperial Valley at the southernmost part of California, but since this too could only be approached through the desolate Arizona plateau, it was an unlikely option. Ultimately the United States would lose the fight and the country would be divided.

Seen as fiercely attacking the American way of life for growing slack from decades of peace and material prosperity, the book sent shockwaves through its readers. Although the content was clearly sensationalized and extreme, its analysis from the viewpoint of military strategy was sophisticated and advanced, and military professionals took it seriously.[111]

Valor of Ignorance was translated into Japanese by a man named Mochizuki Kotarō and published in 1911 by Eibun Tsūshinsha. It was exceedingly popular, selling some 40,000 copies. The Japanese title was *Nichi-Bei hissenron (Genmei: Muchi no yūki)* [Inevitable War between Japan and the United States]. On a complimentary copy of the book that Shibusawa Eiichi received, there is a note in his own hand: "Presented by Mochizuki Kotarō through a messenger in the morning of October 20." Eiichi appears to have perused the book, and although he does not seem to have been closely attracted to the parts about war, there are some pencil marks in the parts related to immigrants.

The story of Homer Lea shows that he was among the most brilliant, if not bizarre, of those Americans of his time whose careers were deeply connected with the history of the Far East. He suffered from physical disabilities but was very uncompromising, and as a child, if he stumbled and an adult attempted to help him, was known to become enraged, refusing all help or pity.[112]

Lea had become fascinated with the study of war in high school and studied at Occidental College and then Stanford

---

[111] See O'Connor, *Pacific Destiny*, p. 322.
[112] This story is told on p. 301 of O'Connor, *Pacific Destiny* and cited to an interview with Marshall Stimson.

University, but answered to the call of adventure before graduating. Having learned Chinese in California Chinatowns, he turned up in China as a champion of its revolution then in the early stages. Lea put his keen intellect and knowledge of war and strategy to use for the revolutionaries, who found him useful and put him to work for their cause, according him the rank of lieutenant general. After escaping to Hong Kong to avoid the chaos of the Boxer uprising (1900), he met Sun Yat-sen and was impressed by the refined Chinese leader's character and political philosophy of the "three principles of the people." He became a faithful supporter of Sun Yat-sen for the rest of his life.

Returning to the United States via Japan, Lea began a fund-raising campaign to back the revolution in China, visiting Chinatowns around the United States to make his case; then he turned to the unheard-of work of recruiting volunteer soldiers among the Chinatown youth. He put out his call in New York, Chicago, Los Angeles and other cities with the plan to form corps of 100 to 150 men per Chinatown and organized their military training as well. He used his contacts to find veterans of the U.S. army to serve as instructors. The volunteer corps gradually increased until it had surpassed 2,000 men in all.

For the United States to permit such a scheme to train – on American soil – a force designed to overturn the government of a foreign country was tantamount to intervention in the domestic affairs of another country, and the fact that no action was taken by Washington is certainly of interest, even though it was suspected that organizing a foreign legionary force within the territory of the United States was against the Constitution. The police and the United States Secret Service apparently did investigate the matter, but did nothing to prevent the activity, suggesting that both the U.S. government and public opinion were in fact in support of the scheme. This attitude toward the activities of Chinese in the United States formed a striking contrast with such Japanese-related issues as the commotion later made over Japanese intentions regarding the rumored emigration to Mexico, testifying to the clear shift

Figure 25
Woodrow Wilson (1856–1924)
became president of the United
States in 1913. Photo: Library of
Congress, United States.

that was taking place in the direction of pro-China, anti-Japan
policy in the United States.

CALIFORNIA PUSHES ON WITH ANTI-JAPANESE LEGISLATION

In the 1912 presidential election in the United States, the
election of Woodrow Wilson resulted in a Democratic administration that replaced the Republication administration of
Taft. Wilson had been president of his alma mater, Prince-
ton University, and then governor of New Jersey, and he was
known as a prominent lawyer as well. After becoming president he is said to have changed the atmosphere of America
through his energetic efforts for the passage of the anti-trust
law, labor laws, and other reformist legislation. A man of
upright and honest character, Wilson was known for his integrity and detachment, although he did have an overbearing and
stubborn streak.

In the New Year, following the conclusion of the presidential election, the California State Legislature again began its now regular frenzy of anti-Japanese legislation. That year nearly 30 bills were proposed that were blatantly anti-Japanese and discriminatory on the basis of race, including those calling for prohibiting the sale of various kinds of liquor to Japanese and prohibiting the hiring of white women by Japanese employers. Among them were eight bills proposed by California state attorney general Ulysses S. Webb, and together called the Alien Land Law bill. The bill was to be brought before both houses of the state legislature.

The purpose of the bill was to prevent foreigners not intending to become American citizens (implying Japanese) from acquiring, occupying, or transferring title to land. Any property acquired in violation of the law, it stated, would be confiscated by the state. Non-Americans were permitted to lease the land but that for a limit of only three years. The bill was blatantly discriminatory; Webb himself declared that the law was to discourage Japanese from entering or remaining in the state.

The California legislature had wanted the U.S. Congress to pass a law completely shutting out Japanese immigrants following the model of the Chinese Exclusion Act of 1882, but Washington, which had its own diplomatic priorities to maintain, was reluctant, so California decided to make the Webb bill a law, thereby discouraging any new immigration and as much as possible pushing Japanese already residing in the state to return to Japan.

As soon as these moves became known in Japan, the Japanese side submitted a strong protest to the U.S. government, and the Japanese Association of America and various influential people began a campaign to prevent passage of the bill. In Tokyo, on April 15, 1913 Tokyo Chamber of Commerce president Nakano Buei, along with Diet member Shimada Saburō and others became promoters for the organization of a group, and Eiichi was made its chairman. Eiichi was ill at the time, but he forced himself to get out of bed to attend the meeting and agreed to serve as chairman.

The group first proposed to take the name "Tai-Bei Dōshi Kai" (Anti-American One-Aim Society), and took a defiant stance vis-à-vis the anti-Japanese trend in the United States, but Eiichi tried to calm the members' passions. One member recalled him saying, "That's not the right way to approach this matter. We have to use reason and good sense to persuade Americans that they are wrong and try to create goodwill between the two countries, so if possible the Society should be open to Americans as well."[113] The others at the gathering agreed with his suggestion and the name was changed to Nichi-Bei Dōshi Kai (Japan-America One-Aim Society).

The first thing the Society did was to send members Soeda Juichi and Kamiya Tadao to the United States on a fact-finding mission. They would meet with key figures at different levels and call on them for understanding, and also meet with Japanese residents in the United States to encourage them to work toward a resolution of the situation. Soeda was a lawyer and president of the Industrial Bank of Japan and one of Eiichi's most faithful collaborators in Japan-America relations issues. Kamiya was affiliated with the Oriental Emigration Company, the Brazil Colonization Company, and other organizations, and thus an expert on immigration issues. Eiichi did his part by writing letters to his friends across the United States, requesting their awareness and understanding of the "California problem" and asking for their help and cooperation in improving the situation.

The Japanese government, too, worked vigorously to influence the American side on the matter through its embassy in Washington. As the issue flared up just at the time of changeover of presidential administrations, however, communications did not go smoothly. On March 4, Wilson was officially sworn in as president, and the very next day Japanese ambassador Chinda Sutemi (1857–1929) sought a meeting with the new president and managed to get the opportunity to urge him to try to persuade the California government to change its tune. Chinda

---

[113] As recalled by Kamiya Tadao, see *Shibusawa denki shiryō*, vol. 33, p. 422.

explained the precedent in which previous president Theodore Roosevelt's intervention in the matter of segregation of Japanese children in the California schools had been successful in bringing about withdrawal of the legislation, and the earnestness of his call for cooperation at the national level apparently duly impressed the new president. Wilson recognized that the Alien Land Law was discriminatory and wrong, and promptly sent his newly appointed Secretary of State, William Jennings Bryan, to appeal to the California legislature.

Bryan was known for his eloquence and persuasiveness and he did what he could, but both the California governor and the legislature were obstinate and refused to change their thinking, so he did not succeed in his mission.[114] Adding to the stubbornness of the Californians was the fact that since the school segregation incident, they had become determined never to have to buckle to intervention from the federal government again, and this further complicated matters. Even Wilson's step of sending a telegram directly to California governor Hiram Johnson was to no avail, and the bill was put up to vote. It was passed by an overwhelming majority – 25 to 2 – in the state's upper house on May 2 and the following day 73 to 3 in the lower house. The law then only awaited signing by the governor, who might have been prevailed upon to delay signing it, but Johnson, who was an advocate of driving out Japanese immigrants from the outset, rejected a review of the matter because the vote had been so clearly in favor, and on May 19, he signed the bill into law.

The Alien Land Law itself was even more racially discriminatory than the school segregation law. Unlike the previous case, the federal government's intervention had virtually no effect in preventing its adoption. The impact on the Japanese side was powerful. The newspapers and journals in Japan attacked the United States for its turncoat behavior and reported it as a huge diplomatic blunder.

When Wilson called in Ambassador Chinda and explained how he had done his best but that the government's efforts had come

---

[114] O'Connor, *Pacific Destiny*, p. 352.

to naught, the shock displayed by the ambassador was so intense that the president quickly realized the gravity of the matter. He had known of the frequent rumors going around of late about the possibility of war with Japan but had assumed they were just irresponsible remarks. Ambassador Chinda's reaction made him realize that they were not entirely groundless.[115] With the situation thus changed, it was hard to tell what Japan would do.

In his *Valor of Ignorance*, Homer Lea had quoted from an article by Kaneko Kentarō (1853–1942), a friend of Eiichi's. Kaneko had been a classmate of Theodore Roosevelt's at Harvard, and during the time of the Russo-Japanese War he had been residing in the United States and in touch with Roosevelt. He had played an important role in communications between Japanese foreign minister and chief delegate Komura Jutarō and President Roosevelt. Kaneko had published an article in the *North American Review* (March 1907) concerning peace and amity between the United States and Japan, arguing that it would be impossible for the two countries to become embroiled in war.[116] He described the mutual economic ties between the two countries as backing up his claim. The United States needed silk and tea from Japan, and Japan could not survive without wheat, cotton, and oil from the United States. There were no areas where their economic interests were in conflict. Both countries would go on to open up markets on the Asian continent, but it was clear to anyone that it would be in the interests of both countries to collaborate rather than compete. So, he concluded, he could not see any reason why the two countries should wage war against each other then or in the near future.

Homer Lea flatly rejected such optimism. No matter how prosperous the trade between two countries and no matter how necessary economic cooperation might be, when two countries decide they have to fight each other, they will do so, regardless. The passions of a country and the dynamics of

---

[115] O'Connor, *Pacific Destiny*, p. 352.
[116] "Japan and the United States: Partners," *North American Review* 184, pp. 631–45. https://archive.org/stream/jstor-25105825/25105825_djvu.txt (accessed 11-10-17)

power are always stronger than the forces of economics. Inasmuch as Japan came to acquire a certain predominant power in the Far East, the momentum of that power could not be stopped. Whether it liked it or not, argued Lea, Japan would be drawn forward by that momentum, either to its glory or to its demise, and could only move as determined by its destiny. If that destiny could be changed, it would only be by the power of some other country.

Homer Lea, Jack London, and Willard Straight were all agreed on this observation. All three of these unusual Americans had had very unhappy childhoods. Straight was an orphan, London had been very poor, and Lea burdened by disability, and all three of them died around the age of 40. All three were men of extraordinary intelligence and persuasive writers. Straight's career was to have an enduring impact on the structure of America's Far East policy. The prophecies of Lea and London pointed incisively to the heart of world history with insights that continue to speak to us even today.

The impressions of Japan and the Japanese presented by these writers may have been somewhat exaggerated in some respects, but by and large they were quite accurate. They were right that at the time, Japan was obsessed with its foothold on the continent – to the point of a kind of hysteria – and that they exhibited an abnormal superiority complex toward Chinese and Koreans. That kind of national obsession and ethnic arrogance made a toxic formula bound to touch off disaster in East Asia.

At that juncture, if Japan had genuinely sought peace and had truly wanted to further the cause of friendship and goodwill, there needed to be not only much greater effort at private-sector diplomacy toward the United States but also a complete review and reassessment of national objectives and policy since the Meiji Restoration. That would have involved the reevaluation of not just the Meiji Constitution and the concept of *kokutai* ("national polity"), but all the ideas regarding the "state." Given the tenor of those times, such an effort would have been impossible. Failing to do so, and simply repeating such euphemistic lines as

"Japan seeks peace" and "there are no reasons for war," ended up complicating the problems.

We do not know to what extent Eiichi was aware of these basic problems and understood their import. He may well have been aware of them but ended up avoiding them as irresolvable problems. Given the Confucian and East Asian-history centered education that had shaped Eiichi's thinking, it may have been, however, that he did not possess the means for grasping the realities of the newly evolving world. And of course there is no doubt about his sincerity. I feel only respect and pride in all the efforts Eiichi made as a human being, but from today's vantage point it is most irritating to see that what he was doing was like shooting into the dark; it looked as if he was engaged in a hopelessly hard and long battle that was destined to defeat.

CHAPTER 7

CULTIVATING THE
FRIENDSHIP OF GIANTS

∞

ON FEBRUARY 14, 1913, the head of the Guomindang (Kuomintang) or Nationalist Party of China Sun Yat-sen arrived in Tokyo. Shibusawa Eiichi was one of the many notables who were at Shimbashi Station to welcome him. On that short wintry day made even colder after the sun had set, Sun alighted from the train in high spirits. His comrades, including Dai Tianchou and He Tianjiong, followed close in his shadow. Sun was 47 that year and despite the long and bitter fight he had been through up until then, he looked healthy and displayed an impressive dignity.

A few years earlier, the story goes, when he had lived in the home of democratic revolutionary Miyazaki Tōten (1871–1922) during his exile in Japan,[117] Sun's face in slumber reminded the members of the Miyazaki household, as well as his comrades, of the majesty of a sleeping lion; the indescribable dignity of his countenance was so impressive that they believed that he would surely lead the Chinese revolution to victory, convincing his followers to keep going despite all the hardships that befell them. He carried the aura of a man endowed with a very special destiny.

This was the man who had overthrown the authority and legacy of the Qing dynasty (1644–1912), and in Japan there were high expectations of the new political forces he led. Eiichi attended many of the numerous welcome parties that were held for Sun for days on end after his arrival.

---

[117] Sun had first visited Japan in 1895, but had lived there in exile on and off through 1899–1903 and 1905–1907.

FIGURE 26
Sun Yat-sen (1866–1925), founder of the National-ist Party of China. Photo: Library of Congress, United States.

On the 15th, in a speech at a banquet held at the Peerage Club by the Tōa Dōbunkai (East Asian Common Culture Association), Sun emphasized the importance of friendship between China and Japan and with great earnestness reiterated how absolutely necessary it was for Japan and China to maintain a mutually cooperative relationship, both for the sake of peace and prosperity in East Asia and in order to maintain a balance of power between the forces of the East and the West in Asia. In the face of the often-irrational "Yellow Peril" rhetoric of the time, Sun believed that the West posed a very real "White Peril" for Asia; if nothing were done, the region would be devastated. The only way to prevent the further plunder of Asia was for China and Japan to work together.

Eiichi was deeply moved by Sun's passion and commitment and profoundly impressed by the sincerity with which he tried to appeal to the conscience of Japan's government and private sector. It would be wonderful if a person like Sun were to assume leadership of the disparate forces in China, making it possible to move forward with the modernization of the country. Still, Eiichi could not help worrying whether that would be really possible. It would be no easy task to shepherd such a complex and massive country toward that goal. It was less than a year since the success of the revolution, and already there were rumors of trouble between Sun and Yuan Shikai, the powerful military leader who had been elected "provisional president" of the new Republic of China.

On February 17, Sun visited Eiichi at his Kabutochō office, bringing He Tianjiong with him. Sun explained that he wanted to consult Eiichi regarding the development of the Chinese economy. The conversation extended to politics as well, and with He acting as interpreter, Eiichi told Sun candidly what he had been thinking over the last several days.

Eiichi agreed with Sun that from now on in order to earn the status and respect of the world, the two countries had to, above all else, grow and develop both economically and in their virtues as nations, and forge mutually supportive relations. If, as Sun said, the situation between him and Yuan Shikai was not harmonious, it would be most unfortunate for the two sides to squabble internally, so Eiichi advised, among other things, that Sun should leave the government to Yuan and devote himself entirely to the economic development of China.[118]

There were still many people in Japan at that time who vividly remembered the turmoil that gripped their country at the time of the demise of the old Tokugawa regime and the rise of the new leadership of the government headed by the Meiji emperor. Some compared the situation in China in 1911 to what had happened in Japan in the mid-nineteenth century. They saw Sun Yat-sen and his followers as the "men of high aspiration" who would overthrow the old Chinese regime the way the leaders of the Satsuma and Chōshū domains, driven by idealism, had toppled the Tokugawa government, and there were many

---

[118] The following summary of Eiichi's remarks to Sun is mentioned in *Shibusawa denki shiryō*, vol. 38, pp. 573–74 and vol. 40, p. 81.

who wanted to help and abet Sun's movement. Eiichi went even further, urging Sun to choose the kind of career he himself had chosen, which was to leave the government and devote himself to the world of business in the private sector.

For the modernization of a still undeveloped country, it was self-evident that nothing was more important than the growth of the economy. But countries that face the task of development invariably have many talented people who are active in the world of politics and government and a serious dearth of people who are capable of playing the role of strengthening the country from below through devotion to the world of business. Perhaps this is because the world of politics and government appears to offer more glory and power, producing results more quickly. It is actually in the world of business, precisely because of the seductive power of money, that people of high principle and patriotism are most keenly needed. Without them, the business world would be left to small-minded people who think only of how quickly they can make a profit, and even if there is good government, the standard of living of the people will not improve.

Eiichi recognized that the role he had played in economic affairs over the last four decades of Japanese history had been effective, and in light of that experience he was convinced that for China's modernization to get off the ground, what it needed was to have people of capacities similar to himself, who could put their personal and private interests aside and pursue the wealth of the nation and take the lead in its economic growth. Eiichi's idea was that if Sun Yat-sen could not achieve what he aspired to in the political sphere, there were sure to be plenty of people who would take care of such matters, so he would do well to leave government to them while he pursued the path of enter-prise – in other words, he should follow a path like that Eiichi himself had taken.

He had heard, Eiichi went on, that China had almost inex-haustible resources. It had a distinguished civilization stretch-ing back 5,000 years. It had capable workers. If it had the right scheme for economic development and the right leaders, there was no telling how great and strong a country it would become.

A person like Sun could accomplish great things capable of changing the very nature of world civilization. China held tremendous possibilities that excited the blood even of 73-year-old Eiichi, and he was eager to see the dream fulfilled by the kind of great leader that he could see in Sun Yat-sen.

Sun Yat-sen was apparently quite moved by Eiichi's suggestion. He had founded the Republic of China after an indescribably long and painful journey, but it was still far from the goal that he had in mind. The rivalry posed by Yuan Shikai was one thing, but the conspiracies and stratagems of the Western powers with whom Yuan had linked hands posed almost insurmountable obstacles to the way forward. And Eiichi's arguments made sense in more than one way. No matter who took the lead in China's government, it was clear that the country had to develop economically. That development would, moreover, go hand in hand with far-reaching social revolution, and was therefore very close to Sun's objectives. Sun Yat-sen could see, too, the desirability of building close ties, through Eiichi's cooperation, with the Japanese business world.

Still, Sun Yat-sen was by nature a man of politics, and he was not endowed with the kind of intuitive sense for economic affairs from which Eiichi had so benefited, so he must have found it difficult to imagine himself as a businessman. He told Eiichi that he would think carefully about which path he should take and for the time being, he earnestly reiterated his hope that Eiichi would offer his cooperation and support for the reconstruction of the Chinese economy.

Eiichi proposed the establishment of a Sino-Japanese joint venture with Sun at the helm. He promptly consulted with Masuda Takashi, Yamamoto Jōtarō, Ōkura Kihachirō, and others, and after discussing the plan with government leaders, he began to make specific preparations.

This was not the first time Eiichi had become involved in projects relating to China. In 1907, he had established the Nisshin (Japan-China) Steamship Company; in 1909 he had organized the Nisshin (Japan-China) Research Society for the Promotion of Enterprise to study conditions for business in China and explore the possibilities for investment there. As the extension of those efforts, he created a company called Toa Kōgyō that assisted with investment for the Nanxun Railway centering on Jiangxi province and an electric power company called Hankou Shuidian Gongsi.

What he undertook in 1913, however, was the first attempt to create a genuine joint-venture company, and it was arranged that there would be the same number of directors from both countries. The corporation would be established with dual nationality under the laws of both countries.

Sun understood what Eiichi had in mind, and on March 3 and 4 Sun himself and the people involved gathered at the Mitsui Shūkaijo, the Mitsui family's guesthouse, to discuss the establishment of the new company. They decided to call it the Chūgoku Kōgyō Kabushiki Kaisha (China Industrial Development Co., Ltd.) and they drafted its by-laws. Meanwhile, Eiichi took every opportunity to explain to Sun about ways to reform the Chinese currency system and bank organization, telling him in detail about Japan's experiences in the early years of the Meiji regime. China might be a gigantic country, but as long as different currencies were circulating in different regions, it would be difficult to build economic foundations for the country. He argued that the currency system ought to be rapidly brought under central control, a central bank established, and finances unified. He did his best to pass on his expertise in as specific terms as possible to his gifted guest.

On March 5, Sun Yat-sen left Tokyo, traveling by train through Japan on his way back to China. Eiichi went to Tokyo's Shimbashi Station to see him off, and Sun bade him farewell with great courtesy. Sun boarded the train at 10:00 a.m. When he reached Nagasaki Station several weeks later, however, sad news awaited him. Song Jiaoren, who had taken over for him during his absence, had been assassinated (March 22). The perpetrators were rumored to be Yuan Shikai's men, and Sun Yat-sen was filled with grief and anger as he wrote straight away to Eiichi saying that he had been deeply impressed by Eiichi's arguments and had been thinking of leaving politics to others and devoting himself to economic construction, but with things having come to this pass, he found that he really could not wash his hands of politics. He was sorry to disappoint Eiichi and that he might not live up to his expectations, but hoped Eiichi would understand.

It was a fine letter, full of feeling, and Eiichi was deeply moved and treasured the letter thereafter, but sadly it was burned in fires that broke out at the time of the Great Kanto Earthquake of 1923. (The letter shown in Fig. 27 is a later example of Sun's correspondence with Eiichi.)

The organization of the joint venture continued on course, however, and the first meeting of its promoters was held on March 20. The following prospectus was sent out to the people concerned:

Chūgoku Kōgyō Kabushiki Kaisha (China Industrial Development Co., Ltd.)

Closer economic linkages will be absolutely necessary in order to forge even closer ties between the two great nations of similar traditions in East Asia and facilitate cooperation and collaboration between them. To this end, leading entrepreneurs of the two countries have come together to show sincerity and commitment toward a great plan for the coming century in East Asia, and hereby propose the establishment of the China-Japan joint venture Chūgoku Kōgyō Kabushiki Kaisha.

Today, a new China has been proclaimed and the enhancement of the strength of the nation is an urgent task. The Chūgoku Kōgyō, therefore, will explore the rich resources to be found in China, examine potential projects that will bring profits, and thereby help to enhance the Chinese economy under the joint responsibility of Chinese and Japanese. We believe we have made clear the purpose and necessity of establishing the company in the by-laws that are attached to this document.

March 1913

Representing the promoters
Sun Wen [Sun Yat-sen]
Shibusawa Eiichi

On the Japan side, the payment for shares in the company was completed by the end of June, a founding office was established, and Eiichi was made chairman of the founding committee. Businessman and later politician Mori Kaku (1882–1932) was active as liaison with the China side, but as Yuan Shikai's pressure against the faction led by Sun Yat-sen intensified and Sun's long-time cohorts Hu Hanmin (1879–1936) and Li Liejun (1882–1946) were exiled and the inevitability of civil war was growing, little progress was made.

In writing to Sun to apprise him of the developments regarding the joint venture in Japan, Eiichi expressed his concern about the suffering of the people and the intervention by the Western powers that were likely to ensue should civil war break out, advising "patience and restraint" and urging him to adhere to endurance and quietly wait for the right time to act. That time should not be far away. In ancient China, Eiichi added, Zhang Gongyun is said to have responded to a question from the emperor by having the character "patience" written 100 times and showing the writing to the emperor. Eiichi thus advised Sun that he should wait for the time for his leadership to ripen. Another letter from Sun, which told about the anguish he was suffering, arrived before Eiichi's letter had reached him, so Eiichi wrote again,

> . . . I do most vividly imagine your present state of mind. It is a most unbearable situation you are in. It is my fervent hope that you will marshal the forbearance to endure [these trials], quietly conserving your energies for the eventual victory that is sure to be yours. As your friend, it goes without saying that I stand ready now, as in the past and in the future, to offer what encouragement and favor I can muster in support of your endeavors.

Since the funds that had been collected to launch the venture could not just be left to lie idle, the founding general meeting of the Chūgoku Kōgyō was convened at the Tokyo Chamber of Commerce on August 11. Eiichi served as chairman of the meeting and Mori Kaku acted as the representative for the Chinese side. Eiichi led the discussion. They decided that there would

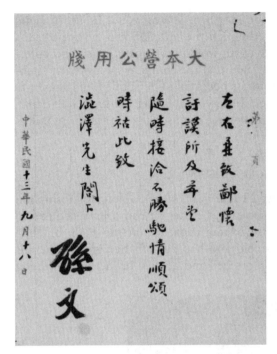

FIGURE 27
A September 18, 1924
letter from Sun Yat-sen
to Eiichi. Photo: Shibu-
sawa Memorial Museum.

be three directors each from the Japanese and Chinese sides and that Sun Yat-sen would be nominated as president, leaving the post vacant for the time being. Kurachi Tetsukichi, former vice minister of the Japanese foreign ministry, became vice president. Eiichi, along with businessmen Nakano Buei and Yamamoto Jōtarō took up the positions of advisors.

In September, the turmoil in China worsened. Yuan Shikai occupied Nanjing and on October 5 was officially named president of the Republic of China, forcing Sun Yat-sen and his faction into exile a second time. In due course, Yuan Shikai contacted Eiichi saying that he wanted the Chūgoku Kōgyō project to stay on course and stating that the new government was ready to underwrite the shares that Sun Yat-sen had planned to provide.

When Eiichi contacted Sun in exile, Sun said that the plan had been aimed at the economic development of China; it would not matter which side, north or south, would be at the helm of the government. Although the situation had developed such that the forces of the north would participate, he had no objections. Since Sun indicated that the company having been established, he was eager for its potential to be fulfilled, the name was changed to Chū-Nichi Jitsugyō Kabushiki Kaisha (China-Japan Business Co., Ltd.), and Yang Ziqi, spokesman for Yuan Shikai, took office as president.

THE DEATH OF TOKUGAWA YOSHINOBU

Then, on November 22 that year (1913), Tokugawa Yoshinobu passed away. From somewhat earlier he had been scheduled to visit Eiichi at his Asukayama residence on the 15th, but had had symptoms of a cold and had put off the visit to rest. His condition suddenly worsened and he died in the early morning

FIGURE 28
Tokugawa Yoshinobu (1837–1913), last of the Tokugawa shoguns. Photo: National Diet Library, Japan.

of the 22nd. Apprised of his condition, Eiichi hastened to the Tokugawa house in Koishikawa Dairokuten, but it was already too late; his former lord and long-time friend was gone.

Throughout Eiichi's life, the man his senior by three years who had been the fifteenth and last Tokugawa shogun had been a special presence – someone for whom Eiichi could show his love and respect without qualification. Their relationship was not one of politics, nor yet framed by economic interests; it had begun as the feudal era came to an end from the age-old sentiments binding lord and retainer and had flourished thereafter into a deep mutual respect. Yoshinobu, moreover, was a man of unyielding character who was never swayed by whatever the affection or respect held in him – he had attained an extraordinarily firm aloofness that was undisturbed by the views of others.

Yoshinobu was an unusual figure, known for his erudition, his keen political acumen, and his capacity for bold decision making. Once the new regime under Emperor Meiji took over, however, he withdrew completely from the public eye and lived a quiet and leisurely life, maintaining contact with only a few people, including Eiichi. In 1910, Yoshinobu had passed on the leadership of the Tokugawa house to his son Yoshihisa, but at Yoshinobu's request, Eiichi served as financial advisor and overseer of accounts for the family.

Publication of the biography of Yoshinobu was a lifelong project for Eiichi, and although initially Yoshinobu tried to avoid involvement, he had begun to take pleasure in the plan; before his death he started reading the manuscript and adding comments, and he had taken to attending the editorial meetings, enjoying responding to questions and telling stories of former times. Eiichi had hoped that somehow the book could be printed while Yoshinobu was still alive so that he could present it to him, and was greatly disappointed that that was not to be.

On December 1, at the funeral hall in Ueno, the purple curtains emblazoned with the white hollyhock-leaf crest that was the hallmark of the Tokugawa family fluttered in the breeze – a once-common sight that had not been seen for many a year. As head of the Funeral Committee, Eiichi had assumed responsibility for the arrangements. The Tokyo City Assembly sent a message of condolence representing the unanimous approval of its members; the City Hall and the streetcars all flew banners of mourning, and citizens refrained from public entertainments in sympathy for the passing of the last head of the long line of shoguns. The funeral was attended by representatives of the emperor, the empress and the empress dowager, as well as by Tokugawa Iesato, heir to the main Tokugawa family, the heads of the Gosanke (the three branches of the Tokugawa Clan) – Tokugawa Yorimichi of Kishū (Wakayama prefecture), Tokugawa Yoshichika of Owari (Aichi prefecture), and Tokugawa Kuniyuki of Mito (Ibaraki prefecture) – along with various former daimyo and numerous former direct vassals of the shogun.

That day, Eiichi presented a poem dedicated to the repose of the soul of his late lord.

> For fifty years a model citizen under the new regime
> That noble countenance is now a divine spirit
> A man so sincere and devoted is assured a place in heaven
> And the echoes of his name resonate far and wide

EIICHI'S 1914 TRIP TO CHINA

On May 2, 1914, Eiichi set sail from Kobe on a ship named the *Chiyō Maru* on a trip to China, stopping by Nagasaki and arriving in Shanghai the morning of the 6th. His account of the voyage tells how from the previous evening the muddy waters of the Yangtze River could be seen mingling with the seas. Even the water supply was muddy and no one had been able to take baths.

In the autumn of the previous year, Eiichi had received a courteous invitation from Yuan Shikai, who had then just become president of the new regime, to visit China. Yuan had said that, with the matter of the Chū-Nichi Jitsugyō Kabushiki Kaisha (China-Japan Co., Ltd.) having been settled, he now wanted to hear Eiichi's advice on the reconstruction of the Chinese economy as well as request Eiichi's cooperation in that endeavor. Having been well-versed in the Chinese classics and familiar with literary references to its landscapes from his youth, Eiichi had been eager to see the sights of China for himself, and he especially had wanted to pay his respects at the grave of Confucius in Shandong's Qufu. However, it had happened that he was suffering from asthma that autumn and was unable to go to China at that time.

By early 1914, Eiichi had recovered his health, and since the problems in China had grown even more entangled and were becoming even more significant factors affecting the future of Japan as well, he decided that he would go and have a look for himself, taking up Yuan Shikai's invitation.

Several decades earlier, Eiichi had stopped by Shanghai, in 1867, on his way to France. He had also visited there with Masuda Takashi in 1877. At the time 36 years old, he had been on audacious business: as president of the Dai-ichi Bank he had gone to extend a loan to the Chinese government. Rebellions had broken out in Shaanxi and Gansu provinces, and Japan had been approached with a request to lend the Chinese government war funds for General Zuo Zongtang (Tso Tsung-t'ang) to put down the rebellion. General Zuo was well known for having suppressed the Taiping Rebellion, and it was rumored that the British-aligned Hong Kong-Shanghai Bank was among sources that were actively providing the general with financial support. The Japanese finance minister at the time happened to be Ōkuma Shigenobu, and Eiichi's 1877 mission to China had been decided when Ōkuma said that the government would come up with the money, but that it would be best for the loan to be negotiated through the Dai-ichi Bank.

Ultimately, the two sides had been unable to agree on terms, so the loan had not been provided, but the Shanghai Eiichi had seen in 1877 was still that of old China. When he arrived in 1914, he found it completely changed. Huge factories and warehouses lined both banks of the Huangpu River, modern port facilities had been completed, and he was surprised to find that the townscape had been completely Westernized.

Shanghai had a chamber of commerce composed of influential persons, and this organization sponsored a welcome for

Eiichi, bringing together people from both government and the private sector. Many leaders of modern Chinese industry were present, including Sheng Xuanhuai (1844–1916), president of the Hanyehping Iron and Coal Corporation; Chinese financial world leaders like Tang Shaoyi (1862–1938) and Wu Tingfang (1842–1922). In the evening there was an exhibit of old calligraphic works and paintings, and poetry writing and painting demonstrations were provided as entertainment, as was typical of traditional banquets in China.

Even among leading figures in China, Eiichi's popularity was rather unusual. Quite apart from the breadth of his knowledge of the classics and the depth of his understanding of China attained through his study of the teachings of Confucius and Mencius, Eiichi was different from most Japanese in that he was not bound by conventions but lived by his own views and convictions. That trait seemed to be transmitted to others even without him explaining himself, creating an affinity between them. A veteran China hand and supporter of Eiichi's activities in China, Shiraiwa Ryūhei (1867–1942) observed that "this gathering of drinking and poetry composition was like nothing held heretofore and was, I believe, an extraordinary moment in the history of Japan-China affairs. It hardly needs saying that Mr. Shibusawa is highly and deeply respected for his virtues among the Chinese people."[119] Eiichi was beginning to carve a special place among Chinese, as he had done among Americans, as the kind of Japanese they could respect.

From Shanghai, Eiichi proceeded by train to Hangzhou, where he visited the grave of the famed Han dynasty general Yue Fei on the banks of the famous West Lake and in Suzhou he toured the Hanshan (Cold Mountain) Temple, celebrated in a famous poem – *Night Mooring at Maple Bridge* – by eighth-century Chinese poet Zhang Ji, and enjoyed tea served by a monk there. Moved by the beauty of the landscape after the rain had stopped, Eiichi composed a Chinese-style poem:

船到楓橋曙色明 *My boat reaches Maple Bridge in a clear dawn*
姑蘇城外雨初晴 *Rain subsides outside Suzhou city*

---

[119] Shiraishi, *Shibusawa Eiichi-O*, p. 168.

新鐘補古寒山寺 *Fresh sounds from old Hanshan Temple*
一杵先聞夜半声 *I earlier heard its midnight bell*

Every sight and sound in the old temple and its vicinity impressed him greatly, and yet he was aghast at the poverty of the people of the region. Was there no one concerned about the situation resulting from turmoil of revolution and rebellion associated with the prolonged decline of the Qing dynasty? he wondered. Many people were emaciated and clad only in rags. The poverty seemed worse in the towns, and the streets were filled with refuse and the worst sort of filth.

While in Suzhou, Eiichi was invited to lunch at politician and businessman Sheng Xuanhuai's villa – a large-scale estate which was called Liu Yuan ("Lingering Garden") because once one entered, its beauty was so entrancing one never wanted to leave.

He then went to Nanjing, a grand metropolis during the Six Dynasties period (222–589), though by 1914 it had been reduced to quite a sorry state by subsequent strife and war. Eiichi got off the train and continued his journey up the Yangtze by boat. There he saw the "Red Cliffs" made famous in a poem by the Song-period poet Su Shi (1037–1101) and the Xunyang river nearby. He enjoyed every moment of the time seeing these and other noted places that were familiar by name to the many Japanese of the day who had gained their education by studying Chinese classics and literature.

Eiichi had known beforehand, of course, how big and vast a country China was, but the reality before his eyes impressed him deeply. He had not quite imagined, for example, the immense and sedate flow of the Yangtze river, or the leisurely tempo of people's lives in the area that was difficult for the always-busy Japanese to fully fathom. He learned of people who would cut down trees in the forests upstream, lash them together into rafts, build a shed on the raft and even a plot of garden and raise their children on it as they slowly floated down the river. When they reached the delta after about a year, they would take apart the raft and sell the timber. Using the money, they would travel back upriver to their origins and start over again – and there were many who lived that way. He had been astonished by the vastness of the United States, but this was something else again.[120]

The Daye Iron Mine, too, was of even more mammoth scale than he had expected. It was larger even than the great Butte mines he had seen in the American state of Montana. The whole mine was iron ore and it was mined in open-cuts in the same way as gravel. Overwhelmed by the gigantic scale and quantity of resources that were hardly imaginable in a small country like Japan, Eiichi could only gaze in amazement.

At Hankou he boarded the train once more. Since he was visiting China at the invitation of President Yuan Shikai, his train travel was funded by the government and his meals on the train were courtesy of China-Japan Business president Yang Ziqi. For 40 hours, the train traveled northward over seemingly endless plains and on May 19 at 5:00 P.M., arrived in Beijing, where

Figure 29
Yuan Shikai (1859–1916), leader of China when Eiichi visited in 1914. Photo: Library of Congress, United States.

[120] *Shibusawa denki shiryō*, vol. 32, p. 591.

he was met by government leaders and leading businessmen, Japanese consul Yamaza Enjirō (1866–1914), councilor Mizuno Kōkichi (1873–1914), and others. He had met Mizuno five years earlier in New York, when he was serving as consul of Japan there. The Ministry of Foreign Affairs had assigned him, along with his wife, to take care of matters relating to the commercial commissioners on their observation tour of the United States.

On May 21, Eiichi was to meet with President Yuan Shikai at his official residence in the Zhongnanhai imperial garden in central Beijing, known even today as the headquarters from which China is ruled. His host was the leader of a massive country, and it would later be rumored that Yuan sought to make himself emperor. Eiichi had assumed that the ritual he would have to perform to meet Yuan would be even more elaborate than that to meet Japan's own emperor. However, it turned out to be very simple. As soon as Eiichi made his appearance, Yuan rose to meet him casually, extending his hand and leading him to a seat. The interview lasted for about an hour and Eiichi recalled finding his host much more modest than he had expected.

Their conversation seemed endless, beginning with Eiichi's itinerary and extending to the subjects of Japan-China relations, economic development, and the famous ancient sites of the city of Beijing. Yuan said that relations between the two countries could be traced very far back and had by no means been built in a day. Still, in order to put their relations on a normal standing, their economic ties had to be very close. It was because he realized this that he had had Yang Ziqi involved in the China-Japan Business Company, and he was eager to benefit even more from Eiichi's guidance on the economy from now on as well. Yuan was extremely kind from the beginning of the interview to the end, promising to facilitate Eiichi's journey and lodgings on the anticipated trip to visit the grave of Confucius.

At the time in Japan, Yuan Shikai was being greatly vilified in the Japanese press, where he was portrayed as a scheming plotter and unscrupulous strategist. Upon meeting him face to face, however, Eiichi found him to be perfectly natural and refined of character, obviously a person of outstanding caliber. Of course, considering that he was the central figure who survived and thrived in the most complicated political situation one can imagine, it would not be surprising that he was skilled at bargaining and likely to deal ruthlessly with his foes. But Eiichi concluded that he was not a fundamentally bad person, but one who would become a central figure in Japan-China relations from then on. The fact that the Japanese media and public opinion tended to heap foul language and abuse even on such figures of a massive country like China filled Eiichi with dread.

Eiichi must have begun to realize that his countrymen had acquired a completely unjustified sense of superiority regarding China and the Chinese people; Japanese arrogance was almost out of hand. His countrymen seemed completely devoid of the sense of love and respect that Eiichi believed was the basis of friendship between peoples. It was unlikely that Japanese would ever win the trust of the Chinese people if they acted like that.

Another thing that worried Eiichi was that Japanese foreign policy toward China was divided into three separate strands. One was that of the Ministry of Foreign Affairs, which focused on dealing with China and the Western powers with interests in China. The second was the foreign policy of Japan's military, which tended to an extremely forceful line oriented to defending and expanding Japan's interests on the continent – especially in Korea and in Manchuria. And the third was the overseas actions of the so-called "Shina rōnin," who protected Chinese revolutionaries exiled in Japan, stirred up trouble in China, and from time to time went off to China where they would get involved in the activities of secret societies and revolutionary militias, appealing hysterically for direct action.[121] And there were no links among these three strands, with each going its own way.

Of course, China was not blameless. The country was in a constant state of turmoil, a near free-for-all of battling factions and shifting loyalties among groups which reminded Japanese

---

[121] Variously translated as "China adventurers" or "China ruffians," these "Shina ronin" were usually agents of a variety of Japanese "patriotic" secret societies.

of their own "Warring States" era of medieval times. Sometimes Chinese pronouncements were quite self-serving, making no attempt to take the interests of other countries in the region into account. Japan would sometimes have to adopt a firm and resolute stance, but still Eiichi could not countenance actions that were cold-blooded and calculating, devoid of all respect for human dignity.

The way things were going, it would be only natural if China, not to mention other countries, came to despise Japan. Even if it might be difficult to completely trust businessmen, a situation must be preserved in which at least they would not be hated. Chinese students in Japan ought to be treated with greater hospitality and friendship. More should be done to cultivate good relations between the two peoples. Between China and Japan, as between the United States and Japan, Eiichi realized keenly in Beijing in the early summer of 1914 that there was an urgent need for private-level diplomacy.

On May 23, the unexpected took place. Councilor Mizuno, who had been busily looking after Eiichi and his entourage until two or three days before, suddenly died. Apparently, he had developed a stomach ulcer and had been rushed to a hospital for an operation, and though Eiichi hastened to pay him a visit, he had already passed away. Mizuno's passing came as a great shock to Eiichi and his entourage.

The plan for May 25 had been to tour the Ming Tombs and see the Great Wall. Eiichi was troubled by what would happen following Mizuno's demise, but he was a traveler so he decided to keep going as planned. They took the train to Nankou and then it was a tiring three-hour ride, tossed in a palanquin, before they reached their destination. The weather was clear and sunny and when around noon the wind picked up, they were engulfed in a dust storm in which they could not open their eyes. They could tell that the term "kōjin banjō" (Ch. *huangchen wanzhang*), or "yellow dust clouds one million fathoms high and deep" was not hyperbole. It was certainly reassuring to have their party protected front and back by several dozen members of mounted guard provided by the government.

Six hours in a dust-filled palanquin apparently took its toll on the 74-year old man, and just after completing the trip from Beijing to Tianjin on the following day, Eiichi's health took a turn for the worse. After a luncheon at the Japanese consulate, by the time he returned to his lodgings, he was totally exhausted and decided to cancel his afternoon itinerary and go to bed early.

The next day it was hot and humid, and from the hotel window they could see a huge cloud of dust hovering over the city of Tianjin. The wind that had begun to blow when they were in Nankou showed no sign of ceasing, and it seemed that not only Beijing and Tianjin but the whole northern part of the country was enveloped in dust storms. Feverish and groaning in his bed from morning, Eiichi was confronted with more shocking news.

Consul Yamaza, who had the very day before seen them off at the train station in Beijing, had had a sudden heart attack and died. The confusion and dismay at the Japanese consulate can only be imagined, and Eiichi and his companions were thoroughly unnerved by this succession of tragic events.

The old saying went that when something happens in twos, there is bound to be a third time as well. Before anything else untoward could happen, argued a senior member of Eiichi's group, Dai-Nippon Beer president Magoshi Kyōhei (1844–1933), the group ought to cut short their plans and return to Japan. Magnanimous and easy-going, Magoshi was known for his forthright way of speaking, but now, apparently thoroughly spooked by the death of the two Japanese consuls, he pressed Eiichi to decide on an immediate return to Japan.

For Eiichi, the main purpose of his sightseeing in China had been the planned visit to Confucius's tomb, and as he did not consider his own illness to be all that serious, he was very reluctant to cancel the rest of the trip. Still, given the hot weather and dust-filled air that was difficult to bear, as well as poor public transport and lodging facilities, Eiichi was "worried that if my chronic condition should take a turn for the worse while we are in Jinan or in some out of the way place on our way to Qufu, it would place the whole group in difficulties; so I thought we had no choice but to follow the urging of the others and change our plans." As soon as Eiichi's condition improved enough, he resolved therefore that they would go by German steamship from Tianjin to Dalian, and from there change ships and go back to Japan.[122] Sadly, this alteration in his travel plans meant that Eiichi was never able to pay respects at the tomb of Confucius, the sage whose thoughts and writings meant so much to him.

WORLD WAR I AND THE TWENTY-ONE DEMANDS

In August of 1914, World War I broke out in Europe. It began as a confrontation between Britain and Germany over their spheres of influence, but its effects had far-reaching impact on politics in the Far East and on the relations among the United States, China, and Japan.

On August 16, Prime Minister Ōkuma Shigenobu invited 40 leading businessmen, Eiichi included, to his official residence. He explained the government's policy regarding the war and asked for their cooperation. Based on its friendship with Britain under the Anglo-Japanese Alliance, he said, the Japanese military would take over all the German colonies and military bases in the Far East and would issue an ultimatum to Germany of its intentions. Of course, German acquiescence to a Japanese take-over was not anticipated and Ōkuma talked as if a declaration of war against Germany would soon be issued, to be followed immediately by attacks on German-held Jiaozhou (Kiaochow) Bay, Qingdao, and islands in the Southern Pacific.

As usual, Eiichi was unhappy with the Japanese proclivity for war. Since the takeover of Taiwan in 1874, Japan had been involved in a war nearly every ten years, and each time, the economy, which Eiichi and his cohorts had finally built up to a certain stage of prosperity, took a serious blow. Although the demand stimulated by the war would seem to partially increase the economy's strength, in fact the toll of raised taxes and the rising cost of goods placed an ever-increasing burden on ordinary people. Of all the post-1868 wars so far, the scars of the

---

[122] *Shibusawa denki shiryō*, vol. 57, p. 121, and vol. 32, p. 550. According to Eiichi's diary, the group left China on May 30.

Russo-Japanese War were the deepest and the country had still not completely recovered from them.

Foreign Minister Katō Takaaki had been repeatedly stating that pursuing territorial ambitions was not part of Japanese foreign policy, but of course that was a complete fiction.[123] One gets the impression that it was from around this time that the number of lies included in statements of the Japanese government began to sharply increase. Indeed, it seemed that officials had no compunction about portraying black as white – what was blatant malfeasance was committed as if it were perfectly righteous. Emperor Meiji, a strong figure who had assumed final responsibility for the country's actions, had died in 1912. After

FIGURE 30
Katō Takaaki (1860–1926), foreign minister in 1914 at the outbreak of World War I. Photo: National Diet Library, Japan.

[123] According to Nish, *Japanese Foreign Policy*, pp. 93–95, Kato was "the leading sponsor" of the policy that Japan should join in the war on Britain's side as Japan could "use this occasion to build up even more strongly her position in east Asia."

that, bureaucratic politics conducted in the name of the (less forceful Taishō) emperor increased. The credibility gap widened even more. Japan completely lost the trust of other countries. That loss of trust was to culminate in the Greater East Asia Joint Declaration of 1943.

No sooner had the much-anticipated deadline for the ultimatum issued to Germany come in August 1914 than Japan sent in a huge army, prepared in advance, and occupied the Shandong peninsula and Jiaozhou Bay. Having obtained that leverage, it launched a mass rush for as many interests as it could obtain throughout China. The Western powers, which had long placed pressure on Japan, preventing it from attaining its ambitions on the continent, had suddenly begun to fight with one another on their own continent; they had abruptly retreated from the Asian stage. Taking advantage of the situation, the Japanese government began to pursue its ambitions virtually unchallenged, leading to the infamous Twenty-One Demands presented to Yuan Shikai in January 1915.

Yuan responded to the unbelievably arrogant and one-sided demands of the Japanese government with supremely skillful bargaining. First, he swiftly published the content of the Twenty-One Demands in the newspapers, completely undermining the desperate attempts of the Japanese side to keep them secret, and after winning over the support of world public opinion, he dragged out the negotiations and began to whittle down the Japanese demands.

Assiduously assisting the Chinese side in this effort was the American consul in Beijing, Paul S. Reinsch. Like Willard Straight of earlier times, Reinsch harbored a fierce anger and hatred toward the high-handed tactics of Japan. To Washington, he sent forceful telegrams urging U.S. intervention in order to protect the territorial integrity of China, and he provided consistent friendship and close advice to Yuan Shikai and his government. So extreme was Reinsch's anti-Japan, pro-China stance that the Japanese embassy in Washington was moved to lodge a protest with the U.S. State Department. The Wilson administration of the time was preoccupied with affairs in Europe and did not take any immediate initiatives, but Reinsch's tenacious pressuring was later to prompt active American efforts to contain Japanese expansion backed up by America's increasing national strength.

On May 7, Prime Minister Ōkuma again invited Eiichi and seven other leading bankers to his official residence. This time he declared that Japan had decided to issue an ultimatum to China, and he looked forward to their cooperation with the war that was sure to come. Since issuing the Twenty-One Demands, Japan had made major concessions, but Yuan Shikai and his government were stubbornly resisting and would not comply with Japan's demands, so the Japanese government had decided that the next step was to declare war.

Eiichi had done his best to cooperate on many occasions before, but this time he balked. Until then he had made it a point not to criticize the government in public venues, but now he answered reporters' questions freely, giving his real and candid views without restraint, and his remarks appeared all at once in many newspapers.

> [Japan] should take neither too soft nor too hard a line with China. Simply squandering money and applying force does not work. We ought to be more thoughtful. Mean-spirited torture of the weak is wrong. Foreign affairs should not be conducted like street peddlers demanding inflated prices; it should be honest and forthright. (*Yorozu chōhō*[124])

The Twenty-One Demands came into being by putting together the wish-lists of the Army, Navy, and the various ministries of the Japanese government, but it was rumored that the situation for Japan had worsened during the negotiations as China tried hard to reduce these various demands. The bargaining reminded Eiichi of the tactics of merchants and customers at fly-by-night street stalls set up at festivals and local fairs.

> Why has the government not presented demands more forthrightly, conditions that could be accepted from the outset without creating misunderstandings in China and forcing Japan to make concessions

---

[124] *Shibusawa denki shiryō*, vol. 48, p. 687.

later? If they had done it properly, it would not have taken 100 days, nor required Japan to deliver an ultimatum, or cause a commotion by sending in troops. The matter ought to have been settled in a matter of 30 days. (*Tokyo Asahi shimbun*[125])

Japanese who talk of China never fail to mention the importance of interdependent relations between the two countries like "lips and teeth; wheels and the cart," but if their behavior is lacking in genuine friendship and amity, there will be no hope of attaining what they so earnestly desire. It can't be helped if the vast disparity between the initial demands and the result leaves the impression that our assertions were "inflated" to begin with. How can we hope to earn the trust of others if we behave like that? And there are certain duties that go along with friendship . . . I believe that our people ought to pay close attention to how they should behave toward Chinese from now on. (*Jiji shinpō*[126])

It is very doubtful, however, that Japanese at that time really understood what it was that so worried Eiichi. They were a people who tended to be easily caught up in boastful talk of pro-war proponents and lose all track of good sense and reason. Even the *Ryūmon zasshi*, published by those who saw Eiichi as their mentor, reported on the meeting at the prime minister's office as follows:

We all, from Seien-sensei [Eiichi] down, agree that, for Japan to be able to lay down a long-term plan for its future and for perpetual peace in the Far East, at this juncture the government should take the toughest stance it could and resolutely pursue all its demands and conditions. We pledge to serve our country unsparingly should diplomatic relations be broken. We hear that the bankers have agreed to be ready any time to provide the market with billions of yen worth of funds. Fortunately, the Yuan government has come to its senses and the problem will likely be settled peacefully, to the benefit for both China and Japan.[127]

Since misguided statements like this were accepted as making perfect sense at the time, it was at this point, we might say, that

---

[125] *Shibusawa denki shiryō*, vol. 48, p. 687.
[126] *Shibusawa denki shiryō*, vol. 48, p. 687.
[127] *Shibusawa denki shiryō*, vol. 48, p. 686.

FIGURE 31
Yūaikai president Suzuki
Bunji. Photo: Courtesy
of Yuai Labor Historical
Museum, Japan.

Japan's fate was decided. With Japanese troops on standby in Manchuria and Shandong and international support for China ineffective, Yuan had no alternative but to accept the latest Japanese ultimatum and sign two treaties which embodied the key components of the Twenty-One Demands.

LABOR AND THE U.S. IMMIGRATION ISSUES

It was around this time in 1915 that Eiichi was busy making arrangements for labor group Yūaikai president Suzuki Bunji to attend the California State Federation of Labor convention. With the passage of the California Alien Land Law in May 1913, the issue of Japanese immigration had entered a new phase, and the idea of making contact with leaders of American labor unions as a means for dealing with it had been advanced by Sidney Gulick, a professor at Doshisha University in Kyoto, and collaborator with Eiichi in the "doll exchange" project. Gulick had gone back to the United States a couple of years earlier and had done some research on the issue of Japanese exclusion before he arrived at the conclusion that the problem was closely related to labor unions in the United States. In other words, he found that at the root of the exclusionism was not only the element of racism but also the fear of losing jobs. So after returning to Japan, he visited Eiichi and other people of influence and suggested that it would be useful if leaders of Japan's labor movement were to make contact with people in American labor groups.[128]

Eiichi quickly consulted socialist Abe Isoo and economist Soeda Juichi on the matter, and they decided that Suzuki Bunji of the Yūaikai would be a good candidate. Suzuki was the figure who could be called the pioneer of Japan's labor movement. After graduating from Tokyo University, Suzuki had joined the socialist movement and was active in the Yūaikai, which he had founded in 1912 as an organization to improve the living conditions and status of workers.

Eiichi had long been seriously interested in the labor movement, but this was his first opportunity to meet someone directly involved in it. He met Suzuki two or three times to encourage him to go to the United States and was well impressed with him. Suzuki was even more serious-minded than he had heard and very willing to take initiatives. For Suzuki's part, he told Eiichi that he had long wanted to see the labor movement in other parts of the world, so he was eager to take up the opportunity. He consulted the leaders of the Yūaikai and decided to go with another leader in the group named Yoshimatsu Sadaya.

During the month of May 1915, Eiichi visited the Ministry of Foreign Affairs twice to talk with vice-minister Matsui Keishirō and appeal for permission for the two to travel to the United States. He had to explain a great deal, because, since the issuing of the Gentlemen's Agreement in 1907, Japan had not issued passports for Japanese workers to emigrate to the United States, and in addition general awareness of what the labor movement in Japan was all about was very poor. Even in the Ministry of

---

[128] *Shibusawa denki shiryō*, vol. 31, p. 421.

Foreign Affairs, the notion that there was a connection between the laws excluding Japanese and the labor movement in the United States was completely new.

Suzuki Bunji later recalled his own encounter with foreign ministry officials.

> The matter was finally settled after a discussion between Trade and Commerce Bureau director general Sakata and myself. Sakata made it clear that the foreign ministry had no intention of asking labor leaders like me to help the ministry solve the immigration problem between Japan and the United States. But he said he had heard that I was dedicated to the welfare of workers, and he thought that was praiseworthy. In recognition of my efforts, he would approve my trip to the United States as a kind of "study abroad." I said I didn't care what the reason was, since whether we were right about the [immigration-cum-labor] problem would eventually become clear; I just hoped he would quickly grant permission for our passports, and excused myself.[129]

On June 19, 1915 Suzuki and Yoshimatsu departed on the *Chiyō Maru* for the United States. After the two arrived in California, they were initially blocked from attending local labor meetings and encountered many difficulties, but eventually they were able to attend the California State Federation of Labor convention and the American Federation of Labor convention as Japanese delegates. Suzuki spoke confidently in English at both conventions. The two apparently made a good impression on the members of the American labor unions and they were able to establish friendly relations with AFL chairman Samuel Gompers and California state AFL secretary Paul Scharrenberg. Setting aside the extent to which these connections were actually effective, their trip did open up a new dimension in efforts on the Japanese side to solve the immigration problem.

The acquaintance with Suzuki that began with this private diplomacy initiative gave Eiichi direct contact with Japan's labor movement for the first time, and it was to open the way for his direct mediation in a number of labor disputes after that time.

---

129 Suzuki, *Rōdō undō nijūnen*, pp. 113–114.

Suzuki, too, was greatly stimulated by what he saw and heard firsthand about the American labor movement, and the Yūaikai rapidly expanded. From about 6,500 members at the time of Suzuki's departure for California it soon grew to more than 10,000.

CULTIVATING FAVORABLE IMPRESSIONS

On October 23 of that year, Eiichi sailed from Yokohama aboard the *Shun'yō Maru* for his third trip to the United States. His diary notes that he left home at 9:00 a.m. and after dropping by prime minister Ōkuma Shigenobu's private residence to bid farewell, arrived around noon at Tokyo Station, the grand new building for which had been completed the previous year, .

On the platform there to see off the 75-year-old Eiichi were the newly appointed minister of foreign affairs Ishii Kikujirō and his predecessor Katō Takaaki, minister of agriculture and commerce Kōno Hironaka, elder statesman (*genrō*) Itagaki Taisuke, along with several hundred leaders of the political and business worlds who had come to join the crowd on the narrow platform.

San Francisco was the venue that year of the Panama-Pacific International Exposition, held to celebrate the opening of the Panama Canal. Chairman of the Tokyo Chamber of Commerce Nakano Buei had been the first to suggest the idea that Eiichi, taking advantage of the chance to see the exhibition, pursue opportunities to cultivate friendly ties between Japan and the United States. The recent troubles in Japan-U.S. relations were like cancer, rheumatism, and other illnesses that might temporarily respond to treatment, but could quickly recur without constant attention. The Japanese delegation of businessmen who had traveled across the United States in 1909 had received a warm welcome wherever they went, and yet it was soon after that that the proposal was advanced by secretary of state Philander Knox to neutralize Japan's Manchurian Railway in China (see chapter 6). Even after that challenge to Japan's interests had been dealt with, trouble soon surfaced again with the enactment of the California Alien Land Law. People like Nakano realized that if matters were left untended, Japan would be left on the defensive at every juncture, and all the efforts of people on both sides to cultivate friendship and cooperation would come to naught.

Eiichi's 1915 trip came at a time when, for better or worse, the number of countries able to participate in the Panama-Pacific Expo had been greatly decreased because of the war going on in Europe; the planners had been delighted when Japan had taken a proactive stance on setting up an exhibit. It was at times like that, Nakano was convinced, that it was desirable to send over a representative of Japan who was popular with Americans and whose appearance would help to create a favorable impression not only locally, in California, but throughout the country.

In July that year, Eiichi had received a similar request from Foreign Minister Katō Takaaki and Prime Minister Ōkuma, too, had informally encouraged him to visit the United States. Eiichi was beginning to feel his age, however, and as he resisted the idea that he needed to take such a high-profile role he did not immediately agree to go. Toward the end of summer, Japan's consul general in San Francisco Numano Yasutarō passed on some interesting news.

Numano said there had been an initiative centering on the San Francisco Chamber of Commerce (SFCC) to create a permanent committee of representatives of business, academia, government, and religious groups that would provide a fair forum for considering the immigration and other Japan-related problems, and come up with measures for solutions where needed. Recently the idea had begun to take concrete shape, said Numano. If nothing were done about the tendency for Japan-U.S. relations to be swayed and worsened by emotional reactions, it would hinder trade and economic exchange, the SFCC worried. SFCC people wanted to do what they could to improve the situation. They proposed that the Japanese side should create a similar organization and engage in activities while keeping in touch with its American counterpart, and the proposal was fielded with the Japanese consul-general in San Francisco.

In the spring of 1913 when the California State Legislature had passed the Alien Land Act denying Japanese, Chinese, Korean, and Indian immigrant farmers the right to hold agricultural land in the state, the Tokyo Chamber of Commerce had responded by creating the Nichi-Bei Dōshikai (Japan-America One-aim Society) of like-minded people to study the situation. As mentioned in chapter 6, Eiichi had been made its chairman, but it did not really achieve much. It was ineffective, they realized, in getting to the heart of a problem to simply try to hold the line of defense after trouble had occurred. As had been proposed by the SFCC, if authoritative groups could be formed on both the Japan and U.S. sides that were able to exchange views and cooperate in their activities, the effect was sure to be much better in solving bilateral problems, and the kind of private-sector diplomacy that Eiichi was always encouraging could be pursued. Hearing about the San Francisco initiative, Eiichi began to think that if he threw his own hat into the ring, it might have some effect, and so he suddenly made up his mind to go to the United States after all.

As noted in Chapter 1, Eiichi had attended the international exposition in Paris in 1867, even before the Tokugawa shogunate had come to an end. At that time, the voyage to Europe from Yokohama had taken them through the Malaccan Straits and across the Indian Ocean, and they had taken the train through the Egyptian desert and embarked on another ship at Alexandria in order to continue their journey to Paris. After that the Suez Canal opened, and the Trans-Siberian Railway was also completed, linking Asia to Europe by an overland route. And now the Panama Canal, said to be the most difficult engineering feat of the century, linked the Atlantic and Pacific oceans. The world had changed greatly in 50 years, and Eiichi must have felt as if the experiences of his youth were something out of a dream.

The Japanese exhibit at the Paris exposition had been rather shabby, tucked away in one corner of the site and consisting mostly of a tea shop where three women dressed in kimono served Japanese tea to visitors and a small number of handcrafted items including warrior armor, helmets, and Japanese swords were on display. In San Francisco in 1915, Japan had been allocated a spacious site of over three acres, giving it a full-fledged national presence. It featured a government pavilion modeled after the Kinkakuji Golden Pavilion in Kyoto and a special display hall imitating the style of Heian Shrine, also in Kyoto, as well as a beautiful Japanese garden, a Japanese tea room, and a Taiwan tea room, among other attractions that turned out to be very popular. In spite of the tensions generated by the discriminatory laws passed in California, the Japanese government had given high priority to the exposition and set aside a sufficient budget for it from several years earlier so that careful preparations could be made. Eiichi himself had been involved in the project, serving as a trustee since June 1914.

Fortunately Eiichi did not suffer from as much seasickness as he had in previous trips, and after a smooth voyage, he and his party arrived in San Francisco on November 8. The very next day he set out for the exposition site.

The sponsors of the exposition were delighted to see Eiichi arrive at the site, and Walton N. Moore, who was both president of the San Francisco Chamber of Commerce and president of the exposition committee, scheduled a program revolving around Eiichi for every day of his visit, treating him to the utmost hospitality. This included hosting a grand luncheon banquet in Eiichi's honor.

On November 13, the famous airplane pilot Art Smith put on an air show in the sky over the exposition site. He performed somersaults and put the plane into a spiral dive, manipulating the plane with the skill and agility of a bird, and leaving Eiichi, who had never seen the like of it before, completely dazzled. And then a white plume began to appear out of the back of the plane and the pilot guided it into a flight that spelled out against the blue sky the letters "B-A-R-O-N" – indicating Eiichi. As the word was completed the assembled crowd all turned toward Eiichi and began to applaud.

After five days at the exposition, Eiichi traveled to Seattle and then to Chicago, and after that visited the major East Coast cities.

For this trip he was accompanied by his second son, Takenosuke, who had just graduated from university, and his third son, Masao, along with their friend Nagano Mamoru and others. In Boston his grandson Hozumi Shigetō (Utako's eldest son), who was studying there, also joined them, so the entourage was made up of people much younger than the 1909 group and and much more affable and relaxing. Eiichi loved playing card games with these young people, and so it was that during the journey, whenever they spent the night on board ship or on the train, they enjoyed playing poker until midnight.

Eiichi quite often played the game of go, but was not a particularly skilled gambler, yet he had nothing against that sort of competition. He became extremely fond of poker, which his sons had taught him after he entered his seventies. In Tokyo, he would often return from a banquet and straight away join his sons playing poker, sometimes staying up most of the night at the game. As the morning light began to dawn, the young ones would take themselves off to bed, but their old father would take a morning bath and change into fresh clothes, and set out with renewed energy to greet the guests who would be arriving to see him from early in the morning – this was the sort of scene often recorded in essays by his fourth son, Hideo.

The prosperity Eiichi observed in the United States in 1915 was greater than anyone in Japan could imagine. The war in Europe was in the process of completely changing the scale of the American economy. As they neared the big cities that were the centers of business – Chicago, Pittsburgh, Philadelphia, New York – Eiichi could see that the number of new and very large buildings had increased, showing signs of how much the cities had grown in the six years since his previous visit. Not only arms, ammunition, and other military goods, but steel, ships, and machine tools sold rapidly; grain stores were quickly sold out, and supply could not keep up with the demand. Stimulated by demand for the war, the already tremendous resources and latent strength of the country were burgeoning, and the faces of Eiichi's old friends in the business world were glowing with excitement and confidence.

As he contemplated the markets toward which the vast energies and newly accumulated wealth would turn next, Eiichi felt an unfathomable sense of alarm. Frank A. Vanderlip, the president of National City Bank with whom Eiichi had been friends since 1902, had already formed a large-scale investment company with the agreement and backing of New York financial circles, and through it was involved in substantive projects for investing American capital overseas. The company, called the American International Corporation (AIC), had something around $50 million that it was ready to invest in mines, railroads, manufacturing, banks, and other sectors in South America and East Asia with an eye to forming international conglomerates.

Whatever the United States' interests were in South America, in East Asia those interests were focused on China. Interestingly enough, the person appointed as vice-president in charge of the Far East at the new company was none other than Willard Straight. When he was younger and working under the Taft administration he had harassed Japan with his ideas for "dollar diplomacy"; later he became acting chief of the Bureau of Far Eastern Affairs of the State Department and set in place policies that were to have long-lasting effects on American foreign policy toward the Far East. After the death of Edward Harriman, Straight had withdrawn from his involvements in Manchuria and while working as an executive for a J. P. Morgan-affiliated company through connections of his wife's family, served as editor for the magazine *New Republic*. It was then that his knowledge and caliber were tapped for the job of vice-president of the new AIC investment company.

On December 3, Straight came to the hotel where Eiichi was staying to pay him a visit. Of course, it was the first time they had met. Apparently Straight was intent on meeting Japan's foremost leader of the business world as a gesture intended to counteract his past reputation as an anti-Japan schemer. It may have been that Vanderlip advised Straight that his very presence could cause the whole Japanese business world to turn a cold shoulder on the new company. The now 35-year-old Straight introduced himself in a modest manner, saying he had always been arguing about foreign policy in the State Department but that now he had to work and show results; he wanted to become "a student" of Shibusawa and was eager to have the benefit of his guidance.

Eiichi laughed off the notion of Straight being his "student," declaring that he had heard about the younger man's exploits and commenting that he hoped he would not play too fast and loose with the fate of East Asia.

Eiichi actually did not have much knowledge of Straight's previous ideology and activities, so his words were simply intended as praise, but Straight would naturally have assumed there was a touch of irony in his remark; he responded by saying he'd already forgotten what went on in the past and that he'd changed his ideas since then, telling Eiichi to put his mind at rest. Eiichi really did not know what Straight was talking about, but simply imagined that the man wanted to put things on a friendly footing from then on.[130]

After Straight left, Eiichi departed by car for a visit to Theodore Roosevelt's villa in Oyster Bay, Long Island, about 30 miles to the east. Roosevelt served Eiichi and his party luncheon in a dining room looking out over an expansive garden, and they enjoyed a relaxing time and leisurely conversation.[131]

Although when Roosevelt left the presidency in 1909 he had backed William Howard Taft as his successor, he had been dissatisfied with the policies that Taft pursued thereafter, and in 1912 he engaged in an intense struggle to prevent Taft from being chosen as the Republican candidate for the next presidential election. He had many reasons for displeasure, but one of them was Taft's Far East policy.

In his autobiography, Roosevelt wrote, "After my term ended, the policies of the government toward Japan were sheer foolishness and did nothing but provoke the Japanese to no good effect whatsoever...."[132] When Taft was chosen as the Republican candidate at the convention in Chicago in June 1912, Roosevelt quit the party

---

[130] *Shibusawa denki shiryō*, vol. 33, pp. 126–27.
[131] *Shibusawa denki shiryō*, vol. 33, p. 125.
[132] *Theodore Roosevelt: An Autobiography*, pp. 379–80. Available at https://archive.org/details/theorooseauto00roosrich (accessed 11-30-17).

and started a new Progressive Party with himself as the candidate for president and took on both Taft and Wilson in the election. The resulting split of the Republican camp handed the advantage to the Democrats, resulting in an easy victory for Wilson.

Roosevelt was still a relatively young man, 18 years younger than Eiichi, but his heyday as a politician was already past. Full of verve and energy as always, he kept himself busy with his scientific studies, writing, and travel. His thinking about U.S. foreign policy, especially toward the Far East, remained unchanged from the time he was president: as a rule he thought the United States had to respect the initiatives that Japan had made in China. He continued to follow the realistic line of thinking that it was wisest for Washington to compromise with Japan on the continent and gain Japan's cooperation in other regards.

During the Long Island visit, Roosevelt remarked to Eiichi that he had recently read a Japanese government report about its five years rule in Korea and found it admirable. He had not thought that Japan had any experience with colonial administration, but it seemed to be doing quite well, he said.

Eiichi's own current concern being the China problem, he wanted to know what Roosevelt thought. He said he was aware that American political leaders were unhappy with Japan's China policies, and reassuring Roosevelt that he was outside politics, hoped the former president would speak frankly.

Saying the issue was very complex and involved, Roosevelt avoided a quick answer, but he did say that he had always thought that Japan was the country that held the keys to peace in East Asia. He thought that probably the leaders as well as the people of Japan also held that view and it was the predominant view in Europe as well. He had always agreed with that view and told Eiichi to imagine, based on that position, his thinking on China.

Regarding the immigration issue in California, Roosevelt told Eiichi that his thinking had not changed from the time he was president. He was against new immigration from Japan, but those already in the United States should be given the right to naturalize and be treated the same as immigrants from Europe.[133]

---

[133] *Shibusawa denki shiryō*, vol. 33, p. 125.

FIGURE 32
Frank A. Vanderlip
(1864–1928), American
banker and journal-
ist. Photo: Shibusawa
Memorial Museum.

Eiichi went on to recall their conversation 13 years earlier during
his 1902 tour of the United States. Roosevelt had praised Japan's
art and its military but said nothing about Japanese industry.
Over the past fifteen years, Japan had been working hard to
develop its industry. It might not have reached the point where
Japanese industry could be praised, but they would keep up their
efforts. Roosevelt said he remembered that conversation and
he was aware of Japan's great strides in economic development;
when he declared that he was now very happy to praise what it
had achieved, host and guest were both in high spirits.

On the following day, December 4, Eiichi was invited to
Vanderlip's beautiful residence on the Hudson River north of New
York City. Vanderlip, who was originally a journalist specializing
in the economy and the author of a number of books, gave Eiichi
a detailed account of recent economic conditions in the United
States. Since the outbreak of the war in Europe, the balance of

international payments had rapidly improved and Vanderlip predicted that the country would soon shift from debtor to creditor. Recently, he said, the central bank system had been set up and the financial market organized, allowing investment funds to accumulate. He believed that a huge fund of about 2 billion dollars would soon be available, and in order to effectively utilize this fund, it would be necessary to launch substantial efforts at overseas investment. He was eager, he said, to pursue investment in China for that purpose.

Eiichi talked about the turmoil in the Chinese political situation and difficulties of dealing with Chinese customs, manners, and popular sentiment, and asserted that Japanese had a long historic relationship to China and a good understanding of its culture. Whatever sort of change was bound to take place in China, handling the situation would be easier if left to Japan. He said he thought it would be better for both Japan and the United States, as well as for China, if Japan and the U.S. cooperated as much as possible regarding future development in China in the form of a joint venture.

Vanderlip nodded as Eiichi spoke, and said that he agreed with what he was saying, but that he had heard that there was recently very intense anti-Japanese sentiment in China, and that Japanese goods were being boycotted. Since the company was setting out to do business with China, it might be a mistake to join hands with a partner that inspired such negative sentiments. But what did Eiichi think? he asked.

Eiichi attempted a defense by explaining that it seemed to be the practice in China's foreign policy to tell the United States it hated Japan even while saying to Japan that it hated the United States. He said it might be hasty to set up a business plan based on the rumor of such shifting sentiments. But even Eiichi realized that his case might not sound very persuasive. In his mind's eye he could see Yuan Shikai's face. Ever since Japan had confronted China with its Twenty-One Demands, Japan-China relations had turned sour, damaging them so much that it was unlikely anything could be done even if the United States wanted to intervene and turn things around to its own liking.

Then Eiichi said to Vanderlip, "One look is worth a hundred words. I am sure you are uneasy about Japan, so I would like you to come and visit us. I will personally serve as your host and guide and show you Japan just as it is. I invite you to plan your business with China after coming to see us."

That conversation was to lead to Vanderlip's visit to Japan in April 1920. On that occasion Eiichi welcomed Vanderlip and his entourage by organizing a full-fledged foreign policy discussion meeting, the Nichi-Bei Yūshi Kyōgikai (Conference of Concerned Japanese and Americans), then something very rare in Japan (see pp. 262–72).

The Philadelphia department store king, John Wanamaker, had met Eiichi and his entourage six years earlier when he visited as leader of the business delegation, but this time he said he wanted to entertain his Japanese friend personally, and on November 28, Eiichi and his companions boarded the train from Pittsburgh to Philadelphia. They arrived at 5:45 P.M., and since it was early winter it was already well past dark. Wanamaker had asked them to come directly from the station to the department store, and when they arrived they found all the floors of the immense building lit up with Christmas decorations as Eiichi alighted from his car, Wanamaker gave him a warm personal welcome at the front entrance. It was a Saturday and a crowd of several thousand had gathered to get a glimpse of Wanamaker's illustrious guest from the Far East. Eiichi recalled that he felt a rush of blood to his head as Wanamaker – a man almost twice his height – drew him through the aisles of the store lined with gaily dressed women looking "like flowers" along their path.

Wanamaker was four years Eiichi's senior but he seemed to be particularly attracted by Eiichi's character, and early the next morning he came to the hotel where Eiichi was staying and they spent the morning together, telling each other about their lives and exchanging ideas. Wanamaker was fascinated by Eiichi's account of his career, which seemed to tell the inside story of the modern history of that far-off island country of Japan. He was intensely curious to know what had been the spiritual foundation that had sustained Eiichi's long and varied life.

Eiichi did his best to explain the thinking of the *Analects* of Confucius, which formed the basis of his life and his business activities, and the world view of the man known as Confucius. Listening gravely to everything Eiichi said, Wanamaker then began to enthusiastically urge him to convert to Christianity. He declared that he had had no idea that people could be cultivated by any faith other than Christianity until that very moment. He recognized that the way Eiichi thought was no different from the way he himself thought about things. The teachings from China, however, must be long dead, he assumed, and he hoped that Eiichi would become a believer in Christianity. If a person like Eiichi would join the faith, he argued with great passion, it would have a tremendous impact for the betterment of Japan and for the Far East.

Like the vast majority of Americans of those days, Wanamaker was a victim of a distinctively Christian parochialism. People who did not believe in the Christian God were not considered fully human. He must have thought he was serving God by converting a famous Asian to Christianity. That afternoon, Wanamaker took Eiichi to visit a Sunday School. In later accounts of his trip, Eiichi often mentioned his exasperation with Wanamaker's repeated urgings that he convert on the stage in front of an audience of more than 1,500 people in the church.[134]

Eiichi was almost about to cynically respond that "your God seems to be active and encourage you to press what you want on others, whereas Confucius, whom I revere, is passive and teaches us not to force the unwanted upon others." But, afraid that such a response might lead to an argument before the audience, Eiichi hastily retreated from the stage.

Nonetheless, Eiichi was deeply impressed with the efficiency of Wanamaker's hospitality. Their activities proceeded according to a prearranged schedule and no time or energy was wasted in

---

[134] For example, see remarks quoted in *Shibusawa denki shiryō*, vol. 33, p. 123.

the process. In a speech on January 27, 1916, he described his impressions of the absence of empty formalities and appreciation for the simple, straightforward way things were done, which he compared favorably with the time and trouble that was taken for the formal greetings, the eating and drinking and so on that characterized social interaction among Japanese. The rational, efficient way of doing things that was part of Wanamaker's inborn character was exactly the way Eiichi tried to do things in Japanese society as well.[135]

On December 6 at noon, Eiichi visited the White House and met with President Woodrow Wilson. It is recorded that he and his party had dressed carefully in their formal morning coats and were nervous about meeting this powerful head of state until the president briskly entered the room, dressed in a rough, stripe-patterned jacket with a red necktie, the picture of American-style relaxed formality. After shaking hands with each member of the party Wilson remarked that the footsteps of travelers help to erase the boundaries between countries and he hoped that the footsteps of such eminent people as they would help to bring down the boundaries between Japan and the United States.[136]

It was their first meeting and it was also a rather formal official visit, and not focused on any major issues, but Wilson brought up the subject of the St. Luke's International Hospital that was under construction in Tokyo at the time. Rudolf B. Teusler, the founder of St. Luke's and a doctor who had contributed for many years to Japanese medicine, was a cousin of his wife and at the time he was deeply involved in fund raising for the hospital in both Japan and the United States.

Considerable effort was being put into the project on the Japanese side, with Prime Minister Ōkuma Shigenobu serving as chairman of the founding committee; Eiichi had also been putting his services to use for it. There had been a 50,000-yen

---

[135] See *Shibusawa denki shiryō*, vol. 33, p. 136, for a record of the speech given at the Bankers Club at the Imperial Hotel.

[136] For an account of this meeting, see *Shibusawa denki shiryō*, vol. 33, p. 151, which appears to be based on "Beikoku ni okeru Shibusawa-ō" (Shibusawa in the United States), by Hozumi Shigeto, as published in *Ryūmon zasshi* 530, pp. 60–62.

donation from the imperial household and Wilson said he was delighted when he heard about it. He also said that Teusler was in New York at the time but that when he came to Washington, he would help him with the fund-raising efforts.

Back in San Francisco, Eiichi met up with Suzuki Bunji and Yoshimatsu Sadaya, who had arrived before him, and through their introduction he met with Samuel Gompers, founder and leader of the labor movement in the United States and chairman of the American Federation of Labor. A banquet was held at the Palace Hotel sponsored by "potato king" Ushijima Kinji, and Gompers brought with him Paul Scharrenberg, who was secretary of the California state Federation of Labor. Being told he was to meet a giant of Japanese capitalism, Gompers arrived looking skeptical and saying he had another engagement and would have to leave around 8:30. But as the conversation went on, he seemed to become intrigued and the talk continued even after 9:00 and then 10:00, until finally he got up to give a speech of welcome to Eiichi and appeared to be in fine spirits.

Gompers was born in London in 1850, making him 10 years younger than Eiichi. His family immigrated to New York when he was thirteen and he had worked in the family cigar-making business. He was a born-and-bred working man, but his thinking was extremely sound and reasonable and he spoke with an authority rooted in long years of experience. Eiichi was impressed to see that workers in an advanced country were of a different order from those of Japan. In Japan, people who had not received an education tended to be regarded "as irrational as a man who plays go without knowing the rules of the game," but there in the United States, it was different. Men like Andrew Carnegie, John Wanamaker, and Samuel Gompers might have little formal education, but they could still present well-thought-out views. The encounter with these men got Eiichi to wondering what the was difference between the cultures and social structures of the two countries.

Gompers believed that the labor movement ought to be aimed at substantive improvement of the lives of workers; he was opposed to getting involved in politics and class struggle. His views were rather conservative, but he was nevertheless highly respected for his character and capacity as a leader. He became the leader of the AFL in 1886 and remained in that post for 38 years until his death.

It is not known whether the meeting between Gompers and Shibusawa actually had any direct effect on the problem of anti-Japanese sentiment and legislation in the western states, but considering that the American labor movement in those days was consistently white-population oriented and openly discriminatory toward non-whites and immigrants, it is of interest that at least some lines of communication were established between the leaders of the movement and Japan.

The journey by train across the American continent had been long, but along the way, wherever the train would stop, Japanese residents of the area would gather to see Eiichi. Apparently word of the efforts Eiichi was making to resolve the anti-Japanese problems in the United States had spread throughout the country through chapters of the Japanese Association of America and the Japan-America One-aim Society. Eager to pay their respects to this eminent man from their homeland who was championing their interests, people often traveled far over poor roads to see him.

Over the long, 74-hour haul between Chicago and Portland, the train passed through vast expanses with little trace of human habitation in Montana and Idaho, but even in such remote inland places Japanese who were working on farms or in mines would turn up at midnight whistle stops, waiting for a chance to see Eiichi. His diary records gifts he received from those who came to see him – a sprig of chrysanthemums, three apples, and so on – with a thoughtfulness that deeply moved him.[137] Thus moved, he thought he could not dare to sleep in the sleeping car; he would stay dressed, dozing in his seat and ready to go out and meet such people. At two in the morning one night, for example, women and couples turned up, having crossed wind-swept plains with children in tow, at some nameless station just for the chance of a brief meeting. Eiichi realized anew, as if he had not realized it properly before, that his countrymen and women were people

---

[137] *Shibusawa denki shiryō*, vol. 33, p. 38.

of deep feeling and sense of obligation. He must have thought that, for the future of people like this, he must try even harder to improve Japan-U.S. relations.

Earlier, on his arrival in San Francisco in November, the San Francisco Chamber of Commerce had waited for Eiichi to arrive in the United States, and on November 11 had convened its first meeting on Japan–U.S. relations. The meeting had been chaired by Wallace M. Alexander (1869–1939), the owner of a huge sugar plantation in Hawai'i. Including six Japanese, there were a total of 19 people present, among whom were Walton N. Moore, who was head of the Chamber and of the World Expo, Benjamin Wheeler, president of the University of California, and Eiichi's old friend James D. Lowman who happened to be there, from Seattle.

The meeting was held on the shared assumption that it was no time for Japan and the United States to be engaged in a prolonged dispute over the immigration problem. Due to war-related matters in Europe, business relations between the two countries were expanding, and the Panama-Pacific International Exposition seemed to be a grand success thanks to Japan's active participation. Japan and the United States were neighbors across the Pacific Ocean, and it was extremely bad for business for their relations to be strained by unjustified emotional issues. Members of the chambers of commerce had been traveling back and forth and found that they had shared affinities, emotional as well as commercial, and mutual understanding of the situation had improved on both sides. The purpose of the meeting was to provide a venue centering on the SFCC to allow people from various viewpoints to present the issues between Japan and the United States, discuss them in a free forum, and take up any proposals for solutions that might be forthcoming at the meeting.

The meeting was exactly the kind of occasion Eiichi had been working hard to encourage. All his efforts from the time he had helped arrange for the visit of members of American Pacific coast chambers of commerce to Japan in 1908 at the request of foreign minister Komura Jutarō had been made in order to build the foundations for meetings of this kind. The dialogue was beginning that day in San Francisco, and when a proposal was presented from the American side that Japan should found a similar group and that the two organizations should work together, Eiichi was fully in favor of it. He promised to found a Japanese committee as soon as he returned to Japan that would fulfill the expectations of all those present.

At the inaugural meeting, the American side called on Eiichi to share his candid views. He presented his own thinking mainly about the immigration problem. As far as Japan was concerned, it had no intention of sending immigrants if they were going to cause problems for American society, and new immigration had been drastically curtailed since the Gentlemen's Agreement (1907) had been concluded. The issues to be discussed should focus on the treatment of Japanese who were already living in the United States. Japan could not tolerate a situation in which its countrymen were discriminated against and not treated equally with immigrants from European countries.

Eiichi reminded those present that it had been the United States that had arrived on Japan's shores bent on opening up the country. The appearance of Japanese people around the world was prompted by the United States itself. Moreover, the United States was a champion of "justice and humanity" and, from what he had heard, it was a nation founded on the grand principle of the "equality of all people." The Japanese people had great respect for this ideal for the founding of a nation; it made utterly no sense to them that the United States should discriminate against Japanese.

If immigrants did not obey the laws of the United States or did not assimilate themselves into American society, then something must be done to remedy the matter, but for those who were already in the United States and were conducting themselves with propriety and making a decent living where they had settled, they should be given the right to naturalize as American citizens. If Japanese could not be given the right to naturalize, then it was the shared wish of the Japanese people that the same treatment would be accorded to immigrants from Europe.[138]

---

[138] *Shibusawa denki shiryō*, vol. 33, p. 125.

The November 11 meeting ended on this note and a second was scheduled to be held on December 14, after Eiichi and his companions had returned from the East Coast. The second meeting was held at the Fairmont Hotel at Eiichi's invitation. Roughly the same people attended, and he presented his plan for founding a similar organization in Japan after returning home. They discussed matters relating to exchange of documents and other specific procedures.

On December 18, Eiichi sent out thank-you letters to the many people who had hosted him and his entourage during their visit to the United States, and then, with a large crowd present to see him off, departed for the return journey to Japan aboard the *Chiyō Maru*.

Leaving Japan on October 23, 1915 and returning on January 4, 1916, Eiichi and his party had traveled for only 73 days, but their schedule had been packed. They had spent 35 days on board ship going and coming and had 10-odd days moving across the United States by train, leaving less than 30 days for the work they intended to do. In that short space of time, they had observed the rapid growth of the United States and met with many people with whom they exchanged candid views. Still, there had been time for closer association with friends they had not been able to visit at leisure during the 1909 business delegation tour – people such as Vanderlip, Roosevelt, Wanamaker, Henry J. Heinz, and Gompers who were top-level leaders in the United States. Eiichi had also had the chance to meet Harvard University president Charles William Eliot and Stanford University president David Starr Jordan and engage in frank discussion of world trends relating to the World War and regarding the nature of civilization in the future. Eiichi may have been hard put to show exactly what had resulted from his trip, but he knew that it had been a valuable journey.

The voyage home was unexpectedly smooth, although the Pacific was known to be rough in the winter months, and as the ship headed westward, Eiichi passed the time reading and in the evenings playing cards. On New Year's Day he woke at 7:00 and went out onto the deck to greet the first sunrise of 1916.

A massive sun that day rose grandly out of a bank of golden clouds that he described as "sukoboru sōkan" – a wonderful sight.

一路帰帆向北溟 *My ship sails on the northern ocean heading straight for home*
船窓除夜夢頻醒 *I wake often during sleep by the window on New Year's Eve*
家人応有送年歓 *My family must be feeling the pathos of the passing year*
不識吾儂迎喜齢 *I barely realize I'm about to turn seventy-seven*

With the coming of the New Year, Eiichi would turn 77 (*kiju*) – by traditional East Asian age reckoning – an auspicious age celebrated with particular honor in Japanese tradition.

With the third year of the war being waged in Europe, the world was changing greatly. No matter which side would win, the map of Europe was sure to change dramatically. And the result was bound to have a tremendous impact on the future of China as well. The encounter of Japan and the United States in China was bound to become ever more complex. Eiichi realized that Japan-U.S. relations would far surpass the matter of immigration alone; they would involve issues with fateful consequences for the world as a whole.

The age of 77 was quite advanced, and yet Eiichi did not feel he was declining mentally or especially physically. He was not so ambitious as to be thinking of launching some new venture or getting involved in any large-scale projects, but as long as he had the will and the stamina to do so, he was determined to work as hard as he could for the sake of Japan and for humankind.

CHAPTER 8

THE JAPANESE-AMERICAN
RELATIONS COMMITTEE

෨

On July 25, 1916, a general meeting of the stockholders of the Dai-ichi Bank was held at the Tokyo Bankers Association. Of 2,858 stockholders, it is recorded, 165 attended and 1,415 sent letters of proxy. As the president of the bank Eiichi chaired the meeting as usual, and reported the business results for the first half (January–June) of that year along with a statement of accounts.

The shipping and munitions industries were flourishing as a result of demand generated by World War I, and other manufacturing industries too had increased their investment in plant and equipment. The country had a large trade surplus of 185 million yen and the surplus went on expanding, so the money market was sluggish. Plant and equipment investment related to silk reeling had increased due to the high price and rising export of silk, but interest rates were falling. Therefore, the Dai-ichi Bank, like other banks, had a hard time implementing effective management of money, but fortunately, the efforts of the staff had enabled the bank to achieve a net profit of 1,092,425 yen for the first half of the year. Combined with the profit carried forward from the previous half year, the profit came to 1,804,305 yen.[139]

The general meeting unanimously approved the statement-related documents and the profit appropriation proposal, and the proceedings came to an end. Then, Eiichi asked for permission to speak. After apologizing for talking about personal matters and

---

[139] *Shibusawa denki shiryō*, vol. 50, pp. 111 ff.

breaking with the conventions of such general meetings and making those present stay longer on a hot day, he announced his decision to resign from the post of president he had held for 43 years.

For him, Eiichi said, the stockholders, especially those who had held stocks in the bank since its early days, were comrades who had given support to the totally new idea of introducing banking to Japan along with other modern ideas of business. Subsequently the bank's business had expanded; society, too, had grown more complex, and relations between the bank and its stockholders had changed, but he had endeavored to maintain sincere and close connections with the stockholders.

He went on, reminiscing about the days of the bank's founding in 1873. In those days Japan had very little in the way of industry worthy of the name, and business was conducted according to the customs and practices of the previous era. In order even to start managing a bank in such a milieu it had been necessary to

Figure 33
Ōkura Kihachirō (1837–1926), founder of the Ōkura *zaibatsu*. Photo: National Diet Library, Japan.

Figure 34
Sasaki Yūnosuke (1854–1943),
second president of the Dai-
ichi Bank. Photo: Shibusawa
Memorial Museum.

teach society as a whole the rudiments and workings of a modern economy.

On behalf of the stockholders Ōkura Kihachirō then gave a speech, expressing gratitude for Eiichi's many years of effort for the bank. Part of the speech went:

> Everyone would go to Shibusawa to find out how to found a company or deal with a bank. He always instructed us with kindness and detail, telling us how to do this and do that. He also advised us that we should no longer stash our money in our houses; we should just put the money in a bank and make payments by check. He taught us such basics we would not have known otherwise one by one with untiring patience. His contribution to raising the cultural standard of the country is really enormous.

Besides teaching others these things, Eiichi himself had had much to learn. Inviting Alexander Allen Shand (1844–1930), a Scotsman who was in Japan working with the Ministry of Finance, Eiichi and other main members of the bank studied in earnest all sorts of things about banking business from basic bookkeeping and calculation methods to the spirit and ethic of the banking business. One class, akin to the corporate training seminars of today, included a young man, not yet 20 years old, whose performance was outstanding. That was Sasaki Yūnosuke (1854–1943).

Sasaki was appointed to succeed Eiichi as president that day. One of Japan's first bankers and an employee at the Dai-ichi Bank from the beginning of his career to the end, he was 15 years younger then Eiichi. Throughout his four-decade career he was a close partner – a veritable brother – to Eiichi. As Eiichi, who was involved with various businesses, was always very busy and frequently away, it would be Sasaki who took care of the bank. Eiichi trusted him deeply for his cool-headedness and quick-wittedness as well as his honesty. Sasaki, for his part, wholeheartedly believed in and respected the great and always-growing reach of Eiichi's way of living and thinking of the whole world as one big family. They fully understood each other's strong and weak points and thought of each other before they thought of themselves. The genuine fellowship they shared remained unchanged throughout their lives.

At the core of the Dai-ichi Bank – which represented the birthplace and the pioneering force of Japan's modern capitalism – there existed harmony and a special teamwork (*hito no wa*), and for a long time that formula must have had quite a significant impact on society. In those days many companies were being run with the Dai-ichi Bank as their ultimate source of support. In the rough-and-tumble environment of the time, rapid growth was being forced to continue on and on. The Dai-ichi Bank demonstrated stable performance and showed solidarity and harmony among its staff and was seen as a big ship that remained stable even in rough seas or as the calm haven for refuge and reinforcement. For those grappling daily with the harrowing difficulties of managing their companies, a visit to the Dai-ichi Bank was known to offer a sense of relief and respite, brief as it might be, that greatly encouraged and inspired them. Whether that is the sort of role a bank ought to perform, I do not know, and the function of banks naturally undergoes great changes with the passage of time. In the formative period of Japan's modern industry, however, those admittedly intangible features of the role played by the Dai-ichi Bank could be said to have been vital.

Having resigned not only from the post of president of the Dai-ichi Bank but from all other roles in the business world including his posts at the Tokyo Savings Bank and the Tokyo Bankers Association, Eiichi freed himself from all of his business obligations. At the general meeting he said, "You may not be much interested in what I am going to do from now on, but when I ask that question myself, it seems that I'm not so senile that I cannot be involved in public affairs. I think, therefore, I shall continue to perform my duty as a citizen of the country until my inevitable demise. I am thinking of endeavoring to play my part as a citizen in such areas as foreign relations, education, or social policy. And that is what I plan to do."[140]

JAPANESE-AMERICAN RELATIONS COMMITTEE AND CHINA

Earlier, immediately after returning in January 1916 from his extended trip to the Panama-Pacific Expo and to the east coast of the United States and back (see pp. 213–31), Eiichi organized the Japanese-American Relations Committee in accordance with the agreement made in the December meeting with the San Francisco Chamber of Commerce. It was decided that the number of Committee members would be limited to 24 at first. Selected from among people with relevant knowledge and experience were those deeply interested in Japan-U.S. relations such as Tokyo University professors Nitobe Inazō and Anesaki Masaharu, House of Representatives speaker Shimada Saburō, privy councilor Kaneko Kentarō, and admiral Uryū Sotokichi, while those selected from the business world were Tokyo Chamber of Commerce president Nakano Buei, Yokohama Specie Bank

---

[140] *Shibusawa denki shiryō*, vol. 50, p. 117.

president Inoue Junnosuke and others.[141] Eiichi and Nakano were to contact each other, taking charge of the management of the Committee.

For a few years after the launch of the Japanese-American Relations Committee, the world's attention was focused on the war in Europe and the situation in the Far East was relatively quiet. The discrimination against Asian immigrants in California seemed to have grown no worse, and it was even rumored that the situation might turn for better. For such reasons the Committee had no real business to attend to. There was almost nothing to do except, for example, hold events such as a welcome party for U.S. Steel president Elbert H. Gary who happened to visit Japan in July 1916 after visiting the Philippines and China.

Gary was 70 years old at that time and traveling with his wife 30 years his junior. Given Gary's stature in the steel industry, they were given both an official and a private welcome. Gary was originally an attorney and ran a large law office in Chicago. In 1898, at the request of financier J. P. Morgan, he had become president of U.S. Steel immediately following its merger, and later became its chairman. He was a staunch advocate of fairness and insisted that the sole key to business success was moral rectitude. That made him a kindred spirit with Eiichi, and they struck up a friendship that was to serve as one of the major links connecting the business circles of Japan and the United States.

In China that year, following the death of Yuan Shikai in June, the political situation grew increasingly chaotic. Having seized the Shandong peninsula (including Jiaozhou Bay) and other German colonies and interests in China at the start of World War I, Japan was doing its best to make sure that as much of that territory as possible would be transferred to its control after hostilities ended. To firmly secure the interests acquired through the

---

[141] Ogata Sadako commented that this group "represented the 'cream' of internationally minded Japanese business leadership as well as a few individuals from academic circles." See "The Role of Liberal Nongovernmental Organizations in Japan," in Borg and Okamoto, eds., *Pearl Harbor as History: Japanese-American Relations, 1931–1941*, p. 461.

"Twenty-One Demands" (1915), the Terauchi Masatake government tried various maneuvers such as giving huge loans (the "Nishihara loan," etc.) or delivering threats backed up by arms, in order to bring Chinese Premier Duan Qirui over to its side.

The previous October, Japan had joined the Declaration of London (a pact that the members of the Allies would not make a separate peace with Germany) and thereby secured the right to attend the peace conference to be held after the war. It hoped thereby to forestall interference from the Allies in China. The bitter memory of the Triple Intervention (by Russia, Germany, and France) when Japan was forced to return the Liaodong peninsula it had acquired through a peace treaty ending the Sino-Japanese War in 1895 was still fresh in Japanese minds. The urgent diplomatic theme for Japan was to make sure it was present at the international conference table and to keep what it had newly obtained.

In January 1917, Japan formed a secret agreement with Britain which assured that in exchange for Japan's recognition of Britain's possession of German colonies south of the Equator, Britain would support Japan's possession of the Shandong peninsula (including Jiaozhou Bay) and other German-held Pacific islands north of the Equator. Japan had signed similar agreements with Russia in July of the previous year and did so with France in February 1917.

Now what about the United States? Paul Samuel Reinsch, U.S. minister to China, fiercely opposed the Twenty-One Demands and tried both openly and covertly to obstruct Japanese activities on the continent. The U.S. State Department did take a compromising attitude toward Japan as needed, but it was easy to see, even at a great distance, that the State Department's thinking was greatly influenced by pro-Chinese and anti-Japanese sentiment. Japan therefore judged it necessary to extract a promise from the United States that it, too, would support Japan's position at the peace conference ending World War I. It then happened that the United States entered the war in April 1917, and seizing this opportunity, the Japanese government sent its former foreign minister Ishii Kikujirō to the United States as a special envoy to negotiate with U.S. Secretary of State Robert Lansing.

As the representative of an American ally, Ishii was warmly welcomed wherever he went in the country. In San Francisco, a large banquet was held for him at the rebuilt Palace Hotel under the sponsorship of the governor of the state, attended by 500 influential people. In New York, at a welcome party held at City Hall, steel tycoon Gary, who had visited Japan the previous year, gave a rather aggressive speech in favor of Japan. Upon reaching Washington, Ishii was invited to both houses of Congress and delivered a speech on Japan's position and policy, drawing enthusiastic applause. On the surface it seemed as if Japan-U.S. relations were once more back on a friendly footing.

But when the negotiations with Lansing began and Ishii touched on the China issue, he felt a huge wall standing in his way. Lansing insisted he would object to any arrangement or agreement that would run counter to the traditional U.S. Far Eastern principle of the "open door" and territorial integrity of China. Interrupting Ishii's rebuttal, he proposed that the United States and Japan jointly make an open-door declaration, obviously implying the characteristic U.S. stance of protecting China from Japanese invasion.

Ishii responded by saying that Japan favored the open-door policy and China's territorial integrity, but that as a matter of reality Japan could not but have a special interest in all political and economic changes that might occur in China, Japan's huge neighbor. Just as the United States had a close interest in Mexico, so Japan had a special interest in China. Ishii stood his ground, insisting that a clause that would recognize that reality, that is, the special interest Japan had in China, would have to be included in an agreement between them.

The negotiations lasted for almost two months, from September 6 to November 2. Ultimately both sides backed down and came up with what is known as the Lansing-Ishii Agreement. The agreement stated that "The governments of the United States and Japan recognize that territorial propinquity creates special relations between countries, and, consequently, the government of the United States recognizes

FIGURE 35
Robert Lansing (1864–1928), U.S.
Secretary of State with whom Japan
negotiated about China in 1917.
Photo: Library of Congress, United
States.

that Japan has special interests in China, particularly in the part to which her possessions are contiguous."[142] Gu Weijun, Chinese minister to the United States, protested to the U.S. government, decrying its sudden change of stance. Japan, on the other hand, welcomed this agreement with open arms, understanding it to mean that the United States recognized Japan's new position in China.

On December 17, 1917 Eiichi, together with other businessmen and interested people, held a welcome home party for Ishii at the Imperial Hotel in Tokyo. It was a formal dinner, with all the guests in white ties and tails and bedecked with medals. Among the guests was Roland Morris, American ambassador to Japan, who praised Ishii's visit to the United States for greatly influencing American public opinion in favor of Japan and, while reserving comments on the content of the agreement, expressing his wish to further strengthen the ties of friendship between the two countries through frank commu-

---

[142] See Nish, *Japanese Foreign Policy*, pp. 114–17. Ishii later wrote in his diary that "These 'special interests' can only be understood in political terms," ibid. p. 286.

nication. Eiichi, too, gave high praise to Ishii's achievements. While referring to Ishii's remark that "the agreement was made possible through sincerity and our meetings were based on honesty," Eiichi said he totally supported such an honest and frank negotiation and that only through such discussion could stability in the diplomatic relations between the two countries be guaranteed.

Indeed, Ishii and Lansing had engaged in long and heated discussions for two months and in a desperate attempt to have its demands accepted, the Japanese side went as far as to reveal Japan's policy objectives vis-à-vis the continent and even the existence of its secret agreements with European countries. This honesty, however, helped not so much to deepen their mutual understanding as to confirm the insurmountable gap in thinking between the two countries. Ishii himself said the negotiations had gone far from smoothly because Lansing had been in favor of China and cautious about Japan throughout. Ishii later wrote that once they had frankly said what they had in mind, they found there existed a huge difference between them. The two sides decided to talk frankly and without reserve from the outset, so the discussion often got very heated and sometimes threatened to reach no agreement at all.[143]

It was President Woodrow Wilson, Ishii thought, who had broken the deadlock. Had Wilson not ordered a compromise, "the negotiation would have ended in failure much earlier, and there's no doubt about that." At that time, Wilson was fully occupied by the war in Europe and could not afford to think about the Far Eastern situation. Rather than coming into unnecessary conflict with Japan, its ally, he thought it better to reach some compromise for now and later reconsider the matter seriously once the war was over. For Japan, too, that was convenient. Later, the results of America's serious reconsideration would take the form of a rupture from which the two countries would not recover. The first sign was to surface in the process of the Allied intervention in Siberia during the Russian civil war.

---

[143] See recollections in Ishii, *Gaikō yoroku*, pp. 142 ff.

In November 1917 the second revolution in Russia that year took place. The seizure of power by the Bolsheviks not only had a serious impact on the European war front but also destroyed the balance of power that had been more or less maintained in the Far East since the end of the Russo-Japanese War (1904–1905). Czarist Russia, which faced Japan across a vast expanse covering northern Manchuria, the Maritime Provinces, and Eastern Siberia, had suddenly collapsed. The ensuing power vacuum in the region offered Japan a great, all-too-thrilling opportunity. Only a little more than three years had passed since it had occupied Germany's colonial possessions in China, including the Shandong peninsula. And now came the chance to establish a sphere of interest in the north – another unbelievable windfall.

Surprisingly, moreover, allies Britain and France asked Japan out of strategic necessity to send its troops into Eastern Siberia. War materiel the Allies had planned to send to the Eastern Front of the war via the Far East was stored in various parts of Siberia. Japan was tasked with preventing this materiel from falling into German hands. Among other things, Japan was expected to suppress the internal conflicts between Bolsheviks, indigenous peoples, Cossack forces, and others that were reportedly occurring within the Russian territory and, if possible, to help restore the Eastern Front.

Even without such a request, the Japanese army had wanted to send troops into Siberia without delay. Given the imperialistic views of national defense current at the time, it was not surprising that Japan should consider the opportunity a logical pretext for extending its influence in the vast northern plains of the continent and, if possible, incorporating some areas into Japanese territory, or at least, creating a neutral buffer zone in preparation for the future.

The United States, however, was opposed to military intervention in Siberia and especially cautious about Japan's dispatch of troops. From Wilson's point of view, an armed intervention in another country's internal affairs was not good, and to make it worse, if Japan sent its troops into Siberia, it would most likely take advantage of the opportunity by stationing them there for a long time and then demanding special rights and interests in the Maritime Provinces, Sakhalin Island, and elsewhere. Britain and France knew what Japan was doing, but they must have thought that Japan, an imperialist country like themselves, might make gains this time but that they could be offset later in future negotiations on expanding their own spheres of influence in China.

Complicated negotiations went on for several months until finally, on July 17, 1918, Wilson could not but agree to the military intervention. Among the reasons was: that the war situation in the Eastern Front had grown so grave that the replenishment of troops was urgently needed.[144] The 50,000-man Czechoslovak Legion fighting on the side of the Allies as part of the Austrian army had left the front and was moving eastward along the Trans-Siberian Railway, and it had become urgent to protect the legion forces.

On August 3, the first British troops landed in Vladivostok, followed by French, U.S., and Japanese troops. The American forces consisted of 9,000 troops, mainly from the Philippines, and included several battalions sent from the home country. William S. Graves was assigned to command the forces. One of the intelligence officers serving under Graves was Robert L. Eichelberger, a name that was to become more familiar to many Japanese as he was the commander of the Eighth United States Army that occupied Japan following the end of World War II.

The official announcement gave the total number of Allied troops sent to Siberia as 28,000, of which 12,000 were sent by Japan. But in fact, Japan landed an exceptionally large army of 73,000 troops, proving American suspicions of its greater ambitions to be well founded from the outset.

Eiichi had visited Prime Minister Terauchi on July 18, 1918 and was told about the government's plans regarding the upcoming Siberian Expedition. As usual, with the welfare of the national economy uppermost in his mind, Eiichi expressed opposition to the squandering of government funds that would result from

---

[144] More detailed discussion of Wilson's motives can be found in Melton, *Between War and Peace*.

Figure 36
Terauchi Masatake
(1852–1919), prime
minister at the time of
the Siberian Expedition
1918. Photo: National
Diet Library, Japan.

sending a large force overseas. But the prime minister before him
was not an old friend like Ōkuma Shigenobu or Itō Hirobumi
but a field marshal of the Japanese Army. Terauchi treated the
venerable business leader to a lecture about government policy
and the meeting ended there. The Siberian situation, moreover,
was so complex that Eiichi could not understand it very well,
and when Terauchi said Japan would send troops overseas under
the order of the emperor, there was no way for Eiichi to say
anything critical. The *Hōchi shimbun* newspaper, dated July 14,
however, carried his remark to the effect that it was crucial to
clearly explain the purpose of such an important matter as the
overseas dispatch of troops.

As Eiichi had sensed, the true motive behind the expedition
was by no means clear. The events were unfolding in Siberia, a
remote, thinly populated region. There was no responsible government there after the revolution broke out and the situation was

extremely fluid. Furthermore, the motives of the Allied powers in supporting the expedition were all different. For France, the purpose was mainly to maintain the Trans-Siberian Railway, in which it had a long-time investment. Britain feared that Bolshevism might make its way to India by way of Siberia and China and sought to put pressure on the new regime by indiscriminately supporting Kolchak, Semenov, and other counter-revolutionary leaders. Japan went along with Britain's thinking but also busied itself in trying to create as favorable a situation for the future as it could in Eastern Siberia and the Maritime Provinces of Russia.

The information of various sorts received by Japan was all too often unreliable and exaggerated. The rumors that German prisoners of war had been released, that they had organized a new army, and that they were very active in Siberia turned out to be virtually groundless. The Czechoslovak Legion safely reached Vladivostok without any Allied assistance and returned home by sea via Japan in 1920. In this army was Ludvik Svoboda, who would later be known as an anti-Nazi resistance hero and serve as president of Czechoslovakia from 1968 to 1975.

These circumstances made it no longer necessary for expedition troops to remain in Siberia, and the Allied troops withdrew one after the other. By March 1920 all the American forces, too, had withdrawn. The Japanese forces alone stayed on, however, and did not seem to be intending to leave at all. Not just that, but using as an excuse the March 1920 Nikolayevsk Incident – culminating in the massacre of hundreds of Japanese expatriates and Russian inhabitants of the town of Nikolayevsk-on-Amur in the Russian Far East – the Japanese army occupied the northern part of the island of Sakhalin as well, and remained on Russian territory until diplomatic relations were established between Japan and the Soviet Union in 1925.

As Eiichi had worried from the outset, Japan's spending on the expedition is said to have been huge: 1 billion yen, roughly 700 times the Dai-ichi Bank's half-year profit (around 1.5 million yen) at that time. That Japan had thrown away such a huge amount of money in Siberia without much planning or foresight testifies to what was already wrong with the management of Japan's political affairs by that point in time. Be that as it may, the Japanese stance toward the expedition showed the whole world Japan's imperialistic intent and further alienated the United States.

PREDICAMENT AT THE PARIS PEACE CONFERENCE

The Paris Peace Conference began in January 1919. The Japanese delegation formally announced its three demands: takeover of the former German colonies in the Shandong peninsula, takeover of Germany's former Pacific islands north of the Equator, and inclusion of Japan's racial equality proposal in the Covenant of the League of Nations.

These demands were strongly backed up by the series of agreements Japan had formed with Britain, the United States, France, and China through careful preliminary diplomacy. Britain and France had already clearly supported Japan's approach. China, too, as far as the Beijing government was concerned, was bound by repeated loans from and agreements with Japan. Such things were taken for granted in the world of imperialistic diplomacy. So, Japan expected its demands to be smoothly incorporated in the peace treaty.

But an unexpected obstacle emerged. At the conference, Chinese representative Gu Weijun (minister to the United States) squarely opposed the Japanese demands, speaking in fluent English and with a clarity and logic mastered from an American education. He called himself a spokesman representing one-fourth of the earth's human population and asserted that Shandong, the birthplace of Confucius, could not possibly be placed under the control of another country. He also insisted that all the former German colonies in China should be returned directly to China.

Opposing the imperialistic ideas that had been entrenched for such a long time, this speech was particularly persuasive in the context of world public opinion at the time. The unprecedented scale of the destruction of World War I revealed that the old-world order – that is, the rule of the world by the big powers – was unbeneficial and harmful. People now wanted a new way of government, a new order that would guarantee peace and happiness for all. This world trend was stimulated partly by the success of the Russian revolution. Under these circumstances Gu Weijun's speech was reported worldwide and won broad and sympathetic support.

Especially the United States both government and people showed sympathy for the position of the Chinese delegation, and the pro-Chinese, anti-Japanese mood finally became firmly established. The protection of China from the invasion of imperialist powers had been the traditional theme of U.S. foreign policy since Secretary of State John Hay had issued the Open Door notes to foreign powers involved in China in 1899–1900. Except for the era of mutual "flattery" (see chapter 4), which was a byproduct of realist Theodore Roosevelt's diplomacy with Japan, successive U.S. presidents and state secretaries had followed that tradition. But the United States was indulging a self-righteous illusion, saying it alone was fair and peaceful in the Far East while all the other powers were guilty of selfishness and aggression. The Chinese representative took advantage of such American inclinations, and the Paris conference, consequently, as far as the Far East was concerned, deviated greatly from discussion of terms of peace with Germany and became an arena of struggle between Japan's demands and opposition to them by the U.S.–China alliance.

There came an additional blow to Japan when on March 1, 1919 a widespread anti-Japanese independence movement started on the Korean peninsula. This further damaged the image of Japan in the eyes of the world. On that day, several thousand intellectuals, young people, and others discontented with Japanese rule assembled at Pagoda Park in Seoul and proclaimed the Declaration of Korean Independence. They were joined by the crowd that had gathered to view the funeral procession of Emperor Gojong, and in no time their numbers swelled to several tens of thousands. Shouting "Mansei" ("Korea forever"), they marched through Seoul's streets. The mood immediately spread throughout Korea and grew into an anti-Japanese movement of unprecedented scale.

Caught off guard, Japan mobilized its army and police in a major crackdown. They clashed with the populace at more than 600 locations across Korea, leaving 8,000 dead and 16,000 injured, and some 50,000 were detained. These events added impetus to the movement for Korean independence among Koreans in exile around the world and led to the establishment of the Provisional Government of the Republic of Korea in Shanghai. In Japan, the government strictly censored news of the crackdown, but detailed reports came out in other countries, most notably in the United States, where news of the anti-Japanese movement in Korea spread widely. Japan was condemned for its brutality, which appeared to be enforcing a reign of fear and terror on the peninsula.

In this way, the war in Europe, which had led at first to what seemed to be glorious opportunities for Japan, eventually pushed the country into a terrible predicament. The end of World War I coincided with an upsurge of anti-imperialism, but Japanese did not sufficiently grasp the strength of that trend, and it put them at a great disadvantage. Not just Japan but Britain and France as well participated in the Paris Peace Conference without having changed their conventional conviction in the righteousness of colonial rule. That dogged stance by the three states was what undermined the ideals of the proposed League of Nations that Woodrow Wilson had made his pet project, and turned the peace conference into an arena of diplomatic bargaining over territory.

Regarding the China issue, too, historically Britain and France, rather than Japan, had led the way in forcing China to cede parts of its territory and sign unequal treaties, but the United States harshly attacked Japan alone. How did Japan come to be the sole target of American enmity?

One reason was probably that Japan was seen as relatively easy to attack. The United States might also have resented the gains Japan reaped from the war, despite having suffered little, compared to Britain and France. Another reason might have been racial prejudice; it must have seemed absurd that although they were both yellow races, Japanese should assume such a superior and oppressive attitude toward Chinese. In those days it was widely felt not just among Westerners but among Asians as well that, while oppression of Asians by the white peoples might not be good, it could not be helped given historical and other circumstances. From the moral standpoint of Westerners, however, it seemed unpardonable for Japan, an Asian country, to rule over China.

The negotiations at the Paris conference became deadlocked and the Japanese delegation was nearly driven to withdrawing from the conference. Finally, due to a compromise made at the personal initiative of U.S. President Wilson himself, the treaty was concluded. Afraid that Japan's withdrawal might knock out the League of Nations, and already severely battered by the ordeals of negotiating, Wilson compromised at the very last minute. As the result, while the racial equality clause was rejected, Japan obtained mandates for the former German islands in the Pacific north of the Equator and retained control of Shandong on the condition that it would later return the peninsula to China. Japan's face was saved.[145]

The compromise reached after such an arduous process, however, pleased no one. Anti-Japanese sentiment intensified further in China and the Chinese delegation refused to sign the peace treaty. Japan, for its part, developed a deep distrust of the United States as a result of its biased attack on Japan, with the whole world watching, one that was both unreasonable and went against international diplomatic custom. The U.S. delegation itself did not conceal its indignation at the compromise made by its own head of state. U.S. Secretary of State Robert Lansing stated bitterly that the president had left China to the mercy of Japanese plundering and delivered a democratic republic into the hands of despotic government. He declared that Japan should be told that if it did not return the German territories taken from China, it would be unwelcome in the League of Nations, and he

---

[145] See Nish, *Japanese Foreign Policy*, pp. 118–23 and Shimazu, *Japan, Race and Equality*.

would be content if Japan decided not to join the body. He was disgusted by the sacrifice forced on China for the sake of saving Japan's face. It was exceptional that a U.S. secretary of state should be so critical of his own president. Around that time, Wilson and Lansing began to drift apart, and eventually Lansing resigned and Bainbridge Colby succeeded him.

Lansing's criticism of President Wilson directly reflected the anti-Japanese sentiment that had quickly escalated among Americans during the peace conference. The image of Japan as the Germany of the East and an aggressive and militaristic country that was an enemy of world peace spread rapidly throughout the United States.

Inevitably, the resistance of Californians to Japanese immigration intensified. Earlier, in 1913, the California Alien Land Law had been enacted, but after Japan declared war against Germany in 1914 and was on the side of the Allies, the anti-Japanese movement had receded, almost as if forgotten. Japanese immigrants, who had felt as if their world was coming to an end when the Land Law was enacted, turned out not to be as much affected as they had thought. On the contrary, as the following figures show, land cultivated by Japanese immigrants increased by about 50 percent in subsequent years. Of the total acreage (281,687) Japanese farmed in 1913, they owned 26,707 acres, leased 205,983, and share-cropped 48,997. By 1919, ownership increased by 22,142 to 48,849 acres, leased acreage increased by 50,931 to 256,914, and that share-cropped by 72,280 to 121,277. Their farm acreage now amounted to 427,040, an increase of 145,353 acres.[146]

Observing the situation, Eiichi even thought the Japanese-American Relations Committee would have little to do regarding the immigration issue, the principal purpose for its establishment. He had begun to consider having the Committee's chief role shift to serving as liaison or coordinator between Japan and the United States regarding the Chinese market, in which their competition was expected to intensify after the war was over.

---

[146] *Shibusawa denki shiryō*, vol. 36, p. 555.

In 1919, however, anti-Japanese sentiment was suddenly rekindled. Vigorous anti-Japanese activity unfolded under the leadership of former mayor of San Francisco and then senator James D. Phelan and California state senator James M. Inman, among others. They quickly won support in the western states, where public opinion had turned against Japan over the events of the Siberian expedition, the transfer of the Shandong peninsula, the Korea issue, and so forth. In September 1919 the Anti-Japanese League, headed by Inman, was established and the movement went into full swing. Its immediate objectives were to wrest from Japanese immigrants the right to the three-year lease of land that had been granted to them under the 1913 Alien Land Law and to prohibit entry to the United States of Japanese "picture brides."

"Picture marriage" was widely practiced in order to bring over wives from the home country for Japanese immigrant men. Photographs would be exchanged, and if both sides assented to the match, the procedures of marriage were completed in Japan in the absence of the bridegroom. In Japan this method of marriage was not considered particularly strange, because arranged marriages were common and it was established practice to choose marriage partners through the exchange of photographs. Americans, however, apparently took it as completely barbaric for a young woman to promise herself in wedlock and cross the Pacific Ocean to the United States to marry a man she had never met. The practice was also decried as a "clever ruse" on the part of the Japanese government, which had abided by the Gentlemen's Agreement of 1907 by voluntarily ceasing to issue passports for immigration to the United States for workers, but had continued to allow limited entry to wives and families of immigrants. Japan was violating the agreement prohibiting immigration, it was charged, by sending over these women under the category of "wives/family members of immigrants."

Children born on American soil to couples brought together by picture marriage were granted American citizenship based on the principle of territorial jurisdiction, so proponents of Japanese exclusionism saw picture marriage as an evasion of U.S. immigration law and an insidious way of limitlessly increasing the number of Americans of Japanese descent. So the Anti-Japanese League included among its objectives the annulment of the Gentlemen's Agreement and the adoption of legislation banning the entry of Japanese entirely and refusing U.S. citizenship to Japanese children born in the United States.

Concerned about the situation, the Japanese government imposed a total ban on the emigration of picture brides on December 8, 1919. That battle won, the Anti-Japanese League decided to take up the farmland issue once again, devoting its energies to the creation of legislation to put economic pressure on Japanese immigrants. In January 1920, the League submitted a proposal to the governor of California that an extraordinary session of the California State Legislature be convened to deliberate Japanese-related bills. The governor, however, refused the proposal due to diplomatic considerations. As an alternative the League resolved to take advantage of the anti-Japanese sentiment running high throughout the state to have anti-Japanese legislation enacted by state referendum.

According to law, if the proposer of a bill collected a required number of signatures (more than 56,000 in the case of California at that time) in support of it, the bill could be called up for a referendum vote. If the bill were supported by a majority, it would go into effect as law. The Anti-Japanese League planned to launch a signature-collecting campaign throughout California with August 4 as the petition deadline and, after collecting a required number of signatures, set up a timetable to hold a referendum in conjunction with the presidential election scheduled for the following month, November (1920), in the hope of quickly making the bill into law. The bill included many items intended to harshly restrict Japanese activities, such as a ban on the three-year lease of land recognized by the 1913 Alien Land Law and a ban against Japanese running businesses on the strength of their rights as guardians of children holding American nationality.

If the petition gained more than 56,000 signatures and the bill was supported by a majority through the state referendum, it would have a decisive impact in pushing public opinion against

Japanese and plunge U.S.–Japanese relations into an even deeper crisis than before. The problem, moreover, was that anti-Japanese sentiment was not confined to the local politics of California but had spread its tentacles throughout the United States in the form of an antipathy to the whole national policy of Japan toward Korea and China.

Eiichi was appalled that the prospects for U.S.–Japan relations looked so gloomy. The long war was over and peace had finally been restored to the world, so why on earth did such injustices have to continue? In neighboring China as well the anti-Japanese movement was as strong as ever. Dissatisfied with the resolution passed at the peace conference concerning the return of the Shandong peninsula, China refused to sign the Versailles Treaty. It also refused to talk with Japan, a country that had stained its hands with the blood of Chinese, unless the Shandong peninsula was returned to China directly at the League of Nations. So, although Japan had achieved its purpose at the peace conference of gaining recognition of its control over the peninsula, it now faced the tricky issue of how and when to return it to China. The longer it did nothing about the return, the stronger the impression that it was clinging to Shandong in violation of the promise it had made in Paris.

In China, meanwhile, demonstrations against Japan were taking place every day. In various parts of the country, people were not satisfied with boycotts of Japanese goods; anti-Japanese activists, mainly students and other youths, broke into shops, seized whatever Japanese goods they found, piled them together and burned them in bonfires in front of crowds. There were numerous incidents of violence and threats against Japanese residents, a situation that was increasingly dangerous. The reaction in Japan was fierce: newspapers and magazines carried strongly worded articles, some calling for readiness for war with China. Sino-Japanese relations were at a perilous stage.

Now that hostilities had been ended, thought Eiichi, all countries should join forces to promote economic growth and social development and realize coexistence through mutual prosperity. Japan, which had built up its strength to some extent during the war, ought to be working hard, he believed, to contribute to the happiness of humankind. Instead, Japan had been branded an imperialist aggressor by both the United States and China, the two countries with which Japan ought to have close relations. Japan had the whole world against it.

Why was Japan so hated by all? Eiichi would often wake up in the night, tossing and turning, sometimes so anxious about the state of his country and its future that he could not resist shedding tears. Ever since the Meiji Restoration he had been working diligently without much rest for the sake of his country's prosperity and happiness. There was still much to do, but he himself saw that the foundations of Japan as a modern state had been laid. He found it difficult to imagine how the result of all that effort had created a country that was now despised by the whole world.

Of course, there were things about Japan's attitude as a country that were not good. Japanese might turn toward militarism, a tendency Eiichi did not like at all. He knew, moreover, that Japan had made many mistakes vis-à-vis China. Some of them had been made because Japan was a developing country, short on experience. Others had been perpetrated out of selfish motives and the headlong pursuit of self-interest. What displeased Eiichi most was the unfounded attitude of Japanese superiority over Chinese. Japanese must humbly reconsider those things one by one for improvement, of course, but Japan was not to blame for everything that had happened. As the old saying goes, "Even thieves have reasons for what they do."

LANDMARKS OF PRIVATE DIPLOMACY

Of course, Japan had its reasons for what it did. Eiichi appears to have thought that it was important to invite experts from the countries concerned and talk things over carefully with them, expressing Japan's position and explaining the reasons behind its deeds. To Eiichi, heart-to-heart discussion from a standpoint of world peace and happiness and free from ulterior political motives and nationalistic sentiments would lead to mutual understand-

FIGURE 37   Wallace M. Alexander (1869–1939), chairman of the American-Japanese Relations
Committee of San Francisco with Eiichi. Photo: Shibusawa Memorial Museum.

ing and discovery of optimal solutions to the problems at hand. Even when finding a solution was difficult, the parties concerned might be able to understand exactly where the problem lay, and that in itself would have had some significant effect.

Eiichi's ardent wish for that to happen led to the holding of two remarkable conferences in Tokyo, one in March 1920 and the other in April of the same year, and attended by leading Japanese and American figures in business, academia, and other areas.

The March conference, the Nichi-Bei Kankei Iin Kyogikai (Joint Conference of the Japanese-American Relations Committees), which lasted for eight days, was a joint meeting of members of the Japanese-American Relations Committee in Japan and the American-Japanese Relations Committee in San Francisco. On March 16, Wallace M. Alexander, chairman of the American-Japanese Relations Committee of San Francisco, together with his party arrived in Japan aboard the *Siberia Maru*. Among the group were Walton N. Moore, who had served as president of the Panama-Pacific International Exposition in San Francisco when Eiichi was visiting there in 1915, and Benjamin Ide Wheeler, president of the University of California, both of whom Eiichi had known for some time, as well as Loyall A. Osborne, vice-president of Westinghouse Electric Company, Walter L. Clark, vice-president of Atlantic Shipbuilding Co., Ltd., and William T. Sesnon, former president of the San Francisco Chamber of Commerce.

Starting on the day following their arrival, the conference meetings were held at the Tokyo Bankers Association for three hours every day from 9:30 in the morning until 12:30 in the afternoon. Eiichi was unanimously nominated as chairman. Kaneko Kentarō was chosen as moderator of the conference and Wallace Alexander and Sakatani Yoshirō were assistant moderators. Agenda items included the immigration issue, the issue of Japanese landholding in California, joint enterprises, the submarine cable, labor-management issues, and exchange of scholars. Participants engaged in free discussion, presenting their frank views on each topic.

The topic of most immediate concern was the referendum likely to take place in California in the fall of that year. The Japanese side expressed its hope of preventing it by all means, but the American side explained the recent upsurge in anti-Japanese sentiment and said it was most likely that the revised Alien Land Law would be passed.

Discussion then touched on the content of the bill, the present status of the anti-Japanese movement, the likely situation after the passage of the bill, and so forth. Then Eiichi asked for permission to comment. He said to the members of the U.S. side, "We would like to hear your honest, unreserved criticism of the shortcomings of Japanese in California. We do have some things to say, too, but first tell us frankly how you feel in this regard."

In response, American members stood up one after the other to express their views. Examples they gave of what they thought were shortcomings of Japanese were plentiful. No matter how long they might live in the United States, Japanese do not assimilate into American society. Japanese in cities and towns tend to concentrate in particular areas and not associate with others.

Their children are fine when they are little, but as they grow up they do not get along well with others. Japanese seem to fundamentally differ from us Americans in the way they live and the way they feel about things. Even children who are born and raised in the United States and hold American citizenship seem to be loyal foremost to Japan, and so on, and so on.

Under Japanese nationality law, too, said the American side, Japanese children born in the United States are Japanese nationals. When they grow up, it seems as if they have a duty to serve in the Japanese military. Such laws only add strength to the arguments of those Americans who oppose according citizenship to Japanese residents. We hear that, while Japan on the surface grants its people freedom of religion, in reality the government interferes in people's fundamental freedoms, such as what one believes in and for what one should live for. The Twenty-One Demands presented to China included a religion-related item, we hear. Such things give an impression that Japanese have different values than Americans, and such impressions work in favor of the anti-Japanese activists. These were the major points.

The Japanese side, on the other hand, argued it was at the request and invitation of the United States that Japanese emigration had begun in the first place; it was hard to understand what the immigrants had done to deserve such complaints. Also, it was American refusal to allow Japanese children to attend public schools and boycotts of Japanese shops that prompted Japanese to form their own neighborhoods and keep to themselves. To turn around and criticize them for not assimilating was unreasonable and hard to accept. The Japanese side tried to counter the criticisms of the immigrants, but their arguments failed to convince the Americans and the two sides' views did not converge.

Ultimately, the recent deterioration of Japan-U.S. relations had little to do with the immigration issue. It stemmed, rather, from the militaristic and aggressive posture Japan had assumed since the Paris Peace Conference. From the point of view of the Americans at the meeting, therefore, the root of the problem had to be addressed and resolved; otherwise, they would get nowhere.

The disagreement over Japanese immigration could be attributed to the differences between the two countries in terms of history and culture, and to the values that formed the basis of life in the two countries. In Japan in those days, supreme value was placed on the state, and the authorities could compel the people to make any sacrifice if it were "for the sake of the country." It was a despotic system of government, but the members of the Japanese side at the conference in Tokyo seemed to see nothing wrong with it. The Americans present explained that they thought such a system, which ignored fundamental human rights, was barbaric, and accepting into their midst as immigrants people who were brought up in such a cultural milieu would be sowing seeds of danger in American society. They thought it was perfectly natural that Americans were wary of Japan.

The conference was intended to identify hints for future directions in Japan-U.S. relations by having both sides speak candidly about what they were thinking. As it turned out, however, the positions of the two sides were so far apart that they were afraid the conference might end up with no agreement at all. In the fourth day session, therefore, Eiichi proposed that the members of the Japanese and American sides temporarily forget about their respective countries' positions and think from a common perspective. In other words, he suggested they stop arguing which side is right or wrong and that, instead, they talk from a shared viewpoint about what should be done in a given situation and what future development would be desirable for all.

The American side promptly agreed. Yes, that's a good idea. Let's think from that point of view. They were very cooperative. As far as the minutes of the session suggests, however, the participants on the Japanese side seemed unable to really understand what Eiichi was getting at.[147]

Take Soeda Juichi, the former president of the Industrial Bank of Japan, for example. Soeda had a Ph.D. in law, could speak fluent English, and had traveled overseas a number of times, thereby gaining a great deal of international experience. Even he defended Japan's position in a loud voice as soon as the

---

[147] *Shibusawa denki shiryō*, vol. 35, pp. 281–85; pp. 292–93.

FIGURE 38
Fujiyama Raita (1863–1938),
president of the Tokyo
Chamber of Commerce. Photo:
National Diet Library, Japan.

discussion turned to the Paris Peace Conference. The anti-Japanese sentiment in Paris, he argued, was solely the result of the Chinese propaganda. The Chinese side sweet-talked Westerners and published a great number of pamphlets designed to cast Japan in a bad light. Japan was reluctant to fight back with similarly vulgar propaganda, he declared, and it had remained silent. That was the reason, he concluded, for the bad impression of Japan that had spread throughout the world.

Fujiyama Raita, president of the Tokyo Chamber of Commerce, took the same position. In spite of the Twenty-One Demands, the occupation of Shandong, the prolonging of the Siberian expedition, and so forth, Fujiyama insisted at the meeting that Japan was peace-loving and did not seek to invade the continent, and he argued that the business world, especially, was committed to peaceful means. He did not think of Japan as "militaristic."

In other words, Eiichi's call on the participants at the conference to put aside the positions of their own countries and think for the sake of all fell on deaf ears among the people on the Japanese side and had little impact on their thinking. That was perhaps because Japanese of those times were so deeply committed to their country that they could not see beyond it.

Eiichi was as good as any Japanese in devotion to his country, but at the same time, he was very well aware of the presence of people other than Japanese in this world. In talking about relations with China Eiichi often used the term "chūjo" (忠恕), which, according to the dictionary, means "to tolerate others; think of others as you do yourself; feeling sympathy or putting oneself in the others' shoes." That is to say, Eiichi's fundamental philosophy of life was consideration for others and getting along with others, and the "others" he had in mind included not just those friendly to Japan, but those who were hostile to it, as well.

Awareness of the needs or realities of other peoples, however, seems to have been seriously lacking among Japanese of those days. Everything revolved around their own country. They were gripped by a great sense of tension, as if the demise of the polity of their country would mean the end of their own lives. That mentality may have been the pathology that was slowly and steadily sickening the lifeblood of modern Japan.

These being the circumstances, what could be gained by talking heart-to-heart was probably limited. The eight-day conference did see a meaningful exchange of views on a number of points, such as submarine cables and labor-management issues, but there were often snags in the discussion on the essential topics relating to landowning and immigration, and in many cases good intentions did not help much. In the end, a joint statement to the effect that both sides would continue to endeavor to improve U.S.–Japan relations was issued and the conference came to an end on March 24.

Concrete results aside, the conference was Japan's first experience in which businessmen, scholars, and others of both Japan and the United States gathered in one place and engaged in serious discussion on relations between the two countries in a

Figure 39
Hara Takashi (1856–1921),
prime minister from 1918
to 1921, followed a policy of
cooperation with the United
States. Photo: National Diet
Library, Japan.

friendly atmosphere. That itself was of great significance. Today, holding an international conference at which experts from different sectors of society in various countries gather and talk is quite ordinary, but in those days such meetings were still very new, and represented a great leap forward in terms of private diplomacy.

Hara Takashi, who had succeeded Terauchi Masatake as prime minister in September 1918 and adopted a national policy of cooperation with the United States, had great hopes for the Eiichi-led private-level conference and welcomed the visiting group of Americans in good faith – such as by hosting a banquet for them – during the period of the conference. Many other events were held in conjunction with the gathering, sponsored by different organizations like the Tokyo Chamber of Commerce and the Japanese-American Relations Committee of Japan. Almost all the time except during session hours the participants were busy attending welcome parties and were besieged by visitors. Starting on March 25, they had a sightseeing tour to Nikko, Hakone, Kyoto, Miyajima, and elsewhere, and a cordial mood pervaded the send-off as they departed Yokohama aboard the *Shun'yo Maru* on April 12, bound for home.

CONCERNED JAPANESE AND AMERICANS

As usual, Eiichi was busy every day. Spring is and was then the season of school graduations in Japan. No sooner had the conference closed than Eiichi's days were filled with attendance at the graduation ceremonies of the schools he was involved in: the Women's Art School, the Futaba Girls High School, the Tokyo Higher Commercial School (present-day Hitotsubashi University), and so on. The Kyōchōkai (Harmony Society), a foundation established in 1919 by Eiichi and others to promote labor-management harmony, had problems of one sort or another at that time and held a board meeting almost every two days. There was also a backlog of tasks that had piled up during the conference period to be taken care of. And there was the usual stream of visitors. The Asukayama area, where he lived, was well known for its cherry blossoms. The trees were in full bloom then, but Eiichi had little time to enjoy them. And in the middle of April he became extremely busy preparing to welcome a prestigious delegation of Americans led by his old friend Frank A. Vanderlip, president of the City Bank of New York and former assistant secretary of the Treasury. This was for the second of the two 1920 conferences, the Nichi-Bei Yūshi Kyōgikai (Conference of Concerned Japanese and Americans), held for six days, from April 26 through May 1.

The American delegation this time consisted of prominent figures, mainly in business, from New York and other parts of the U.S. East Coast. The previous group had included the most important business leaders in California, but the coming group was without doubt more important in terms of influence in the United States as a whole, especially in Washington.

The leader of the delegation, Vanderlip himself, was an outstanding figure in the New York financial world. Other impressive names among the members included former secretary of treasury Lyman J. Gage; Henry W. Taft (brother of President William H. Taft); Cornell University president Jacob G. Schurman; George Eastman of the Eastman Kodak Company; New York Stock Exchange vice president Seymour L. Cromwell; American Exchange National Bank president Lewis L. Clarke; and critic Julian Street of the *Saturday Evening Post*.

The Japanese side attached great importance to the coming of Vanderlip's group. Eiichi brought together leading figures in various circles to form the Welcome Association and took charge of entertaining the delegation. Prime Minister Hara fully supported Eiichi and himself had gone to the trouble of inviting all the people concerned with the planning to a dinner party on March 28 where he asked them to do everything they could to entertain these illustrious guests.

The Welcome Association decided that efforts should be made to have as many of the Americans as possible stay in Japanese homes, rather than at hotels, so that they could actually experience what it was like to live in Japan. Vanderlip, his wife and daughter, and Lyman Gage would stay at the Eiichi-owned Japanese-style residence at Mita Tsunamachi in Shiba ward, Tokyo. At the time my father, Shibusawa Keizō, was living there. Keizō was a University of Tokyo student, and at the order of Eiichi, his grandfather, he together with his brothers, was put in charge of entertaining these guests for more than a week, from April 24, when the Vanderlip delegation was to arrive in Japan, through May 2, the day the delegation was to leave Tokyo.

I remember my father fondly reminiscing about the morning of their arrival. Eiichi was keenly aware of the elements of hospitality, and the morning of the day the guests were to arrive – by which time almost everything was ready to welcome them – Eiichi telephoned Keizō to check on the preparations, reminding him, "Is toilet paper ready? Make sure for yourself."

Cromwell and his wife stayed at the Asano Ryōzō residence next to my father's house; Eastman stayed at the Mitsui Club; Clarke, his wife and daughter at the Kondō Renpei residence in Samonchō, Ushigome ward; Schurman and his wife at the

Ōkura Kihachirō second home in Terajima (Tokyo prefecture); and many others also stayed in private homes. A few, such as Julian Street and his wife, and Henry Taft, stayed at the Imperial Hotel.

Vanderlip was of a new type among men of the business world and had a fairly progressive way of thinking. In a speech at a welcome party hosted by the Tokyo Chamber of Commerce, Eiichi said, "Japan has undergone dramatic changes over the last six decades, and so, as you see, our country is in a state of disorder with both the old and the new existing together. Under your guidance, we will endeavor to keep up with world trends." In his response, Vanderlip observed that old ways of thinking remained firmly entrenched in the United States – i.e., isolationism or egocentric notions ill-informed about other parts of the world. He expressed his hope that the United States would break away from antiquated ideas without delay and acquire the temperament of a great country. Unless it was capable of making the concerns of others its own concerns and the happiness of others its own happiness, the United States would never be a world leader.

Anticipating the Marshall Plan of the post-World War II era, Vanderlip had the idea that the United States ought to take an active role in rebuilding war-devastated Western Europe. Eiichi rated Vanderlip's thinking highly for its innovation and breadth. He recognized how greatly the American financier had matured in thinking and stature compared to the time they had first met when Vanderlip was vice president of the National City Bank of New York under James Stillman. He seemed to have grown even smarter, even more courageous and trustworthy. He now had enough power and was in a position to be able to play a key role as a "pacemaker" of the U.S. economy, which was about to take great and ambitious leaps forward into the world.

Vanderlip, too, thought highly of Eiichi. He trusted him entirely and was firmly in agreement with Eiichi's internationalism. That was why he had persuaded many of his friends into taking time out of their busy schedules to come as far as Tokyo.

When it came to policy matters, however, real heart-to-heart talk was not easy. Vanderlip was too rational and intellectual – a typical American, to be irresistibly charmed by a single person.

Visiting Vanderlip at his home in Scarborough, New York in 1915, Eiichi had proposed that it was desirable for Japan and the United States to make a joint investment in China. Vanderlip had responded by saying he did not think the Chinese would cooperate with Japanese, whom they so abhorred. Eiichi had responded that China, the United States, and Japan should not let themselves be at the mercy of emotional likes and dislikes but that they should rely on more solid foundations and principles in proceeding with a project. In the end, however, he was aware that Vanderlip interpreted what he had said as an attempt to excuse past Japanese actions.

On the surface, Eiichi was aware that he was attempting to make an excuse, and he regretted that, but on a deeper level what he had really wanted to convey was that, in order to bring genuine peace and stability to the Pacific, he firmly believed that Japan and the United States should not be distracted by immediate phenomena but work together in helping to rebuild China. Apparently, he was unable to get that idea across convincingly. Vanderlip would not try to see beyond Eiichi's expressed words to understand his real message. He was very intelligent, which seemed to make it all the more difficult for him to understand those not tuned to his wavelength.

Recalling the conference, Eiichi reflected with great regret, "[In New York], I probably had not tried hard enough, but I am afraid my sincerity did not get through to him." That was why he had decided to invite Vanderlip to Japan to get him to see the reality of the Far East for himself and to try to better explain to him what he had meant. Eiichi wanted to work together with Vanderlip to move toward a shared goal. This thought was what led to the April 1920 conference.[148]

---

[148] For the following summary of the discussion at the conference, see *Shibusawa denki shiryō*, vol. 35, pp. 316–18. See https://eiichi. shibusawa.or.jp/denkishiryo/digital/main/index.php?35#a31030205

The conference was held at the Tokyo Bankers Association's conference hall in Chiyoda ward. Eiichi was chosen as chairman, and Kaneko Kentarō and Vanderlip alternated as moderators. Among the topics on the agenda were the immigration issue, Japan's cooperation in the development of China, Japan's occupation of the Shandong peninsula, the Siberian expedition, and the Korea issue.

The American group this time was from the U.S. East Coast and its members were undisturbed by the anti-Japanese movement in California. In response to Japan's protests against the California referendum and other related matters, their judgment was informed by the fact that the referendum was conducted according to law; they showed little interest in an emotional protest that did not have a legal basis. Kaneko Kentarō complained that the U.S. federal government had not protested strongly against the racist law as Roosevelt had done before. Vanderlip himself then pointed out that Japan, too, practiced racial discrimination, limiting the entry of Chinese and not allowing them to own or lease land. While having such laws of its own, he argued, Japan could not criticize the United States.

This rebuttal momentarily silenced the Japanese side, but Kaneko then countered, saying that since China did not have a Western-style legal system with criminal, civil, and commercial codes of law, Chinese were liable to disobey Japanese laws. Over the past five decades the Japanese had striven hard to meet the civilized Western countries' expectations, and unlike China, Japan was now a safe place where you could safely walk alone at night even in a major city. He argued that it was wrong to treat the hard-striving Japanese on the same level as the Chinese whose country was still "uncivilized" (not modernized).

Kaneko's rebuttal inadvertently revealed the fundamental weakness of Japanese arguments on the whole immigration issue. What the Japanese position boiled down to was that they believed they should be treated differently from other Asians. The American anti-Japanese movement did not make sense to them because they had worked hard for five decades to remake their country in emulation of the West and believed they deserved thereby to be treated on a par with white people. They had completely misread the times. The twentieth century had begun, World War I had ended, and even a communist state had appeared. Their argument was doomed to be received with contempt by white people and arouse only antipathy from other nonwhite peoples. Dividing the world in two, based on the ambiguous and value-loaded concept of "civilized/uncivilized," might not have been totally out of place in the early years of the Meiji era (1868–1912) but was certainly questionable in 1920.

Regarding the Siberian, Shandong, and Korean issues, the Japanese side tried to explain as clearly as possible Japan's position and the actual conditions of the issues, and did its best to correct misunderstandings of Japan as a militaristic, aggressive country. Those explanations were very detailed as well as persuasive, partly because some members of the Japanese side, such as Soeda Juichi and Zumoto Motosada, had actually been to and observed Siberia, and there were also other experts like Megata Tanetarō, former financial advisor to Korea, and Sakatani Yoshirō, who was a former finance minister and familiar with Chinese fiscal affairs.

On the Korea issue, Eiichi himself remarked, "It was no exaggeration that I have devoted myself to the Korean economy for many years. The Dai-ichi Bank, of which I am manager, has long been engaged in Korean financial affairs since it established its branch in Korea in 1878. . . . I am proud to say that it is because of the bank's good management that the circulation of convertible banknotes goes well in Korea."[149]

The first railway line to be built in Korea was the Gyeongin Line between Incheon and Seoul, opened by Eiichi in May 1899. He was sincerely committed to furthering Korean economic development and the project was vivid in his memory. Political relations between Japan and Korea had later become complex, and he had to admit that there were many problems with Japan's Korea policy, but as far as economic affairs were concerned, Japan was not just exploiting the Korean economy but

---

[149] *Shibusawa denki shiryō*, vol. 35, pp. 412–14.

trying very hard to improve it. That was a message Eiichi wanted to get across to the U.S. side.

Today it is obvious to us that no matter how a country may economically aid another, and no matter how good the results may be, if that country deprives the other of its independence and harms its people, anything it might do for the sake of the latter will be blown away in an instant. It may not be fair to blame Eiichi at that time for not being well aware of that principle. In retrospect, however, most of the world was under the colonial rule of a handful of advanced countries in his time, and in economic terms, there were many cases around the world in which exploitation was far more severe than what was going on in Korea.

As for the Chinese issue, Eiichi was determined to persuade Vanderlip to understand the ideas he had failed to get across in New York five years earlier. He spoke with passion and reason. He focused on economic cooperation. He spoke to the point and clearly expressed his thoughts about the most desirable relations between Japan, the United States, and China.

Regarding China, he observed, besides its political instability, the deficiencies of its fiscal and financial systems were also the source of its crisis. If it continued to rely on foreign loans to make up for a shortage of its administrative budget, China would certainly collapse in the not-distant future. The currency in circulation differed from one region to another, and there was no official conversion system in place; such a situation made it virtually impossible to build industry, he said. Eiichi asserted the three prerequisites for China to build up its economy: establishment of a solid fiscal foundation, reform of the monetary system, and improvement of the financial system. Britain and France might provide some aid, but it was the United States and Japan that would be able to really commit to this endeavor.

When two or more countries cooperate in helping another country, said Eiichi, it is vitally necessary for them to have their policy-making decisions based on solid principles and be determined not to change those principles easily.

"If we vacillate in our attitude, sometimes pleasing them and other times angering them, then we will never be able to

Figure 40
Sakatani Yoshirō (1863–
1941), who guided the founding of the Chuo Bank, served
as finance minister; Eiichi's
son-in-law. Photo: Shibusawa
Memorial Museum.

guide China to move forward on the straight and true path,"
said Eiichi. "If China itself does wrong it can't be helped, but
we ourselves cannot change course just to go along with it."[150]
Eiichi said he had expressed the same ideas when Elbert H. Gary,
chairman of U.S. Steel, had visited in Japan, and that Gary had
readily agreed.

The Chinese side, meanwhile, had later planned to reform
its monetary system and organize a central bank, and offered to
invite Sakatani Yoshirō (former finance minister and Eiichi's son-
in-law) to serve as a financial advisor. Eiichi had told Sakatani
that the role of financial advisor would be an extremely difficult
one and that "even if you succeed in performing that role no one
would praise you, while if you don't succeed you will be slan-
dered." He suggested that Sakatani take the post only "if you are

---

[150] *Shibusawa denki shiryō*, vol. 35, pp. 415–16.

ready to 'practice benevolence at the sacrifice of self,'" a phrase from the *Analects* of Confucius. As it turned out, however, Eiichi regretfully told the Vanderlip delegation, the plan had not materialized due to the so-called Sakatani Incident.[151]

In the Japanese government, too, the Terauchi Masatake Cabinet adopted the shameful practice of getting rights from China by providing it with loans without cause. "Taking advantage of another country's financial difficulties through providing loans is far from showing sincerity; on the contrary it violates sincerity," said Eiichi.[152]

The prospects for the future were hard to tell, Eiichi continued, but as far as China's economic construction was concerned, if it were not for the United States and Japan jointly helping it, China would not be able to get construction projects underway, to say nothing of bringing them to completion, as was clear from what had happened in various circumstances before.

Eiichi's logically consistent argument apparently made a strong impression on the American participants. They asked in particular to know the details of the Sakatani Incident from the Japanese side. The Japanese members, however, were not eager to talk about the incident and tried to evade the subject. In retrospect, had the Japanese side explained what had happened more openly, these powerful men of New York financial circles might have been able to shed light on and correct to some extent the traditional pro-Chinese, anti-Japanese prejudice of the State Department. That might have somewhat changed the history of Japan-U.S. relations.

During the six-day conference, the members of the U.S. and Japanese sides asked questions and gave answers amid a generally

---

[151] In 1918, Ishii Kikujirō, special envoy to the United States, had obtained consent from U.S. Secretary of State Robert Lansing to Sakatani's appointment as China's financial advisor, despite the opposition of Paul S. Reinsch, the U.S. minister in Beijing. Several months later, however, Lansing started saying he had *not* consented. As a result, Ishii resigned as special envoy and Sakatani's appointment was cancelled. In Japan this incident is known as the "promise-breaking incident" (*shokugen jiken*). Nish, *Japanese Foreign Policy*, pp. 123–24.

[152] *Shibusawa denki shiryō*, vol. 35, pp. 417–18.

friendly atmosphere. There were detailed discussions, sometimes clashes of views, and other times talk at cross purposes. At one point, Japanese members explained at great length about how unstable and fluid the situation was in China, Manchuria, and Mongolia. But, whenever Japan resorted to some necessary measure or other to protect its Japanese residents and railways it was immediately denounced as imperialist. Hearing this complaint from the Japanese side, Henry Taft swiftly responded that if that was the case, Japan should file a complaint with the League of Nations and let the League settle. No matter what the reason, Japan should not act alone; otherwise such an action would constitute an infringement of Chinese sovereignty.

Theoretically, what he said was right, but it was easier said than done. The United States itself was not a member of the League of Nations, and as of that time, China was refusing to sign the Versailles peace treaty. Filing a complaint with the League of Nations would have made the problem even more complicated and its solution even more difficult. Despite these realities, the proposals and comments of the American side often came across as unrealistic, amusing, disappointing, or even offensive to the Japanese side.

Generally, though, the conference was meaningful. After the conference closed, Vanderlip made a speech. He observed that from the discussions he felt it necessary for the West to stop forcing its style upon East Asia and instead endeavor to harmonize with Asian ideas. The West should deal carefully with various problems in the Far East with due respect. It was also vital that loans to China should be provided with absolute fairness. He appreciated the members of the Japanese side for their honest, modest, and friendly attitudes from beginning to end.[153]

Even today, the age of information, it is not always easy to have Americans recognize that a people different from themselves but just as civilized are living on the other side of the Pacific Ocean. In the early twentieth century, when the superiority of Western civilization was unchallenged and taken for granted, influencing a leading and typical American figure like Vanderlip to change

---

[153] *Shibusawa denki shiryō*, vol. 35, p. 437.

his assumptions to the extent reflected in the speech mentioned above, and bring him all the way to Japan, was noteworthy and was a result of Eiichi's long and conscientious efforts and convictions.

After returning home, the members of the American delegation took various opportunities to spread their new views of Japan in their respective capacities. Henry Taft, for example, wrote an article in the *New York Times* saying that, although Japan might have thought of possessing Shandong during the war, that thought had changed. In terms of international law, as well, Japan's position was coherent, and the current trouble was rather attributable to the stubbornness and inefficiency of China.

In a speech at the Commercial Club in San Francisco, Vanderlip touched on the immigration issue: the Japanese were not complaining about the same restrictions upon them as those on other foreigners, but they were complaining about racial discrimination; the most important thing about this issue was what to do about racial discrimination. Agreements should be made through careful and international discussion based on courtesy and empathy; it was absurd that some American politicians and journalists spoke ill of Japanese and offended them. Vanderlip stressed that the United States, which had been the country to open Japan's doors earlier, had no right to criticize Japan over trifling and unnecessary matters and corner it into closing its doors again.

At a debate on foreign relations held at the Bank of New York Club on July 15, 1920, the issue of loans to China was discussed. There, Henry Taft observed that Japanese understood the United States far more than Americans understood Japan, and urged people to cultivate more correct knowledge of the Far East. Cornell University president Schurman said the U.S.-Japan issue was one of the most difficult confronting the United States as well as an international issue that required utmost care. He expressed great anxiety in seeing Americans dealing with the U.S.-Japan issue as if tossing about a football.

Schurman also made an interesting comment, stating that in Japan there was a struggle going on between military forces and neo-liberal forces centered around businessmen, which was an intriguing situation, and that if Japan managed to overcome this situation it might become a great country with a British-style democratic government.[154]

If such views had had some effect on the policy and attitude of the U.S. State Department, the subsequent developments in U.S.-Japan relations might have been different from what in fact unfolded. Regrettably, the State Department of that time had not moved beyond the overly simplistic principle of the "open door" and the territorial integrity of China, and the anti-Japanese, pro-Chinese mood Willard Straight had set in place was still dominant among working-level diplomats, mainly in the Bureau of Far Eastern Affairs.

As represented in the bitter attacks by Robert Lansing and Paul Reinsch (U.S. minister to Beijing), Japan had committed a number of grave mistakes in its policy toward the continent. From the early Meiji era up to today, Japanese attitudes toward China have often been mistaken, and that is because Japan has not yet laid the correct foundations for relations with China. If U.S.–Japan relations are a history of misunderstandings, Sino-Japanese relations are also a history of repeated, even deeper gaps in understanding. Because of this there clearly were many events that deserved the State Department's criticisms in the early twentieth century.

However, that could not be an excuse for the State Department to take into no account the complicated reality of East Asia and assume a complacent and arrogant stance imposing an overly simplistic logic on Japan and telling it that unless it did what they said, Japan would be a violator of peace. That would get nowhere.

In his *American Diplomacy, 1900–1950*, George F. Kennan wrote:

> Nor would we, over the space of many years, often consent to take into account the significance of what we were asking from the standpoint of Japanese internal affairs. If the price of our frustration of

---

[154] *Shibusawa denki shiryō*, vol. 35, p. 442.

Japan's policies on the mainland was the final entrenchment of the power of the military extremists at Tokyo, that apparently made little difference over the long run. [...] It made little difference if our desiderata touched Japanese feelings in peculiarly sensitive spots. It made little difference that the Japanese soul already bore the wounds of having been deprived of the fruits of victory by outside force after the war with China in 1894. We would not let that worry us when we allowed ourselves to appear again at the conclusion of the war with Russia in 1905 as the frustrators of Japanese victory (which we really were not). We would not let it interfere with our rushing in again, in the wake of World War I – this time as the real leaders of a determined movement to deprive Japan of what she conceived to be the fruits, in terms of betterment of her position on the mainland, of her participation in the war against Germany. (p. 52)

It was against the backdrop of this sad history of U.S.-Japan relations that the two conferences of U.S-Japanese private diplomacy took place in 1920. There, discussions were very frank and honest throughout, sometimes getting to the core of the problems. Businessmen, scholars, and others who were not diplomatic experts engaged in orderly discussion – without any bargaining or bluffing – in a friendly atmosphere. The achievements were the greatest ever that could be expected of private diplomacy, and there was probably no precedent of its kind.

Such private-sector meetings, with no political influence and no binding goals, usually end up in a mood of half-baked goodwill. What kept the 1920 conferences high in quality and appropriately tense from beginning to the end was, of course, partly the discernment and effort of all the participants. But, certainly, one of the factors behind their success was Eiichi's personality and enthusiasm, his earnest aspirations for world peace and happiness.

Writer Julian Street published an open letter in the *New York Times*, severely criticizing the anti-Japanese movement in California and underlining the necessity to normalize U.S.-Japan relations. Later, he wrote his impressions of Eiichi, praising his "clearness of vision, . . . prevision . . . realistic view of life and events, the simplicity and directness with which [he] met all problems, and [his] steadfastness of purpose." Street declared that "Viscount Shibusawa represented in my eyes the sterling qualities of the Japanese race at its best." Recalling his countless charities and generosities, and admiring "his sense of world affairs" and "greatness not restricted to narrow national-ism, Japanese patriot though he was," Street wrote that he would always revere Eiichi's memory as "the sort of nobleman who is a *noble man* – a sort such as the Creator seldom makes."[155]

---

[155] Kyugoro Obata, *An Interpretation of the Life of Viscount Shibusawa.* Tokyo: Daiyamondo Jigyo Kabushiki Kaisha, 1937, pp. 311–13. Reproduced in *Shibusawa denki shiryō*, vol. 35, pp. 443–44.

CHAPTER 9

THE WASHINGTON NAVAL CONFERENCE

ઈ૦

RELATIONS WITH THE United States had deteriorated, in large part over the immigration issue, but it was the actions of Japanese in China, rather than in California, that exacerbated the situation. United States policy, especially after the Paris peace talks ending World War I, had become decidedly pro-China, and the tensions between Japan and China spilled over into Japan's relationship with the United States. Anti-Japanese demonstrations and boycotts of Japanese goods in China were continuing, and the future of trade between the two countries had become a serious concern.

Japanese industrialists launched efforts to try and improve relations with China as well as with the United States. In January 1920, representatives of Japanese businesses trading with China, banks, and eight chambers of commerce in various parts of Japan met to discuss the formation of a nationwide association for that purpose. In June, leading figures from the January gathering founded the Nik-Ka Jitsugyō Kyōkai (Japan-China Business Association) and Eiichi was asked to be its chairman.

The fact that the business community had formed a group to have a say in Japan's diplomatic affairs and actively lobby the government was proof that commerce enjoyed a higher social status than it had in the past and that businessmen were becoming more aware of what they could do. The move was also an expression of business leaders' concern about the increasing militarization of Japan's foreign policy, especially since World War I.

During the long reign of the Meiji emperor, from 1868 to 1912, Japan's military and economic interests had generally coincided, so it had been easy to adopt a consistent foreign policy. But after World War I, government policies became highly strategic, and as plans to create spheres of influence in Manchuria, Siberia, and other areas, or to use the country's strong navy to establish control of the western Pacific came to be seen as urgent matters of national defense, government policies became more aggressive. Japan's actions caused great tensions in relations with China and the United States. Where economic interests were concerned, however, Japanese exports to the United States during World War I had grown four-fold, and imports from America had quintupled. A contradictory situation had arisen whereby Japan's ability to develop as an independent economic power in the future depended on a more cooperative relationship with the United States.

These contradictory stances – aggression versus cooperation – would later affect Japan's worldview and policies. Even ordinary Japanese would be compelled to choose between two opposing alternatives as far as living and thinking were concerned. That dilemma formed the backdrop to the tragic path that Japan would tread between then and the end of World War II.

During Eiichi's long years of trying to improve relations between Japan and the United States, there is no doubt that in addition to the moral and idealistic aims of fostering peace and goodwill, he was also moved – how conscious he was of the fact is hard to know – by the practical motivation of protecting Japan's economic interests. Therefore, participating in the Japanese-American Relations Committee as well as in activities to improve relations between Japan and China was naturally in line with that objective. He would certainly have been willing to chair the group even if he had not been asked, but it happened that he was not in good health at that time in June 1920.

The two initiatives in Japan-U.S. private diplomacy Eiichi had led in the spring that year – the Japanese-American Relations Committee-sponsored joint conference in March and the April visit by the delegation of prominent Americans headed by Frank

A. Vanderlip (see "Landmarks of Private Diplomacy" in chapter 8) – had severely taxed his energies. For more than two months, he had been involved in a dizzying round of activities: three-hour long conference meetings every morning were followed by receptions for one body or another. There were lunches, tea parties, garden parties, and evening banquets in formal wear, events hosted by prime minister Hara Takashi, foreign minister Uchida Yasuya (Kōsai), former prime minister Ōkuma Shigenobu, U.S. ambassador Roland Morris, as well as the Bank of Japan, the Yokohama Specie Bank, chambers of commerce, the Mitsui and Iwasaki families, and so forth. Day after day, Eiichi would return briefly to his office in Kabutochō after an engagement to change for the next function and rush out again, and on top of that he was expected to make a speech at every event where he was present. From early morning, moreover, he would often have to deal with visitors waiting in his office who were there to discuss other matters.

Eiichi determinedly kept up with the frenetic pace during the conferences, but he was severely fatigued. After the last meeting of the second conference on May 1, he took to his bed in the afternoon with a cold. Fortunately, the cold did not lead to complications, but he was now 80 years old. After a stern warning from his doctor and following the entreaties of his family, he decided to stay put at his Asukayama residence and rest for a while. During the whole of May and into June, he saw as few visitors as possible and did not go out at all.

Meanwhile, the formal decision to establish the Japan-China Business Association having been made, three emissaries, Sugihara Eizaburō, vice-chairman of the Tokyo Chamber of Commerce, Itō Yonejirō, president of Nippon Yūsen, and Shiraiwa Ryūhei, an expert in Japan-China relations, called on Eiichi, requesting that he serve as chairman. Itō, speaking for the trio, explained that relations between Japan and China surpassed those between Japan and the United States in importance, and that it was crucial that Eiichi head the group, which industrialists from all over Japan had agreed to join. He said that the Association would have little clout within and outside of Japan without Eiichi, a man of great age and virtue, and that it could not accomplish its goals without him; they pleaded with Eiichi to accept.

Of course Eiichi was well aware of the importance of relations between Japan and China. But he was quite concerned that he was not in good enough health to meet expectations and, besides, his family had been adamant that he take a well-deserved rest following his recent private-diplomacy marathon. He also viewed it as a problem that the world of industry, which was full of many talented individuals, always turned to him to resolve whatever knotty problem it faced. As he was mulling over the matter, Sugihara rose impatiently from his chair, ramrod stiff and with tears in his eyes, and implored him to accept the post, saying that the Association could otherwise not go forward.

Eiichi made up his mind. Healthy or not, we all die one day, he must have thought, and as long as he was living, he could fulfill his long-cherished desire to do whatever he could for Japan and for East Asia. A decisive person by nature, Eiichi apparently felt comfortable with this rationalization. Shiraiwa later recalled that Eiichi accepted the request, saying that although he was sure his family would complain about his being over-extended again, he would do what he could for the Association.[156]

DISASTER AID FOR CHINA

In the autumn of 1920, famine raged in northern China. Severe drought had struck the four provinces of Zhili (later part of Hebei province), Shandong, Shanxi, and Henan, affecting an estimated 20 million people. The previous year's harvest had also been poor, about 80 percent of normal, but in 1920 things got even worse, with harvests only 20 or 30 percent of normal. In some villages there were no harvests at all. Villages were all in a dire state, with everyone selling their furniture and even their children to somehow fend off starvation.

---

[156] See *Shiraiwa Ryūhei danwa hikki* (Record of Conversations with Shiraiwa Ryūhei), as excerpted in *Shibusawa denki shiryō*, vol. 55, pp. 169–170.

The Japan-China Business Association immediately went into action for famine relief. On September 24, Eiichi visited the Prime Minister's office. There he waited for a Cabinet meeting to end and approached Prime Minister Hara and assorted ministers to receive their approval and support for a nationwide charity drive for China. Eiichi was unable to garner sufficient pledges from industry due to the recession after World War I, but, even so, monetary donations reached 400,000 yen by the end of the year and had grown to 650,000 yen by the spring of 1921.[157]

Using the donated funds, the Association set up camps and medical care facilities in Beijing, Tianjin, Jinan and other cities. The camps housed 12,000 people and 680,000 people received medical attention. This goodwill gesture was not for political effect, of course, but it was reported that the Chinese authorities and the general public were appreciative of the gesture (*Asahi shimbun*, June 16, 1921).

Given the overall negative sentiment toward Japan throughout China, however, such gestures were like a drop of goodwill in an ocean of bad. In addition to more private initiatives like those of the Association, achieving true friendship between the two countries would require nothing less than a fundamental shift in Japan's policies toward China.

In June 1921, Eiichi, representing the Association, presented a strongly expressed position statement to the government. The main points of the statement were that Japan needed to establish a consistent policy toward China. At a time when China's domestic situation was so unstable, with two governments competing for control and the Western powers watching closely, any inconsistencies only exposed disunity within Japan itself and invited suspicion and derision on the part of both the Chinese authorities and the public, leading to the misunderstanding that Japan was bent on imperialism and invasion of their country.

---

[157] In 1921, ¥400,000 was worth about US$193,200 and ¥650,000 was about $313,950. Today, in 2016 values ¥400,000 would be equivalent to $44,800,000 and ¥650,000 would be $72,800,000. www.historicalstatistics.org. – ed.

Japan's basic stance should be to avoid unnecessary interference in China's domestic affairs and leave internal issues to the Chinese themselves. Japan should be sincere and show unfailing goodwill and sympathy toward China, and determine to wholeheartedly support its legitimate hopes, even at some cost to Japan itself. If Japan adopted this basic stance and, overcoming various hurdles, made sincere overtures to China in an effort to win over the Chinese public, the efforts would eventually pay off.[158]

As for specific issues, it was Eiichi's recommendation that the Japanese troops guarding the railroad in Shandong retreat, that the railroad be made a joint venture between Japan and China, and that troops at Hankou (Hankow), whose presence was arousing suspicions among the Great Powers, be pulled back immediately.

Eiichi was often doubtful about the government's foreign policy. He realized that diplomacy was a human enterprise, so mistakes were inevitable, but accounts of his views around this time in the early 1920s suggest that he was totally unconvinced by the government's line of thinking. In the past, the government, although sometimes wrong, had taken a clear and easy-to-understand position that he could go along with. He can be heard musing that policy making seemed to be left to the bureaucracy, political responsibilities were not clarified, and no one was taking a strong stand on carrying through on important measures. Even though political parties were becoming more broadly based, different elites, including the military, which had direct access to the Emperor under the Meiji Constitution, were jockeying for power; it was unclear where power really lay.[159]

A prime example of this weak-kneed government was its indifference to the exclusionist moves against Japanese in the United

---

[158] For the above account of Eiichi's position, see *Chūgai Shōgyō shinpō* (Domestic and Foreign Commercial News), No. 12667 (June 21, 1921), "Nis-Shi shinzen hōsaku no kenpaku: Nik-Ka Jitsugyō Kyōkai kōhyō" (Position Statement on Policy for Improving Relations between Japan and China: Japan-China Business Association Publicizes Statement), *Shibusawa denki shiryō*, vol. 55, pp. 183–84.

[159] See also Stockwin, *Governing Japan*, pp. 17–21.

States. In California, a petition to amend the Alien Land Law submitted by the Japanese Exclusion League on August 4, 1920 garnered 83,670 signatures, far in excess of the legally required minimum of 56,000, and as expected, the matter was put up for a state referendum. Eiichi could hardly bear it when he heard about this development, knowing how devastating this would be for tens of thousands of Japanese immigrants in California, but the Japanese government showed no signs of taking any action to intervene.

Japan's foreign ministry viewed the immigration problem as a domestic issue of the United States and felt that making too much of a fuss through diplomatic channels would have the opposite effect of stirring up more anti-Japanese sentiment. Besides, Japanese diplomats could not approach the California State Legislature directly. All that could be done was to watch and wait.

But in Eiichi's view, he and other like-minded Japanese – although they had not been asked – had done their best to approach as many influential Americans as possible through the Japanese-American Relations Committee in order to move public opinion inside the United States. Discussions at the two 1920 conferences for Japan–U.S. private diplomacy had been fairly successful, and Eiichi had taken every opportunity he could that year to explain Japan's position, entertaining congressmen visiting Japan (September 7, 1920) and meeting with newspaper reporters, religious leaders, industrialists and others. He also sent experts such as Harada Tasuku, educator and Christian minister, to California to research living conditions among Japanese immigrants in the state, and continued his vigorous efforts to improve relations between the two countries.

If the Japanese government had the backbone it had shown in the past, Eiichi seems to have believed, it would have carefully assessed the situation and then taken decisive steps to change American sentiment toward Japan. Its actions might not have been successful, but if it took a decisive stance with the country's destiny truly in mind, the private sector – Japanese business and industry – would have found a way to cooperate. If the government continued its litany of empty explanations and avoided taking responsibility, it would soon be too late to do anything, and Japan as a country and its people would be the ones with the most to lose.

And just as Eiichi had feared, the California Alien Land Law was amended as the result of the state referendum held on November 2, 1920, with 668,483 voting for amendment and 222,086 voting against. Anti-Japanese discrimination, which had started with the exclusion of schoolchildren from California's public schools and escalated to the 1907 Gentlemen's Agreement between the Japanese and American governments, and the California Alien Land Law of 1913, had once again entered a new phase, the very development that Eiichi and others had been so concerned about.

Naturally, passage of the law hardened public opinion in Japan. Distrust of the U.S. federal government for its unhelpful stance, which had been growing ever since the Paris Peace Conference, rose to a peak, and the possibility of going to war with the United States began to be entertained in some quarters. It was in fact Japanese in the United States who most worried about this, and on November 8, they sent a telegram to Prime Minister Hara saying that although Japanese on the home islands might be indignant, they implored their countrymen to stay calm and be patient.

In a dispatch to the State Department, U.S. Ambassador to Japan Roland Morris underlined the gravity of the situation and warned that the United States would have to do something if it wanted to continue its activities in Asia. He proposed that a new agreement on limiting immigration be drawn up to replace the Gentlemen's Agreement in order to reliably control inflows of new immigrants and that guarantees be offered for fair treatment of those who were already in the United States. The resultant series of intense negotiations was later known as the Morris-Shidehara Talks (Morris met U.S. Ambassador Shidehara Kijurō 23 times over four months), but anti-Japanese sentiment in the western states was growing stronger by the day, and efforts in Washington to defuse the situation came to naught.[160]

ALLIANCE-SHIFTING BEHIND THE SCENES

The day of the California state referendum was also presidential election day 1920, when Republican Warren G. Harding was elected 29th president of the United States. Harding's victory represented a defeat for the foreign policy of the administration of Democrat Woodrow Wilson, who had played a leading role in establishing the League of Nations. In his inaugural address, Harding declared that the United States would "seek no part in directing the destinies of the Old World"[161] and would accept no political or economic responsibility, definitively shutting the door on the possibility of the United States joining the League of Nations. However, this did not mean that he was rejecting the idea of a collective forum for maintaining peace.

One month after Harding's election, powerful Republican Senator William E. Borah proposed that the United States, Britain, and Japan agree to a large-scale disarmament plan. Referencing this, Harding, in his inaugural speech, said "We are ready… to recommend a way to approximate disarmament and relieve the crushing burdens of military and naval establishments,"[162] hinting that he would hold a new disarmament conference.

At the onset of World War I, construction of warships by the United States had suddenly stepped up. Under the Naval Act of 1916, several large warships were under construction or being planned. During the war, many ships had been lost due to attacks by German submarines, fueling the need for a strong navy, and the opening of the Panama Canal was an additional factor. The Panama Canal had been billed as a means of unifying military preparedness in the Atlantic and Pacific Oceans, meaning that fewer ships would be needed to protect both, but once

---

[160] See Nish, *Japanese Foreign Policy,* pp. 131–32.

[161] See "Inaugural Address of Warren G. Harding," http://avalon.law.yale.edu/20th_century/harding.asp.

[162] Ibid. http://avalon.law.yale.edu/20th_century/harding.asp.

the canal actually opened, maritime transport increased, and the upshot was that more, not fewer, warships were needed.

Once World War I was over and recession had set in, a large-scale naval building program was a huge burden on finances, and there were doubts as to whether the program would be effective for defending the country. If the United States continued to expand its naval power, Britain and Japan would be forced to build their own warships in response and the Anglo-Japanese Alliance would be further strengthened. There was little point in the United States beefing up its own fighting strength if it meant that its rivals would also get stronger. Accordingly, it was to the United States' political and economic advantage to call on Britain and Japan to reduce their forces.

Meanwhile, Britain's military might had been severely depleted by the war and it was in no position to compete with the United States in building warships. If the United States continued to build as planned in 1916, sooner or later it would over-take Britain as the country with the biggest navy. Responding to the call of the United States meant that Britain could keep its naval strength equal to that of the United States: Britain could not have hoped for a better solution to its dilemma. The agreement would allow Britain to remain "master of the seas" if only in name, and even though Britain and the United States would be allowed to build an equal number of warships, the United States would have to deploy its ships in both the Atlantic and the Pacific oceans, effectively halving its strength.[163]

Britain began to approach the United States in earnest soon after President Harding's inauguration, just about the time that rumors about a war between Japan and the United States were rife. The British naval minister made an unofficial overture to the United States through a newspaper reporter, indicating that if the United States was worried about war with Japan and found that it had to shift its Atlantic fleet to the Pacific, the British Navy would step in to protect the Atlantic.[164]

---

[163] See Griswold, *The Far Eastern Policy of the United States,* pp. 270–71.

[164] Griswold, *The Far Eastern Policy of the United States*, pp. 283–84.

This was a very wise move and one that, in the eyes of Britain, succeeded in killing two birds with one stone. In other words, if the United States navy concentrated its forces in the Pacific, Britain would retain its superiority in the Atlantic and could, with the help of American might in the Pacific, hold Japan in check.

These talks between Britain and the United States progressed rapidly in the background as preparations were being made for the opening of the Washington Naval Conference. The Anglo-Japanese Alliance, however, presented a stumbling block. Signed in January 1902, the Alliance had been the cornerstone of Japan's and Britain's policy in the Far East for twenty years, serving to offset the threats posed to Britain by Germany and Russia in China, and to protect its vast holdings and interests stretching from India to Singapore, Hong Kong, and areas along the Yangtze from the possibility of Japanese attacks. For Japan, meanwhile, the Alliance represented backing by the world's greatest power and enabled it to actively implement its policies toward Korea and Manchuria without anxiety.

But the United States viewed the Alliance as a grave impediment. Every time the United States tried to counter Japan's expansionist and aggressive tendencies, through the open door policy and the principle of China's territorial integrity, Japan tended to use the Alliance as cover, leaving the United States unable to pursue matters further. The reason was that if the United States insisted too strongly and went to war with Japan, Britain might join in and support Japan because of the Alliance. Knox's proposal to make the South Manchurian Railway neutral had come to naught due to British objections, and it was all too apparent to the United States that Britain had protected Japan as far as the Siberian Expedition and the Shandong problem were concerned. As it happened, the Alliance was due to expire in July 1921, and the United States had already been pressing Britain to let it lapse or amend its provisions to the United States' liking.

Now that Russia and Germany were no longer a threat, the benefit of the Alliance to Britain was not as substantial, but it would not do to leave its territories and interests stretching from India to Shanghai exposed to Japanese military might without any guarantees. If, as the United States wished, Britain were to end the Alliance, it needed some other security treaty. The agenda for the Washington Naval Conference, from disarmament to security in the Asia-Pacific region, was rapidly taking shape.

Japan, meanwhile, strongly hoped that the Alliance would continue. It was one of modern Japan's most effective foreign policies, providing stability that had lasted for many years. The Alliance had been a lifeline to a fledgling Japan, flung into the world of survival of the fittest. While Britain had been fighting the war in Europe, Japan had stood by its friendship and made few moves to acquire Britain's interests in the Far East. A year before the Alliance's expiration, Japan had begun negotiating with Britain, trying its best to secure its renewal. Initially, Britain had been of like mind, but gradually began to be less responsive. Ultimately it proposed discussing a new framework with the United States, China, and other parties concerned at the Washington Naval Conference.[165]

This was a very unwelcome development for Japan. Indeed, Japan had been well disposed to participate if the conference were dealing only with naval disarmament. It was clear to all that trying to compete with the United States in an unrestricted warship-building race would have been tantamount to economic suicide. Japan's Siberian Expedition had also finally begun to be seen as a failure; it was found that a huge amount of military spending for the expedition had been wasted. It seemed to be in Japan's interest to participate in some kind of collective security organization in order to prevent further foolish adventures. However, discussing the Pacific Far East together with the United States and China was a different issue altogether. Ever since the Paris peace talks, Japan was well aware that the United States had decided to be highly critical of Tokyo over the Shandong problem and various other issues. At the time, Britain had been supporting Japan through thick and thin, allowing it to get out of tight spots. Now it seemed

---

[165] The recognized survey is Nish, *Alliance in Decline*, especially pp. 354–97.

FIGURE 41
Katō Tomosaburō (1861–
1923), navy minister and chief
commissioner plenipotentiary
of the Japanese delegation to
the Washington Naval Conference. Photo: National Diet
Library, Japan.

that Britain had not only been going behind Japan's back and
talking with the United States, but that it had also changed its
policies to pander to the Americans. This demonstrated how
Britain had become less powerful vis-à-vis the United States as
a result of the war and had shifted its foreign policy as a consequence. There were signs that Japan would be isolated, with all
the other participants ganging up on it.

The Japanese government received a formal invitation on July
13, 1921 to the Washington Naval Conference, to be held November 12, 1921 to February 6, 1922, but Japan did not reply immediately, although it obviously could not refuse to attend. To refuse
attendance at this meeting engineered by Britain and the United
States would definitely isolate Japan and put its very future as a
nation in doubt. Japanese officials began lobbying the American
government to create favorable conditions for itself beforehand
with regard to the agenda and the method of proceedings, but to
no avail. On July 26, much later than the other countries, Japan
replied that it would attend. Its delegation consisted of navy min-

FIGURE 42
Shidehara Kijūrō (1872–1951),
Japan's ambassador to the United
States and member of the Japanese
delegation to the Washington Naval
Conference. Photo: National Diet
Library, Japan.

ister Katō Tomosaburō, serving as chief commissioner plenipotentiary, House of Peers president Tokugawa Iesato, and Japan's
ambassador to the United States Shidehara Kijūrō.

Japan's hesitation about joining the conference showed
that the country found itself in an unenviable position at the
beginning of the 1920s. The delegation shouldered heavy
responsibilities, tasked as it was with simultaneously finding
a way to participate in a collective security arrangement without falling behind in the development of the new world order
while also upholding Japan's pride and ensuring the country's
security.

EIICHI GOES TO WASHINGTON

Eiichi was extremely concerned about these developments,
believing that Japan was facing unprecedented diplomatic difficulties. There had never been such ideas as disarmament or a
collective security pact before. There seemed to be new currents

Figure 43
Zumoto Motosada (1863–1943), journalist and member of the Diet; fluent in English, he accompanied Eiichi on his 1921 trip to Washington and New York. Photo: Shibusawa Memorial Museum.

in the world. The great powers appeared to be thinking of how to move along with this new flow, but Japan seemed isolated and had apparently fallen behind. Unless things were turned around, his country might be hit by a great wave and flounder.

Eiichi resolved to go to Washington personally in a private capacity. Ever since retiring from active participation in business at the age of 70, he had devoted his energies to the relationship between Japan and the United States, and on this important historic occasion he believed he could not simply stay idly by in Japan.

He decided to consult the Japanese-American Relations Committee about this matter, whereupon the members enthusiastically endorsed his proposal. The Committee had also felt that one of them should journey to the United States on this occasion and that Eiichi, although aged, was the best choice if his health stood up. Eiichi's prestige in the United States had been growing with each passing year. He was well known, and he was respected and trusted by many influential Americans. He had become known as Japan's "grand old man," a fitting sobriquet. As an individual, not as a powerful politician or a wealthy business-man, he embodied the finest qualities of Japanese.

Eiichi's departure was set for October 13. For the trip he was accompanied by a party that included stalwarts of his personal mission of goodwill between Japan and the United States: Soeda Juichi, a specialist on the economy and law, Zumoto Motosada, the founder and first managing editor of the *Japan Times* news-paper, and Horikoshi Zenjūrō, head of a silk-exporting company who had visited the United States more than 50 times during his career, as well as a secretary, an interpreter, a physician, and others.

Apart from any concrete results that could be expected from his trip, Eiichi was admired and respected for his pluck in set-ting out on such a long voyage across the Pacific at the age of 81. People felt Eiichi would speak for their worries and concerns for Japan's future regarding the outcome of the conference and that he would do what he could for the country. They were con-vinced that he would transmit their sentiments to the Americans and help bring about a favorable outcome. It was uncanny how Eiichi inspired trust among people of so many disparate posi-tions and ideas.

On the 13th, a large crowd gathered at Tokyo Station to see Eiichi off. Attired in his usual frock coat, Eiichi appeared shortly after 8:30 a.m. and was immediately surrounded by hundreds of people. Prime Minister Hara and virtually the entire cabinet – minister of foreign affairs Uchida Yasuya, interior minister Tokonami Takejirō, war minister Yamanashi Hanzō, education minister Nakahashi Tokugorō, agriculture and commerce min-ister Yamamoto Tatsuo, imperial household minister Makino Nobuaki and others – were on hand for Eiichi's departure, as were leading figures from the business world, all thanking Eiichi for his endeavor.

Prime minister Hara gripped Eiichi's hand and wished him safe travels. A mere three weeks later, Hara would be assassinated at the very same station.[166] Eiichi, of course with no inkling of this tragic event, thanked Hara warmly.

Mori Ritsuko and other glamorous actresses who were graduates of the Imperial Theater's school for actresses appeared, clad in beautiful kimono and attracting admiring glances. A contingent of Waseda University students was also on hand and broke out into the school song as Eiichi's train departed. The Waseda connection arose through Ōkuma Shigenobu, the university's founder and Eiichi's old friend. Eiichi had served as chairman of the university's endowment management committee, chairman of the research committee for revising the university's rules in 1917, and had been made a life member of the supporting association of the university in 1918.

Eiichi had known Ōkuma since 1869, during Eiichi's earliest days at the finance ministry. Attending Eiichi's 80th birthday celebration in 1920, Ōkuma had offered his congratulations, saying, "There may be some I have known for fifty years, but [Eiichi] is one of the few with whom I have been on friendly terms for fifty years ever since we met for the first time." Ōkuma had lately been in ill health and was cloistered in his house at Waseda, but when Eiichi called on him in early October to announce his departure for the United States, his old friend pleaded with him to do his utmost so that the United States and Japan would not go to war.

On arrival in both Hawai'i and San Francisco, Eiichi was greeted by a number of old friends, but since the conference would soon be starting, he arranged to visit with them on the return leg of this trip. Traveling by ferry and train, he headed directly for Washington via Chicago, arriving in New York on November 5, and taking up residence at the Plaza Hotel. Soeda Juichi traveled on ahead from Chicago to Washington to prepare for Eiichi's arrival, acting as the party's local liaison in Washington

---

[166] According to Janet Hunter's *Concise Dictionary*, "Increasing accusations of government corruption and scandal culminated in Hara's being stabbed to death in Tokyo in November 1921," p. 55.

and serving as the emissary relaying the conference's proceedings to Eiichi.

On his 1915 trip to the United States, Eiichi had been accompanied by his sons and it had felt like a sightseeing trip, but this time his travels had to be carefully planned according mainly to developments in the conference. Aside from his position as representative of the Japanese-American Relations Committee, Eiichi had no official status, but he hoped to provide as much support as possible from the sidelines by talking with influential people in his private capacity. His small party was composed of knowledgeable people like Soeda and Zumoto, who together with Eiichi, all worked toward the common goal of communicating Japan's needs and aspirations. Unlike on previous trips, Eiichi did not play cards aboard the ship or on the train this time. Instead, he concentrated on polishing his speeches or passed the time quietly reading classical Chinese works of poetry and prose.

Eiichi departed New York for Washington on November 7 to announce his presence. The city was inundated with unusually large delegations from various countries. China, which had been invited to the Conference as an independent country for the first time, had sent a group 300-strong, and the British party, usually a low-key group, had swelled enormously as it now included representatives from its dominions of Australia, New Zealand, and Canada, territories which had a strong interest in developments in the Pacific Ocean. All the hotels in town were full, and Eiichi and his group had only succeeded in booking rooms at the Arlington Hotel through the great efforts of Soeda and the Japanese embassy.

In the afternoon the next day, Eiichi conferred with chief commissioner Katō Tomosaburō, who gave him details about what was to transpire. Eiichi was then notified that he would have a meeting with U.S. president Harding at 3:20 p.m., and he hurried off to the White House accompanied by Japanese ambassador Shidehara. Escorted by a young officer in military garb, Eiichi and Shidehara were ushered into the East Room and then the Blue Room, where Eiichi was surprised to find Harding standing flanked by six military men in resplendent gold-braided uniforms, waiting to greet Eiichi and Shidehara.

Eiichi had met American presidents before – Theodore Roosevelt, William Taft, and Woodrow Wilson – but had never been received quite like this. The previous presidents he had met had been very approachable and friendly, although Eiichi had been tense at the thought of meeting the leader of a powerful country. But as he recorded in his diary, things were different in 1921. Eiichi recollected how, before the Meiji Restoration of 1868, he had accompanied Tokugawa Akitake, shogun Tokugawa Yoshinobu's younger brother, to France where they had met emperor Napoleon III and then King Leopold I in Belgium. Now the White House seemed to be imitating the grave atmosphere of the crowned heads of Europe sixty years before. He wondered why a country espousing a pacifist doctrine and hosting a disarmament conference had started putting on such a show of military brass.

Harding greeted Eiichi in what seemed quite a casual manner, however, expressing amazement at how well he looked at the age of 81. Eiichi explained that he had devoted his life to fostering goodwill between Japan and the United States and hoped that the conference would be successful. But Harding kept the conversation to small talk, again referring to Eiichi's age, saying that in his younger days he had thought that anyone over the age of 50 was positively ancient but that when he himself had turned 50, he realized that age was of little consequence. The meeting soon ended, without the chance to communicate anything of import to the American president. Eiichi had not even been offered a chair, and had stood throughout the "audience" with the president.

Returning to the Japanese delegation office, Eiichi continued to talk with Katō, who explained the importance of the conference and the difficult position that Japan found itself in, but Eiichi's diary recounts how all during that time Eiichi continued to be preoccupied by the strange atmosphere he had just experienced at the White House.[167]

---

[167] *Ryūmon zasshi* 403, pp. 76–78 (December 1921); "Seien Sensei no dōsei" *Shibusawa denki shiryō*, vol. 33, pp. 262–63.

The next day, Eiichi called on an acquaintance, Henry Osborne, a congressman from California, who introduced him to two or three fellow congressmen. Eiichi also went to the Senate office building, where he was introduced to Senator Borah, architect of the conference. The Senate office building was much larger and grander than the congressmen's office building. As soon as Harding was elected, Borah had been one of the first to call for a disarmament conference between the United States, Britain, and Japan, and so he was seen as the first person to propose the Washington Naval Conference. When Eiichi touched on this and expressed his gratitude for Borah's contributions to peace, Borah was very pleased and said that he would do his utmost to ensure the conference's success. Eiichi also received a visit from former secretary of state William Jennings Bryan, then went back to the Japanese delegation's office, and after a jam-packed schedule, returned to New York City on the 3 p.m. train. Reaching the Plaza Hotel where he was staying a little after 9 p.m., Eiichi discovered the bedroom, sitting room and hallway of his suite filled to bursting with flowers and a bouquet of magnificent chrysanthemums decorating a table in the suite. The flowers were a gift from his friend Frank A. Vanderlip, who was currently traveling in Europe and had sent a message saying he would return to New York at the end of the month and looked forward to meeting Eiichi then.

The first session of the Washington Conference opened on November 12. U.S. President Harding opened the conference, and then Secretary of State Charles Evans Hughes plunged into details, citing specific figures and boldly proposing to limit the tonnage of American, British and Japanese warships. He called for immediate scrapping of the three countries' plans for building new warships as well as ships currently under construction. Under his plan, the United States and Britain would be allowed 500,000 tons for their main ships and Japan 300,000 tons, with tonnage for aircraft carriers, cruisers, destroyers, submarines and so forth restricted according to the same ratio.

The Americans had apparently been successful in keeping the proposal secret, as conference delegates were quite astonished when they heard it, and it soon caused a sensation around the world. With just a 30-minute speech, Hughes sank "more ships than all the admirals of the world have sunk in a cycle of centuries," as one newspaper put it.[168] By broaching the issue of reducing fleet size first, the United States had quickly taken the lead in the conference, and Hughes' diplomacy scored a victory.

Hughes' proposal seemed like a mighty gamble, but in fact he had sounded out Britain beforehand as to whether it would accept the same ratio of naval reduction as the United States. Compared to the diplomacy of his predecessors Hay, Knox and Lansing, who had advanced Far East policies independently only to see their proposals repeatedly scuttled by Britain and other European states, Hughes' approach was far superior. Arthur Balfour, Britain's representative at the conference, then took the podium and expressed approval of the U.S. proposal and respect for Hughes's straightforward diplomatic strategy. But to the Japanese side, it meant very poor prospects for the outcome of the conference.[169]

Eiichi believed that Japan should fall into step with the United States and make concessions as much as possible not only over disarmament, but also where its policies toward the Asian continent were concerned, in order to contribute toward peace in Asia and build prosperity and progress within a new order.

On November 17, Eiichi, as the guest of honor at the 153rd regular banquet of the New York Chamber of Commerce, reiterated this idea in his speech.[170] Chamber president that year Darwin P. Kingsley had attended the previous year's conference in Tokyo, and during the dessert course, with Eiichi seated at

---

[168] See http://www.afsa.org/taking-stock-secretary-state-charles-evans-hughes.

[169] Among several surveys of the Washington Conference, Erik Goldstein and John H. Maurer's *The Washington Conference 1921–22* contains a wide range of analyses of various participating countries' motivations and policies. See especially Sadao Asada's chapter on Japan.

[170] *Ryūmon zasshi*, vol. 420 (May 1923), pp. 26–28; *Shibusawa denki shiryō* 33, pp. 265–66.

his right hand, he proceeded to give the 600-strong audience a detailed introduction of Eiichi that also included recollections of his travels to Japan.

In reply, Eiichi alluded to Japan's strong dependence on the U.S. economy. The post-World War II expression, "America sneezes, Japan catches cold" was as apt a description of the situation in the 1920s as it was to be decades later. Eiichi noted that in 1920, U.S. exports to Japan were valued at 370 million dollars, accounting for only 4.5 percent of total American exports. The value of exports from Japan to the U.S., on the other hand, was 410 million dollars, 42 percent of total Japanese exports. In other words, American interests toward Japan amounted to only 4.5 percent, whereas they were ten times higher where Japanese interests toward the United States were concerned. It was obvious from this that friendly relations with the United States were vital for Japan.

Eiichi continued that Hughes, taking the initiative at the Washington Conference currently taking place, was very far-sighted in his insistence on disarmament, and Eiichi believed that this should definitely take place. Spending on armaments, money for which came from people's taxes, could be greatly reduced and the savings directed toward achieving world peace and progress. He said that he was sure that the Japanese people would offer their full cooperation with the United States to ensure the success of this historic conference, and called for the gods to grant conference delegates courage and strength.

Eiichi hoped that Katō Tomosaburō would agree with Hughes' proposal and actively contribute to getting through the agenda. As noted earlier, this came from Eiichi's diplomatic philosophy based on economics, but also based on the impressions he had gained in Washington and reports from Soeda, who had gone to Washington ahead of him, that the United States and Britain had already agreed on how the conference would proceed. Any opposition from Japan would only place it in a more difficult position. If Japan was ultimately going to have to accept the conference's proposals anyhow, it should have the courage to make an overture from the beginning not only for the honor of being among the first to support Hughes's proposal, but also for the sake of goodwill between Japan and the United States.

But the Japanese delegation refused to make its position on disarmament clear. At the conference's second meeting, on November 15, Britain readily agreed with the proposal, while Japan hedged, saying it agreed "in principle." Others wondered what Japan's real intentions were and began speaking ill of it. Eiichi was quite concerned about this and dispatched Soeda to convey his opinion to delegation head Katō, but to no avail. Katō himself did not disagree with Eiichi's thinking, but Japan was in turmoil at the time, and communication with the delegation in Washington was sporadic at best. Prime Minister Hara had been assassinated on November 4 by a rightwing activist, and while finance minister Takahashi Korekiyo now headed the Cabinet, confusion reigned among the leadership just at that crucial time.

In New York for nearly one month, Eiichi met again with many friends. At a reception for Eiichi at the New York Bankers Club, U.S. Steel president Elbert H. Gary, standing in for Vanderlip, who had yet to return from abroad, welcomed Eiichi and entertained him at his home in the city and at his country house on Long Island. Eastman Kodak Co.'s George Eastman, who had visited Japan the previous year, invited Eiichi to his home in Rochester, New York, on November 11 and gave him a tour of his camera plant and the schools, hospitals, and other institutions he had founded with his own money. Eiichi's diary records that snow had fallen in the U.S. northeast that day, so one can imagine the shining mantle of white that covered the landscape through which he traveled.[171] During his stay, Eiichi continued to be showered with hospitality. There was also a reception hosted by Benjamin Strong, governor of the Federal Reserve Bank of New York. Lewis L. Clarke, president of the American Exchange National Bank, who had visited Japan the previous year, invited Eiichi to a lunch party at his home, Eiichi

---

[171] *Shibusawa Eiichi nikki*, November 11, 1921, see *Shibusawa denki shiryō*, vol. 33, p. 231.

was taken to see a horse show, and luscious grapes and other fruit were delivered regularly to him at his hotel.

H. J. Heinz, founder of the H. J. Heinz Company, a manufacturer of processed foods, had already passed away, but his son Howard Heinz invited Eiichi to Pittsburgh, the company's home base, for a visit on November 18. The younger Heinz and his wife welcomed Eiichi as if he were a father to them. Eiichi learned how H. J. had switched from his occupation as a bricklayer to go on to better things, acquiring nearly 160 acres of land where he grew vegetables and setting up a plant to process those vegetables in 1869. They recalled how H. J. had held Eiichi in high esteem, Eiichi shared his own reminiscences, and time flew by as they talked. The next day, Howard's brother Clifford, having cut short a trip for the occasion, joined the party. Eiichi was very pleased at how the children of his old friend had grown into fine men and worked side by side to continue developing their father's business, and the two nights he spent at the Heinz home relieved the fatigue of his travels.

On November 22, Eiichi visited Oyster Bay, home of the late president Theodore Roosevelt who had passed away three years earlier in January 1919 at the age of 61. The hot-blooded Roosevelt had urged the United States to enter World War I. In 1917, when the United States joined the fighting, Roosevelt sent his four sons to the front. One died in action and two were wounded. Roosevelt's widow retreated to Oyster Bay after his death and went into mourning, but she was very happy that Eiichi was visiting the United States and took him to visit Roosevelt's final resting place.

One can imagine a beautiful clear day with a cold wind blowing across the hilltop overlooking the sea where the grave was located. As he laid flowers on the grave, Eiichi must have been thinking back on his friendship with Roosevelt since 1902 and the changes in the Japan-U.S. relationship over the years. He must have noted how simple and plain was the gravesite for a man who had been the head of a great country. Roosevelt's widow, moreover, was living quietly by herself, with only an elderly woman companion. This plain way of life, so far removed from the worship of the powerful that tainted the Japanese body politic, was something that Eiichi especially liked about the United States.

Henry W. Taft, brother of the former U.S. President Taft, hosted a splendid dinner party for Eiichi at his home on November 23. Guests included John D. Rockefeller Jr. and other notables. Ever since the private-sector organized conferences held in Tokyo in 1920 (see pp. 262–75; chapter 8), Henry Taft had had a keen interest in Japan-U.S. relations and later wrote a book titled *Japan and America* (1932).

On the 25th, Eiichi was again invited by Lewis Clarke to a dinner party at his home, attended by U.S. Steel president Gary and his wife and other prominent figures. The food and the hospitality were tasteful and refined and all to the highest standards. Returning to his hotel later in the evening, Eiichi received a telephone call from Frank Vanderlip, announcing that he had just returned from his trip to Europe and inviting Eiichi to his home.

It was raining on Sunday, November 27, but Eiichi set out for Vanderlip's home in Scarborough, upriver on the Hudson about one and a half hours by car from New York. The grand house was situated in a heavily wooded estate. Vanderlip and his family, including his daughter who had accompanied him to Japan the previous year, assembled to welcome Eiichi, and they chatted about memories of Japan and discussed the Washington Conference. In late afternoon, Frank's wife Narcissa showed Eiichi around the Scarborough Day School, a middle school the couple had established on the estate. The couple also entertained Eiichi at dinner in New York City on the 29th and accompanied him to a casino-theater where they all enjoyed entertainment.

On the 30th, the Garys, representing the Japan Society, held a dinner party for Eiichi at their home; the guests included Henry Taft and Darwin Kingsley. Mrs. Gary showed Eiichi around their home, each room splendidly appointed with the finest furniture and casually decorated with sculptures and other artworks, one of them costing as much as 200,000 yen. Eiichi's diary records his amazement, even though he was quite accustomed to lavish

FIGURE 44 Watch received from John Wanamaker, engraved with the message: "Token of affection to Viscount Shibusawa from John Wanamaker, U.S.A., December 5, 1921." Photo: Shibusawa Memorial Museum.

displays, at this evidence of American plenty and accumulated wealth.[172]

At 9 a.m. on the morning of December 3, Eiichi left New York by train for Philadelphia where he met with John Wanamaker. Wanamaker, then 88 years old, seemed very happy at the meeting; wordless with emotion, he tearfully embraced Eiichi when Eiichi entered the department store's office. Even a singularly focused man like him had become sentimental with advancing years.

In the margin of his diary entry for that day, Eiichi noted that Wanamaker, as was his wont, persistently tried to convert Eiichi to Christianity, and that he did his best to parry the proselytizing. Apparently exhausted by Wanamaker's badgering, Eiichi finally pleaded a cold coming on and spent his second night in Philadelphia in a hotel rather than at Wanamaker's home.

On December 5, as Eiichi was preparing to leave for Washington, Wanamaker's secretary called on him and presented him with a gift from Wanamaker: a splendid, specially-made pocket watch from the Waltham Watch Company. Wanamaker had apparently ordered the watch to present it to U.S. President

---

[172] *Ryūmon zasshi*, vol. 407 (April 1922), pp. 32–39; "Tobei nisshi (Seiun-sensei)" [Diary of the Trip to the United States (Seiun-sensei)]; *Shibusawa denki shiryō*, vol. 33, p. 246.

Woodrow Wilson, but he later became disenchanted with Wilson's policies and decided instead to present it to Eiichi, his most respected friend from Asia.

On the 7th, Eiichi had been implored by Dr. Rudolph B. Teusler to attend a fund-raising lunch for Tokyo's St. Luke's Hospital. It was a tight schedule, but Eiichi made a day trip to New York, leaving Washington at 8 a.m. and returning the same day. The lunch was hosted by Thomas W. Lamont of J. P. Morgan, with former U.S. ambassador to Japan Roland Morris, Henry Taft, and others attending for the American side. The Japanese contingent included Eiichi and members of a delegation from the Tokyo Chamber of Commerce including Dan Takuma (director-general of Mitsui), Ōhashi Shintarō (major publisher), and Hara Kunizō (business magnate), who happened to be in New York at the time.

On December 8, Eiichi met with Valentine S. McClatchy, a well-known anti-Japanese activist from California, who happened to be in Washington. McClatchy, born to a prominent Irish family, was the publisher of California newspapers the *Sacramento Bee,* the *Modesto Bee,* and the *Fresno Bee,* and was a very influential figure in northern California and the San Joaquin Valley. McClatchy apparently became anti-Japanese after traveling in Japan and Korea in 1919. McClatchy and his wife happened to be in Seoul during the March 1 Movement protests against Japanese rule, and they witnessed innocent Korean men and women beaten back violently by Japanese policemen and army personnel. They also ran up against the Japanese government's newspaper censorship there, which suppressed news of the uprisings, while Reuters and other foreign wire services were permitted to operate only if they reported favorably on Japan.

McClatchy returned to the United States convinced that the Japanese were the Germans of Asia – ambitious, talented, and intent on conquering the whole of the Far East. He firmly believed that Japanese and Americans could never be integrated and that if they were forced to do so through marriage and other means, the results would be disastrous to both. The more numerous Japanese became in the United States, the more serious the problem would get, he thought, thereby severely affecting friendly relations between the two countries. This attitude was out-and-out racism, akin to the apartheid in South Africa and elsewhere. But McClatchy fervently believed this and later left newspaper work to head the Japanese Exclusion League of California.

Eiichi had heard of McClatchy and was aware of his reputation, so going through Zumoto Motosada, he asked to meet him on this trip. A meeting was arranged, and McClatchy called on Eiichi at the Arlington Hotel.

Eiichi noted in his diary describing the meeting: "I tried to be especially open to the well-known anti-Japanese activist." Eiichi was at pains to be considerate towards his guest, and they had lunch together with Zumoto and Soeda. They spent a long time in conversation, and Eiichi said he would meet McClatchy again in San Francisco when he passed through on his way back to Japan.

Seeing McClatchy off, Eiichi next went to the AFL office to meet Samuel Gompers. Gompers expressed pleasure at seeing Eiichi and they sat and discussed labor issues and other matters. As Eiichi was leaving, Gompers gave him a pamphlet he had written and some magazines. A few days later, Gompers attended a lunch hosted by Tokugawa Iesato, where he met Eiichi once again. Prohibition was in force, and the story goes that Gompers was put out at not being able to have a drink with the meal, but Eiichi calmed him down and they ended up enjoying a fine conversation about the labor movement.

It had been cloudy all day on December 8, and it was already dark when Eiichi returned from the AFL office around 4:30 p.m. Without even time to take a break, Eiichi changed his outfit and set off again, this time for the home of former president William H. Taft. Taft had been appointed chief justice of the Supreme Court during the Harding administration, and Eiichi had gotten to know Taft's brother Henry very well since the previous year's private sector conference in Tokyo and had met him several times in New York. He had first met William Taft, however, back in 1905, sixteen years earlier, when Taft had visited Japan as an emissary for Roosevelt. It was immediately after the Russo-Japanese War, and Eiichi, together with Itō Hirobumi, had entertained Taft at the Kōyōkan restaurant in the Shiba area of Tokyo (1905). They met again in 1907, when Taft was in Japan, and their third meeting took place in 1909, when Taft was U.S. president, in Minnesota, when Eiichi headed the Japanese business delegation visiting the United States (see chapter 5). At this fourth meeting, Eiichi was filled with emotion at the thought of the changes that had taken place in the Japan-U.S. relationship. Most of the people who had led Japan in those days – Itō Hirobumi, Katsura Tarō, Komura Jutarō, Emperor Meiji – had passed away, as had Roosevelt.

Taft was overjoyed to meet Eiichi again, and the two sat in front of the fireplace to talk. They discussed recent political developments in the United States and other subjects, and when their meeting ended after an hour and it was time to leave, it had started to rain. Carrying an umbrella, Taft solicitously escorted Eiichi to the door and saw him off.

SETBACKS FOR JAPAN AND FRUSTRATIONS FOR EIICHI

The fourth session of the Washington Conference took place on December 10. Eiichi left his hotel at 10 a.m. for the spectators' gallery. He later recalled how they found all the seats taken when they arrived, many taken by women. Secretary of State Hughes went over the course of the agenda, followed by American chief delegate senator Henry Cabot Lodge, who announced the signing of the agreement by the United States, Britain, France, and Japan. This Four-Power Treaty contained provisions regarding the security of all the signatory countries' territories in the Pacific. It was like a combined, watered-down version of the Root-Takahira Agreement and the Anglo-Japanese Alliance, but this document formally ended the Anglo-Japanese Alliance.

After Lodge came Arthur Balfour, who recounted that the Anglo-Japanese Alliance had contributed to peace in Asia and security for the world over the past twenty years, and said that it was truly a pity that the alliance had to end now. In a moving speech, he brought the alliance to an end saying "When two nations have been united in that fiery ordeal, they cannot at the end of it take off their hats one to the other and politely part as two strangers part who travel together for a few hours in a railway train."[173]

Balfour, a stalwart of Britain's Conservative Party, had been involved with the Anglo-Japanese Alliance almost since its inception, and he understood the interests of the two countries and was vastly knowledgeable about the political balance of power in the Far East. His address was greeted by great applause, and when he was seated all eyes shifted to the Japanese delegation. The Japanese side had said little throughout the conference, and now there was great expectation that one or the other of the delegates would finally say something. The hall erupted with cries of "Japan, Japan!" – an unprecedented happening for an international conference.

Eiichi waited with bated breath for them to reply to Balfour with a high-flown speech outlining the past and future of Japan's diplomatic policies. The occasion was an excellent chance for Japan to ask for support in the court of international public opinion, but the delegates simply looked at each other and no one stood up to speak. Notwithstanding Eiichi's irritation, an uncomfortable silence set in. Finally, Tokugawa Iesato abruptly stood up and made only the briefest acknowledgment that Japan also regretted that the Anglo-Japanese Alliance had come to an end. Shaking with rage, Eiichi wondered why there was no one who could hold his own and properly represent Japan at such an important juncture. What in the world had Japan's diplomacy come to? Eiichi was usually even-tempered, but that day, he vented his anger when he returned to his hotel. Soeda later wrote of the episode, "King Wen [of Zhou in ancient China] got indignant and his land was ruled in order. His wrath was a righteous indignation. So is the wrath of the Viscount [Eiichi]. He is usually mild-mannered but never have I seen him in such a temper as today."[174]

---

[173] As cited in Nish, *Collected Writings of Ian Nish*, p. 296.
[174] *Shibusawa denki shiryō*, vol. 33, p. 275.

Certainly, a magnanimous speech by the Japanese delegation at the meeting that day might have had some effect. But the Four-Power Treaty was still only at the provisional signing stage, with many loose ends left to be settled, and the negotiations for what became the Nine-Power Treaty dealing with China's territorial integrity and the open-door policy had only just begun. China had already been lobbying vigorously, with the United States supporting it every step of the way, so in Japanese eyes there was no telling how things might turn out. All of Japan's interests now seemed to be on an unstable foundation, so this was no time to be sentimental.

The previous day, Katō had revealed to Eiichi the particulars of an important negotiating point whereby Japan, in return for accepting a reduction of its naval forces, would extract a promise from the other parties not to fortify their territories in the Pacific. Although the 5:5:3 ratio seemed like a good arrangement, if the United States and Britain decided to create military ports in the Philippines, Hong Kong, and Guam and station large warships there, that would immediately threaten the Japanese home islands, making control of Japanese interests on the continent totally out of the question. Given that the United States and Britain controlled virtually all the seas at the time, Japan would have to act carefully as far as its security was concerned lest it fall into a trap. Eiichi was very impressed with Katō's careful calculations as a navy man and how he approached the negotiations, bearing as he did all the responsibility for Japan's defense on his shoulders. As Eiichi noted in his diary that day, "I certainly sympathized with him, his sincerity in both attitude and action."

The U.S. and Britain initially resisted Katō's proposal to make it easier to defend Japan and to restrict their activities in the western Pacific, but Japan would not budge, and in the end they accepted those terms in order to bring about disarmament, and the treaty was finally signed on February 5, 1922.

Eiichi had hoped that the immigration issue could also be placed on the conference agenda to put a stop to anti-immigrant sentiment in America's western states in the future, and he was prepared to remain in the United States for as long as necessary to work for the cause. But after talking the matter over with the Japanese delegation, he came to understand that it would not be possible to do so. After the December 10 session of the Washington Conference, Eiichi met with two members of the U.S. delegation, former secretary of state Elihu Root and delegation leader Charles Hughes, concluding his stay in connection with the conference. The following day, December 11, he bade farewell to the Japanese delegation and took the 10:55 p.m. train from Washington for New Orleans, on his way to Los Angeles.

Eiichi had already crossed the American continent six times by then, going via Chicago from the West Coast, but this was the first time he had gone through the South. Traveling through Atlanta, he reached New Orleans on the morning of the 13th. The warm southern breeze felt pleasant on his cheeks after the winter cold, and the city, with vestiges of its French colonial past and tropical vegetation, struck him as exotic. After an overnight stay and a tour of the city, Eiichi boarded the train once more, crossing the wide Mississippi by ferry, traversing the plains of Texas and heading for New Mexico and Arizona. Bleak desert stretched endlessly ahead, and at stops along the way, he saw that many people were Native Americans and Mexicans. This other face of America was completely new to him, and he was never bored during the long trip. The mountains of the West finally came into view on the afternoon of the 16th, the train continuing on its way into California and finally Los Angeles.

Eiichi spent a few days there, touring Japanese actor Sessue Hayakawa's movie studio and the city of Pasadena, which had by then become known as an upscale residential area. He also visited the University of Southern California and Pomona College. On December 20, he set off for San Diego, where he met Lyman Gage. Gage had been the oldest in the group that had visited Japan the previous year and was six years older than Eiichi. He had been secretary of the treasury under McKinley and it was he who had scouted Frank Vanderlip when he was working at a magazine company in Chicago, named him assistant secretary of the treasury, and later introduced him to New York banking circles. Gage had retired to San Diego, and when he visited

Eiichi at his hotel, they spent three hours reminiscing about the past and discussing the future.

On December 23, Eiichi left warm southern California for the Pacific Northwest states of Washington and Oregon, via San Francisco. His traveling companions were worried that the cold would affect Eiichi, but he caught nary a cold and never found the long train journeys tiring. In Seattle, his old friend James D. Lowman and members of the city's chamber of commerce gave him a warm welcome. After spending two nights there, he set off for Portland on December 29. The days were short in the north, and Eiichi wrote that he had to light a lamp by which to write his diary when he rose at 7 a.m. at his hotel.

On the morning of the 30th, Eiichi toured a sawmill, attended a lunch hosted by the chamber of commerce, and left by train for San Francisco in the afternoon. He spent the 31st entirely on the train, traveling through the snowy landscape of northern California. Arriving in San Francisco after 8 p.m., he spent the night at the Fairmont Hotel. It was New Year's Eve, and the downtown area was filled with noisy revelers.

In the early days of the new year, Eiichi toured a number of cities near San Francisco, including Fresno, Livingston, Turlock, Sacramento, Florin, and Stockton. Old friends Wallace M. Alexander, Robert N. Lynch and others had made prior arrangements, thanks to which Eiichi received a warm welcome at the initiative of the chambers of commerce in each place he visited. In Sacramento, he met with state governor William Stephens. Valentine McClatchy, whom Eiichi had met in Washington, called on Eiichi at his hotel in San Francisco on January 2, and they again discussed immigration issues. Although McClatchy held strong anti-immigration views, he seemed attracted to Eiichi personally and had kindly made arrangements for him in Sacramento. He even asked Eiichi for an autographed photo of himself. Eiichi invited him to lunch, which Charles C. Moore and other friends from the chamber of commerce also joined.

In Stockton, potato king (Ushijima Kinji) George Shima's home base, Eiichi had lunch with Shima at his farm. Ever since the referendum, Japanese had been worried about their future, but they continued working hard and patiently endured the circumstances that swirled around them. Eiichi took every opportunity to visit the local Japanese association and other groups and tried to give their members comfort and courage.

On January 9, Eiichi learned that Ōkuma Shigenobu had passed away. He was saddened at the thought that so many men of his generation who had contributed to creating Meiji Japan were passing on one by one. Ōkuma was one of those whom he had been looking forward to calling on when he returned to Japan to report on his trip.

The same day, he invited friends to the Fairmont Hotel to thank them for their help during his trip, bidding them a formal farewell before returning to Japan. There were over seventy people attending, among them Alexander, Moore, W. T. Sesnon and others from the chamber of commerce; George Shima of the Japanese Association; Benjamin Ide Wheeler, president of California State University; David Starr Jordan, president of Stanford University, and Paul Scharrenberg, head of the California branch of the AFL. Given his age, everyone was conscious that this was likely to be Eiichi's last trip to the United States, and they all said heartfelt words of farewell. In the name of San Francisco's American-Japanese Relations Committee, Alexander thanked Eiichi for his decades-long efforts and presented him with a gift, a gilt-frame plaque inscribed with the following words: "Presented to Viscount Eiichi Shibusawa by his friends. The Japanese Relations Committee of the San Francisco Chamber of Commerce. In grateful recognition of his untiring and unselfish devotion and zeal in the interest of closer and more friendly relations between the peoples of Japan and the United States. January 1922."

The next day, January 10, Eiichi left San Francisco aboard the *S.S. Ventura*, and after a brief stop in Hawaii, arrived in Yokohama on January 30. His trip had lasted 110 days, 78 of them spent on the mainland, and he had attended 91 lunches or meetings and given speeches or made remarks on 81 occasions. This trip had been even more grueling than his previous one, but despite his age, Eiichi had been in fine form and fulfilled all his commitments without incident.

A few weeks later, the Five-Power Treaty committing the signatories to reducing their naval fleets in accordance with specific ratios and the Nine-Power Treaty guaranteeing China's territorial integrity were signed in Washington, marking the conclusion of the Washington Naval Conference. The Japanese and Chinese had been meeting concurrently to agree on terms for the return of the Shandong peninsula to China, that agreement being signed on February 4. Although Shandong had not been on the official agenda of the Washington Conference, negotiations on the issue had been stalled ever since the Paris peace talks because China refused to negotiate directly with Japan, and the United States and Britain had arranged for the two sides to talk privately during the conference. Beginning December 4, a total of 36 meetings took place, attended by U.S. and British observers. The talks came close to foundering several times, but Hughes and Balfour cajoled the parties into signing an agreement.[175]

Over the three months of the conference, Japan had accepted almost all of the United States' assertions and made all the concessions it was willing to make. It had agreed to withdraw its troops from Siberia, and the Lansing-Ishii Agreement guaranteeing Japan's special interests in China was ended. Many of the views and arguments expressed by the Americans were self-serving, but on this occasion Japan had to remain quiet and make an effort to readjust its relations with the United States as much as possible.

The fundamental shift in the world's power relationships that had taken place after World War I was now clearly in evidence. Conditions in Europe had changed, and Germany, Russia and others had temporarily lost their status as Great Powers. The United States, backed by its strong economy, now lorded over all the combatant countries as their creditor. Only Britain had managed to cling to its position as a leading power, but evidently it toed the U.S. line. Japan, as Eiichi had feared, had lagged behind in its assessment of the new situation since the end of the war and lacked a coherent diplomatic philosophy. As a result, Japan

---

[175] For details see Nish, *Japanese Foreign Policy*, pp. 135–38.

had ended up being pushed into a corner by circumstances and became an unwilling part of the new order led by the United States.

But this "new order" was still fluid and was centered on the United States and Britain. Eiichi was dissatisfied with many aspects of it, but, after all, international relations involves counterparts and not everything can go solely one party's way. Given its current position in the world, he believed that Japan should be more or less satisfied. To everyone he met he stressed that what Japan should do now was to resolve the immigration issue and other pending matters as soon as possible so that relations between Japan and the United States could proceed more smoothly.

* * *

In that same year, 1922, when Eiichi completed what was to be his final visit to the United States, another member of the Shibusawa family embarked on a new overseas adventure. My father Keizō, Eiichi's grandson, was transferred to the London branch of the Yokohama Specie Bank, sailing for London from Kobe on September 22. Keizō had graduated from the faculty of economics at the University of Tokyo in March 1921 and had asked Eiichi to get him a job at the bank "because I want to work outside [the direct influence of Eiichi]." Eiichi was very pleased at that; although Keizō had originally wanted to be a biologist, Eiichi had put him on the path of business because he would ultimately inherit the Shibusawa estate. Eiichi was also very happy that Keizō had graduated with unexpectedly good marks.

At a gathering for family and friends to celebrate Keizō's graduation, Eiichi said, "It would have been too kind of an old man like me to worry, but being able to celebrate this young man's graduation and entry into the business world with relatives gathered here today fills my heart with joy. My happiness moves me almost to tears."

Eiichi doted on his grandson Keizō, making an effort to communicate with him by inviting him to lunch or taking him along on trips while he was a student. The influence that Eiichi had as a public figure seems not to have made much impression on Keizō, but in his later years he came to realize the depth and warmth of Eiichi's life.

On the occasion of Keizō's departure on his first trip abroad and doubtless recalling his own memories of visiting Europe, Eiichi wrote the following poem for Keizō as a heartfelt message to his grandson setting out ambitiously onto the sea of life.

Seeing Grandson Keizō Off on His Trip to Europe

You are departing, leaving me loath to part
Your travel clothes will collect many layers of windblown dust
Spring in England's capital, moon over a Paris castle
Bear in mind, your aging grandfather is waiting back at home

CHAPTER 10

THE SUNSET OF PRIVATE-SECTOR DIPLOMACY

ဆ

At noon on September 1, 1923, completely without warning, a massive earthquake hit the city of Tokyo. Working at the Kabutochō office since morning, Eiichi was going over a pile of papers on his desk when suddenly he felt the room shake violently. A large mirror on the mantelpiece fell off and shattered into small pieces. His secretary helped him over the glass-covered floor to the door, where their footing was again shaken by a second violent tremor. The chains on the chandelier hanging high in the center of the room snapped and the fixture crashed to the floor. As they emerged into the swaying corridor, eerie sounds echoed up and down the stairs, as the quake toppled furnishings and twisted the building. One of the gateposts had fallen over into the driveway, blocking the way out of the compound. Eiichi walked to the Dai-ichi Bank, located nearby, and borrowed a car to take him back home to Asukayama.

As he made his way home he thought that although it was quite a big earthquake, it had not done much damage. The Asukayama house was only partially affected. After nightfall, however, when he saw the sky over the city's low-lying *shitamachi* area colored bright red with the blaze of fires, he began to think the scale of the damage inflicted must be extraordinary. The next morning, just as he had feared, it was reported that fires had spread through the Nihonbashi, Kyōbashi, Kanda, Fukagawa, Asakusa, and other areas – all densely populated areas of the city – burning them almost completely to ashes. Indeed, the

Dai-ichi Bank building and Eiichi's own Kabutochō office had not escaped the flames.

The losses were devastating. The Kabutochō office building had originally been Eiichi's private residence. It had been completed in 1888, during the so-called Rokumeikan era, when Europeanization of architecture was at its height. Designed by Tatsuno Kingo, the pioneer of modern Japanese architecture famous for the design of Tokyo Station, the building was a rare example of a private residence in the purely European style at that time. It stood at the edge of one of Tokyo's canals, evoking the atmosphere of Venice with a row of Gothic pillars on the second-floor veranda that reflected on the canal's waters. The building was not that large, with a total floor space of less than 350 square meters, but it was elegantly appointed, with the ceiling of the reception room decorated with Western-style oil painting, and two large rooms on the second floor spacious enough to entertain guests in the Western style, such as with the ballroom dancing that was being introduced to Japan at the time.

Since Eiichi's move to his second residence at Asukayama in 1901, the first floor of the Kabutochō place had been used as the office and the second floor set aside for the project of compiling the biography of Tokugawa Yoshinobu (see chapter 7). In that building, therefore, there had been a large number of documents and records related to the final years of the Edo period, a priceless collection of copies of the *Analects* of Confucius, various commentaries on the *Analects*, and other related books – a total of more than 600 items – amassed over a long period of time, and Eiichi's own related records, letters, and the like. All of them were lost in the fire that night. Among them were many valuable items, including letters from Yoshinobu as well as from Saigō Takamori, Kido Takayoshi, Sun Yat-sen, and other important historical figures with whom Eiichi was on close terms. Eiichi was filled with remorse and berated himself for having left the building without thinking to safeguard such irreplaceable materials.

Tokyo was in chaos. The earthquake and fire left 150,000 people dead and 1,500,000 homeless. The city, police, and other public authorities were paralyzed. Fears of rioting and starvation soon became all-too-immediate reality. On top of it all, Prime Minister Katō Tomosaburō had died about a week earlier (August 24) and the central government was caught in the middle of appointing new leadership.

After consulting with his son-in-law, Sakatani Yoshirō, who had rushed to Asukayama to make sure he was all right, Eiichi sent out messengers to acting prime minister Uchida Kōsai and the home minister Mizuno Rentarō as well as to the superintendent general of the metropolitan police department, the Tokyo mayor, and others, proposing emergency measures to preserve peace and order and provide relief for victims. He also promised them he would call business leaders together and cooperate in whatever way they could.

Rumors circulated that leaders of the socialist movement were plotting a riot to take advantage of the situation, or that groups of Koreans had started setting fires and looting. The rumors, baseless as they most likely were, filled people with alarm. Eiichi's family was worried about their 83-year-old patriarch and suggested that he leave Tokyo and stay in his home town in Saitama for a while until the commotion was over.

"Nonsense!" Eiichi flatly refused. He had just gotten started on his efforts promoting post-disaster relief and reconstruction, assuming total responsibility for the effort. "An old man like me would be worthy to live only if he can be of some use at such a difficult time. How dare you tell me to evacuate to the countryside like a coward?"

Even then, his sons tried to stop him, saying that if he were injured, it would be all over for him. Eiichi finally got angry, saying, "Stop it! How have I been able to live for eighty long years if I was timid and scared in face of a situation like this. At times like this a person has to be useful."

On September 4, a new Cabinet, headed by Yamamoto Gonnohyō-e (Gombei), was formed. The newly appointed home minister Gotō Shinpei sent a group of cavalrymen to Eiichi, asking him to go out with them into the still-smoldering streets. He thus cooperated with Gotō in keeping peace and order. On September 9, the Great Earthquake Disaster Rehabilitation

Association (Daishinsai Zengokai) was inaugurated in collaboration with the Tokyo Chamber of Commerce and the Diet. Its chairman was Tokugawa Iesato, sixteenth head of the main Tokugawa family, and Eiichi was the vice-chairman. They took charge of fund-raising and other relief activities. Eiichi busied himself every day making tours to observe the damage and visiting victims.

Eiichi's friends overseas, especially in the United States, were very worried and sent inquiries about his safety via embassies, news agencies, and trading firms. On September 13, he sent telegrams to twenty-four friends, including Elbert H. Gary (Judge Gary), Frank A. Vanderlip, and Wallace M. Alexander, telling them that he had miraculously escaped the terrible disaster and was now engaged in the rehabilitation of victims through the association he and others had organized for that purpose. He asked for their cooperation since the sympathy and support of American people was much needed.

Eiichi daily received letters of sympathy and friendship from the United States, all expressing relief over Eiichi's safety and promising to extend as much assistance as possible. Rodman Wanamaker, son of Eiichi's friend and department store king John Wanamaker, wrote him a heartfelt letter and had $25,000 in cash delivered to Eiichi by the Wanamaker agent in Yokohama, along with a message that Eiichi could use it in whatever way he liked. Eiichi also received 35,000 cans of vegetables from Howard Heinz, son of Henry J. Heinz of Pittsburgh (founder of the H. J. Heinz Company). A telegram arrived from Darwin P. Kingsley of New York Life Insurance Company, saying that $80,000 in donations from private businesses was being channeled to Japan's relief through the Red Cross and other charitable organizations. Kingsley had also personally sent $1,000 in relief funds for Eiichi, offering to introduce a powerful team of city planning experts to help with post-disaster reconstruction.

New York's silk textile industry offered to donate $400,000. O. M. Clark of Portland said that $200,000 would be donated by the City of Portland and another $100,000 by the lumber association he belonged to. Of the latter amount, he said, $50,000 would be used to buy and deliver timber for reconstruction, and Clark himself was to board the ship that would deliver the wood to Tokyo. J. P. Morgan & Co.'s Thomas W. Lamont reported to Eiichi that his office was in charge of a Japan disaster relief committee and was endeavoring to collect donations. Lewis L. Clarke of American Exchange National Bank wrote that his bank had put up a large Red Cross flag and was conducting a big relief fundraising drive for Japan. He even sent Eiichi photographs testifying to the fundraising drive.

George Eastman, founder of the Kodak camera company, who happened to be traveling in Alaska, quickly sent $25,000, saying that he would send the same amount again if necessary. Henry Taft, Lyman J. Gage, Julian Street, and others also sent Eiichi gracious letters, expressing their concern about the safety of the friends and members of Eiichi's family they had met at the time of the conference held in Tokyo three years earlier in April 1920, for the Conference of Concerned Japanese and Americans (see chapter 8 and chapter 9). They offered to extend as much assistance as they could.

Eiichi's old friend Frank A. Vanderlip said he had been on a camping trip in southern Utah and Arizona and was late in hearing about the earthquake. He asked about the safety of each member of Eiichi's family whom he had come to know in Tokyo when he and Lyman Gage had stayed at Asukayama during the 1920 conference. Besides sending $5,000, he conveyed the deep sympathy for Tokyo's plight that he observed among his countrymen in general, and said he believed the disaster would prompt deepened friendship between the United States and Japan.

As Vanderlip described, there were signs of genuine heart-to-heart sympathy. The ordinarily anti-Japanese Hearst newspapers of California took the initiative in relief fundraising for earthquake victims in Tokyo, calling on people to put the issues of the "race problem" and nationalism aside and extend their sympathies over the ocean. In response to such calls, Robert N. Lynch reported to Eiichi, pledges of $600,000 in donations had already been received from San Francisco citizens.

Eiichi thought it would be unexpectedly fortunate if, as Vanderlip hoped, the disaster might disperse, even if temporarily, the dark cloud hanging over U.S.-Japanese relations. Since the Washington Conference of 1921–1922, relations between the two countries had been rife with problems and difficulties, leaving Eiichi no chance for peace of mind.

Bias against Asians had become pervasive in the United States. Stimulated by the result of the 1920 California referendum voting in favor of the Alien Land Law, other states had adopted discriminatory land laws, not only the neighboring states of Washington, Oregon, and Arizona; even Midwestern states like Kansas and Missouri and other states further east like Louisiana and Delaware, where people rarely saw Japanese, followed suit. In 1922, a long-pending lawsuit over the right to naturalization for a Hawai'i resident named Ozawa Takao, a long pending issue, was finally concluded. Ozawa had lived in Hawai'i for a long time and was a graduate of the University of California; he had been considered to be fully qualified as a U.S. citizen. In a November 13 ruling, however, the U.S. Supreme Court denied him citizenship on the ground that he was not a Caucasian. That decision confirmed that all Japanese were considered ineligible for U.S. citizenship because of their race.

Japan had been steadily growing as a world power since its victory over Russia in 1905. At the Washington Conference concluded in 1922, it had made major concessions to achieve the balance of world power sought by the United States. It had agreed to abandon the Anglo-Japanese Alliance, return the Shandong peninsula to China, withdraw its troops from Siberia, and sign a naval limitation agreement. Eiichi could not help feeling indignant that even though Japan had displayed its sincerity by agreeing to the American-proposed terms at the conference, the United States remained unwilling to shift even slightly its unfair and discriminatory attitude toward immigration from Japan.

On June 5, 1923, the Japanese-American Relations Committee in Tokyo had sent to its friends and acquaintances all over the United States a statement describing the situation and calling for their cooperation to improve relations between the two countries. As a concrete step, it proposed that both the U.S. and Japanese sides organize a "joint high commission" (*rengō kōtō iinkai*) that would examine the immigration issue from all possible perspectives and submit constructive and appropriate recommendations for its resolution to the governments of both countries. This idea came from a recent precedent: when there had arisen the issue of the right to fish off Newfoundland, a U.S.-Canada border issue, and other problems, a joint high commission of members selected from Britain and the United States had studied the issues and proposed measures to solve them. This precedent had been a frequent topic of discussion among members of the Japanese-American Relations Committee since around the time of the private-level conferences held in Tokyo in 1920 (see chapter 8).

The response from the U.S. side varied, including expressions of sentimentalist goodwill and even total embrace of the proposal for a commission. But most of those who responded pointed out that matters of landownership and the right to naturalize were internal affairs of the United States, so it would be difficult to realize the idea of forming a committee some of whose members would be non-Americans. Eiichi himself wrote long letters[176] explaining his thinking and the backdrop of the statement, but they had little effect. Some respondents to the proposal said they could not understand why Japan had such a strong sense of crisis over purely legal issues, adding the cynical suggestion that Japan ought to practice the much-vaunted Oriental serenity over the matter.

Eiichi and others had been thus stymied when suddenly the earth's tremors wreaked disaster in Tokyo, and any efforts at private diplomacy had to be put aside. The total value of relief funds and supplies sent from the United States exceeded 30 million yen, and Japanese public sentiment toward the United States turned more favorable, appearing as it did to be a reliable friend in time of need.

---

[176] *Shibusawa denki shiryō*, vol. 34, pp. 33–34.

DEVELOPMENTS IN CHINA

Meanwhile, the Japan-China Business Association (Nik-Ka Jitsugyō Kyōkai) in Tokyo was preoccupied with the frequent eruption of incidents related to the anti-Japanese movement in China. Although President Li Yuan-hung (Li Yuanhong) of the Republic of China stated that all the issues pending between China and Japan had been resolved with the conclusion of the agreement (1922) that Japan would return the Shandong peninsula, anti-Japanese sentiment did not subside. In June 1923, anti-Japanese riots occurred across the country and the boycott against Japanese goods grew more severe. This time, not only students and young people but organizations like local chambers of commerce appeared to actively support the movement, which spread from the Changsha and Hankou regions to Shanghai, Jiujiang, Xiamen (Amoy), Shantou, and Guangdong. Its influence was also pervasive among Chinese residing in Singapore, Java, and elsewhere.

The Japan-China Business Association had a hard time keeping up with the situation, constantly gathering information from Japanese associations and chambers of commerce overseas and working with the Japanese foreign ministry. On July 3, the Association held a joint meeting in Tokyo of friendly China-related organizations and adopted a resolution calling on Chinese leaders in various fields to reconsider the situation and extend cooperation. Eiichi, as president of the Association, took the podium and spoke candidly, saying that, given the great efforts made since its founding, the Association found it really regrettable that things had come to such a sorry pass. Deeply concerned, he said, "We would not use violence against violence even if our friends show us only enmity in return for what we try to do. But, as far as international relations are concerned, even one error could lead to an irreversible crisis. . . . We are eager to see Chinese people calmly reconsider what they are doing. My sincere hope is that we together will contribute to the peace of the world through a full understanding and alliance between the two great peoples of Asia." His speech was so deeply moving, it was said, that the audience of 500 was struck silent.

Not long after that, the foreign ministry received a report dated August 24, 1923, from Yoshida Shigeru (later prime minister), then consul general in Tianjin. He said that the leaders of the Tianjin chamber of commerce had visited him and asked him to relay the content of a letter they had brought with them. According to the letter, they had heard about Eiichi's July 3 speech and truly regretted that they had made a man of high virtue like Eiichi, who also was familiar with Chinese affairs, feel such bitter emotions; from then onward they would work with Eiichi to ease the bad feelings between the two countries and enhance friendship. Five leading businessmen of the chamber as well as the director general of the local police agency had signed the letter. Yoshida, in his report, said it was truly a remarkable thing that such influential people seriously offered to improve the situation. He suggested that the Japanese side too take this seriously, because their move might occasion the spread of the mood of reconciliation to Hankou, Shanghai, and other places.

Consul General Yoshida happened to be back in Japan after the earthquake, and so, on October 4, Eiichi invited him to the Industry Club of Japan for lunch and heard from him about the situation in China. Eiichi wasted no time in writing a reply (dated October 6) to the letter from the leaders of the Tianjin chamber of commerce. In the letter of reply, Eiichi said he was glad to hear of their willingness to improve Japan-China relations, and that his earnest desire was to see people in business and industry in both countries working together to study the situation and enhance mutual friendship. He continued that people from Japan ought to go to China immediately to promote the exchange of views, but that was difficult given the state of affairs in Tokyo following the earthquake, and so, for now, they should meet Consul General Yoshida upon his return to Tianjin and hear from him what Eiichi proposed.[177]

As was the case with the Americans, the Tokyo earthquake aroused Chinese sympathy toward the citizens of Tokyo and served as a factor in improving Japan-China relations. Eiichi's

---

[177] *Shibusawa denki shiryō*, vol. 55, pp. 220–21.

friend in China, Sun Yat-sen, who at that time was leading the revolutionary government in South China, sent Eiichi a letter, dated September 21, saying to the effect: "I found refuge in your country several times, and hearing that the places I had stayed in those times have been burned down, I feel very sorry and worried. Fortunately, my friends and acquaintances over there seem to have escaped danger. The reconstruction from now will be an immense project. I pray for the safety of you all." Eiichi wrote a reply right away, saying although his office in Kabutochō had been burned down, he and his family and colleagues had all escaped unscathed and that he was pouring his energies into the reconstruction.[178]

The former Qing imperial house and the central Chinese government also sent monetary donations and supplies via the Red Cross or directly to the Japan-China Business Association. Christian missionaries and organizations in China and pro-Japanese Chinese launched vigorous campaigns, holding meetings and movie-viewing events in various parts of the country to make Japan better known to the Chinese public and generate a new momentum for friendship and cooperation between the two countries. Chambers of commerce across China, one after another, offered to make donations. A total value of relief donations from China was over 2.6 million yen, the third largest after only the United States and Britain.

In November, however, news broke of sufficient magnitude to completely overwhelm the mood of growing friendship. In the aftermath of the earthquake, it was reported that several hundred Chinese had been massacred by a Japanese mob in the Kameido area of Tokyo. When newspapers in China reported on this incident, the rancor in Japan-China relations swiftly returned.

The incident had not been made public in Japan for a while, and when the Chinese media reported on it, the Japanese government dismissed it as exaggerated propaganda, making little effort to investigate what had happened, indeed attempting to hush up the incident. On December 7, the Japan-China

---

[178] *Shibusawa denki shiryō*, vol. 40, p. 272.

Business Association invited Kobayashi Shinzaburō and one other Japanese newspaper-related person who had conducted a follow-up investigation on the incident and heard from them what had actually happened.

They reported as follows: Early on the morning of September 3, with two shots fired as a signal, several soldiers came along and took away 200-plus Chinese laborers living in seven common lodging houses in the back alleys at 6-chōme in the district of Ōshima, Kameido (a suburb of Tokyo). Together with a mob, they brought them to an open area near 8-chōme. At around noon, the policemen and the gathered mob surrounded the Chinese, and began slaughtering them with hatchets, fireman's hooks, bamboo spears, Japanese swords, and the like. The corpses were left as they were for several days until September 7, when the Kameido police station ordered a group of construction workers to dispose of the bodies; they poured more than twenty cans of oil over the corpses and burned them completely over the space of two days. They then dug up the earth on the spot and buried the remaining ashes. The number of corpses was not clear, but according to the accounts of many involved, such as the police, *kempeitai* military police, and so on, more than 200, or possibly more than 300, were killed.[179]

Only a few days after news of the incident broke, on December 10, Eiichi visited the foreign minister, Ijūin Hikokichi, at his official residence, and after recounting the reports received of what had happened in Kameido, asked him what the government was going to do. Ijūin said he understood how Eiichi and others felt but that he could not give an immediate answer. The incident was ultimately hushed up.

In the aftermath of the same earthquake, several thousands of Koreans were also killed by Japanese mobs. There were gruesome episodes in Tokyo, Yokohama, and some other places, including one in which Koreans, after being clubbed or slashed by sword, were thrown half-dead into an empty well and then killed by dropping stones from above; in another episode, a man was

---

[179] *Shibusawa denki shiryō,* vol. 55, p. 251.

tortured to death just because he had a Japanese wife; in still another, a pregnant Korean woman was killed, the baby torn from her womb and thrown on the road to die.

Exposed in these horrific acts was the frightening racism and sense of superiority of Japanese toward Chinese and Koreans. It might be that the guilt felt by Japanese because of Japanese aggression in China and Korea since the early Meiji era had turned into an intense fear among some Japanese, and in the extraordinary situation resulting from the earthquake, that fear fueled these atrocities. No matter how hard the Japanese government might try to hide it, that most serious and ugly aspect of modern Japan had reared its head and was clear to see from the outside. These were incidents that stoked fear and enmity of Japan not just in China and Korea but in the United States as well.

THE IMMIGRATION ACT OF 1924

On December 5, 1923, Japan-U.S. relations, which had been temporarily favorable following the earthquake, all of a sudden faced another crisis. Word was received that, that day, two proposals had been introduced in Congress in Washington, D.C. that might establish the discriminatory treatment of Japanese as national policy.

One was a resolution calling for an amendment to the Constitution put forward by a group of Senate and House members, proposing that the children of parents who did not have the right to naturalize could not acquire U.S. citizenship even if they were born in the United States. If such a law were passed in Congress, second-generation Japanese – Nisei – would be denied citizenship, undermining everything Japanese immigrants in the United States had lived and strived for. The other was the draft bill introduced by the House Immigration Committee for a new immigration law to replace the Immigration Act of 1921, due to expire in June 1924. The 1921 act allotted each country a quota equal to 3 percent of the foreign-born population from each country in the United States in 1910. The proposed bill seemed at first glance to pose no particular problems, but a closer look revealed that subdivision (c) of its section 13 stipulated that no alien ineligible for citizenship should be admitted to the United States. Although it made no express mention of Japanese, to Japanese readers, the import was obvious.

The immigration issue was originally a regional political matter centering on California, but now it had officially come up in national policy for the first time in the U.S. Congress. Before things came to such a pass, both the Japanese and the American governments, fearing that the problem might bring them into serious confrontation, had made efforts to prevent policy from taking the form of a law or treaty that would require approval of Congress, and in 1907 they had adopted the exceptional method of the Gentlemen's Agreement to limit the entry of immigrants to the United States, thereby diverting widespread attention from the matter. They had struggled to maintain the Gentlemen's Agreement amid growing anti-Japanese sentiment. The Japanese government had done its part by gradually strengthening numerical restrictions, for example, by imposing the ban on emigration of women as "picture brides" (as described in chapter 8). As long as the issue remained within California, the American government had been able to explain to Japan that the inequities were a local issue – a matter of domestic affairs, not discrimination against Japan by the United States as a country. The Japanese side, too, although not satisfied, had more or less accepted the explanation. If such discriminating treatment was taken up in the form of a Constitutional amendment or a legal bill, however, it would be be established as a national policy.

The Japanese-American Relations Committee in Tokyo held a series of meetings in quick succession and sent a flurry of telegrams, dated December 28, to Vanderlip, Henry Taft, George Wickersham, Darwin Kingsley, Sidney Gulick, David S. Jordan, Wallace Alexander, and others. The messages called for their cooperation in opposing passage of the bill, which threatened to deprive the children of Japanese immigrants born and reared in the United States of their civil rights.

Preoccupied with the harsh language of the Constitutional amendment bill, Eiichi and his cohorts apparently underestimated the importance of the bill for the new immigration act presented to Congress at the same time. Indeed, the distraction it presented may have been the intent of the drafters from the outset. Amending the Constitution was not easy; it required approval of more than two-thirds of the Senate and the House of Representatives as well as more than three-fourths of the state assemblies. So, even when such a resolution was submitted in Congress, its passage was highly unlikely. That knowledge was behind the optimistic letters that Eiichi's American friends sent him, saying that they would do what they could, but anyway they did not think the bill would pass. Henry Taft and David S. Jordan said it was regrettable that such a thoughtless bill had been presented at a time when the Japanese were struggling to overcome the earthquake disaster. Wallace Alexander said he would immediately convene a meeting of the American-Japanese Relations Committee in San Francisco seeking to stall passage of the Constitutional amendment bill.

Meanwhile, the new immigration bill was of the kind that had to be passed prior to the expiration of the Immigration Act of 1921. In adding subdivision (c) of section 13, stating that no alien ineligible for citizenship should be admitted to the United States – something that might have seemed a matter of course to most legislators in the Congress – its backers knew that the whole bill would be impossible to vote down because of objections to one provision alone, even if some in the government and Congress opposed it as detrimental to U.S.-Japan relations. The bill apparently had been carefully crafted with that calculation in mind.

Even after announcing the bill, the House Immigration Committee held further deliberations with the competent government agencies and, on February 7, 1924 the final draft was adopted and sent to the plenary session of Congress. Subdivision (c) of section 13 was left unchanged.

The U.S. government was concerned about the gravity of the matter, and Secretary of State Charles E. Hughes wrote a letter to the chairman of the House Immigration Committee, Albert Johnson, saying that if the bill were passed with section 13 left as it was, everything they had achieved in the successful signing of the Washington Treaty and all the sympathetic efforts at relief by Americans toward Japan at the time of the Tokyo earthquake would have been wasted. He warned further by adding, "The Japanese are a sensitive people, and unquestionably would regard such a legislative enactment as fixing a stigma upon them."[180]

In Tokyo, the Japanese-American Relations Committee was surprised at how seriously the situation had developed and met frequently for discussion. The members all agreed that such unwarranted discrimination was totally unacceptable and decided that someone influential among Americans of both the public and private sector should go immediately to the United States to do what could be done to prevent passage of the bill.

On February 13, Eiichi, together with privy councilor Kaneko Kentarō, met with Foreign Minister Matsui Keishirō to discuss the situation and urged that a special envoy be sent to Washington. While many suggested that Eiichi should be the one to go, Eiichi himself thought Kaneko should go this time. Eiichi had done all he could there only a couple of years earlier, and even if he went again, there might not be much more he could do. Kaneko, on the other hand, who had been a schoolmate of the former U.S. President Theodore Roosevelt at Harvard, knew many in U.S. political circles. He had done a good job as a government envoy at the time of the 1905 peace conference in Portsmouth to end the Russo-Japanese War. He spoke and wrote in English well. He was most eager to prevent the passage of the bill. He deplored the bill, declaring heatedly that if it were passed, the Japanese people would be looked down upon as inferior forever; such dishonor would be done to the Yamato race that Japanese would be ashamed to appear before the world.[181]

---

[180] Griswold, *The Far Eastern Policy of the United States*, p. 371.
[181] *Shibusawa denki shiryō*, vol. 34, p. 141.

Perhaps fearing that sending a man of such strong feelings as an envoy might have an effect contrary to what was desired, the foreign minister would not say yes to that idea. On March 3, Eiichi and Sakatani Yoshirō visited Prime Minister Kiyoura Keigo and Foreign Minister Matsui and talked with them for more than two hours, but the government's stance was not clear at all. It was not until March 17, when Eiichi, accompanied by Sakatani and Dan Takuma, visited Foreign Minister Matsui at his invitation, that Matsui told them that he had received a telegram from Hanihara Masanao, Japan's ambassador in Washington, requesting that the dispatch of an envoy be postponed this time for fear of arousing the anger of anti-Japanese advocates. Matsui stated that the Cabinet had made the decision accordingly not to send an envoy. For the Japanese-American Relations Committee it was a regrettable development, but since the government had made its decision, there was nothing it could do. They decided to wait and see for the time being while at the same time requesting people they knew in the United States to do their best in revising the bill.

One response to their request was led by Sidney Gulick among a group of pro-Japanese individuals in New York who called on all quarters to delete or revise the provision in question. Their approach, however, was not so much to oppose the provision of the law itself as to criticize the procedure and attitude with which the matter had been handled. Considering that Japan was an ally tied to the United States by a Gentlemen's Agreement and a trade treaty, it was underhanded and totally lacking in courtesy and human feeling to introduce such legislation without the slightest discussion with that ally in advance. It was like a slap in the face, they argued, and could only injure the pride of that country, sparking feelings of resentment. Still, the group's efforts delivered little punch as an opposition movement.

By contrast, V. S. McClatchy, J. D. Phelan, and other anti-Japanese agitators, believing the victory of their strategy imminent, ran an even bigger campaign pushing for the bill to be passed without revision. They engaged in energetic activities including lobbying Congress, organizing anti-Japanese gatherings in various places, and circulating printed matter. Articles in major newspapers such as the *Los Angeles Times* and *Chicago Tribune* emphasized the economic and racial threat of Japanese immigrants to American society.

The House Immigration Committee, ignoring the protests of the secretary of state, submitted a recommendation to the plenary session of Congress that the bill for the new immigration act be passed in its original form. In the Senate, meanwhile, David A. Reed of Pennsylvania and other politicians of "good conscience" were opposed to discriminatory provisions and presented an amendment to section 13 of the bill. This led, in April, to heated debate on the matter in the plenary session. Driven by local pressure and public opinion, California's Senator Samuel M. Shortridge and former governor Hiram W. Johnson, expressed strong opposition to the revision.

Fearing the direction of these developments, Japan's ambassador Hanihara wrote to Secretary of State Hughes on April 10, requesting him to make a special effort to stop passage of the bill. Unfortunately, the wording in this letter was later used against Japan in Congress. In that "fateful" letter the ambassador said in effect that: the new immigration act would be taken as a serious insult to Japan; that now it no longer mattered whether the new act would allow entry of smaller numbers of Japanese; and that what did matter was that the new act would brand Japanese as an inferior race, a race not worthy of inclusion in American society. If the bill were passed in its original form, he continued, it would have "grave consequences" for Japan-U.S. relations, which had been favorable for past several decades.[182]

Hughes accepted the purport of the letter and sent copies to both houses of Congress. It was too late for the vote in the House

---

[182] Mizutani Ken'ichi, "1924-nen Imin Hō ni okeru 'Nihonjin mondai'" ("Japanese Problems" Associated with the U.S. Immigration Act of 1924), *Doshisha American Studies*, March 20, 1997, pp. 73–89; NII Electronic Library Service, http://ci.nii.ac.jp/naid/110000198930 (accessed 12-13-17), p. 85. For the English text of Hanihara's letter, see *Papers Relating to the Foreign Relations of the United States, 1924, Vol. II.* https://history.state.gov/historicaldocuments/frus1924v02/d280.

of Representatives, where on April 12 the bill had been passed in its original form, with 323 supporting it and 71 against. In the Senate, deliberations were still going on, and a group led by Senator Henry Cabot Lodge of Massachusetts referred to the passage in the Hanihara letter that included the phrase "grave consequences," which they interpreted as a "veiled threat."[183] They argued that the United States could not change its position on domestic affairs because of a foreign threat. The atmosphere of the Senate quickly turned grim. Even Senator Reed, who had been opposed to the bill and submitted an amendment to it, ended up reluctantly supporting passage. The Senate voted in favor of the new immigration act by a large margin, 71 to 4.

Aghast at the effect of his letter, ambassador Hanihara immediately wrote a letter to explain, but it was too late. The new Immigration Act was formally passed through both houses of Congress and had only to be signed by the president.

When this news reached Japan, where people had been waiting anxiously to see how things would develop, the shockwaves of the law's passage quickly spread throughout the country. Everyone, young and old, men and women, felt directly and immediately a sense of affront to their country such as they had never experienced before. The insult of summarily shutting Japanese out of the United States seemed unforgivable. With the single provision of a law, the United States had trampled upon the pride of the entire Japanese population, and they felt the hurt as deeply and acutely as if it had been delivered by physical violence.

The U.S. government could no longer cite the excuse that the discriminatory provisions were necessary due to the special circumstances of California. The United States as an entire culture had hurled this insult at Japan with obviously ill intention. No matter how Americans of "good conscience" might try to deny that ill intent, Japan would no longer trust their word. Japan now came to understand that, of the two faces of America, the face of goodwill was after all a sham. The face it had showed

---

[183] Griswold, *The Far Eastern Policy of the United States*, p. 374.

Japan with the 1924 Immigration Act, an ugly and arrogant Caucasian face, was the real face of the United States. The law became known in Japan as the "Japanese Exclusion Act." British historian and philosopher Arnold Toynbee, who was then in Japan, described the situation at the time as follows: "The news of the enactment aroused the nation for several weeks to a dangerous pitch of excitement . . . ."[184]

For Eiichi it was a cruel blow. At first he tried his best to believe it wasn't true. Wasn't the United States the country that had "championed justice and humanity and set an example to the world since its founding"?[185] He could understand it if it had been the work of overzealous state politicians, but for the U.S. Congress – especially the Senate – which was supposed to be composed of men of solid good sense, to make such a decision, Eiichi thought, "could never happen." Later, however, when he read a detailed report of the sequence of events, he realized not only that his expectations had been betrayed but that indeed all his efforts over the last two decades had come to naught. His heart felt as heavy as a rock, and he did not even notice the tears pouring down his face.

On April 17, Eiichi gave a speech, as planned, at a luncheon held by the Pan-Pacific Association at the Imperial Hotel. He began by saying, "It may be inappropriate for a person like me – unable to speak or read a foreign language – to talk about foreign relations. But, please listen to the disgruntlement of an old man involved in this matter over a long period of time." He then spoke, sometimes haltingly, about Japan-U.S. relations since the time he had heard, as a fourteen-year-old boy working on a farm in the countryside of northern Saitama, about the arrival of the Black Ships led by Commodore Perry off the coast of Edo (now Tokyo). He told how he had been involved in private-level diplomacy over the past two decades, including heading a delegation of Japanese businessmen to the United States, entertaining American guests in Japan, leading the activities and discussions of the Japanese-American Relations

---

[184] See ten Broek, et al., *Prejudice, War, and the Constitution*, p. 28.
[185] *Shibusawa denki shiryō*, vol. 34, p. 308.

Committee, and the like. "When I heard about the passage [of the Immigration Act] through the U.S. Congress, all my efforts [to forge friendship between our two countries] suddenly seemed like a stupendous waste. I was so disappointed I almost wanted to give up living, even wanting to complain to the gods and buddhas for not watching over us. . . . I had done my best to somehow prevent the worst from happening, but the situation just got worse and worse. I thought that although the House of Representatives had passed the bill the Senate would refuse to approve it. When I heard the Senate, too, had passed it with a large majority I could not help wondering if it would have been better if Japan had turned away the Americans' Black Ships seven decades ago."

The audience was silent, filled with sadness as they listened to the candor of the eighty-four-year-old man and contemplated the difficulties that lay ahead for their country.

"But I believe," said Eiichi, shaking his small body to steady himself, "that truth will be victorious. Let me express my earnest hope here, that the U.S. president will have the wisdom to exercise his veto power and then take steps to fundamentally resolve the issues between the U.S. and Japan. That, I firmly believe, would be the best way not only for Japan but for both of our countries."

On April 19, the Japanese-American Relations Committee met at the Bankers Club and discussed what they should do now that the "deplorable" Japanese Exclusion Act had been passed. The members around the table were filled with indignation that their earlier request for dispatch of a special envoy had been refused by the government and disgust that the letter written by ambassador Hanihara – the man who had rejected the idea of an envoy – had ended up adding impetus to passage of the bill. Among the members, Yamada Saburō, a lawyer, urged that ambassador Hanihara be either immediately recalled to Japan or made to resign, that the Cabinet take responsibility and resign en masse, and that the United States be called on to think the matter over again. Fujiyama Raita, president of the Tokyo Chamber of Commerce, said that the latest development meant rejection not just of Japanese immigrants but of the Japanese people as a whole. The impact on the economy would be great; already the exchange rate had fallen below $40 against 100 yen and Japanese government bonds were steadily decreasing in value. He was worried that Japan might no longer be able to receive loans from the United States and that the very foundations of economy-oriented diplomacy Japan had been building since World War I would be shaken. The Committee concluded that since the American public appeared to be not necessarily in support of the new Immigration Act, it behooved Japan to launch a propaganda campaign to influence public opinion; and since the U.S. president had yet to sign the bill into law, the Committee would send telegrams to influential Americans, asking them for their cooperation.

On the same day, the Tokyo Chamber of Commerce, too, met and discussed the same subject. It accused the government of diplomatic failure and deliberated on what to do. At the meeting, Ōkura Kihachirō, co-founder of the chamber together with Eiichi, made the intriguing observation that the real motive behind the U.S. exclusion act was to intervene in and disrupt relations between Japan and China and ultimately get China on its side.

On April 21, the Japanese-American Relations Committee sent telegrams in Eiichi's name to sixteen influential Americans – including Elbert H. Gary, Vanderlip, and Kingsley – asking them for last-ditch efforts to prevent the Japanese Exclusion Act from being put in force. "We fear all past efforts for promotion of goodwill between the two countries will be nullified," the telegram said.

On May 2, Prime Minister Kiyoura invited Eiichi, Kaneko Kentarō, Dan Takuma, Uchida Kōsai (former foreign minister), Shidehara Kijūrō, and others to his official residence to hear their views on Japan-U.S. relations. Uchida made a perceptive comment, "Japan and the United States have been on friendly terms with each other since the Gentlemen's Agreement, but beneath the surface there was always something awkward. Between the two countries there is probably a cancer that most people in Japan and the U.S. are totally unaware of, and the two countries have mutually suffered pain from it over many years."[186]

Eiichi criticized the Japanese government on that day, honestly stating his views. The successive cabinets, he said, had done things in a haphazard manner without any consistent policy; the result of that was what they saw now. In dealing with the immigration issue, the government had relied only on bureaucratic negotiations with the U.S. Department of State; never had it understood the importance and danger of the issue, nor had it taken any thoroughgoing steps to change anti-Japanese sentiment in the United States. On the other hand, continued Eiichi, when the private sector had offered remedial proposals like the establishment of a "joint high commission" or dispatch of a special envoy, the government was always vague and evasive. How could the government properly handle diplomatic issues – the decisions that would determine the destiny of the country – by such prevarication?[187]

Later, in response to questions from news reporters about the meeting, Eiichi said, "I am generally quiet, like a cat, but thinking it necessary to show my claws once in a while, I did not mince words." The major newspapers reported on the meeting with sensational headlines like "Government Impotence Is To Blame" (*Hōchi Shimbun*). "Foreign Ministry Rejected Proposal for Special Envoy to Conceal Its Impotence: Now Is Too Late for Regrets" (*Yomiuri Shimbun*), and "Three Men from Private Sector Take Japan's U.S. Policy to Task" (*Jiji Shimpō*).

On May 22, in the attempt to avoid a rupture in Japan-U.S. relations, the Japanese-American Relations Committee sent telegrams again to the United States expressing its fervent hope that U.S. President Calvin Coolidge would veto the bill. The telegrams called for last-ditch efforts to block the lamentable immigration bill from becoming law for fear that it would harm friendship between the two countries.

---

[186] *Shibusawa denki shiryō*, vol. 34, p. 232.
[187] *Shibusawa denki shiryō*, vol. 34, pp. 232–33.

These ardent efforts on the part of the Japanese notwithstanding, on May 26, 1924 President Coolidge signed the Immigration Act into law. Intending to minimize its impact, the president did meet with leading figures in Congress, seeking to shelve the controversial provision, but they would not accept the idea, saying that the bill had been passed with an overwhelming majority as it was. When the president signed, he added a note saying to the effect that if the provision related particularly to Japan had been separately presented he would have vetoed it but that since it had been part of the whole he could not.

Ultimately, such gestures mattered little. The Japanese reaction to the act was intense. Distrust and antipathy toward the United States began to spread far and wide in Japan. "The United States has branded Japan an inferior state and openly insulted its people." "It is tantamount to a declaration of war." "If we are challenged to fight, we will certainly take up the challenge." "Let us fight, ready to sacrifice everything." Such were the sensational remarks – made by even eminent scholars and politicians – that met with thunderous applause from the masses. Many meetings and demonstrations in protest took place. One young man hated the United States so much that he committed suicide. There was an incident in which two unknown men forced their way into the site of the former American embassy, and dragged down and stole an American flag.[188] Stores began to put out signs that said, "We do not sell American goods."

All these things became news in the United States, and were often reported in exaggerated ways, adding further to the strain on relations between the two countries. The *Chicago Tribune*, dated May 28 (1924), reporting that the Japanese government had allegedly called up 3 million in army reserves, clamored for the strengthening of the U.S. Navy in preparation for imminent war with Japan.

Within Japan, the people most deeply wounded by the passage of the law, however, were the many pro-American Japanese

---

[188] See Minohara, *Hainichi iminho to Nichi-Bei kankei*, pp. 290–91.

leaders in various fields. For a long time they had trusted the United States, understood its quirks, and sought to shape Japan's future by cooperating and working with it. The Japanese Exclusion Act betrayed the very foundations of such thinking and shattered their admiration for and trust in the "civilization" they had envisioned with the United States as its model. To show how deeply they were wounded, Eiichi wrote in a letter to Sidney Gulick: "It is of course unbearable to see how painful and deep-seated the Japanese reaction has been – something far beyond the imagination of the Americans."[189]

It was probably at this time that the era of "civilization and enlightenment" (*bunmei kaika*) came to an end in Japan. Since the beginning of the Meiji era, Japan had followed a path guided by adoption of the "civilization" of the West that had seemed so superior and important in the world. In the 1920s and 1930s, it became clear that "civilization" was, after all, something that served only to benefit the Western world and the white peoples. Betrayal and hurt turned Japanese minds away from reason; increasingly they became inclined toward zealotry and violence.

The intense reaction in Japan startled and worried Americans. Horikoshi Zenjūrō, a businessman who happened to be visiting New York on business at the time, wrote a long letter to Eiichi to convey the local atmosphere. According to him, one day when he met Judge Gary, he found him in an unexpectedly bad mood. Gary complained about a telegram he had received from Eiichi; citing the passage in the telegram that said "We fear all past efforts for promotion of goodwill between the two countries will be nullified," Gary said it could be interpreted as a threat that Japan would sever its diplomatic ties with the United States and wage war. Such a telegram was only embarrassing for those who received it, said Gary, and given that earlier the phrase "grave consequences" in ambassador Hanihara's letter had produced a great reaction in the Senate, Japanese should have known better. They should be more careful, Gary advised. Sidney Gulick, too,

---

[189] *Shibusawa denki shiryō*, vol. 34, p. 422.

told Horikoshi that he could not make public Eiichi's telegram because of the inappropriate expression.

Reading Horikoshi's letter, Eiichi was stunned, and at the same time could hardly believe the story. He knew Gary to be one of the most magnanimous persons in the American business world; he was widely known as a man of high moral fiber and noble character. If even Gary reacted that way to the telegram, Eiichi wondered if ultimately Japanese feelings would never be understood.

Not long after that, Eiichi received a long letter, dated June 11, from Gulick. He had found it quite embarrassing, he wrote, that Japanese had become so emotional over the new Immigration Act. Americans had no intention to "insult" Japan in passing the law, except perhaps for some who had presented the original bill. Despite it being a time when tolerance and calmness were most needed, the Japanese public's distorted view of American intentions was aggravating the situation, making things worse than they were. His wording was polite, but he clearly expressed his dissatisfaction with Japanese attitudes.

Gulick continued: The United States had made a procedural error in unilaterally annulling the Gentlemen's Agreement. This was obviously a rude way of doing things, and Americans of good conscience would never approve it. However, the fundamental issue was whether immigrants would be accepted or not, and that was something the United States could decide on its own free will. It was not a matter in which Japan had a right to interfere. Japan should understand this. Gulick's letter was worded as a critique of Japanese journalism for sensational reporting, but the content was clearly intended to urge Eiichi and his friends to think the matter over again.[190]

---

[190] The letter, an excerpt of which follows, is preserved in the *Shibusawa denki shiryō*, vol. 34, pp. 259–76. "Japanese editors write as though Congress purposely and wantonly insulted Japan and all Asiatic peoples. Deplore and criticise, as I do the action of Congress, I am confident that there was no such purpose. I will go further and say that, with a few possible exceptions, they did not for a moment realize that what they were doing would be so interpreted. The reactions in

Eiichi felt as if he were seeing the bottom of the chasm of relations between Japan and America for the first time. It seemed to him as if his efforts over many decades in the form of private-level diplomacy had been of almost no use in filling in the depths of that chasm.

Like other Japanese who called the 1924 Immigration Act the "Japanese Exclusion Act," he was not looking at the broader picture of immigration to the United States the law was created to address. He could not fathom how anyone could say "no insult was intended" to Japanese by the Act.[191] In his eyes, the entire issue boiled down to just one thing: discriminatory treatment – racist insult. Above all else, Japan wanted to be accorded the status of first-class country, treated the same way the European countries were; nothing less would be acceptable. In a letter to David S. Jordan, president of Stanford University, Eiichi protested that placing Japan in the same league as countries that the United States considered inferior was cruel and rude, leaving an old man like himself only to moan with disappointment.[192]

The overweening pride that filled Eiichi and others in the 1920s and 1930s may be hard for people today – even Japanese – to understand. During subsequent decades, of course, having undergone humbling experiences of all kinds, Japanese themselves have matured as a people, and values have greatly changed worldwide. Today, being Caucasian – with all its accompanying burdens – is no longer necessarily superior or enviable. Back then, however, assertion of their rightful stature in international society was something for which people would lay their lives on the line. How many hundreds of thousands of young Japanese, driven by the determination that their country be recognized as a first-class country in the world, died on battlefields during the Sino-Japanese War or later? How many people worked them-

---

Japan astonish them. They do not understand why she feels so deeply. They accordingly give a reason which is not correct, namely, that she is clamoring for free immigration to the United States." (p. 260)

[191] Ibid., p. 261.

[192] *Shibusawa denki shiryō*, vol. 34, pp. 291–92.

selves to the bone, rising early and going to bed late over many years to achieve that aim?

Eiichi had no inkling at that time that the Japanese inferiority complex toward Caucasians and groundless superiority complex over other peoples of color would eventually earn Japanese the enmity of not just white but colored peoples and lead to the devastation of the country in the mid-1940s. He believed that an unfair insult justified anger, and that he ought to be angry not just for the sake of Japan but also, as a friend, for the sake of the United States. Thinking that even in the United States thoughtful people would surely be as indignant as Japanese, he intended to work with these justice-loving Americans to fight against an evil that he felt was darkening the world.

Eiichi felt that the Gulick letter must have been wrong in that basic regard. But in that he went to the trouble of writing at such length and in such detail, Gulick was better than others in the American business world whom Eiichi had trusted as comrades but whose response to his telegram had been brusque and cold. Some wrote that the climax of the issue having been over, there was no point in making a fuss, that it would be better to accept the defeat and think of what to do next. Vanderlip remained silent, but apparently that did not mean his friendly feeling toward Eiichi had weakened; he was realistic and had decided that making a fuss over the issue would no longer be of any use.

Eiichi gradually came to the realization that Americans and Japanese differed in their sensibilities, attitudes, and ways of thinking, and that what Japanese thought to be absolutely right might not necessarily be right for Americans. Until then, Eiichi had had the vague understanding that there were two types of Americans, good and bad. The bad Americans did bad things like excluding Japanese, while the good Americans fought against them under the banner of idealism and humanism.

Looking back over the way the immigration issue had developed, however, Eiichi could not but admit that his understanding had been flawed. Now he saw that while it was true that the members of the U.S. Congress whom the Japanese side had considered to be "men of good conscience" had been opposed to discriminatory legislation since the time of Theodore Roosevelt, they had done so out of diplomatic considerations, thinking that overt friction with Japan should be avoided. In terms of their fundamental views – that Japanese immigrants should be excluded from entry – they did not much differ from the outright advocates of Japanese exclusion. The Japanese side, however, had naively assumed that they were pro-Japanese and comrades in the fight for justice. Such assumptions were hasty, self-serving, and wrong.

No wonder, Eiichi began to see, that the attempt to mobilize such people to further the Japanese cause had lacked the expected decisiveness. No wonder the Japanese side had suffered one loss after another in California – the passage of a regulation requiring children of Japanese descent to attend racially segregated separate schools (1906), the Alien Land Law of 1913 prohibiting Japanese and other aliens from owning agricultural land or possessing long-term leases over it, and the majority support for the state referendum (1920) amending the Alien Land Law. Passage in the U.S. Congress of the 1924 Immigration Act was the last straw. Now it was very clear that the American side did not take the matter as seriously as did Japanese. If that was the case, Eiichi realized, any attempt to appeal to the American tradition of humanism by direct display of righteous wrath was futile in the first place, and not only that, a direct display of one-sided indignation would end up alienating the few in the United States who had been friendly toward Japan.

THE RESETTING OF PRIVATE DIPLOMACY

On June 18, the Japanese-American Relations Committee met to discuss what policy should guide it from then on. Almost all the members of the Committee were filled with anger and resentment; they all felt they had been terribly betrayed by the United States. Declaring, "It's all over," Kaneko Kentarō resigned in protest as president of the Committee. Nitobe Inazō, who had once studied in Hokkaido under William S. Clark, the third president of the Massachusetts Agricultural College (now the

FIGURE 45
Nitobe Inazō (1862–1933), agricultural economist, educator, diplomat, and Christian, who became disillusioned with the United States after the passage of the 1924 Exclusion Act. Photo: Shibusawa Memorial Museum.

University of Massachusetts Amherst), and had endeavored to spread among Japanese the spirit of Christianity he had learned from Clark, deplored the "death" of the American spirit, declaring that as long as the Japanese Exclusion Act was in effect, he would never set foot on American soil again. Zumoto Motosada, the journalist, urged that the Japanese-American Relations Committee be dissolved, saying that such actions insulting to Japan taken by the U.S. Congress, the highest political body in the land, essentially negated the raison d'être of the Committee, and declared that they should dissolve it once and for all and issue a statement to make Americans realize how humiliated Japan felt.

Eiichi had been listening quietly, but he finally stood up and tried to soothe their anger as much as he could. He told them that they all should firmly resolve to come to terms with a new phase of Japan-U.S. relations, that they might have little room for doing anything about the Immigration Act, but that there were many things for the Committee to do otherwise.

He went on to express his recent concern about the rapid rise of nationalism, militarism, and anti-Western Asianism in Japan. These trends were increasingly pronounced in the tone of newspapers and magazines. Given that the masses of the country were much inclined to belligerent agitation, he was extremely worried about the future. Dissolving the Japanese-American Relations Committee, widely seen as a moderate organization, at such a time, could end up adding fuel to the fire, Eiichi said.

Dan Takuma agreed with Eiichi, and also advised caution, warning that a single misstep in dealing with this issue might lead to a serious crisis for Japan. Fujiyama Raita and Soeda Juichi followed suit. It was decided to keep the Committee in existence and to study the Committee's future direction of activity at the initiative of executive members Eiichi and Fujiyama.

On June 16, in response to a protest about the Immigration Act lodged by the Japanese government two weeks earlier, U.S. Secretary of State Hughes sent a brusque reply saying that the new law represented the exercise of the legislative power of Congress over the control of immigrants and was not much different from the Gentlemen's Agreement in terms of actual application. The reply said it considered this matter to have been settled. The Gentlemen's Agreement had been an agreement between the governments of Japan and the United States drawn up without a resolution passed in Congress, and, although the entry of Japanese immigrants had been regulated by the agreement for many years, it has been the target of criticism in Congress. The reply ended by saying that it did not wish to create friction with the Congress, and the implication was that the Department of State was unable to say more on the matter.[193] Compared with the cautious attitude of Secretary of State Hughes at the time the bill was under deliberation and the hesitancy of President Coolidge in signing it into law, the once-friendly United States seemed to the Japanese side to have suddenly turned cold. Many Japanese familiar with the situation felt bitterly the loss of a long-valued ally.

Japanese efforts in private-level diplomacy had to adopt a fundamental change in stance. Now that the U.S. government had made its position clear and considered the issue formally settled, any Japanese expression of discontent with the immigration issue would inevitably be considered interference in internal affairs.[194] There was little choice but to work within the bounds of this restriction.

Until then, Japanese concerned with issues pending between the United States and their country had been able to communicate with friends and comrades across the Pacific and present a united front with Americans who shared common cause with them. As in the Tokyo conferences of 1920, they had been able

---

[193] Letter dated June 16, *Papers Relating to the Foreign Relations of the United States, 1924* (711.945/1124), vol. 2, pp. 403–408.

[194] Foreign Minister Shidehara wrote to Ambassador Hanihara later in June that the government would refrain from a reply to Hughes' note as "any further exchange of correspondence . . .would only tend to arouse popular agitation in both countries and to complicate further the situation without serving any useful purpose." Nish, *Japanese Foreign Policy*, pp. 291–92.

to deepen mutual understanding by candidly expressing what they had felt and thought. There had been a broad measure of freedom enabling both sides to speak candidly. Now that freedom and mutual regard had been lost. Eiichi mused that it was as if you could be cut down with a sword but were not allowed to fight back. It was as if you had to face whatever arrows might be aimed in your direction undefended and unarmed. Whatever tears and blood you might shed, you were barred from complaint but ought to endure everything and wait until the United States changed its mind. That could hardly be called diplomacy, he thought; it was more like the self-inflicted suffering of a religious ascetic.

As if trying to convince himself it was true, whenever Eiichi gave a lecture or speech he would reiterate his conviction that justice would ultimately emerge victorious. But he sometimes could not but feel his confidence waver. The circumstances surrounding Japan were growing increasingly difficult, and he could not see the light of hope anywhere. He nostalgically recalled the old days when Japan-U.S. relations had been based simply on the principle of cooperation. In those days everything had been simple and direct, without the complications that now beset them. People had looked austere and dignified like giant, old weather-beaten trees. Eiichi often remembered Townsend Harris, the first U.S. consul general to Japan, who was for him a nostalgic "champion of fairness and humanism."[195]

By the mid-1920s, America's allegiance and attention had shifted to China, leaving it room only for criticism and suspicion of Japan. Helping China build a democratic and modern civilization in Asia became an American passion. It had been pouring funds into the continent, and tens of thousands of American missionaries and doctors were devoting themselves to China's aid. It was a huge social development project. To those engaged in it, Japan looked only like a vicious beast trying to disrupt peace in China and obstruct the goodwill and affection of Americans

---

[195] *Shibusawa denki shiryō*, vol. 34, p. 369.

toward Chinese. The scenario envisioned by Japanophobe Willard D. Straight was now unfolding in reality.

The United States had become a great power, but its likes and dislikes shifted constantly, making for a capricious diplomacy. It would treasure a country as long as it was suitably submissive and obedient, but discard it like a worn-out rag should it grow too outspoken or confident. The triangular relationship produced in the Pacific by American capriciousness led eventually to the great storm of the Pacific War.

That same year, illness prevented Eiichi from one last chance to contribute to the future of China. In November 1924, Sun Yat-sen sent a message that he wanted to see Eiichi during a stop-over in Kobe on his way by sea, via Shanghai, to Beijing to attend a national conference on the reunification of China. The coming conference would determine the destiny of China, he said, and as he thought, "at a time when the world situation has been cease-lessly evolving very fast, the peoples of East Asia should achieve a grand unification," he wanted to see Eiichi by all means to seek his advice. Sun was scheduled to arrive at Kobe port at five on the afternoon of November 24 on board a ship named *Shanghai Maru*. Unfortunately, Eiichi had been very ill and was not able to go to Kobe, so he had the Dai-ichi Bank Kobe branch deliver a message to Sun.

Sun Yat-sen was firmly committed to forging cooperation among the peoples of East Asia to defend against the incursions of the white peoples. His Nationalist party had approached the Soviet Union out of political and military necessity in an effort to reunite China, and Sun's Russian friend Mikhail Borodin was very active as an adviser of his party. Borodin provided theoreti-cal background and modern objectives to Sun's anti-white senti-ment. Sun, therefore, had been sad when Japan proved so eager to join the Western camp of world powers. At a press conference in Kobe, Sun said the people of both China and Japan ought to join hands and call for international equality for the sake of Asian people, or broadly for all the oppressed peoples in the world. Only based on such objectives was China-Japan friend-ship possible and meaningful.

On November 30, after a further exchange of telegrams with Eiichi, Sun left Japan for Beijing. Soon after the opening of the conference in Tianjin, however, he fell ill and on March 12 of the following year, 1925, died in Beijing, ending his hardship-filled life.

Himself ill in bed, Eiichi had sent condolence gifts and messages to Sun through the Japan-China Business Association and the China-Japan Industrial Development Company. After Sun's death, Eiichi sent a large bouquet of flowers to be presented at his funeral, and prayed for the repose of his soul.

During that autumn and early winter of 1924, the Japanese-American Relations Committee had been holding meetings to discuss the painful questions of what to do following passage of the U.S. Immigration Act. It finally decided to suspend all of its U.S.-related activities for the time being but without disbanding the Committee. On December 25, copies of a letter Eiichi wrote on behalf of the Committee were sent to seventy individuals in the United States who were in close association with the Committee, telling of the Committee's suspension of activity and Eiichi's thoughts. It was a respectful and heartfelt letter. The gist is as follows:

> In this year of 1924, which is drawing to a close, the new Immigration Act was regrettably enacted but the Committee would like to express its sincere gratitude for all kinds of friendliness and encouragement sent to us from various quarters in the United States. The warm words received were like a light in the darkness, giving us the hope and courage that kept us going.
>
> The subsequent development of the situation, however, makes it clear that any form of activity on the Japanese side concerning the Immigration Act would only invite suspicion and become a source of misunderstanding; the Japanese-American Relations Committee has decided, with reluctance, to suspend its activities for the time being. This, needless to say, does not mean any decline in our enthusiasm for amity between our two countries. Our conviction that close cooperation between the two countries is essential not just for Japan and America but for the peace and prosperity of the whole world has not changed in the least. Specific activities, particularly activities in the United States, will be left to the initiative of

the American side. We hope that you will continue your efforts in promoting peace in the way you consider best. If there are things we can do to cooperate with you without inviting misunderstanding, please call upon us at anytime.[196]

Many American friends were moved by Eiichi's heartfelt message and responded with letters promising to cooperate with him. Already in the United States voices had grown louder opposing the way the Immigration Act had come into being. Gulick wishfully said that in a few years it was not unlikely that the controversial subdivision (c) of section 13 of the act would be amended so that the quota system might be applied to Japanese immigrants as it was to other countries.

Subsequently, too, Eiichi continued until the end of his life to do his utmost to promote goodwill between the two countries by such means as entertaining American visitors to Japan. The traditions and forms of private-level diplomacy that had been accumulating over the two decades were brought to an end in that year of 1924. The termination of their endeavors was almost unbearable for Eiichi and the many friends and colleagues who had thought Japan-U.S. cooperation to be a core part of Japan's national policy. It came as a shock from which they thought they would not recover.

When a project one has been devoting one's efforts to fails due to the thoughtless actions of others, one cannot help blaming heaven and despising people. Bitterness and frustration shut up the heart, cloud one's vision, and put a pall over everything one tries to do. The more important one finds one's work, the more likely one is to be deeply affected by success or failure. On that score, Eiichi was a bit unusual. When he suffered failure, he grieved as much as anyone, but that state of grief rarely affected him at his very core. Whatever dilemma he might have faced, he would set out to solve the problem and continue in search of the next path on which to move forward. This attitude was probably the secret to his many achievements over the many avenues he followed throughout his career.

---

[196] *Shibusawa denki shiryō*, vol. 34, pp. 418–22.

In any case, private-level diplomacy was back to square one. Circumstances in Japan were increasingly fluid and difficult. As ultra-rightist forces gained momentum, letters to the editor of a threatening tone began to appear in newspapers describing Eiichi's pro-Americanism a "sell-out" of his country. From then on, Eiichi thought, he would probably have to direct more of his attention inward toward Japan, to do what was obligatory, however difficult it might be. But he was now eighty-four years old and increasingly felt the rapid changing of the times and his advancing age.

CHAPTER 11

RAINBOWS OVER THE OCEAN

ഇ

In 1924, while passage of the Immigration Act cast Eiichi and his colleagues in Japan into despair and disappointment, Japanese immigrant families in the United States were making lives for themselves with courage and forbearance. The immigration issue had entered a new phase and the era of the Nisei had begun. They were busy opening up new paths for their lives with no need to rely on backing of their parents' homeland. In the late 1920s and 1930s, their worldview and lifestyles were growing far apart from the nationalism that was then intensifying in Japan.

Nishiyama Sen (1911–2007), pioneer in simultaneous interpreting of English and Japanese and well known for his interpreting for NHK during the live telecast of the Apollo landing on the moon in 1969, spent his boyhood in Salt Lake City, Utah. The 1910s and 20s was the time during which anti-Asian racial discrimination grew intense, culminating in the enactment of the Immigration Act in 1924 that shut the door on immigration from Japan. He was a Nisei, or second-generation Japanese, the population of which was growing in various parts of the United States at that time.[197] Unlike in California at that time (around 1925), in Utah students of Japanese heritage were apparently attending public schools.

---

[197] Translator's note: The author, a long-time associate and personal friend of Nishiyama's, recalls that when he was writing this book, Nishiyama shared recollections of his boyhood; the anecdotes narrated below are based on these personal conversations, which took place in 1970.

Nishiyama was in the seventh grade when one day his class went swimming at a heated pool, an appealing feature of a newly built municipal gymnasium. Like his classmates he was in high spirits. The gatekeeper to the pool allowed all of them entry except for Nishiyama, insisting that the white students were allowed to swim in the pool but not Japanese. The teacher who accompanied the students was embarrassed and tried his best to negotiate with the gatekeeper, but without success. Nishiyama had to give up swimming and went home alone.

When he went to school the following day, he was immediately called to the principal's office. The principal, a middle-aged woman, sincerely apologized to him, saying how sorry she was that her country could allow such discriminatory treatment. After she heard what had happened, she said, she was so disturbed that she couldn't sleep all night. The school had just decided that from then on it would never use that pool again and instead use another pool where Nishiyama could enjoy swimming like everyone else. She then told him she hoped that he would try to put up with the situation this one time and not let it get in the way of his good spirits and his studies. His classmates, too, were shocked by the incident and a number of them joined in signing a written protest to the mayor through their Boy Scout troops, condemning such baseless discrimination in their country that championed freedom and equality.

When Sen went home and told his family what had happened, his father gave him a scolding. Sen had been thoughtless to go into a public place like a city-run swimming pool where there was likely to be a "no Japanese" rule. "You were not only humiliated as a Japanese," the father said, "but you also caused trouble to your school, the Boy Scouts, and others. You're already thirteen years old, so you should understand your place in society and avoid going to where you are likely to cause trouble."

Sen's father was among the first generation of Japanese immigrants to the United States, and this was typical of their thinking in those days. His reaction to his son's experience reflected in part the extreme fear of being humiliated in public and in part the time-honored Japanese tradition of refraining as much as possible from causing trouble to others. It was also a form of self-protection amid the upsurge of anti-Japanese sentiment. As an unwelcome minority in American society in those days, first-generation Japanese immigrants found a way to survive by working together to avoid incurring the displeasure of white people and patiently waiting for times to change. They looked forward to the day when their Nisei children, who held U.S. citizenship, would grow to adulthood to protect them in turn. This was the doleful situation of the weak, who must band together to protect their young and defend themselves against the strong.

Another incident that illustrates the thinking of first-generation Japanese immigrants to the United States was a robbery that took place in a small town in Idaho. Evidence found at the scene of the crime seemed to indicate that a certain Japanese was the culprit. But the thief had disappeared with the stolen money, and despite vigorous police investigation, he was not found. The newspapers began attacking the police for their incompetence. Then, although no request had been made for their cooperation, local Japanese voluntarily issued a circular to other Japanese in neighboring states, and together they carefully tracked the criminal until he was caught and turned in to police. What this reflected was their sense that a crime committed by a member of their group was a disgrace to all Japanese, and their determination to restore their own honor by catching the criminal and preventing accusations likely to be leveled by white people against the Japanese as a whole.

Being born and raised in such circumstances was never easy for the Nisei. It was difficult to bear a level of racial discrimination under which public institutions could post signs like "No Japanese allowed," and was the cause of both anger and distress among Japanese. But Nishiyama Sen observed that, having been brought up in such a world from the beginning, he had not felt as offended as others might think. He and his fellow Nisei learned to avoid going to swimming pools or theaters or any other place where they were likely to be discriminated against. Nishiyama himself had no memory of having felt serious annoyance or despair because of discrimination. It might have been because of the basically optimistic social sensibility in the United States at that time. Not just the Nisei but all Americans shared the idea – indeed, the strong conviction – that the United States was a country of hope, a country full of opportunity, where, even if they had a hard time, they would surely be better off if they worked hard enough, Nishiyama said.

That was why, as soon as they were of an age to understand what was going on around them, the children of Japanese immigrants became eager students, determined to be first-rate citizens. Their common goal was to get better grades than their white classmates. In his junior high school, said Nishiyama, when a Nisei student was not getting good grades, the other Nisei students would get together to encourage and help him or her improve. As was the custom in those days, local newspapers published the names of young people of the community who had graduated from university, and among the high-achieving graduates there were always many Nisei, much to the surprise of anti-Japanese advocates.[198]

Another expression of this Nisei mentality may be found in the heroic record of Nisei soldiers on the Italian front during World War II. Although most Japanese in the western part of the United States were interned during the war in detention camps, some young Japanese men and women volunteered to serve in the U.S. military forces. Despite cruel and difficult battle conditions, they made great contributions to the U.S. cause with unparalleled courage, patriotism, and organizational ability. One Japanese-American unit, the 442nd Infantry Regiment, was the most decorated unit in the war.

The valor of the Nisei made a deep impression in American society. The fact that the children of Japanese immigrants who had been despised and persecuted in U.S. society for a long time risked their lives to protect their American homeland with outstanding achievements stirred a sense of guilt and soul searching among many Americans. This, along with the eventual defeat in the war of the immigrants' home country and the disappearance

---

[198] O'Connor, *Pacific Destiny*, p. 428.

of radical nationalism there, helped put an eventual end to anti-Japanese sentiment and the restrictions imposed upon them.

An outstanding self-made man among Nisei in the United States was Mike Masaru Masaoka (1915–1991). His name became known among Japanese for his role as a lawyer at the time of the Tokyo war crimes trials held following Japan's defeat. Masaoka also grew up in Salt Lake City and was a boyhood friend of Nishiyama Sen. He was the third oldest of seven children. When the oldest brother, George, was twelve, their father was killed in a traffic accident. After that George took the lead in the family, encouraging his younger brothers and helping their mother run the produce and fish market the father had managed. Neighbors saw the boys going out early every morning to purchase goods at the wholesale market to sell in their store.

In what must have been the 1920s and 1930s, just as anti-Japanese prejudice was peaking in the United States, the teen-age George was busy working and sending his brother Mike to university. The second oldest brother, Ben, was later killed on the Italian front during World War II. After the war, their mother was chosen "Mother of the Year," an award recognizing a best wife and mother devoted to the education of her children. One mother was selected every year from throughout the United States. Nishiyama Sen frequented the home of Mike and his family, and recalled that whatever predicament they faced, Mike and his family were always cheerful and happy.[199]

TRIBUTE TO TOWNSEND HARRIS

In the autumn of 1927, Eiichi traveled to Shimoda on the Izu Peninsula, accompanied by his eldest daughter, Utako, his grandson Keizō (this author's father), and others, to attend a ceremony unveiling a stone monument dedicated to Townsend Harris (1804–1878), the first United States consul general to Japan. The idea of erecting a monument to honor Harris's achievements had been proposed by a Chicago businessman named Henry M.

---

[199] http://articles.latimes.com/2001/may/20/local/me-331

FIGURE 47   Ceremony unveiling the stone monument dedicated to Townsend Harris at
Gyokusenji temple, Shimoda, site of the first U.S. consulate (Eiichi, center in
the front row). Photo: Shibusawa Memorial Museum.

Wolf during a visit to Shimoda. Eiichi had been consulted on the
proposal via Edgar A. Bancroft, U.S. ambassador to Japan. Eiichi
had admired Harris from early on. He had even paid his respects
at Harris's grave in New York, composing poems on the occasion (see p. 144). Upon hearing about Wolf's proposal Eiichi
had immediately agreed and taken the lead in doing everything
from fundraising and negotiating with local people, to designing the monument and making preparations for the unveiling
ceremony.

The memorial stone was erected on the grounds of Gyokusenji temple where Harris had been in residence for one year
and a half. The inscription was prepared by Wolf, Bancroft, and
Eiichi. An excerpt from Harris's diary entry written on September 4, 1856, is inscribed on the front of the monument. It says
on the previous night he could not sleep from excitement and
the "enormous" mosquitoes and that at half past two p.m. on
September 4, with "a reinforcement from the ship" he erected
a heavy flagstaff in the middle of the precincts of Gyokusenji

temple and raised the U.S. flag on Japanese soil for the first time. The paragraph ends with: "Grave reflections. Ominous of change. Undoubted beginning of the end. Query, – if for real good of Japan?"

On the back side of the monument is a long inscription by Eiichi that records Harris's achievements, and praises the sincerity and courage exhibited at the time of the anti-foreign samurai killing (January 1861) of the Dutch-American consulate interpreter Henry Heusken (see pp. 8–9). It also describes Eiichi's visit to the Harris grave in New York in 1901. It had been late autumn and the colors of the maple trees around the grave were bright and beautiful. The inscription concludes with the waka poem he had composed during his visit to the grave. The entire inscription in Eiichi's own calligraphy was carved onto the stone, and the monument was ready for its unveiling ceremony.

The Izu Peninsula in autumn was especially beautiful. Concerned about the health of eighty-seven-year-old Eiichi, his group decided to stay overnight at the Shuzenji hot spring resort on the night of September 30 and cross over Mount Amagi to Shimoda by car the following day. His daughter Utako, a young girl of seventeen at the time of former U.S. President Ulysses S. Grant's visit to Japan in 1879, was now sixty-four. Lonely after the passing of her husband, Hozumi Nobushige, the previous year, she had decided to accompany her father on his Izu trip; it had been a long time since they had traveled together.

At the Shuzenji Inn the group spent a quiet and relaxing night. In her diary, Utako reflected on the sight of her father leaning on the railing and tossing crumbs to the carp in the pond after he returned from the bath. His was a figure that evoked many fond memories. It had carried him through a brilliant career, but at the same time was that of a simple, unassuming old man full of human warmth. Once, she recalled, the pressures of his role as a public figure had seemed overwhelming, and when she had tried approaching him she had felt the tension he carried. But over the last several years, he had suddenly seemed to her to have become a mild, gentle old man. Riding together with him in the car, she realized that he no longer exuded that tension; she felt entirely at ease.[200]

It was a fairly long way to go from Shuzenji to Shimoda. I later heard that out of concern about Eiichi, my father, Keizō, had gone ahead, driving the road in advance to check the traffic conditions, how long it would take to reach Shimoda, the location of rest stops, and other such details. Utako's diary tells how there were long tunnels along the way and the road was unpaved. It was pitch dark in the tunnels, and when the car's headlights illuminated the rough surface of the inner tunnel wall made by chipping away at the rock, they could see water trickling down the walls here and there. Somewhat spooked by the sight, she found herself nestling up to Eiichi sitting next to her, thinking "My father is here, so I'll be fine." What a silly woman, she recalled wryly, to act like a young girl instead of the mature woman she had become.

At Shimoda, a grand unveiling ceremony started at 3 o'clock, attended by Charles MacVeagh, U.S. ambassador to Japan, and many members of the U.S. embassy, Tokugawa Iesato, president of the America-Japan Society, and many other guests including Kabayama Aisuke, Ōkura Kihachirō, and Hattori Kintarō.[201] Gyokusenji head priest Murakami Kibun's four-year-old son Yasumichi, lifted the red and white curtain to reveal a beautiful granite monument made by the Shimizugumi construction company. Eiichi stood up and gave a speech. He first expressed his appreciation for the efforts of the many people who had made possible the monument's completion and the grand ceremony. Referring to the quoted paragraph of Harris's diary, Eiichi then said:

---

[200] *Shibusawa denki shiryō*, vol. 38, pp. 343–50 and pp. 384–400.

[201] Translator's note: Kabayama Aisuke (1865–1953). Educated in the United States and Europe, he became a businessman in 1927 and was a member of the House of Peers and of the Privy Council; Ōkura Kihachirō (1837–1928), was an entrepreneur and investor in the Imperial Hotel as well as an avid collector of art who built Japan's first private museum of art in 1917; Hattori Kintarō (1860–1934), founder of the Seiko timepiece company, member of the Tokyo Chamber of Commerce, and a philanthropist in later life.

In response to Harris's words "Query, – if for real good of Japan?" I think it my duty to answer that query. I would say: [the opening of the country] proved very good for Japan. We will never forget your thoughtfulness. And please accept our appreciation. Together with you all here I would like to loudly declare our appreciation to Harris's soul in heaven. . . . Looking back at the changes that have taken place in Japan during the seven decades since the arrival of Harris, so many emotions fill my heart. I was right there when these changes occurred, and therefore I am all the more impressed with how much Japan has advanced.[202]

It was his conviction that the world was always advancing and that, even if difficulties occurred for a while, things were still improving as a whole. Despite the bitter experience of failure in his efforts of private diplomacy, he remained faithful to that basic conviction. Given the complex web of conflicting interests in Eiichi's time, it may be understandable that he had fond memories of Harris's persona and the logical consistency of the American that was so reminiscent of the samurai of old. It was not something like an old man's cynical attempt to implicitly censure the society of his own time by speaking highly of previous times.

"There was nothing dark or gloomy about my grandfather," Keizō often said. "It was not naïve optimism either, but rather a kind of cheerfulness and composure as if deeply rooted in the soil. When I was beside him I felt everything was all right, I felt naturally safe and secure. He was great indeed." It may have been a cheerfulness and beauty allowed only to people like Eiichi, who had seen with their own eyes the unprecedented process of advancement from the closing years of the Tokugawa shogunate and who had devoted everything in their lives to that advancement.

Unlike Eiichi, my father Keizō was a modern man brought up amid the contradictions and confusion of the Taishō and Shōwa eras (1912–1989). Not long after Eiichi's death, Keizō had to watch the utter destruction of the Japan that Eiichi and others of his time had so painstakingly built up. Immediately after the

---

[202] *Shibusawa denki shiryō*, vol. 38, pp. 357–59.

FIGURE 48
Chiang Kai-shek (1887–1975),
Chinese statesman who visited
Japan in 1927; with Eiichi (left).
Photo: Shibusawa Memorial
Museum.

war, he got involved in cleaning up the mess as finance minister in the second postwar cabinet. He had to endure a number of unhappy developments in his personal life, and he could not be as sure, as Eiichi had been, that the world was always advancing – that it would always get better. For this very reason, he was all the more attracted to the cheerful and fulfilled way of living Eiichi had had in his final phase of life.

EIICHI AND CHIANG KAI-SHEK

On October 26, 1927, not long after Eiichi returned from Shimoda, Chiang Kai-shek (Jian Jieshi), leader of the Chinese Nationalist Party (Kuomintang), visited Japan, and bringing with him his comrade, Chiang Chun (Zhang Qun; later premier of the Republic of China), he went to see Eiichi at the Asukayama residence. Chiang was just forty years old and was in the middle of fighting in North China to unify his country by conquering or forging alliances with local warlords. He was leading the Northern Expedition in the wake of the death of Sun Yat-sen.

Eiichi heartily welcomed these visitors from China and entertained them while recalling Sun Yat-sen's visit to the Asukayama residence, among other topics. It had been Eiichi's ardent wish since his tour in China in 1914 that Japan and China would form friendly ties, but unfortunately their subsequent relationship had been full of confusion, tension, and estrangement. There had been virtually no sign of improvement in their relations. That was partly because the Chinese political situation was extremely messy, but also because arrogant and self-centered attitudes on the part of some Japanese made normal diplomatic relations almost impossible.

Japan's relations with the United States were also fraught with problems, but at least channels of communication were still open between them; there were groups of influential people in the two countries who could talk candidly and respectfully with each other, whatever difficulties might trouble relations between their governments. In Japan's relations with China at that time, however, it was not only difficult to communicate with Chinese friends but also to find partners for dialogue among Chinese. It might be that if two countries do not get along with each other, their people, too, find it hard to get along. Although Japan and China, which had a common culture and shared traditions, ought to have been able to work together to carry on Asian civilization, their relationship had come to a most troubled state, and it made Eiichi very sad and regretful.

The difference in age between Eiichi and Chiang might have been too large, but Eiichi tried to show his sincerity as much as he could and encourage Chiang, too, to be frank with him. Confucius, when asked what was essential to human relations, is said to have immediately answered it was "shu" (恕; Jap. *jo*), explaining, "What you do not wish for yourself, do not do to others." Eiichi completely agreed with this idea. In recent years, he told Chiang, both Japan and China had been trying to do to the other what they did not wish for themselves. He said he would endeavor to correct this tendency and restore the principle of "shu" to improve Japan-China relations. He then asked Chiang to explain this point to people in China so that they, too, would endeavor to establish friendly ties with Japan.[203]

Chiang must have been greatly surprised to hear the ancient classic of his country cited in such earnest and sincere terms by the eighty-seven-year-old man before him – so much so that he may have suspected he had just heard a mean joke. He knew very well that if there was a country that would stand in the way of the reunification of China that he and his compatriots were struggling so hard to achieve, it was Japan. Although agreement had been reached in principle with world powers at the Washington Conference, the Japanese were not at all willing to give up its special interests on the continent. Complex and difficult diplomatic efforts were needed to solve each of many issues, including tariffs and matters of the foreign settlements. It was the unpleasant price China, which had belatedly joined the family of modern nations, had to pay in order to establish its presence as a nation-state in world affairs.

China's relations with Japan were far more difficult than those with the United States. It was obvious that Japan had no intention of letting go of the special interests in Manchuria and Mongolia that it had struggled hard to accumulate over many years. Not just that, but a desperate empire like Japan's would grab for whatever it thought was necessary to its national interests, no matter whom it might belong to. That nascent empire was the greatest obstacle standing in the way of Chiang's movement. (Indeed, he spent most of his entire career feuding with Japan; even after World War II, he had to face all kinds of difficulties stemming from Japan's past acts.)

Little had he expected, therefore, that he would meet a citizen of Japan, of all countries, who would speak to him seriously, quoting Confucius's teaching that what you do not wish for yourself, you do not do to others. Age had by no means addled

---

Shibusawa denki shiryō, vol. 39, p. 29.

his brain. No, this small old man wearing a warm smile – already a towering figure in history as one of the founders of Japan's modern industry – was stating his convictions with all sincerity. He was not using flowery words but talking about basic principles gained from his rich experience in commerce and industry as well as from his long and eventful life. Chiang found himself attracted by Eiichi.

Chiang began to think that people in the Japanese business world might be worth talking to. Later, he made a request to meet Eiichi again and asked him to introduce him to Japan's business leaders if that was possible. Eiichi readily agreed, and on November 4, a meeting took place at the Bankers Club in central Tokyo, attended by Kodama Kenji and Soeda Juichi among others.

On that day, soon after he introduced Chiang to those present, Eiichi had to leave midway due to a prior appointment, leaving them to talk together. Chiang was disappointed to find that all of the Japanese business leaders present, except for Eiichi, were more or less supporters of Japan's imperialistic state policy. Even Kodama, president of Yokohama Specie Bank and known as a liberal and a moderate engaged in broad, international work, insisted on his Japan-centered views and ignored Chinese interests when it came to the Manchuria and North China issues where Japanese and Chinese interests directly clashed. What made Chiang especially sad was that they did not even question such thinking and that they took it for granted that it would benefit China to follow the guidance of and cooperate with Japan and thereby reap the fruit of "coexistence and co-prosperity." They uncritically believed China would be willing to do so. Here there was no possibility of civility-based, person-to-person dialogue. Chiang left the Bankers Club feeling grim and misunderstood, although he had half expected such a result.

Chiang's interest in Eiichi remained, however. There was something special in Eiichi that he could not find in the other Japanese he had met. As he saw it, Eiichi was a broad-minded, gentle, kind-hearted, and marvelously modest man. Chiang saw something of an ideal form of Japan in this old man.

FIGURE 49   Chiang Kai-shek and Shibusawa Keizō (1956). Photo: Shibusawa Memorial
Museum.

If the day came when even a little of Eiichi's heart was reflected
in Japan's foreign policy and China and Japan could truly collaborate on an equal footing, then the landscape of Asia would
certainly change. It was a beautiful dream like a colorful rain-
bow arching briefly in the sunset sky, a dream most unlikely to
come true.[204]

---

[204] In this connection, ten years later, in 1937, when a Japanese business
delegation led by Kodama Kenji visited China it was welcomed in
Nanjing by the Chinese government. At that time, Chiang Kai-shek
gave a speech as Chairman of the National Military Council of the
Nationalist Government, stressing the importance of China-Japan
friendship. In the middle of the speech he put his manuscript aside and
suddenly began talking about Eiichi. He proposed "a silent moment of
prayer for the repose of the soul of Japan's great man we all respected."
It might have been Chiang's pointed message toward Japan, which –
contrary to the words Eiichi had expressed – was at that very time
forcing upon China what Japan would not have wished for itself. Or, it
might have been Chiang's eager desire to make Eiichi's fellow Japanese
realize what Eiichi had truly wanted to see.

That year (1927), Judge Gary (Elbert Henry Gary, a key founder of U.S. Steel) died. Upon hearing the news, Eiichi sent a heartfelt message of condolence. He had not been on very close terms with Gary, but Gary had been a top leader of New York business circles along with Frank A. Vanderlip, and so Eiichi had relied on him on various occasions. Gary, too, had valued his ties with Eiichi and done what he could for him. Several months prior to his death, Gary had all of a sudden summoned Horikoshi Zenjūrō (founder of the Horikoshi trading company with overseas offices in New York and elsewhere), and said he wanted to see Eiichi again somehow, wondering if it was possible to ask Eiichi to come over to the United States once again? Gary gave no particular reason for wanting such a meeting, but Horikoshi responded by saying that Eiichi was very old, and that since Gary was younger, perhaps he should go to Japan to see Eiichi. The matter had been left as it was, and not long after that, Gary passed away.

Having reached the advanced age of eighty-seven, Eiichi had survived many of the people he had become acquainted with in the United States. Among businessmen were James Stillman, John Wanamaker, Henry J. Heinz, and E. H. Harriman. Among politicians were Theodore Roosevelt, Woodrow Wil-

---

Years later, after the end of the terrible war, in the summer of 1956, my father Keizō visited Chiang, then president of the Republic of China, at his residence on Mt. Yangming in the suburbs of Taipei. Then, another ten years later, in the autumn I had the chance to meet President Chiang Kai-shek at the presidential office in Taipei. He had just turned eighty years old. He asked my age and then said he was about the same age when he had visited my great grandfather. "Your great grandfather was several years older than I am now," he said. When I presented him with a photographic edition of Eiichi's handwritten copy of the *Analects*, Chiang told me about that episode of Eiichi referring to the Confucian idea of "What you do not wish for yourself, do not do to others," and then said to the effect that China and Japan, while preserving the traditions of East Asia, should contribute to the advancement of world civilization.

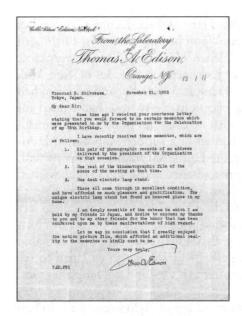

FIGURE 50
Thomas Edison letter to Eiichi
(1928). Photo: Shibusawa
Memorial Museum.

son, and Warren G. Harding; Lyman J. Gage had just died in
January (1927). Except for Wanamaker and Gage, they all had
been younger than Eiichi.

Inventor Thomas Edison died a few years later, in 1931. Eiichi
had been acquainted with him ever since they met during Eiichi's
1909 trip to the United States as the leader of the Japanese business delegation. They often exchanged letters. In 1922, Eiichi
served as head organizer of a gathering held in Tokyo to celebrate
Edison's seventy-fifth birthday.

Eiichi had passed on his connection with Edison when Mikimoto Kōkichi, well known for his pearl culturing business, traveled to the United States, writing Mikimoto a letter of introduction to the famed inventor. With that letter, Mikimoto obtained
an interview with Edison, declaring that he too was an inventor.
The story goes that upon meeting Edison, he spread out many
large pearls on the table and launched into an elaborate explanation of the pearl culturing process. Impressed by his zeal, Edison
agreed that Mikimoto indeed was an inventor and that invention

dealing with a living creature was something he himself had never tried. They were photographed together at the time. Soon afterward Mikimoto started a large sales campaign in the United States with leaflets quoting words of the famous Edison. "Mikimoto Pearls" were to become widely known in American society, no doubt largely due to this effective publicity stunt. Aside from the question whether Mikimoto really was the inventor of pearl culturing, his shrewdness as a businessman was certainly striking.

On October 1, 1928 a ceremony was held to honor Eiichi's eighty-eighth birthday, an age traditionally celebrated for its auspicious number. The sign identifying the sponsors claimed the backing of "everyone in the business world throughout the country." The venue was the Imperial Theatre, hired exclusively for the occasion. Among the guests were the prime minster, the ministers of his cabinet, and representatives of foreign countries. All the influential people in Tokyo were gathered here. It was a tremendous and glittering occasion.

The age of eighty-eight was, and still is, a fairly long life and well worth a major celebration. Still, that such a grand event was held for an old man who had had nothing to do with power politics and who had been quietly living out his life after retirement from his business involvements was like a grand finale representing the great prestige and overwhelming popularity he had enjoyed through his long life.

The stage that day was festooned with colorful decorations of skillfully arranged pine, bamboo, and plum – plants with symbolic and auspicious meaning. At the back somewhat right of center were seated Eiichi and his wife. Sitting behind them were their family members. At the left of the stage were the prime minister and other important guests. The audience seats were filled, long before the opening of the ceremony, with numerous guests and other people coming from around the country for that occasion. At 5:00 p.m. the curtain opened and Dan Takuma made an opening address, followed by Prime Minister Tanaka Giichi's congratulatory speech, which was not the usual perfunctory formality, but a very thoughtful speech that praised Eiichi's achievements based on a careful perusal of them. Now it was Eiichi's turn. At a sign from Nakajima Kumakichi, master of ceremonies, Eiichi stood from his seat and, as he approached the podium smiling, the hall exploded with thunderous applause.

Whenever he appeared on such a gala occasion, this old man exhibited the splendid performance of a veteran actor. Perhaps he had something of the actor within him. His movements, gestures, and bearing were neither exaggerated nor suppressed; he always kept them adequate and moderate. His whole body, moreover, was overflowing with cheerful modesty, toward which no one could feel offense or displeasure.

"I am very happy, so much so I cannot find words to express my appreciation," Eiichi began, and again a storm of applause arose and continued long, leaving Eiichi standing without speaking for a while at the podium.

He was good at speaking, another talent of his. What you like to do, you will do well, the saying goes. Eiichi loved talking with people by nature. His speeches were consistent and rich in expression. In addition, since he kept in mind who was in his audience and what their interests were and spoke to their hearts, those who were listening to him were quite naturally captivated by what he spoke of. On that day, as usual, he spoke without notes, making a fairly long speech smoothly from beginning to end, often interrupted by loud applause.

Starting with his boyhood, he then talked about his trip to France, employment in the government, and how he eventually entered the business world and devoted all his time and energy to endeavoring to achieve two major objectives – advocacy of *gapponshugi* and the breakdown of the long-entrenched practice of "revering the government and despising private (business)," the *kanson-minpi* described earlier in this book (see chapters 3 and 5). "With my humble ability I couldn't have done much," he demurred. But, backed up by the trends in the business world, the economy had undergone far greater improvement and advancement than he had expected over the last six decades. Not just business had expanded but the personality and attitude of those engaging in business had changed greatly, he said:

> You have come today to celebrate my eighty-eighth birthday. For this tottering old man, retiring from business long ago, the Prime Minister came and delivered a speech of congratulations. This fact alone is enough to show how closely the government and the private/business sector have been linked.

Another big round of applause filled the hall. Deftly and almost imperceptibly Eiichi switched the celebration from one of his personal honor to the remarkable focus of advancements made in Japanese history. By so doing, the life of Eiichi, the man of the moment, became a kind of shared heritage of the Japanese people, which enabled him to express joy and gratitude without reserve.

> Thinking this way, I now clearly see that what I had vaguely thought Japan should be like after I returned from Europe at the beginning of the Meiji era was not at all an illusion but a very correct vision.

With Eiichi's gentle, dignified figure before them and images of his eventful life overlapping with the tumultuous modern history of their country filling their minds, the audience was intoxicated. Eiichi concluded his speech by adding,

I am certain that the day will come when equality will prevail. My strong conviction that the status of people engaging in business should be raised has proven correct. Even more pleasing than the celebration of my small life is the celebration of our country.[205]

It would be wrong to assume, however, that Eiichi's popularity was due to some great success in specific business projects. The prestige that he had gained, which was almost a national prestige, was derived from something more fundamental, from the very way he had lived. It might be closer to truth to say that the hopes, aspirations, fears, joys, and sorrows he had carried through his long life were very close to the national emotions felt throughout the country at each phase of the history Eiichi had lived through. A look back on the national life of Japan since the start of the Meiji era seems to show there were threads in it that were inseparable from Eiichi's life.

One of those threads might have been the ardent wish he had held his whole life to break with the long tradition of unquestioned respect for officialdom and disdain for the private sector (*kanson minpi*). Many Japanese tacitly understood that respect for the individual and establishment of a democratic society were indispensable, not just because they could help to control autocracy, but because they were essential to modernization, which was the only hope for Japan's future. In 1873 Eiichi had left the government and joined the private, business sector, which was at the time a most daring thing to do. Some people acutely and correctly grasped the meaning of Eiichi's action. What someone had to do for the sake of Japan, Eiichi took the initiative and did. Never again did he take a post in the government; he remained in the business sector for the rest of his career. It was the kind of dogged spirit for which Japanese have great admiration.

Eiichi by nature had a dignity and strength that made people feel safe and secure. People suffer from worry and anxiety in a rapidly changing world. Japan of that time was no exception.

---

[205] *Shibusawa denki shiryō*, vol. 57, p. 316.

Japanese did know the necessity of modernization, but seeing the traditional system of values passed on by their ancestors being torn into pieces in exchange for modernization made them anxious and insecure. Change was frightening but being left behind as modern events sped forward could lead to the ruin of their country. Eiichi seemed able to reassure those who suffered from that dilemma.

Eiichi's theory of "the inseparability of morality and economy," insofar as he himself talked about it, was not the clichéd, superficial meaning – i.e., merely the moral management of the economy – but had the power to bring composure to the minds of people torn apart by the conflicting forces of new and old. People sensed that within Eiichi there coexisted a natural harmony of modern rationalism and traditional East Asian values. As long as Eiichi was that way, as long as he felt no sense of anxiety, they were able to think things would work out. As the result, people's expectations of Eiichi were excessively high: since he knew well enough about the new and old worlds, as long as they left everything to him, he would surely come up with reasonable solutions to satisfy them all.

Soon after Eiichi's death, a Shibusawa relative took a taxi, and the taxi driver, not knowing who he was, of course, remarked, "So Shibusawa-san has passed away . . ." He then added sadly, "I've never met him, but somehow I feel as if I owe a great deal to him." Around the same time, a waka poem that went "I really hate capitalists, but you, only you, should have lived longer," was found in the Asukayama residence mailbox. It was signed, "a leftist." The poem seemed to say that Eiichi had something that touched the hearts of people on the street.

COMMEMORATING THE GRANT TREE PLANTING

On May 10, 1930 a monument in memory of General Grant's tree planting was erected in Ueno Park, Tokyo. Eiichi and Masuda Takashi were the joint promoters of the event. When former U.S. president Ulysses S. Grant had visited Japan in 1879, a half century earlier, Eiichi had been thirty-nine years old, and together with Masuda and Fukuchi Ōchi, had organized a big welcome event on behalf of Tokyo citizens. On August 25 that year, a great pageant had been held in Ueno Park with the Emperor and Empress Meiji and General Grant and his party as guests of honor and featuring the ancient martial arts of *yabusame* (archery on horseback) and *inuoumono* ("dog shooting"), and other attractions (see pp. 55–61). Grant and his wife had taken part in a tree-planting ceremony held to commemorate their visit, and the trees had since been treasured by Tokyo citizens, who had nicknamed them the "Grant Cypress" and the "Grant Magnolia." In that half century, the trees had grown very large.

The fresh foliage of spring was beautiful on that day in Ueno Park in May 1930. Red-and-white curtains customarily used at auspicious occasions hung at the back of the spacious Takenodai lawn, and the Japanese and American national flags fluttered in the breeze. The Grant Cypress and Grant Magnolia trees were wrapped in decorative cloths dyed in stripes. Among the guests gathered by the time the ceremony started were acting U.S. ambassador to Japan Edwin L. Neville, foreign minister Shidehara Kijūrō, vice foreign minister Yoshida Shigeru (later prime minister), former ambassador to the United States Hanihara Masanao, and other diplomats, as well as business leaders such as Dan Takuma, Ikeda Shigeaki, and Sasaki Yūnosuke. Governor of the Bank of Japan Hijikata Hisaakira was also present. The captain of a ship named *President Grant*, of the American President Line, which happened to be in port at Yokohama that day, was invited as well.

Jane McIlroy, daughter of a military attaché at the U.S. embassy, unveiled the monument carved with the portraits of General Grant and Emperor Meiji. Then Eiichi made a speech, reminiscing about the 1879 welcome for Grant and explaining the background of the monument's construction. Following congratulatory speeches by ambassadors and the foreign minister, Tokyo City social affairs bureau director-general Yasui Seiichirō (later governor of Tokyo) delivered a speech on behalf of the mayor in which he promised that Tokyo City would take responsibility for and protect and preserve the monument and the two trees from then onward.

After the ceremony, a memorial tea party was held at the Seiyōken restaurant nearby. Those present fully enjoyed sharing their reminiscences. Eiichi was particularly interested in a story told by a man named Kuki Ryūichi. At the time of Grant's visit, Kuki had been a young diplomat stationed in Europe. He had been ordered by the foreign ministry back home to join Grant's entourage and accompany Grant to Japan. On the way he was to make secret inquiries into Grant's stance toward China and Japan and send a report home. In those days Japan and China were engaged in tension-filled negotiations on the territorial issue of the Ryukyu Islands.

On the way, Grant spoke with Kuki about various things to pass the time on the ship and made the following prescient observation. China was the largest country in the world, with a population of 400 million and limitless resources, and in the eyes of Europeans and Americans it was a country thousands of times greater than Japan, Grant said. Even if Japan fought with China it had little chance of winning. Of course, if Japan lost, that would be a big problem. But if Japan were to win, that would be an even bigger problem, because of what it would mean about the state of China's civilization and people. And the whole world would swarm into China, scrambling for its resources. The result, said Grant, would be that not just China would be in great trouble but that Japan, too, would face unsurmountable difficulties. It would be wisest and best for Japan to be very patient and avoid war with China by all means.

Born in rural Ohio, Grant was a man of simplicity and solidity, but he also seemed to have a special spark of genius. Whether or not this story of what he told Kuki has been exaggerated or embroidered with the passage of time is hard to confirm, but we cannot help noticing that events between Japan and China subsequently unfolded almost exactly as Grant had predicted, and relations remain strained even today in 2018.

THE ADVENT OF THE *SHIBUSAWA EIICHI BIOGRAPHICAL MATERIALS*

Eiichi's grandson, Keizō, after graduation from university, entered the employ of Yokohama Specie Bank, was assigned to its branch office in London, and went to Britain in September 1922. He hoped to train hard in London for four or five years and then work in the United States for a while. Back home in Japan, however, Eiichi was growing weaker with age and also had health problems, so Keizō got permission from his bank and returned to Japan in the summer of 1925. At that juncture, he decided to leave the Specie Bank and enter the Dai-ichi Bank with the intention of following in Eiichi's footsteps.

When Keizō returned home he found Tokyo completely changed in the wake of the powerful earthquake that had hit Tokyo in September 1923, resulting in devastating fires and destruction. Not only the townscape but the people of the city looked different too. After three years, Eiichi, too, seemed different. He was weaker physically, walking with more difficulty, but more than that, he seemed to have somehow risen above the bonds of earthly humanity and secured a place in a loftier realm.

Eiichi in his seventies had remained physically energetic despite his very advanced age. He would take Keizō, then a university student, out for dinner and eat such luxuries as conger eel (*anago*) tempura or juicy beefsteak with gusto. He had been mild in nature and rarely showed any ill temper. He had always worn a smile. Even so, when giving someone advice or warning or giving instructions, he had made sure his message had been gotten across, leaving no doubt as to his intent. He had achieved great maturity and mellowness, but the vital force of his personality and ambitions could still be felt.

When Keizō returned to Japan after three years away, however, he saw that the raw edges of Eiichi's personality had been smoothed. Keizō and others around Eiichi found themselves guessing and doing what Eiichi wanted them to do even without him asking for or saying anything. They did it quite spontaneously, and there was no problem, and it seemed as if everything proceeded smoothly.

"I wouldn't use words like saintly or spiritual. Transparency might be closer. It seemed that what could be called the 'glare' or worldliness that Grandfather [Eiichi] had always emitted gradually faded. Instead, we could observe something like his inner personality coming out from deep within him," wrote Keizō.[206]

"When I went out with him I mostly followed him, walking behind, and I felt I could observe something different about him from behind," he continued. "He walked with his head tilted slightly to the left, his hair soft like that of a child and blacker than was typical for his age hanging thickly over his white collar. There was a different pitch in the sound of his right and left footsteps, for reasons unknown. Watching his back as we walked, I felt I was gazing not so much at a famous figure of history as a solitary old farmer from the Chiaraijima hamlet (Eiichi's birthplace) with a life rich with accumulated experience spanning an unimaginably long period of time. His back seemed to convey a poetry and a childlike innocence that I couldn't have detected by looking at him from the front."

Several biographies of Eiichi had been published while Eiichi was alive, but none of them had satisfied Keizō. No matter how many successful cases in his career might be enumerated, Eiichi as a flesh and blood human could not be fully portrayed, nor could the Japan and the period he had lived through be sufficiently depicted. He was a man with an extraordinarily broad range of interests and a very long period of activity. That does not mean that he was a workaholic; he was a highly cultivated man with a sophisticated mind and gentle sensibilities. He was not someone who could be measured by a single yardstick.

Reconstructing Eiichi's activities as they actually were against their historical backdrop and correctly appraising them would require a huge amount of broad-ranging materials, which would then have to be properly organized. Inasmuch as Eiichi's life was inseparable from the modern history of Japan, Keizō thought it

---

[206] "Sofu no ushiro sugata" (The Figure of My Grandfather), *Ryūmon zasshi* 530 (November 1932), p. 6.

necessary as a close relative to collect such materials as fully as he could so that people of later times would be able to access them. To fulfill that need and express his love and respect for Eiichi, Keizō embarked on the compilation of the unique and voluminous *Shibusawa Eiichi denki shiryō* (Shibusawa Eiichi Biographical Materials), on which I have heavily relied in writing this book.

Keizō was a great believer in source materials. In his activities as a researcher in the areas of folklore studies and the economic history of fisheries, he considered the collection and organizing of documents and artifacts to be the most important step. He devoted most of the time and money invested in those studies to the collection and organization of such materials. As he saw it, his mission was to gather and process the primary sources – like ore from a mine – to make it easier for other people to access the information, and felt the work of refining the "ore" and producing fine finished products could be left up to others.

Keizō applied this policy to compilation of Eiichi's biographical materials. Even while Eiichi was alive, he and his colleagues embarked on the collection of wide-ranging materials under the leadership of Tsuchiya Takao, a university classmate of Keizō's who had become professor of economic history at the University of Tokyo. The work was interrupted by World War II but was resumed afterwards. It went on quietly and inconspicuously, for more than thirty years, with investment of a considerable sum of money. Keizō died in 1963 before the *Shibusawa denki shiryō* was completed in 58 volumes in 1965; 10 supplementary volumes were published in 1971.

To my knowledge, it is one of the most voluminous and well organized biographical archives of a single individual in the world. Before World War II, a staff of 21 led by Tsuchiya launched the project; after the war, it was continued by Keizō with a staff of 43. It must be rare as well for such a large number of people to work together at such an unheralded endeavor for such a long time. In 1966, the work received the Asahi Culture Award from the Asahi Shimbun newspaper company.

I am very proud of my father's commitment and devotion to its completion.

FRIENDSHIP FRUSTRATED

In the summer of 1931, an unusually long spell of rain hit many parts of China. Water levels at rivers gradually rose and in July embankments burst along major rivers including the Yangtze (the Chang Jiang), the Yellow River (the Huang He), the Huai River (the Huai He), the Pearl River (the Zhu Jiang), and the Songhua, causing devastating property damage and loss of life. The Yangtze, it was said, had not witnessed such massive flooding in eighty years. Inundated areas across the country covered 59,000 square miles, which was equivalent almost to the whole territory of Japan. An estimated 34 million people had been affected by the disaster and 4 million houses damaged.[207] Seventeen percent of the cultivated acreage in China was reportedly flooded. Having hit in the summertime, the flooding had devestated crops, according to the Chinese government. Given damage to stored grain, the impossibility of autumn rice planting, and so forth, the total losses went over 2 billion yuan. The "three Wuhan cities" – Wuchang, Hankou, and Hanyang – were hit hardest; in the evening of July 27 the embankments along the Yangtze broke, and by August 10 reportedly a total of 3,000 people had drowned and 300,000 were driven from their homes.

In Japan, the Tokyo Chamber of Commerce and Industry took the initiative to establish the Chūka Minkoku Suigai Dōjōkai (Charity for the Flood Disaster in China) on August 24. Eiichi became president and Gō Seinosuke chairman. Partly because of the generosity of the Chinese side in providing

---

[207] The flooding was the largest-scale natural disaster anywhere in the world in the twentieth century. Even Chinese experts admit that accurate data is difficult to obtain. One recent extensive survey of the various contemporary reports and later analyses suggests that probably around 52 million Chinese were affected, with about 2 million deaths from drowning, disease or starvation. Chris Courtney, "Central China flood, 1931," http://www.disasterhistory.org/central-china-flood-1931.

donations of several million yen in relief at the time of the 1923 Great Kantō Earthquake (Tokyo earthquake) and partly in an attempt to improve Japan's relations with China, many Japanese organizations, including the Japan-China Business Association (Nik-Ka Jitsugyō Kyōkai), the Red Cross Society, and the Industry Club of Japan, willingly joined the Dōjōkai, providing full cooperation for flood relief fundraising.

The news that a vast area "the size of Japan" had been inundated and that 10 million people were starving sent a new wave of shock throughout Japan, arousing an eagerness among Japanese to provide relief to flood victims in China. The emperor donated 10,000 yen for relief of Japanese residents in China and 100,000 yen for relief of Chinese victims. The Dōjōkai transmitted the money to Shigemitsu Mamoru, Japanese minister in Shanghai, via whom it was sent to Song Ziwen, chairman of the flood relief committee on the Chinese side.[208]

The flood damage seemed to grow more severe each day, and the Dōjōkai launched an extensive fundraising campaign calling on numerous economic organizations, women's groups, newspaper companies, news agencies, and others to contribute. On September 5, Dōjōkai vice-chairman Kodama Kenji visited Eiichi at the Asukayama residence and reported on the status of fundraising. He then suggested that, in order to make the purport of the fundraising campaign fully known to people throughout the country, Eiichi speak to them via JOAK (now NHK) radio and call for their support. By then Eiichi was ninety-one years old, and that year there had been many days when he did not feel well; he had tended to stay at home most of the time. In July he began to suffer from asthma, and on his doctor's advice he rested at home; going out was ill-advised. Through great efforts on the part of the Dōjōkai secretariat, an unusual arrangement was made with JOAK that Eiichi's talk would be aired from his house on September 6. In those days it was totally unheard of for

---

[208] See documents included in a Chinese appeal to the League of Nations, September 23, 1931, http://biblio-archive.unog.ch/Dateien/CouncilMSD/C-592-M-236-1931-VII_EN.pdf.

broadcasting equipment to be brought into a private home to air a nationwide broadcast.

Health problems kept him from taking a bath every day, but this was an important occasion. He bathed and readied himself, seated on an armchair in the reception room, waiting for the broadcasting time. At six-thirty, the broadcast started with introductory remarks by announcer Matsuda Yoshirō. Despite the worries of those around him, Eiichi's voice was firm and articulate. He began talking first about why he had become president of Dōjōkai despite his advanced age and poor health, and then about the importance of Japan-China relations, the friendship displayed by Chinese at the time of the Tokyo earthquake, and the details of the devastating damage in China caused by the flooding. He urged full cooperation of listeners across the country. Once in a while his windpipe made a whistle-like sound peculiar to an asthma patient, but otherwise his voice was quite all right. He spoke for some minutes. His honest and sincere broadcast was very well received.

> At the time of the Great Kanto Earthquake and Fire of 1923, Japan received a tremendous outpouring of sympathy from China and donations amounting to more than ¥2,500,000. Not only because we received such generosity at that time, but also out of our desire to soothe the calamity suffered by the people of a neighboring country, it goes without saying that we should help out of fellow feeling as well as our moral duty. I believe this is the obvious thing to do if we hope to maintain good relations between Japan and China.[209]

Response to the fundraising campaign sharply increased after the broadcast.[210] Elementary school children donated small sums of 10 or 20 sen. A poor woman living in Sugamo, Tokyo made a donation saying she had been wanting to do something for the

---

[209] Excerpt of speech as transcribed in the *Shibusawa denki shiryō*, vol. 40, pp. 77–78.

[210] Exchange rates fluctuated dramatically in 1930–32 after the global Great Depression, but 10 sen was probably worth about US 5 cents in 1931 or the equivalent of US$7 today.

flood victims in China but had had no chance to do so, but that, learning on the radio the previous evening that "Shibusawa sensei," whom she had always respected, was president of the Dōjōkai, she made up her mind to make a donation, hoping that even a small amount might help a little.

Using the money thus collected in the campaign, the Dōjōkai purchased a huge volume of relief goods, chartered a ship, the *Amagi Maru*, and filled it with the goods, and the ship left for China with Fukao Ryūtarō, one of Dōjōkai members, aboard. It was scheduled to enter port in Shanghai on September 20, leave there on the following day, and go upstream on the Yangtze to Wuhan, the central part of the most severely afflicted area. The Song Ziwen-led flood relief committee on the Chinese side, appreciating the goodwill of Japan, was waiting, fully prepared for reception of the relief goods.

Other events, however, betrayed and obstructed Japan's relief effort. On the pretext of a bomb explosion in the suburbs of Mukden on September 18, the Japanese army (Kwantung army) stationed in Manchuria seized control of the city. The Mukden Incident developed into a full-fledged Japanese invasion that led to the occupation of all of Manchuria. Japan had launched upon the grave path of invasion and ruin, and there was no turning back.

The occupation of Manchuria was something the Kwantung army had been maneuvering to achieve from years before. The Kwantung army was intent on occupying Manchuria and securing Japan's interests and influence there before the revolution by the Chiang Kai-shek-led Chinese Nationalist Party (Kuomintang) spread to the region. The Kwantung army's activity ignored the sovereignty of the Nationalist government and challenged its policy. Naturally the Nationalist government hardened its stance, and as an expression of its strong resistance to Japanese actions, it refused to receive the relief goods carried on the *Amagi Maru*.[211] Dōjōkai member Fukao, on board the ship, tried his

---

[211] See documents included in a Chinese appeal to the League of Nations, September 23, 1931, http://biblio-archive.unog.ch/Dateien/ CouncilMSD/C-592-M-236-1931-VII_EN.pdf

best to persuade the Chinese side to receive the relief goods, stressing that they were an expression of the friendship of the Japanese general public and had nothing to do with the Japanese army's policy. The Chinese side, however, thought that the Japanese army had launched the offensive in Manchuria despite, or rather to take advantage of, the great suffering inflicted from the unprecedented disaster. Their anger was deep and irreconcilable; there was no room for acceptance of the boatload of relief goods fully expressing Japanese generosity at such a time.

At the Dōjōkai headquarters the board of directors held an emergency meeting to discuss the matter and concluded that they could do nothing under the circumstances; they decided to have the *Amagi Maru* return to Moji, Kyushu with its cargo. There naturally arose the burdensome problem of repayment of the relief money to the donors. Most of the money had been turned into relief goods, and so these goods had to be sold immediately to obtain cash for repayment. As it turned out, donations of less than 100 yen were fully repaid, but for the donations of 100 yen and over it was decided that the amount repaid would be determined after subtracting part of the loss of purchase and sale of relief goods and transportation-related costs.

On October 16 the Dōjōkai sent a note, signed in Eiichi's name, to all donors, reporting on the sad fate of the voyage of the *Amagi Maru*, giving details of repayment of donations, and asking for their understanding. On that day Eiichi himself was reaching his last. In early October he had developed symptoms of acute intestinal obstruction and on October 14 had had a simple operation, performed by Dr. Shiota Hiroshige. The operation itself went smoothly, but the patient's age made it a very rare case in the world of medicine. On the 16th, his temperature rose, robbing him of appetite, his fatigue visible. His condition turned critical.

That the last phase of the private diplomacy in which Eiichi had been actively involved came to such a sad pass was very regrettable. But the wheels of history had already begun taking a major turn that no one could stop. The actions of the Japanese military in China betrayed not only the flood relief drive but all the efforts in Japanese diplomacy that had been made since the start of the Meiji era, bringing them to a catastrophic end.

The tough body that had sustained Eiichi's activity for ninety-one years was weakened. At the beginning of November, he developed a high fever that continued and was complicated by bronchitis. On November 8, hearing that many visitors had gathered at the house worried about his condition, Eiichi sent them his last words:

> Thank you very much for your long years of support. I wanted to live to be 100 years old and work till then. But I am afraid I will never get up again. It is illness, not I, that is to blame. Even after I die I will protect the business and health of every one of you. I hope you will think of me from now on, too.

Eiichi's room was strangely bright and quiet, with little sign of impending death. Rather, there was only a beautiful stillness as when the sun sets behind the mountains to the west, leaving its golden glow lingering in the sky. "I felt my dying grandfather taking the lead for us, who were going to live on," Keizō often told me. At the moment Eiichi breathed his last, Keizō felt very sad, but at the same time, a strange sense of calm and relief came over him, he said. Eiichi died at 1:50 a.m. on November 11, 1931.

On November 15 Eiichi's body was buried at Yanaka cemetery in Ueno. Burial in the earth was Eiichi's wish. Seeing his coffin being covered with soil, Keizō recalled the dramatic changes that had taken place in the country during Eiichi's life.

That age of turbulent change was over, mused Keizō, thinking he would never experience such a radical change. Little did he dream that only ten years later, in December, Japan would declare war on the United States with the surprise attack on Pearl Harbor, which would eventually lead to the devastating defeat of Japan and subsequent occupation by Allied forces. Such a development a decade later was beyond his wildest imagination.

In the autumn of 1963 it was my turn to bury the ashes of my father, Keizō, at Yanaka cemetery. It was a chilly day, the clouds hanging low. I remembered his words. Things are peaceful today, Keizō had told me not long before his passing, to the extent that people compared it to the Genroku era, the most peaceful of the eras of the generally peaceful Edo period. He hoped such a peaceful time would last long and that Japanese, who had been racing fiercely toward one goal or other for such a long time, would once in a while be able to sit back and enjoy their lives.

He was afraid, however, that the era of peace would not last long and that, on the contrary, the storm of change was escalating. The same problem over which Eiichi had so anguished remained unsolved; it had returned to trouble us in a different guise. In his book, *American Diplomacy 1900–1950*, published in 1951, George F. Kennan wrote:

> It is an ironic fact that today our past objectives in Asia are ostensibly in large measure achieved. The Western powers have lost the last of their special positions in China. The Japanese are finally out of China proper and out of Manchuria and Korea as well. The effects of their expulsion from those areas have been precisely what wise and realistic people warned us all along they would be. Today we have fallen heir to the problems and responsibilities the Japanese had faced and borne in the Korean-Manchurian area for nearly half a century, and there is a certain *perverse justice in the pain we are suffering* from a burden which, when it was borne by others, we held in such low esteem. What is saddest of all is that the relationship between past and present seems to be visible to so few people. For if we are not to learn from our own mistake, where shall we learn at all?"[212] (emphasis added)

Perverse justice indeed. The United States was then facing the worst crisis since its founding. The very country that was once so full of self-confidence, attacking other countries in a high-handed manner as if to teach them the ABCs of civilization, found the very raison d'être of its society challenged. For Japan, it was not someone else's problem; it was geographically and politically closely implicated. Not just the United States but

---

[212] Kennan, *American Diplomacy*, pp. 48–49.

Japan, China, and all countries needed to join hands and minds in order to keep civilization from collapsing. The path would be one of struggle and hardship, but the time had finally come for the real beginning of the private diplomacy of which Eiichi once dreamed. That path, to which this author committed his own efforts in subsequent decades, constitutes yet another story.

REFERENCES

சு

Baxter, James. "Informal Diplomacy in Meiji Japan: The Visits of General Grant and Crown Prince Nicholas Alexandrovich." In *Interpretations of Japanese Culture: Views from Russia and Japan*, James C. Baxter, ed. Kyoto: International Research Center for Japanese Studies, 2009, pp. 217–46.

Borg, Dorothy and Shumpei Okamoto, eds., *Pearl Harbor as History: Japanese-American Relations, 1931–1941*. New York: Columbia University Pres, 1973.

Buell, Raymond Leslie. "The Development of Anti-Japanese Agitation in the United States" (1922). https://archive.org/stream/jstor-2142459/2142459_djvu.txt.

Conroy, Hilary, Francis Conroy, and Sophie Quinn-Judge. *West Across the Pacific: The American Involvement in East Asia from 1898 to the Vietnam War*. New York: Cambria Press, 2008.

Courtney, Chris. "Central China Flood, 1931," http://www.disasterhistory.org/central-china-flood-1931.

Daniels, Roger. *Asian America: Chinese and Japanese in the United States since 1850*. Seattle: University of Washington Press, 1988.

Fletcher, William Miles. *The Japanese Business Community and National Trade Policy, 1920–1942*. Chapel Hill, NC: University of North Carolina Press, 1989.

Fridenson, Patrick and Kikkawa Takeo. *Ethical Capitalism: Shibusawa Eiichi and Business Leadership in Global Perspective*. Toronto: University of Toronto Press, 2017.

Goldstein, Erik and John H. Maurer. *The Washington Conference 1921–22: Naval Rivalry, East Asian Stability and the Road to Pearl Harbor*. Portland, OR: Frank Cass, 1994.

Griswold, A. Whitney. *The Far Eastern Policy of the United States*. New Haven: Yale University Press, 1938.

Harris, Townsend. *Complete Journal of Townsend Harris*, p. 207. https://archive.org/details/completejournalo00harr

Hesselink, Reinier H. "The Assassination of Henry Heusken," *Monumenta Nipponica* 49:3 (1994), pp. 331–51.

Hozumi Shigeyuki. *Hozumi Utako nikki 1890–1906: Meiji ichi hōgakusha no shūhen [The Diary* of Hozumi Utako 1890–1906: The World of a Meiji Era Scholar of Law]: Tokyo: Misuzu Shobō, 1989.

Hunter, Janet. *Concise Dictionary of Modern Japanese History.* Tokyo: Kodansha International, 1984.

Ihara Toshiro, *Meiji engekishi* [A History of the Meiji Theater], Waseda Daigaku Shuppanbu, 1933.

Iokibe, Makoto and Tosh Minohara, eds. *The History of US-Japan Relations: From Perry to the Present.* Singapore: Springer, 2017.

Iriye, Akira. *Across the Pacific: An Inner History of American-East Asian Relations.* New York: Harcourt, Brace and World, 1967.

Iriye, Akira. *Japan and the Wider World: From the Mid-Nineteenth Century to the Present.* London: Routledge, 2014.

Iriye Akira, *Nihon no gaiko* [Japanese Diplomacy]. Chūo Kōron Sha, 1966.

Ishii Kikujirō, *Gaikō yoroku* [Diplomatic Commentary]. Tokyo: Iwanami Shoten, 1930.

Kennan, George K. *American Diplomacy 1900–1950.* University of Chicago Press, 1951.

Kennedy, David M. *The American Spirit: United States History as Seen by Contemporaries.* 2 vols. Boston: Cengage, 1956.

Kennedy, Robert C. "On This Day," http://www.nytimes.com/learning/general/onthisday/harp/1110.html.

Mahan, Alfred Thayer. *From Sail to Steam.* New York: Harper and Brothers, 1907. Available at http://www.gutenberg.org/files/25122/25122-h/25122-h.htm.

Melton, Carol Wilcox. *Between War and Peace: Woodrow Wilson and the American Expeditionary Force.* Macon, GA: Mercer University Press, 2001.

Minohara Toshihiro, *Hainichi iminho to Nichi-Bei kankei: "Hanihara shokan" no shinso to sono "judainaru kekka"* [The Japanese Exclusion Act and U.S.–Japanese Relations: The Truth behind the "Hanihara Note" and its "Grave Consequences"]. Tokyo: Iwanami Shoten, 2003.

Mizutani Ken'ichi, "1924-nen Imin Hō ni okeru 'Nihonjin mondai'" ["Japanese Problems" Associated with the U.S. Immigration Act of 1924], *Doshisha American Studies*, March 20, 1997, pp. 73–89. Available at NII Electronic Library Service, http://ci.nii.ac.jp/naid/110000198930.

Neu, Charles E. *An Uncertain Friendship: Theodore Roosevelt and Japan, 1906–1909*. Cambridge, Mass: Harvard University Press, 1967.

Nish, Ian. *Japanese Foreign Policy, 1869–1942: Kasumigaseki to Miyakezaka*. London: Routledge & Kegan Paul, 1977.

Nish, Ian. *The Origins of the Russo-Japanese War*. London: Longman, 1985.

Nish, Ian. *Collected Writings of Ian Nish: Part 2: Japanese Political History*. Richmond: Japan Library, 2001.

Nish, Ian. *Alliance in Decline: A Study of Anglo-Japanese Relations, 1908–1923*. London: Bloomsbury, 2012.

O'Connor, Richard. *Pacific Destiny*. Boston: Little, Brown, 1969.

Reckner, James R. *Teddy Roosevelt's Great White Fleet*. Annapolis: Naval Institute Press, 1988.

Roosevelt, Theodore. *Theodore Roosevelt: An Autobiography*. New York: Charles Scribner's Sons, 1922.

Roosevelt, Theodore. *Letters*, vols. 4 and 5, edited by Elting E. Morison. Cambridge, MA: Harvard University Press, 1951.

Roosevelt, Theodore. Naval War College address, June 2, 1897. Accessed 12-21-17 at http://www.theodore-roosevelt.com/images/research/speeches/tr1898.pdf#search='theodore+roosevelt+naval+war+college+speech'.

Shibusawa Eiichi. *Seien hyakuwa* [One Hundred Essays by Seien]. Tokyo: Dōbunsha, 1912.

Shibusawa Masahide. *Three Women of the Shibusawa Family*. Tokyo: Shibusawa Eiichi Memorial Foundation, 2009.

Shimazu, Naoko. *Japan, Race and Equality: The Racial Equality Proposal of 1919*. Oxford: Nissan Institute/Routledge, 2002.

Shiraishi Kitaro. *Shibusawa Eiichi-O* [The Life of Shibusawa Eiichi]. Tokyo: Tōko Shoin, 1933.Available at http://d.hatena.ne.jp/tobira/20140519/1400455515 (accessed 11-8-17).

Shurtleff, William and Akiko Aoyagi. *How Japanese and Japanese-Americans Brought Soyfoods to the United States and the Hawaiian Islands: A History (1851–2011)*. Lafayette, CA: Soyinfo Center, 2011.

Statler, Oliver. *Shimoda Story*. Honolulu, HI: University of Hawaii Press, 1969.

Stockwin, J. A. A. *Governing Japan*. Oxford: Blackwell, 1999.

Suzuki Bunji. *Rōdō undō nijūnen* [Twenty Years of the Labor Movement]. Tokyo: Ichigensha, 1931.

Taft, Henry W. *Japan and America*. New York: Macmillan, 1932.

ten Broek, Jacobus, Edward N. Barnhard, and Floyd W. Matson. *Prejudice, War, and the Constitution: Causes and Consequences of the Evacuation of the Japanese Americans in World War II*. Berkeley: University of California Press, 1954.

Thompson, J. Lee. *Theodore Roosevelt Abroad: Nature, Empire, and the Journey of an American*. London: Palgrave Macmillan, 2010.

Tobei Jitsugyōdan shi [A Record of the Honorary Commercial Commissioners of Japan to the United States of America], Tōkyō Shō kaigisho, Iwaya Sueo, ed. Tokyo: Tōkyō Shōkaigisho, 1910.

Treat, Payson Jackson. *Japan and the United States, 1853–1921*. New York: Houghton Mifflin, 1921.

Twain, Mark. *Roughing It*. http://www.gutenberg.org/files/3177/3177-h/3177-h.htm

Warner, Dennis Ashton and Peggy Warner. *The Tide at Sunrise: A History of the Russo-Japanese War, 1904–1905*. London: Routledge/Frank Cass, 2002.

United States Government. *Papers Relating to the Foreign Relations of the United States, 1924*. Available at https://history.state.gov/historicaldocuments/frus1924v02/d310.

Young, John Russell. *Around the World with General Grant*. 1879. https://archive.org/details/aroundworldgrant02younuoft

Wollenberg, Charles. "'Yellow Peril' in the Schools (II)." In *The Asian American Educational Experience: A Sourcebook for Teachers and Students*, Don T. Nakanishi and Tina Yamano Nishida, eds. New York: Routledge, 1995.

APPENDIX 1. ITINERARY OF THE HONORARY COMMERCIAL COMMISSIONERS TO THE UNITED STATES (1909)

∞

September 1, sunny, cold: Arrived Seattle, lodgings at Washington Hotel.

September 2, partially sunny: Observed a fire department demonstration.

September 3, cloudy, cold: Visited a beer factory and other places.

September 4, sunny, hot: The entire city greeted us, setting aside the day as "Japan Day" at the Alaska-Yukon-Pacific Exposition.

September 5, sunny, hot: Visited farms and other sites. Boarded the 10:40 P.M. special night train, sleeping en route.

September 6, sunny, cold: Arrived Tacoma at 7:30 A.M. Visited Mt. Rainier National Park. Slept on the train.

September 7, sunny, cold: Returned to Tacoma at 2:00 P.M. Visited Tacoma Chamber of Commerce. Lodgings at Hotel Tacoma.

September 8, partially sunny, cold: Visited lumber mill and other locations. Departed Tacoma late at night. Slept on the train.

September 9, sunny: Arrived Portland early morning. Toured sights of the city. Lodgings at Portland Hotel.

September 10, rainy, cold: Visited the nearby town of Vancouver. Departed at 4:30 P.M. Slept on the train.

September 11, sunny, cold: Arrived Spokane at 4:00 A.M. Visited Spokane Chamber of Commerce and other places. Lodgings at Hotel Spokane.

September 12, sunny, cold: Toured sights of the city. Attended a play in the evening. Slept on the train.

September 13, sunny, cold: Visited Potlatch, Idaho. Returned to Spokane at night. Slept on the train.

September 14, sunny, cold: Arrived Anaconda at 8:30 A.M. Visited copper mine, and stopped by Butte. Slept on the train.

September 15, sunny, cold: On train entire day, heading out of Montana into North Dakota. Slept on the train.

September 16, sunny, cold: Arrived Fargo at 7:45 A.M. Visited agricultural experiment station. Arrived Grand Forks at 2:20 P.M. Visited local agricultural school. Slept on the train.

September 17, sunny, cold: Arrived Hibbing at 6:00 A.M. Visited the Stevenson Iron Mine. Arrived Duluth in the afternoon. Hotel lodgings.

September 18, sunny: Visited the city and ports along Lake Superior. Departed at 11:30 P.M. Slept on the train.

September 19, sunny, cold: Arrived Minneapolis at 6:00 A.M. Met with U.S. President William Howard Taft, and visited factories. Hotel lodgings.

September 20, sunny, cold: Met with the mayor. Visited the University of Minnesota. Slept on the train.

September 21, lightning storm, cold: Arrived St. Paul at 5:30 A.M. Visited the city, and attended the delegation welcoming party. Visited manufacturers and wholesalers. Departed at 11:30 P.M. Slept on the train.

September 22, rainy, cold: Arrived Madison at 8:30 A.M. Visited the University of Wisconsin. Arrived Milwaukee at 2:00 P.M. Hotel lodgings.

September 23, sunny, cold: Visited steel works and other locations. Departed in the evening. Slept on the train.

September 24, sunny, cold: Arrived Chicago in early morning. Visited banks and the steel works. Lodgings at the Congress Hotel.

September 25, sunny, cold: Visited the University of Chicago, newspaper company, and other locations. Hotel lodgings.

September 26 (Sunday), sunny, cold: Visited Jackson Park. Hotel lodgings.

September 27, sunny: Attended the Chicago Association of Commerce and Industry's welcome party. Visited art institute, schools, hospitals, etc. Departed by train at 1:30 A.M. Slept on the train.

September 28, cloudy: Arrived South Bend (Indiana) at 6:30 A.M. Visited the University of Notre Dame. Slept on the train.

September 29, cloudy: Arrived Grand Rapids at 6:00 A.M. Visited a furniture factory and other sites. Slept on the train.

September 30, sunny: Arrived Detroit at 8:00 A.M. Attended Parke Davis welcome party and other events. Lodgings at Cadillac Hotel.

October 1, cloudy: Visited a park and a seismometer factory. Attended Detroit Chamber of Commerce banquet and other events. Slept on the train.

October 2, sunny: Arrived Cleveland at 9:00 A.M. Visited the grave of former Secretary of State John Hay. Lodgings at Hollenden Hotel.

October 3 (Sunday), sunny: Rested. Hotel lodgings.

October 4, sunny: Attended the Cleveland Chamber of Commerce dinner party. Attended by Mr. John D. Rockefeller. Slept on the train.

October 5, sunny: Arrived Dunkirk at 7:00 A.M. Visited railway company, toured grape fields and winery. Arrived Buffalo at 3:00 P.M. Slept on the train.

October 6, sunny: Visited Niagara Falls. Slept on the train.

October 7, sunny: Arrived Rochester at 6:30 A.M. Visited the Eastman Kodak Company. Slept on the train.

October 8, sunny: Arrived Ithaca (New York) at 7:30 A.M. Visited Cornell University. Slept on the train.

October 9, cloudy: Arrived Syracuse at 3:15 A.M. Reception at 8:30. Visited power plant and other sites. Slept on the train.

October 10 (Sunday), sunny: Rested. Visited the city of Manlius in the afternoon. Slept on the train.

October 11, sunny: Arrived Schenectady at 4:00 A.M. Visited the General Electric Company. Slept on the train.

October 12, sunny: Arrived New York Grand Central Station at 6:30 A.M. Lodgings at Astor Hotel.

October 13, sunny: Welcome party given by raw silk importers' association. Visited the grave of General Ulysses S. Grant. Lodgings at Astor Hotel.

October 14, sunny: Attended Chamber of Commerce reception and other events. Hotel lodgings.

October 15, sunny, windy: Visited the harbor. Hotel lodgings.

October 16, sunny: Attended New York Peace Association welcoming party. Visited the Hippodrome Theater. Hotel lodgings.

October 17 (Sunday), sunny: Took part in the Tokyo Commercial College reunion. Hotel lodgings.

October 18, sunny: No events scheduled. Hotel lodgings.

October 19, sunny: Visited silk weaving factory. Had dinner at the Nippon Club. Hotel lodgings.

October 20, sunny: Lunch at the Lawyers' Club. Visited the grave of Townsend Harris. Hotel lodgings.

October 21, sunny: Attended the Jacob Schiff welcome party. Slept on the train.

October 22, sunny: Arrived New Haven at 4:00 A.M. Visited factories and Yale University. Arrived Providence at 1:50 P.M. Slept on the train.

October 23, cloudy: Arrived Boston at 8:00 A.M. Visited the Waltham Clock Company and Harvard University. Hotel lodgings.

October 24 (Sunday), rainy: Day trip to Newport, visited the grave of Commodore Matthew C. Perry. Hotel lodgings.

October 25, cloudy: Visited various factories. Slept on the train.

October 26, sunny: Arrived Wooster at 8:00 A.M. Visited the sewage purification plant. Arrived Springfield 2:00 P.M. Received official telegram informing us about the assassination of Ito Hirobumi. Slept on the train.

October 27, sunny: Arrived Newark at 9:00 A.M. Met with Thomas Edison. Attended welcome party. Arrived Reading (Pennsylvania) at 9:00 P.M. Slept on the train.

October 28, cloudy: Arrived South Mount at 8:00 A.M. Attended welcome party. Returned to Reading at 10:00 A.M. and attended their great welcome party. Arrived at Philadelphia at 6:30 P.M. Lodgings at Bellevue Stratford Hotel.

October 29, sunny: Visited the Mint Bureau, the University of Pennsylvania, Gerard College, and other sites. Hotel lodgings.

October 30, sunny: Attended the mayor's reception and visited the Navy arms factory. Attended the Manufacturers' Club welcoming party. Hotel lodgings.

October 31 (Sunday), sunny: Slept on the train.

November 1, sunny: Arrived Washington D.C. at 9:20 A.M. Met with Secretary of State Knox and others. Lodgings at Willard Hotel.

November 2, sunny: Attended the Metropolitan Club dinner party and other events. Hotel lodgings.

November 3, sunny: Attended the party for the Emperor's Birthday hosted by the Japanese Embassy. Mr. Knox also attended. Departed at midnight. Slept on the train.

November 4, sunny: Arrived Baltimore at 3:00 A.M. Attended welcoming party at Belvedere Hotel, Baltimore, and other events. Slept on the train.

November 5, cloudy: Arrived Pittsburg, at 8:50 A.M. Visited the Homestead Steel Works and other sites. Lodgings at Schenley Hotel.

November 6, cloudy: Visited glass factory, Heinz food factory et al. Departed at midnight. Slept on the train.

November 7 (Sunday), sunny: Arrived Cincinnati at 7:00 A.M. Lodgings at Sinton Hotel.

November 8, rainy: Attended Cincinnati U.S.A. Regional Chamber of Commerce reception. Departed in the evening. Slept on the train.

November 9, sunny: Arrived Indianapolis at 6:00 A.M. Attended welcome party and other events. Slept on the train.

November 10, sunny: Arrived St. Louis at 7:30 A.M. Attended various welcome parties. Hotel lodgings.

November 11, sunny: Visited factories, and attended a theater. Departed at night. Slept on the train.

November 12, rainy: Arrived Kansas City at 7:30 A.M. Attended various welcome parties. Slept on the train.

November 13: Arrived Omaha at 7:50 A.M. Attended reception, and visited factories. Took part in the commercial club dinner party. Hotel lodgings.

November 14 (Sunday), snowy: Arrived Denver at 7:30 A.M. Welcomed by local Japanese residents. Hotel lodgings.

November 15, snowy: Visited schools and other sites. Attended a welcome dinner party. Departed past midnight. Slept on the train.

November 16, sunny: Rode over Rocky Mountains on train. Slept on the train.

November 17, sunny: Arrived Salt Lake City at 8:00 P.M. Departed for Nevada through Ogden. Slept on the train.

November 18, sunny: Arrived Sacramento at 11:00 A.M. Met with Japanese countrymen. Arrived San Jose at noon. Arrived and rested at Delmont at 5:00 P.M. Slept on the train.

November 19, sunny: Arrived Santa Barbara at 7:30 A.M. Arrived Los Angeles at noon. Caught a cold. Hotel lodgings.

November 20, sunny: Day off due to cold. Hotel lodgings.

November 21 (Sunday), sunny. Day off. Returned to train at 9:00 P.M. Slept on the train.

November 22, sunny: Arrived San Diego at 7:00 A.M. Attended Chamber of Commerce welcome party and other activities. Slept on the train.

November 23, sunny: Arrived Riverside at 8:00 A.M. Arrived Redlands at 11:40 A.M. Departed at 2:00 P.M. Slept on the train.

November 24, sunny: Arrived Williams at 9:00 A.M. Arrived at the Grand Canyon at noon. Departed at 9:00 P.M. Slept on the train.

November 25, rainy: Arrived Barstow at 1:00 A.M. Met with local Japanese residents. Arrived Bakersfield at 4:00 P.M. Slept on the train.

November 26, sunny: Arrived Oakland at 6:00 A.M. Visited the University of California, Berkeley, and other sites. Attended reception. Lodgings at Fairmont Hotel.

November 27: Sightseeing in city and other activities. Visited Golden Gate Bridge. Hotel lodgings.

November 28: Attended welcome reception. Hotel lodgings.

November 29: Visited companies and factories. Hotel lodgings.

November 30: Departed for Japan on board the *Chiyo Maru*.

APPENDIX 2: LIST OF THE HONORARY COMMERCIAL COMMISSIONERS OF JAPAN TO THE UNITED STATES OF AMERICA

ဆ

TOKYO

Baron Shibusawa Eiichi, president of Dai-ichi Bank
With Shibusawa Kaneko [wife];
Attendants: Masuda Meiroku and Takanashi Takako
Nakano Buei, member of the House of Representatives, president of Tokyo
  Chamber of Commerce, and president of the Tokyo Stock Exchange
Attendant: Katō Tatsuya
Hibiya Heizaemon, vice-president of Tokyo Chamber of Commerce and
  president of Kanegafuchi Spinning Co. Ltd.
Attendant: Iiri Raisaku
Satake Sakutarō, member of the House of Representatives, special member
  of Tokyo Chamber of Commerce, and president of Tokyo Gas Co. Ltd.
Attendant: Natori Wasaku
Iwahara Kenzō, director of Mitsui & Co. Ltd.
Nezu Kaichirō, member of the House of Representatives, member of Tokyo
  Chamber of Commerce, and president of Tobu Railway Co. Ltd.
Attendant: Ueda Sekizō
Horikoshi Zenjūrō, owner of exporting firm Horikoshi & Co.
With Horikoshi Shinako
Koike Kunizō, member of Tokyo Chamber of Commerce and president of
  stock brokerage firm Koike & Company
Attendant: Iida Hatarō
Hara Rinnosuke, manager of construction firm Shimizu Gumi
Attendant: Tanabe Junkichi
Machida Tokunosuke, member of Tokyo Chamber of Commerce and silk
  dealer

Takatsuji Narazō, director of Kanegafuchi Spinning Co. Ltd.

Watase Torajirō, owner of Tokyo Konoen [agricultural machines and supply company]

Baron Kanda Naibu, professor, Gakushuin University and professor, Tokyo Higher Commercial School

With Kuma Chiyoko

Minami Takajirō, doctor of agriculture, professor, Agricultural College of Tohoku Imperial University

Iwaya Sueo, staff member of Hakubunkan [major publisher] and lecturer, Waseda University

Kumagai Taizō, assistant in the Medical College Hospital, Tokyo Imperial University

OSAKA

Doi Michio, president of Osaka Chamber of Commerce and president of Osaka Electric Light Company

Takaishi Shingorō, chief secretary of Osaka Chamber of Commerce

Nakahashi Tokugorō, special member of Osaka Chamber of Commerce and president of Osaka Merchant Marine Co. Ltd.

Attendant: Murata Shōzō

Oi Bokushin, member of the House of Representatives and president of Tokyo Sulphur Co. Ltd.

Ishibashi Tamenosuke, member of the House of Representatives and employee of Osaka Asahi Newspaper Company

Iwamoto Einosuke, stock broker

Matsumura Toshio, lawyer, and special member of Osaka Chamber of Commerce

Sakaguchi Heibei, silk manufacturer

KYOTO

Nishimura Jihei, member of the House of Representatives, president of Kyoto Chamber of Commerce, and president of Shoko Chochiku [Commerce and Industry Savings] Bank

Nishiike Nariyoshi, chief secretary of Kyoto Chamber of Commerce and president of Rakuhoku Hydro-power Electric Company

Fujie Nagataka, director of Kyoto Municipal Ceramics Laboratory

YOKOHAMA

Ōtani Kahei, president of Yokohama Chamber of Commerce and president of Japan Tea Manufacturing Company
Attendant: Kameda Kōzō
Sōda Kinsaku, member of Yokohama Chamber of Commerce and president of the Soda Bank
Hara Ryūta, doctor of engineering, and engineering chief of Yokohama Waterworks Bureau
Shidō Akira, director of Silk Inspection Laboratory, Ministry of Agriculture and Commerce

KOBE

Matsukata Kōjirō, president of Kobe Chamber of Commerce and president of Kawasaki Shipbuilding Company
Taki Kumejirō, fertilizer manufacturing
with Unoko
Tamura Shinkichi, owner of Tamura & Company, exporting business

NAGOYA

Kamino Kinnosuke, member of Nagoya Chamber of Commerce and president of Meiji Bank
Kadono Tominosuke, vice president of Nagoya Chamber of Commerce
Itō Morimatsu, director of Itō Bank

ABOUT THE AUTHOR

ɕɔ

MASAHIDE SHIBUSAWA (B. 1925) graduated from the Department of Agricultural Economy of the University of Tokyo in 1950. Closely involved in organizations dedicated to facilitating international exchange and dialogue, he was executive director of the MRA (Moral Re-armament) Foundation from 1964 to 2013, executive director of the Language Institute of Japan from 1968 to 1997 and director of the East-West Seminar (run by the MRA Foundation) from 1970 to 1997.

An active supporter of education and research in international relations in East and Southeast Asia, he has held positions such as Director-CEO of the Tokyo Jogakkan Schools for Women (1994–2003), Research Fellow, Royal Institute of International Affairs (Chatham House), London, visiting professor at the University of Alaska and visiting professor, School of Business Administration, Portland State University. He was a founding member on the Japanese side in the Trilateral Commission. He became president of the Shibusawa Eiichi Memorial Foundation in 1997.

In addition to the present work, his publications include *Chichi: Shibusawa Keizō* (Memories of My Father Shibusawa Keizō; Jitsugyō-no-Nihon, 1968), *Asia in the World Community* (English), ed., with Prachoom Chomchai, (Chulalongkorn University, Bangkok, 1973), *Japan and the Asian Pacific Region* (Royal Institute of International Affairs, London, 1984), *Taiheiyō-Ajia: Kiken to kibō* (Pacific Asia, Perils and Promises; Simul Publications, 1991). He also translated Taufik Abdullah's *Shinjitsu no Indoneshia: Kenkoku no shidōshatachi* (The Truth about Indonesia: The Leaders Who Founded the Country, from Indonesian *Manusia dalam kemelut sejarah;* Simul Shuppankai, 1978), and Charles Morrison's *Tōnan Ajia itsutsu no kuni: Sono seizon senryaku* (The Five Countries of Southeast Asia: Their Strategies for Survival, from the English *Strategies of Survival: The Foreign Policy Dilemmas of Smaller Asian States* by Charles Morrison (Simul Shuppankai, 1981).

INDEX

დ

* **Bold** page numbers refer to figures.

Abe Isoo 211

Africa 24

Aguinaldo, Emilio 16, 74

Alcock, Rutherford 9

Alexander, Wallace M. 228, **255**, 256, 308, 309

Alien Land Law: 1913 law 179, 181, 210, 214, 250–52, 282–83, 340; revised 1920 256, 283, 318, 340

Allied intervention in Siberia (1918) 241 (*see also* Siberia: Japanese expedition)

American Asiatic Association, Journal of the 165

American Exchange National Bank 317

American Federation of Labor 212

American International Corporation (AIC) 218

American-Japan Society 356

American-Japanese Relations Committee (San Francisco) xi, 255, 309, 326

Analects of Confucius xix, 224, 270, 314, 363

Anesaki Masaharu 236

Anglo-Japanese Alliance (1902) 89, 205, 285–87, 304–305, 318

Anti-Japanese League (California) 251–52

Around the World with General Grant 38

Arthur, Chester A. 27

Asabuki Eiji 35

Asian Magazine 165

Asukayama (Ōji) house 66, 108, 194, 262, 278, 317, 376, 369; Chiang Kai-shek 1927 visit 358–59; Harriman 1905 visit 160; home hospitality for the Grant party (1879) 52–**54**, 55; King Kalakaua 1882 visit 71; Knox 1912 visit 166; in 1923 earthquake 313–15; West Coast chambers of commerce 1908 visitors 129

Atlantic Fleet (U.S.) 123, 129, 137, 144, 285

Atlantic Monthly 172

Australia 123, 293

Balfour, Arthur 296, 304–305, 309

Bancroft, Edgar A. 354

Bank of Japan 67, 117, 168n, 278, 370

Bank of New York Club 272

Beijing 200, 201, 203, 204

Bethell, Ernest 158

Bierce, Ambrose 26

Bliss, Cornelius N. 82

Bonaparte, Charles J. 118

Borah, William E. 284, 295

Borodin, Mikhail 345

Boxer Rebellion (1900) 79, 80, 177

Brady, Anthony N. 81, 82

Brazil Colonization Company 180

Britain: 21, 21, 49; as ally of Japan 97, 205; confrontation with Germany 205; fears of Bolshevism 245; Iwakura Mission in (1871) 13–15; navy of 123, 125; 1921 Washington Conference 284–88, 295–96, 305–306, 310; and Opium Wars 158; Paris Peace Conference 246, 248; Russo-Japanese War and 147;

secret agreement with Japan in 1917 238; Shibusawa Keizō in (1922) 372; and Singapore 99
Brown, William C. 136
Bryan, William Jennings 181, 296
Bryn Mawr College 86
Butte mine (Montana) 200
Bälz, Erwin 106, 108

California Federation of Labor 170, 210, 212, 226
California Grange 170
California State Legislature 25, 27, 120, 169, 179, 215, 282
Canada 115, 123, 293, 319
Carnegie Steel Company 76
Carnegie, Andrew 16, 76, 226
Central Pacific Railroad 24
Chamber of Commerce (London) 89
Chiang Chun 358
Chiang Kai-shek xvii, 55, **358**–61, **362**, 378
Chiaraijima 1, 373
Chicago: Eiichi 1902 visit 63, 75–76, 82; Eiichi 1909 visit 140–41, 149; Eiichi 1915 visit; 216, 217, 227; Eiichi 1921 visit 292; Elbert H. Gary 237; Homer Lea 177
China xviii, xx, 1, 64; anti-Japanese movement in 253, 320, 276; Boxer Rebellion 80; boycott of Japanese goods 276; dispute over Ryukyu Islands 47–49; Chūka Minkoku Suigai Dōjōkai fundraising campaign 375–78; earthquake in Tokyo 321–22 (*see also* Kameido massacre); Eiichi's 1914 trip to 196–205; Eiichi's ideas on 186–89, 221–22, 260, 268–69, 359–62; Eiichi's projects on 189–94; German colonies in 237, 242, 246, 249; immigration to United States 26–29; independence 23; investment in 159–60, 164, 265; Ishii-Lansing negotiations on 238–

41, 310; Japan's wars with xvi, 64, 19–20, 28, 89, 152; 1920 disaster aid for 279–80; Opium Wars 158; South Manchurian Railway 161; Twenty-One Demands 208–210, 238, 257; Ulysses Grant ideas on 371; United States and 21–23, 125–26, 153, 163–64, 218, 247, 344; Washington Conference 1921 presence at 293
Chinda Sutemi 180–82
Chinese Exclusion Act (1882) 26n, 27, 114, 179
Chinese-American Publicity Bureau 162
Christianity 20, 28, 39, 225, 301, 341
Chōshū (domain) 3, 15, 18, 67, 68, 104, 146–47, 187
Chūka Minkoku Suigai Dōjōkai (Charity for the Flood Disaster in China): 1931 fundraising campaign 375–79
Chū-Nichi Jitsugyō Kabushiki Kaisha (China-Japan Business Co., Ltd.) 194, 196, 200, 201
Chūgoku Kōgyō Kabushiki Kaisha (China Industrial Development Co., Ltd.) 190–94
Civil War (American) 10, 25, 31, 38
Clark, Walter L. 256
Clark, William S. 14, 340
Clarke, Lewis L. 263, 298, 300
Colby, Bainbridge 250
Commercial Club (San Francisco) 272
Conference of Concerned Japanese and Americans (Nichi-Bei Yūshi Kyōgikai; 1920) 165, 223, 262–72, 317
Confucius xix, 198, 224–25, 246, 360; grave of 197, 201, 204, 205; sayings of 132, 270, 314, 359
Consolidated Tobacco Company 81–82
Coolidge, Calvin 334, 343
Cornell University 149, 158, 263, 272; Eiichi visited 389
Cromwell, Seymour L. 263
Crédit Lyonnais 97
Czechoslovak Legion 245

Dai Tianchou 185

Dai-ichi Bank (First National Bank) xv, 35n, 108, 117, 145, 197, 236, 345; capital of 81, 84, 245; Eiichi retirement 131, 133, 235; Korea investment 267; 1916 stockholders meeting 232; 1923 earthquake 313–14; Shibusawa Keizō and 372

Dai-ichi Kangyō Bank 67

Daily Mail (London) 90

Dalian (Port Arthur) 92, 110, 205

Dan Takuma 302, 333, **347**, 366, 370

Daye Iron Mine (China) 200

Dewey, George (Admiral) 16

Diamond Head (Hawai'i) 72

Diaz, Porfirio 173

Dorman, F. W. 130

Doshisha University 210

Duan Qirui 238

Duke, James B. 82

Dōjōkai (*see* Chūka Minkoku Suigai Dōjōkai)

Eastman, George 263, 298, 317

Echigoya (Mitsukoshi) 44

Edison Electric Company **141**

Edison, Thomas xviii, 141; Eiichi 1909 meeting 139, 390; letter **364**–65

Eichelberger, Robert L. 243

Eighty-eighth birthday ceremony for Eiichi (1928) 365–68

Eisenhower, Dwight D. 20

Eliot, Charles William 230

Elkinton, Mary Patterson 166

Elliot, Howard 136

England: Eiichi 1867 visit 36; Eiichi 1902 visit 87–95

Enryōkan 36, 47

First National Bank (U.S.) 164

Five-Power Treaty 310

Fleury-Hérard, Paul 96

Foreign Affairs, Ministry of (Japan) 203, 211

Four-Power Treaty (1921) 304, 306

France 3, 7, 9, 97, 238, 242–43; Eiichi 1867 visit 10–**11**, 294, 367; Eiichi 1902 visit 97–98; investment in Trans-Siberian Railway 245; at Paris Peace Conference (1919) 246–48; Russian ally 97; Washington Conference (1921) 304

Fujiyama Raita **259**, 332, 342

Fukagawa residence 114

Fukuchi Gen'ichirō 12, **13**, 35, 45, 51, 56, 57

Fukuzawa Yukichi 48

Futaba Girls High School 262

Gage, Lyman 82, 263, 307, 317, 364

Gary, Elbert H. 237, 269, 298, 300, 316, 333, 336–37, 363

General Electric 137

Gentlemen's Agreement (1907) 120, 127, 211, 229, 283, 325, 328, 333, 337, 343,

George Shima (*see* Ushijima Kinji)

German Far East colonies 205, 206, 246, 249; possessions in China 242; Southern Pacific islands 205

Girard College 85

Girard, Stephen 85–86

Gojong, Emperor (Korea) 157; funeral (1919) 247

Gold Rush 24, 25

Golden Gate Bridge 29, 168

Gompers, Samuel xviii, 16, 212, 226, 303

Gong, Prince (Korea) 47

Gotō Shinpei 161, 168

Grant, Ulysses S. 31, 32, 33 36, **37**–63; Eiichi's visit to grave 62; Grant Cypress 370; Grant Magnolia 370; Harris sword given to 10; Horace Capron 14; 1930 monument in Ueno Park 369, 371

Graves, William S. 243

Great Earthquake Disaster Rehabilitation Association (Daishinsai Zengokai; 1923) 316–19

Great Kantō Earthquake of 1923 191,
    313–19
Great Northern Railway 136
Great White Fleet 123, 174–75
Greater East Asia Joint Declaration
    (1943) 207
Gu Weijun 246–47
Gulick, Sidney 210–11, 325, 328,
    336–37, 339, 347
Guomindang (Kuomintang; Nationalist
    Party of China) 185, 358, 378
Gyeon-gin Line railway (Korea) 267
Gyokusenji temple 5, **6, 354**

Hagino Yoshiyuki 134
Hale, Eugene 119
Halsey, William 124
Hama Detached Palace 124
Hangzhou 198
Hanihara Masanao 328–30, 332, 336,
    343n, 370
Hankou 281
Hankou Shuidian Gongsi (power
    company) 190
Hanshan (Cold Mountain) 198
Hanyehping Iron and Coal Corporation
    198
Hara Kunizō 302
Hara Takashi **261**, 263, 278, 291;
    assassination 292n, 298
Harada Tasuku 282
Harding, Warren G. xviii, 284–85,
    295, 303, 364; Eiichi 1921 meeting
    293–94
Harriman, Edward 85, 136, 162, 164,
    218, 363; Eiichi 1902 meeting 84;
    1905 visit to Japan 159–60,
Harris, Townsend 4–10, **7**, 11, 144, 344;
    monument 353–**354**, 355–58
Harvard University 139, 149, 230
Hashimoto Tsunatsune 107
Hattori Kintarō 356
Hawai'i: annexation 70, 71; Eiichi 1902
    visit 70–72; U.S. bases in 17

Hay, John 22, 80, 247, 296
Hayakawa, Sessue 307
Hayashi Tadasu 147, 157
He Tianjiong 185, 187
Heinz, H. J. 299, 316, 363
Heusken, Henry 5, 8–10, 355
Hijikata Hisaakira 370
Hill, James 136
Hirata Tōsuke 67
Hitch, Caroline 72
Hitotsubashi University xvi, 262
Hitotsubashi Yoshinobu (see Tokugawa
    Yoshinobu)
Homestead Steel Works 76
Honorary Commercial Commission-
    ers of Japan to the United States of
    America (Tobei Jitsugyōdan) 136–51
Horikoshi Zenjūrō 291, 336–37, 363
House Immigration Committee (U.S.)
    326–27, 329
Hozumi Nobushige 43, 355
Hozumi Shigetō 43, 217, 223
Hozumi Utako 1, 43–45, 55, 57–60,
    217, 353, 355–56
Hu Hanmin 192
Huangpu River 197
Hughes, Charles Evans 295–96, 297,
    304, 307, 326, 342–43

Ideals of the East 100
Ikeda Shigeaki 370
Imanishi Kenji 72
Immigration Act of 1921 324
Immigration Act of 1924 (Japanese
    Exclusion Act) 324–40, 341, 349
Imperial College of Engineering 41, 43
Imperial Hotel 120, 124, 156, 226, 240,
    264, 331, 356
Imperial Theater (Teikoku Gekijō) 132,
    133, 292
Industrial Bank of Japan 67, 180
Industry Club of Japan 321, 376
*Influence of Sea Power on History,
    1660–1783* 17

Inman, James M. 251
Inoue Junnosuke 237
Inoue Kaoru 36, 46, 67, 68–**69**, 84, 92,
    103–104, 135, 147
Ishii Kikujirō 213, 270n, 238–41
Itagaki Taisuke 213
Itakura Katsushige 18
Itō Hirobumi 32, **34**, 36, 67, 68, 112,
    139, 156, 244, 304; assassination
    (1909) 139, 144–**148**, 149, 390;
    finance ministry 67, 34; Iwakura
    Mission (1871) 12; in Korea 156,
    121–22
Itō Yonejirō 278
Iwakura Mission (1871) 12–14
Iwakura Tomomi 3, 12, 31, 36
Iwasaki Hisaya 124
Iwasaki Yatarō 42
Iwaya Sueo (Iwaya Sazanami) 99, 138
Izu peninsula 353, 355

Japan Society 300
Japan Women's University xvi, 133
Japan-America One-Aim Society
    (see Nichi-Bei Dōshi Kai)
Japan-China Business Association
    (see Nik-Ka Jitsugyō Kyōkai)
Japan-Korea Treaty (Japan-Korea
    Protectorate Treaty) 156
Japanese Association of America **167**,
    179, 227
Japanese Exclusion Act (see Immigration
    Act of 1924)
Japanese Exclusion League 116, 282, 303
Japanese Foundation for Cancer
    Research (Japan) 133
Japanese-American Relations
    Committee (Japan) 236, 237, 250,
    255, 261, 277, 282, 290, 293,
    318–19, 325, 327, 328, 332, 334,
    340, 341, 342, 346
Japan–U.S. security treaty 154
Jardine Matheson & Company 89
Jesup, Morris K. 81

Jiaozhou (Kiaochow) Bay 205, 207,
    237–38
Jikei University School of Medicine 106
Jinzhou-Aihui (Chinchow-Aigun) line
    164
Johnson, Hiram 181
Jordan, David S. 230, 309, 326, 338

Kabayama Aisuke 356
Kabukiza Theater 109, 123
Kabutochō office 66, 114, 135, 278;
    1923 earthquake 313–14, 322;
    Kodama Gentarō 1903 visit
    101–103; request to join Tobei
    Jitsugyōdan (1909) 136; retirement
    announcement (1909) 131–34; Sun
    Yat-sen 1913 visit 187
Kalakaua, King 70–71
Kameido massacre (1923) 322–23
Kamiya Tadao 180
Kanagawa, Treaty of (1854) 4
Kaneko Kentarō 120, 182, 236, 256,
    266, 333, 342; and Roosevelt 327,
    340
Kantō Earthquake (see Great Kantō
    Earthquake of 1923)
Katsura Kogorō 3
Katsura Tarō 70, 84, 124, 135, 161;
    Katsura-Taft Memorandum 113, 124
Katō Takaaki **206**, 213, 214
Katō Tomosaburō **288**–89, 293, 294,
    297–98, 306, 315
Katō Tsunetada 138
Kawatake Mokuami 51
Keifu (Seoul-Pusan) Railway Company
    92, 93
Keio University 124
Kennan, George F. 381
Kido Takayoshi letters from 12, 314
Kingsley, Darwin P. 296, 300, 333
Kinkakuji (Golden Pavilion) 216
Kiyokawa Hachirō 8
Kiyoura Keigo 66
Knapp, George O. 82

Knox, Philander C. 55, 137, 213, 296; as Secretary of State 162–66
Kobayashi Shinzaburō 323
Kodama Gentarō 101, **102**–106, 109
Kodama Kenji 361, 376
Komura Jutarō 66, 84,110–111, 124, 127, **128**, 135, 137, 182, 228
Kondō Renpei 106, 263
Korea: anti-Japanese independence movement 247–48; Declaration of Korean Independence (1919) 247; Eiichi's ideas on 108, 267–68; Itō Hirobumi in 122, 148, 152, 156; Jack London in 171; Japan-Korea Treaty (Japan-Korea Protectorate Treaty) 147, 156–57, 158; Japan's occupation of 122; Japanese annexation of xvi, 92, 93, 113, 147; Japanese expansion 152–53, 324; Provisional Government of Republic of 248; railways 267; Russian interests in 21, 92, 105; Taft promise to Japan 121 (*see also* Korean peninsula); Theodore Roosevelt on 220; Willard Straight in 158–59
Korean Daily News 158
Korean peninsula 113, 125, 152, 153, 154, 162, 247; independence movement 247–48, 268; Russia and 92, 105, 147, U.S.-Japan memorandum 113
Kuki Ryūichi 371
Kuomintang (see Guomindang)
Kurachi Tetsukichi 193
Kusumoto Masataka 36, 57, 69
Kwantung Army 378
Kyoto 2, 18, 88, 262; chamber of commerce of 129; Doshisha University 210; Fushimi-Momoyama grave 166; Golden Pavilion of 216; meeting at Yamagata's Murin'an villa 93
Kyōchōkai (Harmony Society) 262

Kōyōkan (restaurant) 111–112, 121, 304; West Coast chambers of commerce group 129
Kōzu (Odawara): Eiichi convalescence in 107

Lamont, Thomas W. 302, 317
Lansdowne, Lord 89
Lansing, Robert 238–41, **240**, 249–50, 270n, 273
Lansing-Ishii Agreement 310
Lea, Homer 171, 174–77, 182–83
League of Nations xiii, 248, 249, 253, 271, 284
Lee, Robert E. 31, 38
Li Hongzhang 47
Li Liejun 192
Li Yuan-hung 320
Liaodong peninsula 153, 238
Liliuokalani, Queen 70
Lincoln, Abraham 39, 77
Lodge, Henry Cabot 16, 116, 173, 304, 330
London Bridge 91
London, Jack 87, 91, 171–72, 183
Low, Seth 82
Lowman, James D. 228, 308
Lynch, Robert N. 317, 308

MacArthur, Douglas 20
MacKenzie, John D. 169
MacVeagh, Charles 356
Magoshi Kyōhei 204
Mahan, Alfred T. 17, 18–20, 30, 123, 183
Makino Nobuaki 291
Manchuria xvi, 277; Japan's advance into 159; Japan's special interests in 300; Japan's occupation of 378; railways in 164
Manchurian Railway (*see* South Manchurian Railway)
Mao Zedong 171
Maritime Provinces 243, 245

Marshall, George 20
Masuda Takashi 35, 197, 369–70
Matsuda Yoshirō 376
Matsudaira Katamori 18
Matsudaira Sadaaki 18
Matsugen (restaurant) 59
Matsumura Shōnen 98
McClatchy, Valentine S. 302–303, 308, 328
McKinley, William 17
Megata Tanetarō 267
Meiji Constitution 183, 281
Meiji Restoration xv, xvi, 89, 107, 134, 183, 254, 294
Meiji, Emperor xvi, 31, 47, 55, 108, 120, 137, 206, 277; Ueno Park pageant 370
Metcalf, Victor H. 118–19
Mexico 239; secret treaty rumor 173, 177
Miike mines 99
Mikasa (flagship) 124
Mikimoto Kōkichi 364–65
Minobe Tatsukichi 98
Minomura Risuke 35
Mita Tsunamachi residence 263
Mitsubishi zaibatsu 42, 117, 124
Mitsui Club 263
Mitsui Hachirōemon 124
Mitsui Trading Company 99
Mitsui zaibatsu 35, 99, 117, 124, 166, 190, 278, 342
Miyajima 262
Miyazaki Tōten 185
Mizuno Kōkichi 138, 201
Mizuno Rentarō 315
Mongolia 271; Japan's special interests in 300, 360
Monroe doctrine 48
Moore, Walton N. 216, 309, 228, 255
Morgan, J. P. 76, 78, 137, 164, 237, 317
Mori Arinori 36
Mori Kaku 192
Mori Ritsuko 292
Morimura Ichizaemon 168

Morris, Roland 278, 283, 302
Morris-Shidehara Talks 283
Morton Trust Company 81
Morton, Levi P. 81
Mukden 110; Straight as consul 159–60
Mukden Incident 378
Murai Brothers Shōkai 82

Nagano Mamoru 217
Nakahashi Tokugorō 291
Nakajima Kumakichi 366
Nakamura Yoshikoto 162
Nakano Buei 120, 128, 135, 179, 193, 213, 236
Namamugi (incident) 15
Nanjing 362n; Eiichi 1914 visit 199; Yuan Shikai occupation of 193
Napoleon III 3, 10, 94, 95, 294
Narushima Ryūhoku 35
National City Bank (New York) 81, 82–84, 164, 218, 264
Native Americans 24, 307
Native Sons of the Golden West 170
Navy, United States 119, 123, 174, 286, 335
Neville, Edwin L. 370
New Republic (magazine) 165, 218
New York City 87; Eiichi 1915 visit 217; Roosevelt birthplace 77
New York Bankers Club 298
New York Central 136
New York Chamber of Commerce 79, 80, 82, 296,
Nichi-Bei Dōshi Kai (Japan-America One-Aim Society) 180, 215, 227
Nichi-Bei Kankei Iin Kyōgikai (Joint Conference of the Japanese-American Relations Committees) 255
Nichi-Bei Yūshi Kyōgikai 165, 262
Nichi-Bei hissenron (*Genmei: Muchi no yūki*) 176
Nik-Ka Jitsugyō Kyōkai (Japan-China Business Association) 276, 278, 280, 320, 322–23, 346, 376

Nikkō 47, 262
Nikolayevsk Incident (1920) 245
Nimitz, Chester 20
Nine-Power Treaty 206
Nippon Yūsen (NYK) 105–106, 117, 278
Nisei 324, 349–53; 442nd Infantry Regiment (U.S. Army) 352
Nishino Keinosuke 132
Nishiyama Sen 114, 349–53
Nitobe Inazō 14, 166, 236, 340, **341**
North America Review 182
Northern Pacific Railroad 84, 136
Numa Morikazu 56
Numano Yasutarō 214

Odaka Atsutada 2
Odaka Chiyo 1 (*see also* Shibusawa Chiyo)
Ōe Taku 92
Ōhashi Shintarō 302
Ōji Asukayama 52
Oji Paper Company 35, 53
Okakura Kakuzō 99–100
"open door" (of China) 22–23, 80, 125, 153, 163–64, 239, 247, 273, 286, 306
Ōkubo Toshimichi 12, 32, **103**–104, 145
Ōkuma Shigenobu 33, **34,** 197, 205, 213, 214, 223, 244, 278, 292, 309
Ōkura Kihachirō 67, 168, **233**–34, 264, 333, 356
Opium Wars (1840–1842; 1856–1860) 1, 28, 89, 158
Oriental Emigration Company 180
Osaka Mint Office 145
Osborne, Henry 295
Osborne, Loyall A. 256
Oyster Bay (Roosevelt residence) 219, 299
Ozaki Yukio 120
O'Brien, Thomas J. 121, 166

Pan-Pacific Association 331
Panama Canal 123, 213, 215, 284; construction project 77, 80
Panama-Pacific International Exposition 213, 214, 228, 236
Paris: Eiichi 1867 visit 10, 215; Eiichi 1902 visit 94–98; international exposition 10, 94; Paris Peace Conference 246–49, 257, 259, 276, 283, 287, 310
Parkes, Harry Smith (Sir) 3, 33–34, 49, 58
Pearl Harbor: attack on 184
Peoples Gas (Chicago) 82
Perry, Commodore Matthew Calbraith 1, 4–5, 14, 112, 139, 143–144, 331
Pershing, John J. 20, 166
Phelan, James D. 252, 328
Philadelphia 224, 301, 390; Eiichi 1902 visit 85–86; Eiichi 1919 visit 140; Eiichi 1915 visit 217,
Philippines 16, 17, 20, 24–25, 211; Japan's ambitions for 117, 173; Taft and 111–113; U.S. occupation of 74, 78
Pierce, Franklin 5
Pittsburgh 217, 316; Eiichi 1902 visit 76; Eiichi 1909 visit 140, 390; 1915 visit 217, 224; Eiichi 1921 visit 299
Pomona College 307
Port Arthur (Dalian) 110, 205
Portsmouth, New Hampshire 84, 111n, 160–61, 327
Progressive Party 220
Pruyn, Robert Hewson 15

Qing dynasty 185, 199, 322
Qingdao 205

"Red Cliffs" 199
Red Cross Society 117, 316–17, 322, 376
Reinsch, Paul S. 207–208, 238, 273; Sakatani Incident 270n

Roches, Léon 3
Rockefeller, John D. Jr. 300
Rockefeller, William II 82
Rocky Mountains 75, 391
Rokumeikan 46, 314
Roosevelt, Theodore xviii, 16, 77, 85, 116, 118–20, 159, 219–220, 363; diplomacy 247; Eiichi visit on Long Island 219–220, 299; and Russo-Japanese War 110; Syngman Rhee interview 157
Root, Elihu 80, 124, 307
Root-Takahira Agreement (1908) 79, 80, 124–25, 162, 304
Ross, Edward A. 170
Russia: East Asia 153; Japan's negotiations with 101; Japan's victory over 155; 1917 revolution 242, 247; threat to Japan 21; war with 106, 110
Russo-Japanese War 78, 84, 147, 155, 156, 173, 242, 304; annexation of Korean peninsula 113; deserter rate 175; impact of 206; Jack London observed 171–72; Japan's victory 116; loans for 159; rumors of war 172; surgery during 133
Ryukyu Islands 47–49, 371

Saigō Takamori 2, 3, 69; letters to Eiichi from 314
Saigō Tsugumichi 36, 69
Saionji Kinmochi 68, 121
Sakatani Yoshirō 256, 267, 269, **269**, 315, 328; Sakatani Incident 270
Salt Lake City (Utah) 74, 94, 114–15, 140, 349, 353, 391
Samuel, Marcus 92–93
San Francisco Board of Education 116, 118, 120, 127
San Francisco Chamber of Commerce 214, 216, 228 256
San Francisco Chronicle 72, 116, 129
San Francisco earthquake (1906) 117–118, 119

San Francisco Examiner 72
San Francisco Labor Council 170
Sanjō Sanetomi 31, 47; wife 44
Sapporo Agricultural College 14
Sasaki Yunosuke 108, 131, **234**–35, 370
Satsuma domain 15, 18
Scharrenberg, Paul 212, 226, 309
Schmitz, Eugene 170
Schurman, Jacob G. 263, 272
Scriba, Julius 107
Seattle 26, 129, 136; Eiichi 1909 visit 140, 387; Eiichi 1915 visit 216, 228; Eiichi 1921 visit 308; Knox 1912 visit to Japan 166
Seien hyakuwa (One Hundred Essays by Seien) 150
Seikanron 152
Seiyōken (restaurant) 371
Seoul: Pagoda Park 247
Seoul-Pusan Railway (see Keifu Railway Company)
Sesnon, William T. 256, 309
Seward, William H. 5
Seward-Burlingame Treaty (1868) 24, 25
Shand, Alexander Allen 234–35
Shandong peninsula 207, 237, 238, 242, 246, 249, 251, 253, 259, 272, 281, 287, 318; agreement on return of 310, 320
Shanghai 21, 197, 378; Eiichi 1914 visit 196–98; Korean Provisional Government in 248
Sheng Xuanhuai 198, 199
Sherman Antitrust Act 85
Shiba Detached Palace 36, 120, 137
Shibusawa Chiyo 44, **53**, 55, 57
Shibusawa Eiichi Biographical Materials (*Shibusawa Eiichi denki shiryō*) xviii-xix, 374–75
Shibusawa Eiichi denki shiryō (see *Shibusawa Eiichi Biographical Materials*)
Shibusawa Hideo 217
Shibusawa Kaneko **65, 66,** 70, 87

Shibusawa Keizō 88, 109, 311–12, 356,
    357, 372–73, 380
Shibusawa Kotoko 57
Shibusawa Masao 217
Shibusawa Takenosuke 217
Shibusawa Tokuji 57
Shibusawa Utako (*see* Hozumi Utako)
Shidehara Kijūrō 283, **289**, 293–94,
    333, 343n, 370
Shigemitsu Mamoru 376
Shima, George 308, 309
Shimbashi Station 36, 66, 51, 70, 110,
    186, 190
Shimoda 4, 5, 6, 353–56
"Shina rōnin" 203
Shinobazu pond 59
Shintomiza theater 41, **50**
Shiraishi Kitarō 141
Shiraishi Motojirō 160
Shiraiwa Ryūhei 198, 278–79
Shōnin Dōshikai (Businessmen's Society)
    71
Shunkan no ruiseki (Accumulated
    Moments) 88
Shuzenji 355
Siberia 277; Eastern 242, 245; Japanese
    1918 expedition 242–46, 251, 286
Siberian Railroad (see Trans-Siberian
    Railway)
Singapore 21, 99, 286, 320
Sino-Japanese War (1894–1895) 19, 79,
    81 93, 97, 99, 105, 153, 156, 238,
    338
Smith, Art (pilot) 216
Soeda Juichi 180, 211, 258–59, 267,
    291, 292, 298, 305, 342, 361
Sone Arasuke 66
Song Jiaoren 190
Song Ziwen 376
Sonoda Kōkichi 138
South Manchurian Railway Co. Ltd.
    (Mantetsu) 92, 160–162, 164–65,
    213, 286, 286; neutralization
    demand 160–62, 166

Southern Pacific Railroad (U.S.) 84
Soviet Union 145, 245, 345
Spain: territory of Philippines 20; U.S.
    war with 16, 175
Spanish-American War 73, 80
St. Luke's International Hospital (Tokyo)
    223, 302
Standard Oil Trust 78
Stanford University 230
State, U. S. Department of 158, 162,
    164, 238, 334–35, 343; Far Eastern
    Affairs 218, 219, 273; Willard
    Straight 158
Stephen Girard Bank 86
Stephens, William 308
Stewart, John A. 82
Stillman, James 81, 82, 164, 363
Straight, Willard 158–60, 162–65, 166,
    172, 183, 207, 218, 219, 273, 345;
    meeting with Eiichi 218–19; South
    Manchurian Railway 162
Street, Julian 263, 274, 317
Strong, Benjamin 298
Suez Canal 63, 98, 215
Sugihara Eizaburō 278
Sun Yat-sen xvii, 185, **186**–94; death of
    346, 359; Homer Lea meeting 177;
    letters from 314; 1924 letter to Eiichi
    345,
Suzhou 198
Suzuki Bunji xviii, **210**–13, 226
Svoboda, Ludvik 245
Syngman Rhee 157

Taft, Henry 263, 271–72, 300, 302,
    317, 326
Taft, William Howard xviii, 80, **111,**
    219, 303–304; governor-general of
    Philippines 111; re Korea 122; 1907
    visit to Japan 120–23; re Philippines
    122; U.S. president 162
Tagore, Rabindranath 55
Taiping Rebellion 197
Taiwan: Japanese takover 205

Takahashi Korekiyo 135, 166, 168, 298
Takahira Kogorō 79, 124
Takaishi Shingorō 138
Takaki Kanehiro 106, 107
Takamine Jōkichi 73
Takeuchi Tsuna 92
Tanaka Giichi 366
Tang Shaoyi 198
Terauchi Masatake 161, 238, **243,** 261, 270
Teusler, Rudolf B. 223–24, 302
Tianjin 203–205, 20; chamber of commerce 321
Tōa Dōbunkai (East Asian Common Culture Association) 186
Tōa Kōgyō 190
Toba-Fushimi, battle of 18, 94
Tobei Jitsugyōdan (*see* Honorary Commercial Commissioners of Japan to the United States of America)
Tōgō Heihachirō 18, 121, 124
Tokonami Takejirō 291
Tokugawa Akitake 10, 36, 65, 94–96, 294
Tokugawa Iesato 196, 289, 303, 305, 316, 356
Tokugawa Ieyasu 48
Tokugawa Keiki (*see* Tokugawa Yoshinobu)
Tokugawa Yoshinobu 10, 18, 36, 94, 108, 146, **194,** 294, 314; biography project 134; chooses Eiichi to go to Paris 11; death of 194–96; Eiichi served as a retainer xvi
Tokugawa shogunate 32, 187, 215
Tokutomi Roka 155
Tokutomi Sohō 155
Tokyo Bankers Association xvii , 232, 236, 266;
Tokyo Bankers Club 361
Tokyo Chamber of Commerce xvii, 35, 63, 120, 127–28, 135, 179, 192, 213, 215, 259, 261, 264, 302, 316 332

Tokyo Chamber of Commercial Law 35
Tokyo City Assembly 196
Tokyo Gas Company 81
Tokyo Higher Commercial School (later Hitotsubashi University) 262
Tokyo National Museum 58
Tōkyō Nichinichi shinbun 12, 35n, 42, 56
Toynbee, Arnold 331
Tokyo Prefectural Assembly 35
Tokyo Savings Bank 236
Tokyo Stock Exchange 128
Tokyo Welcome Committee (for Grant) 35, 41, 43
Tokyo Yōikuin xvi, 85, 133–34
Trans-Siberian Railway 215, 243, 245
Treaty of Amity and Commerce 8
Treaty of Kanagawa (see Kanagawa, Treaty of)
Triple Intervention 238
Tsuchiya Takao 374
Tsushima, Battle of 110, 124
Twain, Mark 16
Twenty-One Demands 207, 208, 210, 222, 238, 257, 259

U.S. Far Eastern Fleet 16
U.S. Mint 13
U.S. Steel 76, 137, 237
Uchida Kōsai 166, 278, 291, 315, 333
Uchimura Kanzō 14
Ueno Park 55, 59, 60; 1879 pageant 370
Ueno Suesaburō 118
Union Iron Works (San Francisco) 73, 123
Union Pacific Railroad 84, 136
United Nations xiii
United States xvi–xx, 1, 3, 4, 5; anti-Chinese movement 26n, 29; anti-Japanese tendencies 167, 253–54, 324–40; China stance 49, 153, 163–64, 165, 247; Constitution 324–26; disarmament plan 284; Eiichi compares with Britain 13–14, 87, 90; Eiichi 1902 visit 63–86;

Eiichi 1909 visit 134–51; Eiichi 1915 visit 213–31; Eiichi view of 11, 149–51; Eiichi 1921 visit 291–309; Eiichi prestige in 290; Great White Fleet 123, 129; Iwakura Mission 1871 visit to 12; Japanese immigrants in 24, 27–28, 114–20, 125, 251, 257–58; in Korea 159; "Open Door" 153; Philippines 20–23, 122, 124; recognition of Japan's sovereignty over Korea 113, 122; and Siberia 242; Treaty of Amity and Commerce 8; view of Japan 14–15, 23, 51, 154, 246, 248, 343; war with Japan, rumors of 173–74, 283, 285; war with Spain 16; as "white man's country" 25

University of California 228

University of Chicago 149

University of Southern California 307

University of Wisconsin 149

Uraga 1, 4

Uryū Sotokichi 236

Ushijima Kinji (George Shima) 167, 226, 308

Utako (see Hozumi Utako)

Valor of Ignorance 174–176, 182

Vanderlip, Frank A. 82, 218, **221**–223, 262, 263–67, 268, 272, 295, 300, 307, 316, 333, 339, 363

Versailles Treaty 253, 271

Vietnam, War in 40, 74

Villette 95–96

Vladivostok 243, 245

Waltham Clock Company **65**, 139, 301

Wanamaker, John 224–25, 226, 230, **301,** 316, 363–64

Wanamaker, Rodman 316

Waseda University 124, 292

Washington, George 39, 48, 77

Watanabe Kinzō 166–68

West Coast chambers of commerce 129–31

Western Labor Union 115

Wheeler, Benjamin Ide 228, 255, 309

White House 120; 1902 Roosevelt meeting 79; 1915 Wilson meeting 223; 1921 Harding meeting 293–94

White Star Line 86

Wilhelm, Kaiser 19

Wilson, Woodrow xviii, **178**, 180–81; Eiichi 1915 meeting with 223, 241, 248–50, 284, 302, 363

Wolf, Henry M. 354

Women's Art School 262

Working Men's Party (WMP) 170

World War I 205, 277, 284–85; Paris Peace Conference 246, 248–49, 257, 283; start of 237, 238

World War II: relocation camps 174

Wu Tingfang 198

Yamagata Aritomo 32, 67, 68, 146–47

Yamamoto Gonnohyō-e 315

Yamamoto Jōtarō 193

Yamamoto Tatsu 67

Yamanashi Hanzō 291

Yamaza Enjirō 201

Yang Ziqi 200

Yangtze river 21, 196, 199, 286, 375, 378

Yasoshima Chikanori 107–108

Yasuda Zenjirō 35

Ye Wanyong 157

"Yellow Peril" 186

Yokohama 1, 63, 70, 129, 151, 215; dyke building project 15; Foreign Chamber of Commerce 35; Grant arrival 36; Great White Fleet at 123–24, 144; Heusken affair (1861) 8–9; Namamugi incident (1862) 15; 1923 earthquake incidents 323; Tokyo-Yokohama industrialists 111; young Eiichi plot and 1–2;

Yokohama Foreign Chamber of Commerce 35

Yokohama Specie Bank 278;
  Shibusawa Keizō 372
Yonekura Ippei 35
Yoshida Shigeru xviii, 92, 321, 370
Yoshikawa Akimasa 67, 69
Yoshimatsu Sadaya 211, 226
Young, John Russell 37–39

Yūaikai 210–13
Yuan Shikai xvii, 187, 193, **200**, 201,
  207, 208, 209–10, 222, 237

Zhang Gongyun 192
Zumoto Motosada 267, **290,** 291, 303
Zuo Zongtang (Tso Tsung-t'ang) 197